Children & the Law

Balancing a child's welfare interests and rights so as to ensure recognition and respect for his or her autonomous identity, while facilitating family unity, has become a major challenge for modern family law. This book, following on from *The Principle of the Welfare of the Child: A History*, examines, contrasts, and compares the response of England and Wales and Ireland to that challenge. It does so by applying the same matrix of indicators to explore, in each country, the distinction between welfare interests and rights and to trace changes in the balance between them. By profiling the nations in accordance with the same indicators, it reveals important jurisdictional differences in the extent to which welfare interests or rights determine how the law is currently applied to children.

Kerry O'Halloran, recently retired, has for 13 years been Adjunct Professor at the Australian Centre for Philanthropy and Nonprofit Studies, QUT, Australia.

Children & the Law

Shaping the Modern Welfare Principle in the British Isles

Kerry O'Halloran

Routledge
Taylor & Francis Group
LONDON AND NEW YORK

First published 2023
by Routledge
4 Park Square, Milton Park, Abingdon, Oxon OX14 4RN

and by Routledge
605 Third Avenue, New York, NY 10158

Routledge is an imprint of the Taylor & Francis Group, an informa business

British Library Cataloguing-in-Publication Data
A catalogue record for this book is available from the British Library

ISBN: 978-1-032-21488-7 (hbk)
ISBN: 978-1-032-21489-4 (pbk)
ISBN: 978-1-003-26864-2 (ebk)

DOI: 10.4324/9781003268642

Typeset in Times New Roman
by Deanta Global Publishing Services, Chennai, India

Thanks for your patience, Elizabeth.

Contents

Acknowledgements

This book owes much to the groundwork laid in earlier publications including *The Welfare of the Child: the Principle and the Law*, *The Politics of Adoption*, *Child Care and Protection: the Law & Practice in Northern Ireland*, and my earlier contribution to this series. Given the not-dissimilar subject matter and related case law, focused on much the same jurisdictions, there is inevitably some degree of overlap and I thank the publishers concerned for their understanding.

There were many who contributed along the way to making this a better book. Particular thanks are due to those who offered comment on draft chapters or related text, particularly Geoffrey Shannon and Julie Doughty. Their encouragement, support, and advice have meant a lot, and this book and its author would have suffered without them.

I am very thankful to Routledge, particularly to Siobhán Poole, for commissioning the book and the series. Responsibility for any mistakes, inconsistencies, or other faults, and for all views expressed, must unfortunately rest wholly with me.

Introduction

Neither nationally nor internationally has the development of the law relating to the welfare interests of children been determined exclusively by judiciary or legislators. Nor, in the latter case, has it been due solely to changes implemented through provisions specific to children.

Changes directed by statute towards improving the legal position of children are the most conspicuous, the legislative intent is more clearly discernible and the impact usually readily identifiable. Changes in ideas, the breakthrough in knowledge that brings a deeper and more sophisticated understanding of what might constitute a child's needs and thereby generate an improved 'child welfare' response, can be more difficult to grasp and their significance only fully appreciated with hindsight. Changes directed more generally towards improving the rights, the health and living conditions, institutions, and access to services infrastructure, for all persons and with overlapping effects, can be the most difficult to identify, trace, and measure in terms of their particular consequences for children. Moreover, the change agents are not always those in the foreground – legislators, policy makers, and judiciary – often, in the background, there are advocates and organisations strategically applying the pressure needed to move things forward. The role of voluntary organisations in promoting changes to the law relating to children has not always been given the recognition it deserves.

This book, in four parts, builds upon the foundations laid by its predecessor.[1] It sets out to bridge the gap between the developmental history of the welfare principle, as examined in Book 1, and the contemporary role of that principle in the law relating to children, to be addressed in future books in this series. It aims to take account of the change agents – ideologies, new concepts, organisations, and professions – that contributed to what is generally viewed very largely in terms of evolving legislation and case law. It does so by continuing the narrative that traced the history of the principle in the context of the evolving law relating to children in England and Wales.

The first part, in two chapters, considers the gradual shift in law and policy away from the early and rather negative focus on parental rights and duties: in a private

1 O'Halloran, K., *The Principle of the Welfare of the Child: A History*, Routledge, 2022.

DOI: 10.4324/9781003268642-1

family law context, as regards criteria for parenting arrangements following marriage breakdown; in its public civil counterpart, as regards parental failure to ensure protection and provide an adequate standard of care; and in the public criminal arena where the law has tended to oscillate between welfare and justice, treating needs, or punishing deeds. It explores the Christian origins of 'charity' and assesses the role and effect of national, long-established voluntary organisations – such as the NSPCC and Barnardos – in researching, raising awareness, and lobbying for change in society's approach to the welfare and rights of children.

The second part, also in two chapters, focuses on the influences brought to bear to effect change. It begins by reflecting on the significance of the common law cultural legacy that bequeathed to the nations being considered in this book, the same understanding of what constituted a 'family' and the roles of parent and child within it. This is followed by a review of key government reports and official recommendations, identifying and assessing the various domestic pressures that led to legislative change at the end of the twentieth century. It then takes account of those developments outside the domestic legal field – leading to changes within it – that profoundly altered the interpretation and weighting given to the principle of the welfare interests of the child. This leads into a consideration of the international influences that challenged, and did much to change, the domestic laws and social attitudes towards children. In the main, it does so by taking account of some of the many key decisions taken by the European Court of Human Rights (ECtHR) and their consequences for child welfare law. It then considers the significance of advances in medicine, particularly in psychiatry and psychology, that transformed our understanding of childhood. These advances alerted the judiciary, legislators, and all with a concern for children's welfare, to the importance of interpreting children's needs, and their corresponding welfare requirements, in relation to the developmental stages of childhood and to the framework of relationships and social context that provide the setting for that development.

The third part, constituting more than half of the book, again consisting of two chapters, maps the role and function of the welfare principle in the contemporary public and private family law of England, the progenitor common law jurisdiction, and then similarly in relation to contemporary law in the neighbouring jurisdiction of Ireland. This core part is crucial as it: works through the legislation and case law, providing a descriptive account of national law and practice; classifies the welfare related material in accordance with the civil and criminal areas in which the principle applies; and applies a matrix of indicators to identify and measure the nature and effect of the role played by the welfare principle in England and Wales and in Ireland.

Finally, the concluding part, in one chapter, conducts a comparative analysis of the jurisdictions profiled in Part III. It identifies and considers the main issues and the primary themes of jurisdictional difference and commonality. In so doing, this part validates the approach to be taken in assessing the role and function of the welfare principle in the range of other jurisdictions to be considered in this series. In conclusion, the book ends by benchmarking the distinctive characteristics and primary jurisdictional differences against the principles established by the Convention on the Rights of the Child 1989.

Part I

Moving away from a traditional interpretation of welfare

1 Children

Their welfare interests and the law

Introduction

The perennial debate – in academia[1] and government[2] – as to whether the needs and deeds of children require a similar state response to safeguard and promote their welfare, or a differentiated response focused on either punishment/rehabilitation or on safe family-based care, respectively, is probably highly influenced by cultural context. Similar contention surrounds those regarded as best placed to speak for what might constitute the welfare interests of a child: parent, local authority, judiciary, or the child; and, if the latter, then with or without expert mediation. Then there are questions as to how to weigh welfare interests relative to other matters. The choices to be made, or the balances to be struck, and whether or not other matters come into play, will vary from country to country and within any country from time to time.

This chapter first explores the origins and evolving role of welfare interests then the interface between welfare and justice. It considers changes in its function: from acting as little more than a brake on the exercise of parental rights; to a factor to be taken into account in circumstances of criminal conviction and public health and safety; to becoming the paramount goal for the court in any issue affecting a child's upbringing. It concludes by examining the ways in which the developing role and weighting of welfare has forced adjustments in the inter-relationships between parents, child, and the state.

Welfare and children

The law initially had some difficulty in recognising that a child might have a legal status – separate and distinct from that of their parents – and in the main only did so in circumstances of parental absence. An orphan, most usually a prospective

1 See, for example, Rutter, M. and Giller, H., *Juvenile Delinquency: Trends and Perspectives*, London, Penguin, 1983 and Muncie, J., *Youth and Crime*, London, Sage, 2004.

2 See, for example, the Home Office: *The Child, the Family and the Young Offender*, London, HMSO, 1965; *Children in Trouble*, London, HMSO, 1968; and *Youth Justice – the Next Steps*, London, HMSO, 2003. Also, see, the Treasury, *Every Child Matters*, (Cmnd 5860), London, HMSO, 2003.

DOI: 10.4324/9781003268642-3

inheritor of property or a prospective bride, was first acknowledged in the courts of Chancery as having interests which the law could be called upon to protect: but it was not their welfare that then attracted judicial protection; it was their prospective rights. The doctrine of *parens patriae* as exercised in wardship,[3] enabled the judiciary in Chancery – followed eventually by legislators – to recognise the separateness of children's interests and, because of their innate dependency, determine that those interests should be given some priority in law.

Wardship and the origins of the welfare principle

Like its origins, the extent of the *parens patriae* powers are equally uncertain, but it is clear they extend beyond the parental duty of care and protection to warrant the taking of positive steps to safeguard and promote the interests at risk.[4] Inherently vested in the monarch, exercised by the Chancellor, delegated to the Court of Chancery, then administered by the High Court and devolved to the Attorney General:[5]

> the King is to be considered as the *parens patriae*; that is he is the protector of every part of his subjects, and that, therefore, it is the duty of his officer, the Attorney General, to see that justice is done to every part of those subjects.

These powers have been described as "theoretically limitless"[6] because they "spring from the direct responsibility of the Crown for those who cannot look after themselves."[7]

Parens patriae

It seems probable that these powers originated as an incident of the feudal system of tenure. From perhaps the fourteenth century, the monarch – as ultimate landlord to whom all lords, yeomen, serfs, and others owed allegiance and paid fealty – was responsible for those declared *sui juris* and who, because they lacked the necessary capacity, could neither protect their own interests nor fulfil their feudal duties and therefore "belonged to the King as *pater patriae*, and fell under the direction of this court, as charities, infants, idiots, lunatics, etc."[8] In practice

3 See, for example, Seymour, J., '*Parens Patriae* and Wardship Powers: Their Nature and Origins', *Oxford Journal of Legal Studies*, Vol 14, No 2, 1994 at pp 159–88.
4 See, further, O'Halloran, K., *The Principle of the Welfare of the Child: a History*, Routledge, 2022, at chapter 2.
5 *Ludlow Corp. v. Greenhove* (1827) 1 Bli. NS 17, at p 48.
6 See *Re W (A Minor) (Medical Treatment)* [1992] 4 All ER 627 at 641. Also, see, *Re X (A Minor) (Wardship: Restriction on Publication)* [1975] 1 All ER 697 'no limits to that jurisdiction have yet been drawn,' *per* Denning LJ, at p 705.
7 Ibid, *per* Denning LJ, at p 411.
8 See *Falkland v. Bertie* (1696) 2 Vern 333 *per* Lord Somers LC at 342; 23 ER 814 at 818.

it was the property rights of those within such groups that attracted an exercise of the *parens patriae* powers: protecting property from abuse or misuse by officials entrusted to safeguard it – such persons becoming known as 'guardians' – was initially the main concern.

Welfare of the child

From the outset, unlike any other form of judicial proceedings, it was the welfare of the child that was central to wardship: it was concerned with protecting the person as well as the property of its wards. The issue of a wardship order vested in the Chancery court the parental duty to maintain, protect, and educate a child and was exercisable on behalf of the court by its appointed guardian throughout childhood. Should that appointed guardian neglect or abuse their position of trust then the Chancery court would intervene. That intervention – in relation to guardians rather than parents – was significant in two respects. First, while the child's welfare was not itself a ground for intervention, any suspicion that a guardian's conduct was to the detriment of a child's interests would warrant Chancery intervention. Second, while recognising that the jurisdiction was exercisable for the benefit of the child, the Chancery judges were at the same time prepared to accord some weight to the views of the parents.

The principles gradually worked out in the context of a guardian's duties towards a ward eventually came to be extended to the parent/child relationship. In time the Court of Chancery made the step of determining that a father, like a guardian, could be deprived of his position of trust in relation to a child if found guilty of abusing that trust. As Lord Eldon LC declared in *Lyons v. Blenkin*:[9]

> It is certain that the court will interfere against the acts of a guardian, if acting in a manner inconsistent with his duty; and it is equally clear that the court will control a parent if acting in a manner in which he should not.

The duties of parents came to be viewed by the judiciary as synonymous with those of guardians. The welfare interests of the child, at least in a negative sense of preventing their abuse, came to provide the justification for ultimate judicial control of the father as it had done in respect of the guardian. As his lordship later explained, "it has always been the principle of this Court, not to risk the incurring of damage to children which it cannot repair, but rather to prevent the damage being done."[10] Thus the Court of Chancery in the eighteenth and early nineteenth centuries, before the era of statutory reforms, can be seen to have developed a jurisprudence in which both a guardian and a father were viewed as holders of an office of trust in relation to a child. Moreover, that trust was a continuing one: the welfare of a child was not simply a matter for once-off adjudication, it

9 (1821), Jacob 245 at p 253.
10 *Wellesley v. Duke of Beaufort* (1827) 2 Russ 1, at p 18.

required continual re-appraisal and ongoing management; a precursor, perhaps, to the current interpretation of welfare in an adoption context as the projected lifetime goal for the child concerned. The welfare of the child remained the principal, if not the sole, concern of the Court of Chancery in all circumstances where, for one reason or another, parental rights were irrelevant, secondary, or unimportant or where an appointed guardian had defaulted on their responsibilities.

Transfer of jurisdiction from Chancery to the High Court

For centuries, the Court of Chancery developed the *parens patriae* jurisdiction of wardship and the responsibilities of guardianship while the High Court, exercising its statutory powers and duties, continued to adjudicate on paternal rights of custody. Chancery courts employing a flexible and discretionary approach to the welfare needs of a particular child. Common law courts applying precedents, adjudicating on statutorily prescribed duties and enforcing their judgments by use of *habeas corpus*. This dual judicial system, both dealing with matters affecting the welfare of a child, continued through the eighteenth and nineteenth centuries.

The Supreme Court of Judicature Act 1873

This legislation unified the court systems of equity and the common law. The statutory fusion of equitable and common law principles included a directive that, in the event of a conflict between them, the principles of equity should prevail.

By the end of the nineteenth century it was the case law of equity rather the common law that had established the welfare interests of the child as a benchmark against which continued entitlement to exercise parental (in practice, paternal) rights would be measured.[11] The judiciary in the Court of Chancery provided the foundations for the future evolution of the welfare principle: a guardian, even if a parent, held a position of trust in relation to a child; the exercise of rights inherent in such a position was conditional upon first fulfilling a basic duty of care owed by a 'guardian' to a 'ward'; failure to fulfil the duties of a guardian would justify removal of the rights even from a parent.[12]

Developing a legal role for the welfare interests of a child

At first the interest of the state in family affairs turned on matters of status: the law was primarily concerned with the grounds authorising a change in the legal relationships that bound family members together. The welfare of the child operated as little more than a caveat to that concern. State intrusion into family affairs was thus very largely restricted to the grounds prescribed by criminal law for policing conduct between family members – usually abuses of parental

11 See *Re Agar-Ellis* (1883) 24 Ch D 317, CA.

12 See, further, *The Principle of the Welfare of the Child: A History*, op cit, at chapter 2.

responsibilities – until the introduction of matrimonial proceedings: effectively when divorce first became widely available and state intrusion extended to abuses of the spousal relationship as grounds for marriage dissolution.

Because of their innate dependency, children have always had their welfare interests defined and determined by others. Family law identifies the welfare related areas in which decisions may need to be taken, sets the parameters and processes for decision-making and identifies or authorises those who may make the decisions. While for present purposes the law as it applies to family and criminal matters is most relevant, this is not the only law relating to the welfare interests of children. By extension of its protective remit, the law has also developed a health and safety strand to provide protective measures in a much wider social context. Its early concern to apply the welfare principle in relation to spheres of activity such as education, health, and employment continue to evolve.

Public family law: custody

By the end of the nineteenth century the courts had become accustomed to upholding the general principle that 'it is for the child's welfare to be in the custody of unimpeachable parents'[13] *ergo* for custody to be denied the parent/s first had to be impeached. Consequently, the law was interested only in the circumstances whereby a parent, invariably the father, could be held to have forfeited custody rights by particularly reprehensible behaviour. That is to say, the courts were concerned more with applying criminal law sanctions against a father – in order to defend socially approved standards of behaviour – than with protecting or promoting the welfare of his child in any recognition of the latter's separate and legally defensible interests.

Negative role for welfare

The emergence and consolidation of the common law concept of custody as the main parental right was accompanied by the corollary that a child's welfare was, in a sense, only taken into account by the judiciary *in absentia*. Not until welfare interests had been seriously violated did they come into play as a factor capable of disentitling parent or guardian from their office of trust in respect of that child. The role played by the welfare principle was thus both negative and secondary in the context of custody proceedings. Having determined that the father's behaviour was in breach of the law, the courts turned to examine the effect of that behaviour on the child and it only then went on to consider arrangements which might safeguard the child's future welfare. The first step was court recognition that a fixed objective threshold – represented by the criminal law – had been breached by the father; perhaps by causing his child criminal injury, or neglect. This breach licensed the second step by which judicial discretion

13 See, for example, *Re Flynn* (1848) 2 De. G & Sm. 457; *Barnardo v. McHugh* [1891] A.C. 388; *Ward v. Laverty* [1925] A.C. 101; and *Re Thain* [1926] Ch. 671.

was exercised to take into account the welfare interests of the child concerned when concluding the proceedings.

The Prevention of Cruelty to, and Protection of, Children Act 1889, commonly known as the Children's Charter, was probably the first legislative iteration of that approach. Section 1 decreed that any adult – parent or not – who 'wilfully ill-treats, neglects, abandons, or exposes such child, or causes or procures such child to be ill-treated, neglected, abandoned, or exposed, in a manner likely to cause such child unnecessary suffering, or injury to its health, shall be guilty of a misdemeanor'. It thereby made parental abuse or neglect of a child a public law matter. Other provisions safeguarded welfare interests by imposing restrictions on the employment of children, prohibiting others from using them for begging purposes, and empowered a court to issue a 'fit person order' in respect of a child. Interestingly, s 8 provided for a child to be heard by the court without any stipulated age criteria. It declared that 'the evidence of such child may be received, though not given upon oath, if, in the opinion of the court, such child is possessed of sufficient intelligence to justify the reception of the evidence, and understands the duty of speaking the truth.'

This profoundly negative interpretation of welfare, existing only as a measure of an abuse of parental rights, defined and confined the legal role initially assigned to the welfare interests of a child, but it gave the state an initial foothold in family affairs. It was from this judicial approach that eventually a more positive affirmation of the separate legal interests of a child was to grow.

Private family law: matrimonial proceedings

Divorce first became widely available with the Matrimonial Causes Acts of 1923 and 1937,[14] even if restricted to fault based grounds; it was then broadened by the Divorce Reform Act 1969 and its grounds of two years separation and irretrievable breakdown, as consolidated in the 1973 Act; leading to the Family Law Act 1996, which established the present 'no fault' grounds, making divorce an elective option for any dissatisfied spouse. However, as the law relaxed – in stages – its approach towards spouses wishing to free themselves from marital ties, it correspondingly increased the requirement that this be conditional upon them first satisfying the court that satisfactory arrangements had been made for the future care of any children of their marriage. This approach was firmly established by the Guardianship of Infants Act 1925, s 1, which stated – in what was probably the first legislative mention of 'paramountcy' – that 'in matters regarding custody and upbringing, the welfare of the infant should be regarded by the Courts as the first and paramount consideration.' It was an approach that was sustained until the volume of custody proceedings (marital and non-marital) caused the state to retreat from status based concerns and restrict intrusion to circumstances where the parties (not necessarily parents) self-declared a conflict regarding care arrangements for children.

14 Divorce was in fact first available under the Matrimonial Causes Act 1857 but on very restrictive grounds.

Positive role for welfare

The legislative reference to 'paramountcy' in the 1925 Act grounded the decision in *Cammell v. Cammell*,[15] when Scarman J based his decision to some extent on the following proposition:

> In my view, however, the court in construing the statute should have regard [not only to … but also] to the policy of the law that, where in any proceeding before any court the custody or upbringing of an infant is in question, the court, in deciding that question, shall regard the welfare of the infant as the first and paramount consideration.

A few years later, in the landmark ruling *J v. C*,[16] the House of Lords, on appeal from wardship proceedings, held that even if the parents were 'unimpeachable' the welfare interests of the child were still of paramount importance.[17] Thereafter the paramountcy principle was established as the governing consideration in custody disputes, in effect elevating welfare interests to become a legal threshold for marital dissolution. Under the Matrimonial Act 1973, s 41, other grounds having been satisfied, the only remaining obstacle to a spouse obtaining a divorce decree was satisfying the court's 'welfare test' in respect of their children. For some years the judiciary, armed with the authority of the *J v. C* ruling and assisted with representation for the child provided by both a guardian *ad litem* and a solicitor, accumulated a body of jurisprudence as to what did and did not constitute welfare compliant arrangements. This judicial focus was radically affected by the introduction of the Children Act 1989 which sharply curtailed the volume of custody cases requiring adjudication. On the one hand the Act applied the requirement that when determining any issue affecting the upbringing of a child the court must, as stated in s 1(1), regard the welfare of that child as the paramount consideration. On the other, by amending the 1973 Act, it removed the need for the judiciary to apply a mandatory welfare test in the majority of such proceedings.

Restricting the welfare role

In a private family law context, the scale of state retreat from involvement in family affairs licensed by amending s 41 of the 1973 Act was huge.[18] Thereafter, judicial scrutiny of welfare compliant arrangements for children was restricted to those parents who declared an inability to reach agreement. Given the additional delays and costs involved, few had an incentive to do so. Other than the small minority prepared to so declare, the welfare test became marginalised as

15 [1964] 3 All ER 255.

16 [1970] AC 668.

17 See, further, *The Principle of the Welfare of the Child: A History*, 2022, op cit, at chapter 4.

18 Consolidated by the Family Law Act 1996 which removed the fault grounds for divorce, leaving only the ground of irretrievable breakdown.

it defaulted to a 'tick box exercise' whereby solicitors acting for the parties routinely stated that they had agreed satisfactory arrangements for their children.

Private family law: adoption etc.

Again, the state's concern in adoption matters was initially very much about legal status: transforming that of a child from 'illegitimate' to 'legitimate'; divesting the birth parent/s of parenthood; and vesting full parental responsibilities, together with name and inheritance obligations, in the adopters. Since its statutory initiation under the Adoption Act 1926, until its latest statutory formulation under the Adoption and Children Act 2002, this legal process has mostly treated the welfare test as a matter of marginal significance: to be satisfied by the eligibility criteria of the parties involved; and by the suitability of the adopters in terms of evidence of their capacity to provide a secure family environment. Much the same welfare considerations applied in relation to guardianship.

Welfare as the paramount consideration

After many decades of judicial resistance to any suggestion that welfare should be the overriding consideration in adoption proceedings, the introduction of the Children Act 1989, s.8(4)(d), defining adoption as falling within the definition of family proceedings, in effect made adoption subject to the paramountcy principle. Any doubt remaining as to the application of this principle was removed by the 2002 Act, s.1(2), which aligned adoption law with the 1989 Act, applied the principle to all decisions made in the adoption process, making a transformative step for adoption law in this jurisdiction.

Public and private: wardship

Aligning child protection and adoption laws was also a highly significant step for state intrusion into family matters: it underlined a decisive change in a policy which, for almost the entire lifetime of adoption as a statutory process, had regarded it as primarily a private family law proceeding; indeed, the most private of all such proceedings. Henceforth, adoption was to be levered into public law: mainstreamed into local authority child protection processes; retaining only a marginal relationship with its traditional private family law constituency.

The paramountcy of welfare as a public/private bridge

The 1989 Act, s 1, established the governing authority of the paramountcy principle, stating that 'when a court determines any question with respect to (a) the upbringing of a child or (b) the administration of a child's property, or the application of any income arising from it the child's welfare shall be the court's paramount consideration.' Of note is the fact that under the 1989 Act the principle was binding on the court alone, other bodies such as a local authority were not so bound, and that it applied only to matters concerning the child's 'upbringing' and 'property.'

Imposing the paramountcy principle on the adoption process necessarily raised the likelihood that in many circumstances court orders of lesser magnitude would be judicially regarded as more appropriate – such as the s 8 orders available under the 1989 Act and the Special Guardianship Order – in circumstances where step-parents, kinship applicants, and others would previously have opted for adoption. The sharp reduction in annual intercountry adoptions together with the availability of special guardianship and such like resulted, as intended, in the reduced use of adoption as a private law, first party, resource.

Also as intended, the annual rate of non-consensual adoptions from the public care system increased as the rights of the birth parent/s became subordinated to the welfare interests of their child. This adjustment to the role and weighting of the welfare principle – positioning it to bridge the private and public sectors of family law – stands as a remarkable landmark in the development of the welfare principle.

Developing third party liability for the welfare interests of a child

A natural extension of state intrusion into family affairs, on the grounds of safeguarding child welfare, was that it should follow into those areas where the child, with family permission, was to be found. It is probable that initially the extension was pursued with a view to holding parents accountable for the exploitation of their children – in the context of employment, thieving, prostitution etc. – which in due course led to third party liability for those who failed to provide adequate protection for the welfare of children on their premises. From such beginnings – a negative monitoring of breaches in child welfare – the state developed a more positive role by legislating for the promotion of child welfare in a public services context.

Health and safety laws

The employment of children, as an extra pair of hands to help their neighbours by working with crops in the fields or with livestock, has been an accepted part of family life in all societies. Their employment and exposure to exploitation by third parties, in factories and mines etc. most probably began on a large scale with industrialisation.

The Factories Acts

Industrialisation, in the early part of the nineteenth century, brought with it employment opportunities for children, readily availed of by the many parents living in poor social conditions and often in poverty. It has been shown that, on average, children in England then started work at ten years of age, but in industrial areas they started work even younger, most often at age eight.[19] By the 1830s

19 See Griffin, E., *Liberty's Dawn*, Yale University Press, 2014.

a general concern regarding the working conditions of young children in factories, cotton and woollen mills, and in coal mines was generating public pressure for reform. The Factory Act 1831, limited the working day to 12 hours for all children younger than 18 years of age but, like earlier legislation, it failed to provide enforcement measures. Its successor, the Factory Act 1833, prohibited the employment of children under the age of nine in factories and set limits: a maximum working week of 48 hours for children aged 9 to 13, limited to eight hours a day; and 12 hours a day for those aged 13 to 18. The Act also required children under 13 to receive elementary schooling for two hours each day. Importantly, it established a regulatory system to ensure both protection for children and employer liability. This was followed by the Mines Act 1842 which raised the starting age of colliery workers to ten years. Subsequent improvements were triggered by the report of a Royal Commission of Inquiry into the employment of children,[20] leading to the Factory Acts of 1844, 1867, and 1878, the latter of which prohibited work before the age of ten in all trades.

Public services

It would be hard to overstate the contribution of national public service provision as a safety net for ensuring and raising basic child welfare standards. It created a floor, where there was none before, that prevented very many children and their families from succumbing to the perennial threat of illness and destitution.

Education

The education of children is held to be an essential component of their welfare and became so by law in 1880 for those up to ten years of age. This mandatory national requirement may well have provided many children with opportunities for improving their prospects but, if nothing else, it safeguarded the welfare of all those who might otherwise have been sent out to work. Subsequent amendments raised the school-leaving age to 12. In this jurisdiction, while a state education system with a national curriculum provides a basic platform for the education of all children, this was long preceded by charity schools, by an elite sector of fee-paying 'public' schools reserved for a privileged few and, more recently, has been accompanied by a growing sector of faith schools.

Health and social security

The duty of public authorities to intervene when a parent is failing in their duty to ensure the health of their child has been evident since at least 1899[21] when a

20 See *Report of the Royal Commission on the Employment of Children and Very Young People in Mines and Factories*, 1842.

21 *R v. Senior* [1899] 1 QB 283.

member of the Peculiar People sect was convicted of the manslaughter of his baby by neglect as he had refused to provide the child with medical aid or medicine. Shortly afterwards – 1904 to 1916 – the government launched the beginning of its programme of major health and welfare reforms, building on the national framework first laid down in the series of Poor Laws.[22] A minimum wage, introduced in 1909 for certain low-wage industries, was expanded by 1920 to numerous industries including farm labour, but not until 1945 was a national family allowance scheme launched.[23] This was followed by legislation that put in place the foundations of the present National Health Service that has undoubtedly contributed greatly to the welfare of children.[24] Among the social problems addressed during this period was the plight of unmarried and widowed mothers, whose circumstances had worsened after the Poor Law Amendment Act of 1834 had made it much harder to claim child support benefits, leaving adoption as the only option available to secure the welfare of their child.[25]

Welfare, justice, and children

Contention as to whether 'welfare' and 'justice' are conflicting paradigms, alternative philosophical approaches, opposite ends of the same continuum etc. have polarised debate to little effect for many years.[26] Lately, government policy statements have tended to stress that welfare and justice are complementary[27] which – accepting that the balance between the two will require adjustment in relation to the child and their circumstances – would seem the better approach.

Justice

Law, let alone justice, had at best a peripheral relationship to children until the early decades of the twentieth century.

Traditional justice

Initially the law did not recognise children as such: babies and very young children were viewed as incidences of the property rights of their parents, any issues

22 See *Royal Commission into the Operation of the Poor Laws, 1832*, at: https://victorianweb.org/history/poorlaw/royalcom.html
23 The Family Allowance Act 1945.
24 Among the laws passed were the National Insurance Act 1946, the National Insurance (Industrial Injuries) Act 1946, and the National Assistance Act 1948.
25 See, for example, Gordon, L., 'Single Mothers and Child Neglect', *American Quarterly*, Vol 37, No 2, (1985), at pp 173–92.
26 See, for example, Adshead, G. and Sarkar, S.P., 'Justice and Welfare: Two Ethical Paradigms in Forensic Psychiatry', *Australian & New Zealand Journal of Psychiatry*, Vol 39, Nos 11–12, 2005.
27 For example: 'Preventing Offending Promotes the Welfare of the Individual Young Offender and Protects the Public' (Home Office, 1997).

arising in relation to such a child would be pursued against the parent; older children were for most purposes considered to be adults. Historically, the legal system in this country has a doubtful record, as a means for ensuring that children are treated in a manner that is morally correct or fair[28] and their conduct met with proportionate punishment, and/or correctional intervention, applied objectively and impartially; though probably little different than in other countries at that time. From being regarded until the mid-nineteenth century as small adults and flogged, imprisoned, or hanged for petty offences,[29] to being transported as orphans or vagabonds to the colonies of the British Empire well into the twentieth,[30] children suffered greatly as the 'justice' meted out to them was often cruel, took no account of their childhood and less of their welfare.

Tempering justice with welfare

Children, those aged seven years or more and found guilty of an offence, were liable to be treated as criminals until 1933 when the age threshold for criminal liability was raised to eight years and then to ten in 1963 where it remains. The process of ameliorating punishment with welfare considerations began at the end of the nineteenth century.

Reformatories and industrial schools

From 1866 a child in trouble with the law – because he or she had been found guilty of an offence or of being a vagrant – was defined as 'out of parental control,' which allowed the state to assume parental rights. A series of statutes – the Youthful Offenders Act 1854, the Reformatory Schools Act 1854, and the Industrial Schools Act 1868 – provided courts with a welfare option enabling them to send a child to either a reformatory school if found to be a delinquent, or an industrial school if a vagrant, to be 'reformed' or 'trained,' respectively, as an alternative to the punishment of jail.[31] This distinction between 'delinquent' and 'destitute', reflecting the corresponding institutional focus on deeds and needs,

28 Definition of 'justice' provided by the *Cambridge Advanced Learner's Dictionary and Thesaurus* at: https://dictionary.cambridge.org/dictionary/english/justice.

29 See Morris, A. and Giller, H. *et al*, *Justice for Children*, Macmillan, London, 1980, at p 3, where they recount that in 1833 'a 9-year old boy was sentenced to death for pushing a stick through a cracked window and pulling out some printer's colours, the value of which was two pence.' Also, see, Morris, A. and Giller, H., *Understanding Juvenile Justice*, Croom Helm, London, 1987, at p 6, where it is mentioned that on one day in 1814, five children aged between 8 and 12 were hanged in England for petty larceny.

30 According to the House of Commons, *Child Migrant's Trust Report*, 'it is estimated that some 150,000 children were dispatched over a period of 350 years—the earliest recorded child migrants left Britain for the Virginia Colony in 1618, and the process did not finally end until the late 1960s.'

31 These residential institutions operated separately from the 1850s until 1933: reformatory schools were intended for delinquent children and industrial schools for the destitute, but in practice there was some overlap; they were merged under the Approved Schools Act 1933.

marked out the binary justice and welfare approaches that is still in place today (see, further, below).

The Children Act 1908

The provisions of this legislation, also known, along with the 1899 Act, as 'the Children's Charter,' list the offences that, presumably, the carers of children were then associated with: from 'baby farming and the suffocation of infants; to cruelty, begging, burning, prostitution, smoking and being habitually drunk.' Under the Act, children who had allegedly committed an offence were dealt with in court separately from adults. It established the juvenile courts and finally abolished the death penalty (s 103) in respect of children and young persons. A large part of this Act dealt with the powers of the court to commit children – aged 12 to 16 – to reformatories, industrial schools, to the care of a 'fit person,' or probation officer – as alternatives to the previous options of 'poorhouse' or prison – and prescribed the treatment regime to which they would then be subject. It also re-affirmed the right of 'any parent, teacher, or other person having the lawful control of a child or young person to administer punishment' to them (s 37).

The Children and Young Persons Act 1933

This legislation, consolidating the provisions of the 1908 and 1920 Acts, though heavily amended, remains in force (see, further, Chapter 5). Part 1, being concerned with the prevention of cruelty to children and preventing their exposure to physical and moral danger, specifies and proscribes the range of conduct and circumstances which could give rise to offences. It introduced a more generalised protective function by limiting the types of employment suitable for children and the hours they may work. The Act drew a distinction between children: defined as either juvenile offenders, or in need of care and protection, or considered to be 'refractory'; and prescribed a corresponding range of court disposal options.

The most innovative provisions of the 1933 Act, for present purposes, were to do with the onus placed on the courts, by s 44, to have regard to welfare interests:

> (1) Every court in dealing with a child or young person who is brought before it, either as being in need of care or protection or as an offender or otherwise, shall have regard to the welfare of the child or young person and shall in a proper case take steps for removing him from undesirable surroundings, and for securing that proper provision is made for his education and training.

The specific requirement that the welfare test be applied to offenders – and that consideration be given to possible education and training – was a legislative milestone.

The Children and Young Persons Act 1969

Government policy had, by the 1960s, been much influenced by the work of child psychiatrists and developmental psychologists (see, further, Chapters 3 and 4) and moved towards recognising child offenders as more in need of treatment than punishment. Consequently, whether appearing before the court because of their deeds or needs, there was a growing consensus that first consideration should be given to the disposal option best suited to a child's particular welfare interests.[32] This approach found legislative endorsement with the Children and Young Persons Act 1969 which is still in effect, if heavily amended.

The 1969 Act placed the welfare principle front and centre of all proceedings relating to children and young persons – whether for care and protection or for criminal offences – by requiring the judiciary to consider the relative merits of a treatment rather than a punishment order following the conviction of a juvenile offender for certain offences. This approach was, in due course, judged to be a failure: by the professionals concerned (judiciary, social workers, and probation officers) who considered that juvenile criminals were escaping the consequences of their actions; and by the latter, who preferred brief punishment to protracted welfare supervision.

The Children Act 1989

Under Sched 2, para 7, local authorities are required to take reasonable steps to reduce the need to bring criminal proceedings against children and further preventative duties are placed on them under the Crime and Disorder Act 1998. It is of considerable significance that the lead role for this preventative strategy was given to local authority social workers rather than to the probation or police services. The governing principle for crime prevention in relation to children and young persons had been designated as oriented towards welfare rather than justice.

Tempering welfare with justice

Following the failed experiment of the 1969 Act, which sought to apply the welfare principle equally to both juvenile offenders and children in need of protection, the Children Act 1989 restored that distinction when it drew a principled line separating the law's response to a child who had committed an offence from one with welfare needs: involving different courts, different application of the welfare principle, and different court disposal options. However, the distinction was not watertight, there were some checks and balances.

The Children Act 1989

The 1989 Act returned the law to an affirmation of the welfare principle as being most appropriately applied to children in need of care and protection (see, further, Chapter 5). By abolishing care orders in criminal proceedings, s 90 of the Children Act 1989 made a clear and firm legal distinction between welfare needs and criminal behaviour. Nonetheless, as mentioned above, the preventative duties

32 See, for example, the government White Papers: *Child, Family and the Young Offender*, Cmnd 2742, London, HMSO, (1965); and *Children in Trouble*, Cmnd 3601, London, HMSO, (1968).

were assigned to local authorities and under s 31(2)(b) a care order could be granted in respect of a child 'out of control.'

Otherwise, the 1989 Act re-affirmed the requirements of criminal justice. This had always remained grounded on general considerations of the public interest, it had assiduously guarded against any obscuring or diminution of a defendant's rights and insisted on a high standard of proof to secure a conviction. Almost all children and young persons, aged ten or older, the perpetrators rather than the victims of criminal offences, would thereafter be very largely excluded from proceedings initiated under the 1989 Act.

Adjusting relationships between parents, child, and state

The most notable change in this set of relationships has been the legislative drive to promote a degree of convergence between the public and private sectors of family law, and more overall coherence for that body of law, through strategic use of the paramountcy principle, a common set of court orders, and by structural changes to the court system.

Parents, child, and state

Arguably, while the state has for some decades been in the process of retreating from private family law – having put in place an elaborate menu of processes and court orders for the parties to choose from to 'fix' or limit aspects of the damage caused by family breakdown – it has moved more assertively into the area of public family law and increased judicial and local authority powers in respect of children and young persons: both juvenile offenders and those considered to be in need of care or protection; and has also increased the representation available to them in court proceedings.

Child and parent

The landmark decision of *Gillick v. West Norfolk and Wisbech Area Health Authority*[33] changed the traditional legal relationship between parent and child from its exclusively parental rights basis to an approach based on tapering parental responsibility relative to the age and understanding of the child. The House of Lords then ruled that in some circumstances a doctor could prescribe contraceptives for a child under the age of 16 without consulting the child's parents. Consequently, the legal standing of a child in a decision-making process affecting his or her interests has since, for most purposes, depended on their age and their understanding of the issues involved. As Lord Scarman explained:

> a minor's capacity to make his or her decision depends upon the minor having sufficient understanding and intelligence to make the decision and is not to be determined by reference to any judicially fixed age limit.

33 [1986] 1 AC 112, HL.

The *prima facie* presumption that a child below the age of 16 is non-competent may be rebutted by evidence based on age and understanding: a child over that age will be presumed to have the necessary competence; but, if aged 16 or younger and deemed to be '*Gillick* competent,' the law now requires that his or her consent is sought in relation to the matter at issue. The *Gillick* ruling, preceding the 1989 Act, was the first step away from the objectification of the child within a paternalistic welfare philosophy and towards welfare as a matter capable of subjective interpretation, and of justifying action as a right, by the child concerned (see, also, Chapter 5). It signified the beginning of a children's rights approach in this jurisdiction and the beginning of a re-adjustment of legal responsibilities for welfare related matters between older children, their parents, and the state.

Parental responsibility

The concept, as much as the order, has altered the previous 'all or nothing' perception – that had continued to cloud the functions of care and custody orders – and substituted a legal bond between parent and child that endures beyond the making of any public or private family law order (excepting adoption). In an era of what for some children are often transient and serial parenting arrangements, this concept/order is an important means of retaining links and responsibilities between birth parent and child.

Child and state

The rationale of the *Gillick* ruling allowed it to transcend its parent/child context and establish the principle that – at least in the law of this jurisdiction – the consent of a discerning child aged 16 or younger, with a capacity to understand the complexities of an issue and its probable consequences, must be sought when determining that issue; whether it arises in the context of their relationship with parents, a third party, or the state. This principle is now constantly in play and has become particularly challenging in the context of 'looked after' teenage girls in local authority residential accommodation.

The effect of case law and practice resulting from the two Conventions has further reinforced this approach and is continuing to redress the balance between the rights of parents, child, and state. The United Nations Convention on the Rights of the Child (UN CRC), adopted by the UN General Assembly in November 1989 and ratified by the UK in December 1991, influenced the shaping of some of the more formative principles governing the 1989 Act.[34] The Human Rights Act

34 Article 5 of the Convention, for example, recognises the inherent mutuality between the rights of parents and the welfare of their children in its declaration:

> States Parties shall respect the responsibilities, rights and duties of parents … to provide, in a manner consistent with the evolving capacities of the child, appropriate direction and guidance in the exercise by the child of the rights recognised in the present Convention.

See, also, Article 12 which deals with the right of a child to freely express his or her opinion, and have that opinion taken into account, in any matter or procedure affecting him or her.

1998, which gave effect to the Convention for the Protection of Human Rights and Fundamental Freedoms and came into force in October 2000, thereafter became a potent force for guiding the modern evolution of children's rights.[35]

Civil and criminal jurisdictions

While the welfare of the child provided a natural unifying principle in respect of children's needs (in the contexts of care and protection and family breakdown) it also served to distance that nexus from the law relating to children's deeds: in that respect, the gap between the civil and criminal jurisdictions would seem to have widened.

These two jurisdictions are governed, respectively, by: the Children Act 1989; and the Criminal Justice Act 1991, the latter reinforced by such ancillary legislation as the Criminal Justice and Public Order Act 1994 and the Crime and Disorder Act 1998. However, there are areas of overlap. As mentioned earlier, local authorities are specifically required to direct preventative services towards children at risk of offending as well as at children in need. Also, the consequences of the uncontrolled behaviour of a child or young person may give rise to either civil or criminal proceedings and the outcome may lead to two different forms of secure accommodation: for children and young persons being 'looked after' by a local authority; and for those convicted of, or on remand in relation to, a criminal offence; both accessed only by order of the court (see, further, Chapter 5).

Parent and state

Whereas the distribution of authority and responsibility – between parent and state – in relation to the parenting of young children has not altered greatly in recent generations, even allowing for the impact of the twin thresholds of 'children in need' and 'children at risk of significant harm,' it has necessarily been adjusted by the above *Gillick* ruling and the accompanying UN CRC generated 'rights ethos' in respect of older children.

Local authority and parent: prevention and promotion

Local authority investment in ways and means of preventing a breach of the welfare threshold, and in promoting opportunities for furthering the welfare of children, has become much more pronounced since the introduction of the 1989 Act. The high visibility of its child protection activity perhaps detracts from the more discrete community-based funding, support, and regulatory supervision directed towards the range of voluntary organisations with a brief for children and parents

35 See O'Halloran, K., *Children & the Law: European Perspectives on Child Welfare and Rights*, Routledge (forthcoming).

which are now much more prevalent in all urban areas than formerly (see, also, Chapter 2).

Local authority and parent: parental participation in decision-making

In *W v. UK*[36] the court stressed that, under Article 8 of the ECHR, parents had the right to participate in any decision-making likely to impact upon their family life with their child. It explained:[37]

> What has to be determined is whether, having regard to the particular circumstances of the case and notably the serious nature of the decisions to be taken, the parents have been involved in the decision-making process, seen as a whole, to a degree sufficient to provide them with the requisite protection of their interests. If they have not, there will have been a failure to respect their family life and the interference resulting from the decision will not be capable of being regarded as 'necessary' within the meaning of Article 8.

Family re-unification post-care order

Again, the sharp end of child protection allied with the push to promote adoption from care may deflect attention from the scale of local authority investment in psychologists, family care centres, family aides, and play therapists that mediate in that uncertain space between a child becoming the subject of a care order and their failing parents. Nonetheless, there is good reason to suspect that this jurisdiction is less attentive to the rehabilitation of children in care with their birth families than other European countries.

Control

The responsibility to exercise control, so as to ensure that the behaviour of a child or young person does not breach socially acceptable norms, is in law now distributed with some uncertainty between the child, their parents, and the state. This legal function has its origins in private family law – in the doctrine of parental rights – it is a natural corollary to the parental duties of care and protection, and is essentially negative. As such it continues to be partly a matter for the civil jurisdiction of the courts.

However, 'control' has grown to represent a significant public law interest in the protection of third parties from the unreasonable behaviour of children and young persons. A real change has been the shift from the focus on the offender in isolation to a broader approach by also holding parents accountable for their failure to exercise adequate control, by making room in proceedings for the views of victims, and by requiring offenders to make direct reparation. This public law

36 (1988) 10 EHRR 29.
37 Also cited in *P, C and S v. UK* [2002] 2 FLR 631 at para 119.

dimension has become a significant and contentious area for modern social policy and more complicated in the aftermath of the *Gillick* ruling. Depending on the nature of the uncontrolled behaviour and its consequences, this may be a matter for either the civil or the criminal jurisdiction of the courts which in turn will determine the role to be played by the welfare principle.

Role of the welfare principle

Reviewing the history of this principle discloses certain immutable benchmarks for the content of a child's welfare interests.[38] The most obvious of these were concerned with safeguarding physical integrity. It detailed the record of legislative and judicial attention to such welfare functions as care, protection, health, safety, control, custody, and maintenance of children. These may be divided into those that are essentially negative in their effect and those that are positive.

Negative

From the earliest times, the law has prioritised the attention given to those areas with negative connotations for children because of the possible consequences for their physical welfare. This is still the case. Public civil legislation proscribes things, circumstances, and behaviour held to be detrimental and sets the threshold for intervening in family affairs on behalf of any child whose welfare has been, or is at risk of being, impaired. In a criminal context the prescriptive approach is aimed at identifying the circumstances in which a child may impair the welfare of others and in so doing compromise their own, even if that is a secondary consideration. State intervention on welfare grounds generally occurs after the event, justified by the fact of harm caused. Orders are then made to remove legal authority from those found to have defaulted on their responsibilities and to vest it elsewhere so as to best afford the child protection from future abuse, neglect, or from an environment conducive to their criminality.

The negative role played by the welfare principle in public law will undoubtedly continue in its traditional form within a modernised, highly structured, densely professionalised and tightly calibrated system for balancing public and private interests in relation to the needs of children. It will remain largely focused on determining entry to, and exit from, child protection proceedings, and in moderating exit from criminal proceedings, when judicial decision-makers will determine where authority will thereafter lie in respect of the children concerned.

Positive

In relatively recent times the law has also developed a positive approach to welfare interests. This is evident to some degree in public law where legislation

38 See, further, *The Principle of the Welfare of the Child: A History*, 2022, *op cit*.

requires preventative state intervention, makes provision for support services and welfare benefits to vulnerable children and families, and regulates general child care facilities such as playgroups, crèches, etc. Consensual state intervention in family affairs, to prevent further weakening of adequate (or underpin 'good enough' parenting) child care standards and maintain family based care arrangements, has been a very significant development in the role of the welfare principle. Additionally, the legislative emphasis on promoting the welfare interests of children in the care of the state, while proving to-date more aspirational than realisable, also indicates an awareness of a need to improve rather than to just monitor existing rudimentary care standards.

Welfare and cultural context

The intrinsic relativeness of 'welfare' is thrown into sharp relief when the particular needs of the child concerned are not representative of the cultural context within which they are being assessed. This contrast is most obvious where welfare issues arise in a UK court concerning a child from a developing country. This may also occur when the child is a UK citizen but part of a discrete minority as, for example, where he or she is disabled, a member of a religious sect, or of a family caught in the 'poverty trap.' In the cultural pluralism of contemporary Britain the upbringing of many children conforms to the values of their immediate social group and are not representative of the broad mainstream of society.

Pluralism and multiculturalism

Michael Freeman has written lucidly and with passion about the consequences of such cultural disparity and has drawn attention to cases which graphically illustrate the scale of the problem.[39]

Among such cases was that of *Alhaji Mohamed v. Knott*[40] involving a Nigerian Muslim couple, married in Nigeria: he in his mid-twenties, possibly married polygamously; she perhaps 13, maybe 11 and suffering from venereal disease contracted as a consequence of her husband's promiscuity. Following their arrival and after taking up residence in England, a successful application for a 'fit person order' was made in respect of the girl under the Children and Young Persons Act 1933, s 62, on the grounds that she was in need of care, protection, and control and was exposed to moral danger within the meaning of the Children and Young Persons Act 1963, s 2. On appeal, by way of case stated, the Divisional Court decided that the marriage was recognised as valid by English law[41] and reversed the

39 Freeman, M., *The Rights and Wrongs of Children*, Pinter Pub Ltd., 1983.

40 [1969] 1 QB 1. See, also, *Re S (A Minor)*, (1993) 1 FLR 297.

41 Subsequently, the Immigration Rules 1986, were amended (HC 394 at para 277) prohibiting persons under the age of 16 from entering the UK in reliance upon their status as a spouse.

decision of the magistrates, explaining that the couple were validly married and – within the context of their culture – the girl would not be considered to be sufficiently at risk to warrant coercive state intervention. In justifying the decision, Lord Parker CJ said that "decent-minded English men and women, realising the way of life in which the girl and the man were brought up, would not inevitably say that the continuance of their association, notwithstanding the marriage, is repugnant." That same year a West Indian father, charged with assaulting his 12-year-old disobedient son by punching him in the face, was found not guilty on the grounds that within his culture this would constitute acceptable chastisement.[42] Some 30 years later the words of Wilson J in *Re D (Care: Threshold Criteria: Significant Harm)*[43] offered evidence of a different approach which strongly suggested that cultural context should be discounted and seemed to promise a more uniform application of the welfare test; at least as far as the threshold of significant harm is concerned.

> Today in England and Wales we are not a collection of ghettoes, but one society enjoying the benefit of the composition of very many racial and cultural groups and one society governed by one set of laws. It would concern me if the same event could give rise in one case to a finding of significant harm and in another to a finding to the contrary.

This approach is difficult to fault if the principles of equality and non-discrimination are to prevail, even – perhaps especially – in a multicultural society. Nonetheless, after decades of exposure to human rights law, the numbers of young girls still undergoing female genital mutilation and forced marriage would suggest that the welfare principle – and benchmarks for its application – have yet to be fully established as a cross-cultural norm.

This anomaly, contradicting the logic of the paramountcy principle, whereby welfare may be viewed by the law as conditioned by its context, rather than applied objectively as a *grundnorm*,[44] is evident in other areas. The tendency to merge the welfare interests of a child with that of the mother or parents increases in proportion to the dependency of the child. Whether the dependency is due to being a foetus, a young baby, or suffering from a serious but treatable disability, or being so severely incapacitated as to be on a life support machine, there are many examples of a judicial willingness to impute the welfare interests of the child to the parent. In such circumstances a decision compatible with the interests of a parent, unaccompanied by any evidence of wilfulness or recklessness on the part of the latter, will quite often be held to be synonymous with the welfare interests of the child. Somewhat tangentially, this tendency to contextualise welfare is also evident in the poverty debate. For those who support the argument that a high proportion of

42 *R v. Derrivierre* (1969) 53 Cr. App. Rep. 637.

43 [1998] Fam Law 657.

44 See Kelsen, H., *The Pure Theory of Law*, (first published in 1934), The Lawbook Exchange, Ltd. (2009).

child care problems are a consequence of parental poverty then government aspirations to eradicate poverty or to 'level up' offers hope that it will thereby also substantially reduce those problems, on the 'rising tide lifts all boats' principle.

The movement against the contextualising of welfare has been assisted by the Conventions which have now gained widespread ratification, being incorporated wholly or partially into the domestic law of some countries. So, for example, when the ECtHR in *A, B and C v. Ireland*[45] determined to uphold the decision of an Irish court to deny a Lithuanian resident in Ireland access to an abortion – a decision shielded by the margin of appreciation rule – because of the "acute sensitivity of the moral and ethical issues raised by the question of abortion or as to the importance of the public interest at stake,"[46] this was challenged by a minority of six judges. They argued, to no avail but with some conviction, that such reasoning justified exactly the opposite approach and pointed out that[47]

> it is the first time that the Court has disregarded the existence of a European consensus on the basis of "profound moral views". Even assuming that these profound moral views are still well embedded in the conscience of the majority of Irish people, to consider that this can override the European consensus, which tends in a completely different direction, is a real and dangerous new departure in the Court's case-law.

In the long run this powerful voice of dissent would seem to be growing steadily more persuasive (see, also, Chapter 5).

Consequently, a shift away from contextualising welfare and other morality benchmarks has brought a degree of specificity to inform understanding of what constitutes 'welfare interests' and to allow a more uniform acceptance of the standards by which they may be defined and measured. There are now legal forums and frameworks for holding national governments accountable – if only on a 'name and shame' basis – for a failure to measure up to recognised welfare standards (e.g. Russia's refusal to tolerate same sex adopters). The international dissemination of national welfare audits provides a mechanism for encouraging national compliance with set, uniformly applicable, international norms.

Welfare interests in relation to other interests

Reference to the 'welfare interests of a child' carries two implications. First, that a child has interests additional to those of 'welfare.' Second, that there is a need to make room for a child's interests in the context of interests other

45 [2010] ECtHR (GC) (No. 25579/05) (16 December 2010).
46 Ibid.
47 Ibid. Joint dissenting opinion of Judges Rozakis, Tulkiens, Fura, Hirvea, Malinverni, and Poalelungi at para 9.

than those of children. Essentially it points up the fact that a child's welfare interests cannot be considered in total isolation: other factors have to be taken into account; balances must be struck. Where welfare interests are governed by legislative priority setting, usually by a direction that they be treated as the matter of first consideration or of paramount importance, then it might appear that the balance to be struck is self-evident and pre-set. But, in some circumstances, judicial creativity has blurred the distinction between welfare and other interests by judgments which assert that only by ruling in favour of the latter can effect best be given to the former.

Interests of a child other than those of welfare

Under the 1989 Act, the requirement to give paramount importance to welfare interests is binding only on a court and then only when it's considering issues relating to a child's upbringing or property. Outside 'courts of law' there is a vast range of tribunals and forums dealing with other matters affecting children, which are not bound by the paramountcy principle; for example, immigration tribunals, social security, housing, schools, and health care. It is sufficient for each that they give precedence to performing their respective statutory functions. In so doing they may take into account welfare interests insofar as this does not deflect from giving effect to their functions which are ancillary to, but distinct from, such interests. Schools, because of their prolonged influence on all children, are particularly important. They clearly focus on addressing children's educational interests but are not statutorily required, when doing so, to give any specific role or weighting to their welfare.

In public family law there is no legislative obligation on a local authority to give priority to a child's welfare interests. This, in conjunction with the directive to 'promote the upbringing of such children by their families' and the 'no-order' presumption of the 1989 Act, allows it to give precedence to other interests; for example, preserving family unity or the partnership basis of its relationship with parents. It may well take the view that maintaining a marriage or keeping siblings together would be more important in the long-term for all parties concerned than giving priority to a particular child's immediate welfare interests. A local authority may also, of course, simply choose to allocate its resources for purposes other than addressing the welfare needs of a particular child.

In private family law the tension between welfare and other interests has been growing steadily more pronounced. Because paramountcy is restricted to matters affecting 'upbringing' and 'property' it therefore has no bearing on other issues. As demonstrated in a number of cases in recent years, the presumption favouring the preservation of life must give way to the welfare principle. In effect, the courts may – and frequently do – find that the welfare interests of a child, with complex health needs and reliant upon medical intervention, are best addressed by measures designed to result in his or her death. Also, the welfare interests of a child who is not the primary subject of proceedings will remain subordinate to those of the child – perhaps a sibling – who is.

Interests other than those of children

The courts are steadily extending the list of exceptions to the legislative requirement that welfare interests be given priority.

Public law proceedings provide numerous examples of areas where other interests take priority over those of children. Most obviously in a criminal context the welfare interests of a child are now clearly subordinate to the interests of justice; judicial attention focuses on accountability, punishment, proportionality, reparation, and social rehabilitation rather than on the indices of welfare. In applications for secure accommodation orders, matters other than welfare, such as public safety, govern the outcome. Similarly in the context of immigration issues, priority is given to upholding the government's immigration laws rather than to welfare. The courts have even adjusted the balance between the weighting given to welfare interests and to the standard of proof required in civil cases. This occurred in *Re H and R*[48] when the House of Lords, confirming that the standard of proof required was the normal balance of probabilities, went on to state a new rule that the more serious the allegation the more substantial the evidence should be.

In private law there would now seem to be a general retreat from judicial intrusion into parenting matters, unless clear notice is served of circumstances in which welfare interests may be compromised. There has been no development carrying as much significance for the welfare interests of children, in terms of reducing the proportion of judicial decisions affecting those interests, than the removal of the welfare test in uncontested matrimonial proceedings. In that context welfare interests have been made subordinate to the right of parents not to have their privacy invaded. In contested private proceedings the legislature's decision not to provide parity with public proceedings, by standardising arrangements for the representation of welfare interests, indicates an intent to respect those interests as being presumptively private and therefore not necessarily requiring equivalent resources. In adoption, against the trend, the law has changed to place greater importance on welfare interests than on the availability of parental consent when determining whether the legal criteria for an order are satisfied. Welfare interests now give way to: property rights in applications for ouster orders; to principles and laws regulating immigration; and to comity between nations in the context of applications made under the Hague Convention.

The courts have also given much attention to balancing welfare interests against the rule that all parties should make a full disclosure of information known to them that have a bearing on the proceedings.[49] For example, in *Re D (Minors) (Adoption Reports: Confidentiality)*[50] the House of Lords ruled that welfare interests could not prevail against the fundamental principle of fairness that a party was entitled to the disclosure of all materials which might be taken into account by a court when reaching a decision adverse to that party; the principle applied

48 [1996] 1 FLR 80.

49 [1995] 2 FLR 687.

50 [1995] 4 All ER 385. See, also, *Re G (A Minor) (Social Worker: Disclosure)* [1996] 2 All ER 65.

with particular force to adoption proceedings. This increasing tendency to treat a child like any other party has also been evident in cases such as *Oxfordshire County Council v. M*[51] and *Re L (Police Investigation: Privilege)*[52] where the court ordered disclosure of documents and other material relevant to the future of the child concerned.

Weighting

The weighting attached to the child's welfare interests threatened to destabilise family law at the close of the twentieth century. The directive, in the 1989 Act, that when deciding any issue concerning a child's upbringing (or property) the court should treat the welfare of the child as the matter of paramount importance, correspondingly reduced the relative significance of all other factors and of all other decision-makers. In particular this served to devalue the rights of parents and undermine from within the fundamental premise of family law that the integrity of the family unit was entitled to protection in law (see, further, Chapter 5). It also re-positioned the powers of the local authority relative to those of the court: unlike the latter, the decisions to be taken by a local authority would be free from the requirement to subordinate all other considerations to that of furthering the welfare interests of a child. The welfare principle had come to assume the position of a new reference point, not unlike the governing and centrifugal influence once exercised by 'paternal authority.'

Arguably, however, there has been a steady withdrawal from this position. The application of the paramountcy principle is being judicially reined-in as the number of exempted circumstances increase (see, further, Chapter 5).

Conclusion

Family law – governing parenting arrangements and care and protection measures – provides the main arena for settling issues relating to children's welfare interests. Youth justice is also significant. Its twin frames of reference – welfare and justice – govern the legislative response to the needs and deeds, respectively, of children. Other laws such as those relating to education, health, safety, and employment also have an important, if more generalised, bearing.

This chapter has shown how the welfare principle has served to both promote the integration of family law while also widening the divide between it and youth justice. State intrusion into family affairs would seem to have become more assertive in relation to the latter, as it has with care and protection, but to have retreated considerably from private parental care arrangements following family breakdown. What is a great deal harder to judge is whether the relentlessly rising volume of cases is itself gradually diluting and ultimately devaluing the currency

51 [1994] 2 FLR 175.
52 [1996] 2 WLR 1235.

of the principle. As judicial application of the paramountcy principle in adoption is extended for a few children and prospectively estimated on a lifetime basis, the welfare shelf-life for the very many subject to other family law proceedings is shrinking, in keeping with the unsustainable relationships of their parents, and left to be addressed by single issue court orders. The security and durability of a child's welfare interests remain inexorably dependent upon the stability of their parents' relationship.

2 Advocates for change

Introduction

This short chapter makes the point – often overlooked or understated – that changes to law and social policy owe a great deal to the leverage exercised by the voluntary sector: its institutional organisations and its leadership. While legislators and the judiciary, domestic and international, are the most visible architects of law in liberal democratic societies, they build on foundations laid by majority public opinion as channelled through political processes that are open to lobbying from influential entities such as those that represent the interests of the voluntary sector (or 'third sector' or 'nonprofit sector'). Developments in the role and weighting of the welfare principle, a key component of the law relating to children, can be attributed – at least in part – to the pressures exerted from that quarter. More recently, the public sector has assumed a share of the advocacy role as national Ombudsmen – or other such bodies – have followed the example set by Norway in 1981 and established similar offices.

The chapter is in two parts. Beginning with a brief outline of the relationship between law and society, the first part considers voluntary organisations – particularly charities – their origins in Christianity, the significance of the Statute of Charitable Uses 1601, and their evolving role as agents for promoting social change. The second part focuses on the role played by specific leading child welfare charities, their distinctive contributions to promoting the welfare interests of children, and as advocates on behalf of those interests.

Law and society: balancing public and private interests

Maintaining order is the business of law. It does so, in contemporary liberal democracies, through the enforcement of values-compliant conduct, by authorising judicial and other forums to arbitrate and mediate disputes and by establishing the related rules, processes, and procedures. It is also an important, perhaps the most important, means of promoting social cohesion and continuity while also being a conduit for facilitating social change. To achieve and maintain a level of coherence and homeostasis in a context of constant social fluidity, law and social policy must remain open and responsive to pressures for change, much of which

DOI: 10.4324/9781003268642-4

is exercised by voluntary organisations. Some of the more significant adjustments to the law relating to children have been a consequence of such pressure.

Law and society

In a contemporary common law context, the law is based on principles of social justice, is intimately linked to the democratic political process, and is increasingly governed by human rights provisions embodied in domestic legislation and a raft of international instruments. Clearly, this was not always the case.

Christianity and the family: voluntary organisation beginnings

Initially, church rather than state undertook responsibility for family matters.[1] Births, marriages, sexual relationships, parenting, dying and death were all areas administered for countless generations in accordance with religious laws by denominational clergy; for some religions – mainly Muslims, Evangenical Christians and, to a lesser extent, Jews – this continues to be largely the case. As has been said, in words that, arguably, continued to apply in most common law nations well into the twentieth century:[2]

> The enormous status and prestige of the early and mediaeval church enabled her to assume jurisdiction over whole areas of social life which today would rightly be considered the concern of secular government. Indeed not until the mid-nineteenth century did the ecclesiastical courts in England lose their jurisdiction over marriage and matters relating to the probate of wills.

In respect of child welfare, this provided a context which generated related 'good works' by religious organisations in the form of orphanages, mother and baby homes, etc.

Public/private

The legal systems of the democratic nations must balance public and private interests. As Wigram VC declared more than 150 years ago: "many things of public utility may be strictly matters of private right, although the public may indirectly receive a benefit from them."[3]

Public benefit acts such as gifts to the poor or clothes for orphans were often motivated by private concerns, being underpinned by prayers to the church for

1 See, further, O'Halloran, K., *The Principle of the Welfare of the Child: A History*, Routledge, 2022, at chapter 3.

2 See Brady, J., *Religion and the Law of Charities in Ireland*, Northern Ireland Legal Quarterly, Belfast, 1976, at p 6.

3 *Nightingale v. Goulburn* (1847) 5 Hare 484 at p 490.

the redemption of the benefactor's soul. Masses offered for the dead, for example, were accompanied by alms for the poor of the parish, chantries[4] by endowments for the church and monasteries, and guilds[5] by bequests of property for the use of the church. Private and public interests were thus harmoniously balanced in their Christian origins. Altruistic activity also served as a discrete social mechanism for reinforcing the roles, relationships, and status of those involved while instilling a common morality in the community.

The secularisation of voluntary organisations – a process that owed much to the Statute of Charitable Uses 1601 – brought with it charitable status, regulatory supervision,[6] an assumption that organisational purposes be for the public benefit, and tax exemptions, all of which formally stamped such entities as being more public than private.

Christianity and voluntary organisations

To be a Christian has always entailed a duty to love one's neighbour, this being an inescapable requirement for salvation of the soul. "Love thy neighbour as thyself" (Matthew19:19; Leviticus 19:18) is an iconic biblical exhortation that has echoed down through the ages. Both the Old Testament and the New gave this commandment more particular expression in their repeated admonitions for the faithful to care for the poor, widows, orphans, sojourners, and other *personae miserabiles* (Deuteronomy 10:18; 24:17–21; James 1:27). "As much as you do for the least of these you do to me," Jesus said to his followers (Matthew 25:31–46). This inescapable requirement to care for the needs of others as a condition for the salvation of one's own soul became in time the driving force for Christianity's social role. Only by demonstrating love, through good works, could eternal salvation be assured. Saving lives in this world as the gateway to eternal salvation in the next has always been a paradigm of central importance for Christianity.

Given the strength of the linkage between Christianity and family matters it is unsurprising that this should be represented by Christian voluntary organisations with a mission to support family life in general and to provide for the needs of neglected, abused, or abandoned children in particular.

4 A 'chantry' (from the Chanting of the Mass) was a religious service founded and endowed by a benefactor for the repose of the soul of one or more persons. It was an important institution of the mediaeval Church and very popular in the fourteenth and fifteenth centuries. See, Wood-Leigh, K., *Church Life under Edward III*, 1934, at p 91; cited in Brady, J, *Religion and the Law of Charities in Ireland*, op cit, at p 12.

5 See Westlake, *The Parish Gilds of Mediaeval England*, 1919, where mention is made of 'the gild of the Blessed Virgin Mary in the parish church of St Botolph at Boston founded in 1260 gave a yearly distribution of bread and herrings to the poor in alms for the souls of its benefactors'; cited in Brady, J., ibid, at p 14.

6 The Statute of Uses established a body of Commissioners with powers to supervise and inspect charitable trusts.

Voluntary organisations

As explained in the Children Act 1989, 'a "voluntary organisation" means a body (other than a public or local authority) whose activities are not carried on for profit.'[7]

Such organisations and their activities have been in existence for at least the last millennium, but within a common law context their essential elements evolved in pre-Reformation England when church and monarch were the twin institutions governing society. At that time, it was the outreach facilities of the Catholic Church – centred on parishes, monasteries, guilds, hospitals, orphanages, and other church-run networks of poor relief – that formed the 'voluntary sector' and tended to the needs of the poor and destitute. These were largely replaced by secular parish based relief systems during the latter half of the sixteenth century following the Protestant Reformation. Arguably, therefore, one of the consequences of the Reformation and dissolution of the monasteries was a shift in the status of voluntary organisations from private to public as the majority of Englishmen 'reflected less on their souls and became more concerned with the worldly needs of their fellow men.'[8]

Nonetheless, in a society rigidly structured by feudalism, with wealth and power distributed accordingly, religious and secular organisations functioned to some extent as a buffer offsetting the gap between rich and poor, acting as a necessary solvent – mediating between the powerful and the powerless, articulating grievances, and providing supplementary resources – that helped maintain social stability.

The Statute of Charitable Uses 1601

This statute[9] legislatively established the respective responsibilities of voluntary organisations (designated 'charities') and state for repairing social infrastructure and alleviating the suffering of the English poor following the ravages of war and the dissolution of the monasteries. The statute, or at least its essential principles as applied by the courts, travelled with the armies of the Crown to provide a framework for voluntary organisations and their activities throughout the common law world (see, further, Chapter 3). The Preamble to this Act set the legal parameters for the subsequent four centuries of 'charity,' and continues to influence the reshaping of its role in response to the challenges of emerging social need. The purposes then declared to be charitable, and therefore appropriately pursued by charitable bodies, included the 'releife of aged impotent and poore people … and the educacion and prefermente of orphans.'

7 S 105(1) F48.

8 See Jones, G., *History of the Law of Charity 1532–1827*, Wm. W. Gaunt & Sons, Inc., Holmes Beach, Florida, 1986 at p 10 and also Leonard, E.M., *The Early History of the English Poor Relief*, Cambridge University Press, Cambridge, 1900 at p 9.

9 Also known as the Statute of Elizabeth, 43 Eliz 1, c 4.

From such beginnings in the early seventeenth century, voluntary organisations in England were legislatively assigned some responsibility for protecting and promoting the welfare interests of children, a responsibility which transferred to their counterparts throughout the common law world, reinforced by caselaw precedents forged in English courts. Such precedents being an entrenched aspect of the common law with an extensive history, as noted by Richard Fitz-Nigel in the twelfth century who reputedly observed, "there are cases where the course of events, and the reasons for decisions are obscure; and in these it is enough to cite precedents."[10] Following the codification of Preamble enumerated purposes in the *Pemsel* ruling,[11] which embedded the public benefit test as the legal hallmark of charity, the shift in the status of voluntary organisational activity from private to public was virtually complete. Subsequently, religious organisations and their activities were assumed to have charitable status even though legally exempted from that test. Such was the growing importance of charities' social role that, as has been said:[12]

> Essentially, the institutions of early eighteenth-century charity were still those first set in place after the sixteenth-century Reformation. The structures established then and the functions they performed were based on locality; and inherited from the mediaeval parish system.

Voluntary organisations: child welfare functions

Primarily, voluntary organisations have been founded to satisfy an unmet social need by filling a gap in existing service provision, supplementing government provision, or by pioneering a new approach to a specific social issue.

Charities and public benefit services

Being exempt from the rule against perpetuities,[13] charities may in theory exist forever. Many have existed for centuries and in the process accumulated vast assets, data banks of irreplaceable worth, and close bonds of mutual understanding with those socially disadvantaged whose interests they were established to serve. Free from the exigencies of government, and to some extent also from the

10 Fitz-Nigel, R., *Dialogues de Scaccario*, 1177–79; cited by Dias, R.M.W., *Jurisprudence* (5th ed.), Butterworths, London, 1985 at p 56.

11 *Commissioners for Special Purposes of Income Tax v. Pemsel*, [1891] AC 531.

12 See Deakin, N., *In Search of Civil Society*, Palgrave, London, 2001. See, also, Chesterman, M., *Charities, Trusts and Social Welfare*, Weidenfeld and Nicolson, London, 1979 at pp 40–53.

13 This rule dates from the statute of *Quia Emptores* 1290 when the judiciary and legislature set limits on the ability of persons to impose alienation constraints on their property to take effect after their death. It requires ownership to vest within the 'perpetuity period'; fixed at life or lives in being plus 21 years or just 21 years where there is no life in being. Once vested, a charitable trust enjoys the considerable legal privilege that it may continue in perpetuity.

competitive pressures of the commercial marketplace, unaccountable to shareholders or constituency, while entrusted with funds from private donors and the public purse, the responsibility rests squarely with a charitable organisation to provide appropriate resources, promote the interests and publicly champion the cause of those they represent.

Pioneering service provision

From at least the time of the Reformation until local authorities were established in 1929, the responsibility for meeting the needs of the poor, the ill, the disabled, and abandoned children and those otherwise disadvantaged fell mainly to charities. By the end of the nineteenth century, while the state continued to provide facilities such as workhouses in the towns and the funds and the officials to manage care facilities such as hospitals, it was charities that were the primary providers of health, social care, and education services for the socially disadvantaged. As financially independent, mission driven bodies, supported by public donations and armies of volunteers, charities were free and able to pioneer service development, to take initiatives, and shape services to fit emerging patterns of social need. They established and staffed hospitals, mother and baby homes, orphanages and other facilities that offered care and protection for children in need. Mary Carpenter, for example, in the 1840s, established a number of charitable organisations to provide education for poor children – known as the 'Ragged Schools' movement – in urban areas.[14] Such services, privately initiated by charities – schools, hospitals, etc. – often, in due course, passed to the public sector as government assumed responsibility for what had been proven to be an essential public service.

The role of charities was defined and expanded through judicial precedents, established in the courts of England, and derived authority from the provisions of the 1601 Act or more precisely from the principles articulated in the Preamble to that statute. These precedents were assiduously followed throughout the common law world and over the ensuing centuries they did much to build a shared pool of jurisprudence until adjusted by a spate of late-twentieth-century national law reform processes designed to ensure a better fit between charities and contemporary forms of social need. Such organisations provided – and continue to provide – a similar 'voluntary sector' platform among the common law nations which includes a focus on child welfare.

Advocacy

Voluntary organisations did not necessarily confine their activities to poverty relief and the provision of public benefit services. It is unlikely that there was any

14 See Carpenter, M., *Reformatory Schools for the Perishing and Dangerous Classes and for the Prevention of Juvenile Delinquency*, (1851), Routledge, London, 1969.

government pressure on them to do so. Indeed, during the Victorian era, many important initiatives resulting in social policy changes by government were led by voluntary organisations. Although charities were, and continue to be, prohibited from having political purposes, they were able to lead by example – e.g. by providing adoption services long before the first legislation introduced a legal framework for meeting the needs of unwanted children – and by advocating on behalf of a particular social cause, provided this was ancillary to their charitable purpose.

Social change

There will always be a tension between the role of law to maintain the *status quo* through rules, processes, and institutions that aid predictability and its role as independent guardian of principles of justice which require it to be open and responsive to the unpredictable. In the latter case, whether this occurs as a consequence of a shift in government policy or in circumstances, the law has a role in providing a bridge for social change followed by legitimising that adjustment and then establishing the new rules, etc. necessary for a new phase of integration. Alternatively, instead of being merely responsive, law may itself be the instrument for effecting social change as when used to transform attitudes towards the welfare needs and deeds of children.[15]

Agents of change

Non-government bodies – not-for-profit entities in general but particularly those with charitable status – are well placed to apply pressure on government to effect change in law and social policy. Being established as autonomous entities – with an additional legal requirement on charities that they maintain independent governance – and very often functioning as public benefit service providers on behalf of government, voluntary organisations mediate between the latter and the socially disadvantaged. They know the needs of their client group, have earned their trust over many generations, and have a vested interest in advocating on their behalf to government for such adjustments as may be necessary to re-align law, policy, and service provision with client need.

The voluntary sector: the contribution of child welfare organisations to social, legal, and professional change

The social activism of charities and other voluntary organisations – complementing their service provision role – became more pronounced in the latter half of the

15 For example, the legislative intent underpinning the Children and Young Persons Act 1969 was to establish the principle that the commonly held distinction between children who presented as 'depraved' or 'deprived' was misguided and instead the courts should treat all young children in accordance with their welfare needs.

nineteenth century. Protests against the practice of 'baby-farming' and against the conditions suffered by children employed in factories or as chimney sweeps, etc. were led by charities such as Barnardo's and the NSPCC. The Infant Life Protection Society, founded in 1870, provided such support as was then available for the protection of newly born babies in workhouses and it campaigned for the introduction of the Infant Life Protection Act 1872. The Society for the Suppression of Juvenile Vagrancy (later called the Children's Friendly Society), established in 1830 and aided by the social activist Mary Carpenter, challenged the harshness of the vagrancy legislation and the practice of transporting juvenile offenders overseas.[16] The Charity Organisation Society, founded by Octavia Hill and Helen Bosanquet in 1869, was a good example of reflective philanthropy at work; mixing provision for the poor with a sociological analysis of the causes of poverty. This Society, which pioneered individual casework, is credited with being the seed-bed of social work as a profession. These and the many child welfare organisations are each important in their own right but also, for the purposes of this book, their aggregate significance lies in the cultural context they created. They established a climate of general public awareness of what constitutes child neglect and abuse, directed private donations towards public benefit child welfare causes[17] while also, and importantly, empowering children with the means to express their concerns regarding such matters.

Then as now it was not necessary to be poor to be socially disadvantaged and this was reflected in the lobbying activities of charities and other voluntary organisations. They were to the fore in supporting the suffragette movement, in the battle for political reform (which resulted in the famous 1832 Reform Act) and in the anti-slavery campaign when campaigners compared the treatment of mill-workers, including children, to that of slaves.

By the early decades of the twentieth century, the role of charities as public service providers was fading. Partly this was due to the state gradually assuming more responsibility – the public service contribution of charities has waxed and waned in accordance with that of the Welfare State – but it was also due to the fragmentary effect of the emerging myriad forms of voluntary organisations.[18] By the end of that century, however, the position was reversed as government turned to such organisations – particularly charities – as a means of delivering the public benefit services that it could no longer afford to provide. Government

16 See, further, Carpenter, M., *Juvenile Delinquents, Their Condition and Treatment*, W. & F. G. Cash, Oxford, 1856.

17 See, for example: *A-G v. Minshull* (1798) 4 Ves 11 and *A-G v. Wansay* (1808) 15 Ves 231 (apprenticeships for poor children); *Rolls v. Miller* (1884) 27 Ch D 71 (homes for working girls); *Re Coulthurst* [1951] Ch. 661, C.A. (widows and orphaned children); *Re Elliott* (1910) 102 LT 528 (10 blind boys and 10 blind girls resident in a specified area); and *Re Sahal's Will Trusts* (1958) 1 WLR 1243 (children's homes).

18 Such as: Industrial and Provident Societies; Friendly Societies; Royal charters; Co-operatives; private trusts, unincorporated associations, community foundations, and a variety of social enterprises.

funded social care provision, delivered by tax exempt charities, subsidised by public donations and by volunteer staff, became the accepted norm in the developed nations facing the dilemma created by inexorable demographic trends, outsourced manufacturing, and falling tax revenues. Arguably, as charities became more dependent upon government contracts and funding, they also became more hesitant to criticise government policy. This was an era referred to by some as characterised by 'the muting of dissent' from the voluntary sector.[19] Whether true or false, this should not detract from recognising the record of achievement of leading child welfare voluntary organisations – all legally constituted as charities – in contributing to changes in the law relating to children both domestically and internationally. Furthermore, many of the UK lead charities eventually opened branches in other common law nations, extending their mission and political influence to the same effect in other social contexts. In short, it would be difficult to overstate the importance of the contribution made by these organisations to leveraging change in the law relating to children. This was particularly true of the larger institutional charities, long embedded in their respective constituencies, which could speak truth to power with some credibility and authority.

Coram

Founded by Thomas Coram in 1739, the Thomas Coram Foundation for Children – probably the oldest charity for children in the UK – began by establishing the Foundling Hospital in London for abandoned babies, followed by the opening of several branch facilities across England, and has since evolved into a cluster of separate charitable organisations. These include: an adoption agency; a foster care programme; a legal advice centre; and family support facilities.

Agency response to child welfare issues

The agency was founded in response to the plight of abandoned babies and children starving and dying in the streets of London. It lobbied for, and was instrumental in achieving, legislation for regulating provision for single mothers and their children.

Adoption and foster care

Coram pioneered 'concurrent placements' the process whereby dual approved carers (approved for adoption and for fostering) would undertake responsibility for children in the public care system on the understanding that their status as foster carers may or may not be transformed into adopters. This has facilitated the

19 See, for example, the Commission on the Future of the Voluntary Sector in England, *Meeting the Challenge of Change: Voluntary Action into the 21st Century* (the Deakin Report), NCVO, London, 1996.

adoption of many children who would otherwise have remained subject to care orders. For the past 40 years, Coram has been registered as an adoption agency and has grown to become one of the largest in the UK.

Pioneering new approaches to promoting child welfare

This charity has developed innovative approaches to childcare and education, informed by developments in child psychiatry which highlighted the importance of children's emotional wellbeing and their need for a secure family placements.

Input to professional education

From the outset, one of Coram's primary objectives has been to assist in the training of those with a professional care responsibility for children. Most often this has taken the form of education programmes for foster carers but, following its recent amalgamation with the British Adoption and Fostering (BAAF), Coram has taken responsibility for publishing *Adoption & Fostering* the quarterly journal for child care social workers and others. This has increased its capacity to disseminate good practice guidance among the professions concerned.

The National Society for the Prevention of Cruelty to Children

Founded by Benjamin Waugh in 1884, as the London Society for the Prevention of Cruelty to Children (London SPCC), this charity is one of the largest UK voluntary organisations dedicated to child welfare and the sector leader in the field of child protection. Unlike all other child welfare organisations, the NSPCC was the only UK charity to be granted statutory powers under the Children Act 1989 allowing it to apply to the court for care and supervision orders.

Agency response to child welfare issues

The NSPCC was formed in order to lobby the government to introduce child protection legislation. Following five years of campaigning, the organisation's success was marked by the introduction of the first UK statute – the Prevention of Cruelty to, and Protection of, Children Act 1889 – specifically directed towards affording protection to children from neglect and abuse.

Child sexual abuse

Perhaps as a result of its enquiries into a series of sexual abuse cases in Rochdale in the early 1990s, the NSPCC has since acquired a reputation for professional leadership in this particular field. It frequently operates in tandem with local authority social workers, providing specialist expertise, with indicators of abuse, to support local social work teams, police, teachers, church bodies, youth clubs, and others working with children.

Advocacy work with children

The NSPCC operates a national Child Helpline service to receive phone calls from children who may be suffering abuse or neglect, or who believe they are at risk. It has recently launched an additional helpline dedicated for use by school children which has generated heavy usage. The organisation provides support and guidance for helpline callers, enabling them to take appropriate action.

Advocacy work on behalf of children

The NSPCC lobbies government on issues relating to child welfare and frequently launches campaigns to raise public awareness on child protection issues.

Barnardos

Founded by Thomas John Barnardo in 1866, and grounded in Christian beliefs, this British charity was initially established to provide a 'ragged school' where poor children in London could get a free basic education. From that first step the charity moved to provide residential care for vulnerable children, sometimes in the form of communities or 'cottage homes' where children could be supported to live in small, family-style groups looked after by a house 'mother.' The Barkingside 'garden village,' with 65 cottages, a school, a hospital, and a church, providing a home and training for 1,500 girls, was launched in 1900 as a model of its kind. By the time of Barnardo's death in 1905, the charity had 96 homes caring for more than 8,500 children. Until 1967 Barnardos was also playing a leading role in the transport of some 130,000 British children to other common law countries; a questionable contribution to promoting the welfare interests of children.[20]

Agency response to child welfare issues

Barnardos' primary contribution to child welfare was its provision of a homely model of residential care for the many thousands of abandoned and orphaned children for whom no safe alternative care was possible. Though it has to be acknowledged that some of these children were in fact 'abducted' – without parental consent or court order – from parents whose standard of care Barnardos considered to be unacceptable and some of its homes have recently been the subject of historical child abuse enquiries. Towards the end of the twentieth century this agency closed the majority of its residential care facilities – the last in 1988 – and instead concentrated on adoption, foster care, and family support services. It is reputed to be the largest UK child welfare agency in terms of annual expenditure, estimated to be approximately £200 million.

20 See, further, Constantine, S., *Child Migration: Philanthropy, the State and the Empire*, at: https://archives.history.ac.uk/history-in-focus/welfare/articles/constantines.html#f1.

Initiating foster care

Barnardos' is credited with initiating foster care through the practice developed by that agency in 1887 of 'boarding out' children from its homes with host families which led to the Assisted Boarded Out Scheme being launched in 1891. This was an attempt to support first-time, unmarried mothers, then often ostracised by society, by giving them funding to pay for private foster carers in their local area, while still working, so that on their days off they could spend time with their child. This form of family based care in approved foster homes, supervised and supported by residential home staff, is currently the preferred model in many countries in continental Europe. By 1905 more than 4,000 Barnardos' children were boarded out.

Adoption and post-adoption support services

From the middle decades of the twentieth century, Barnardos was involved in adoption and became a registered adoption agency in 1947. During the period 1949–1976, some 4,220 adoptions are recorded as having been processed by that agency. In more recent years, Barnardos has developed post-adoption tracking, reunification, and counselling services.

Pioneering child therapy services

Direct therapeutic work with troubled children has become a leading agency service. This approach, which treats children – suffering from bullying, abuse, bereavement, or other forms of trauma – at home and in family centres, as part of their family unit, has developed into a resource greatly valued by local authority social workers. Involving parents in creative play therapy – in settings such as converted double decker buses – proved a popular attraction for disadvantaged children and an acceptable medium for engaging with their parents.

Children's Society

Founded by Edward Rudolf in 1881, as the Church of England Children's Society, this Christian charity was initially concerned with the effects of poverty on children and in 1882 opened its first home for 'waifs and strays.' It went on to create a number of such small homes, run by parental figures, as a refuge and an alternative to the harsh environment of workhouses. By 1919 it had established 113 homes, catering for some 5,000 children, though by 1950 this provision had shrunk to 34 residential nurseries. In keeping with the practice of other institutional UK child welfare voluntary organisations, the Society was found to have been implicated in historical child abuse arising from its role in facilitating the migration of 3,700 children to Australia, Canada, and Zimbabwe.[21]

21 See the Independent Inquiry into Child Sexual Abuse (IICSA), 2017 at: www.iicsa.org.uk.

Agency response to child welfare issues

As with other child welfare voluntary organisations, the Children's Society began by setting up residential facilities allied to adoption services. It operated on the principle that children should not become long-term residents in homes, but instead should be fostered or adopted. By the late 1960s the Society had become one of the largest adoption agencies in the country. Again, in keeping with similar agencies, it moved away from both residential care and adoption in the 1970s.

Pioneered day care centres

In 1969 the Society opened its first day care centre to provide support for single-parent families and those affected by illness, stress, or severe poverty. This led to similar centres being established across the country hosting facilities such as advice centres, play groups, and youth clubs. By the end of the twentieth century this had become the Society's core form of service provision.

Research

The Society has been responsible for generating child welfare related research projects, especially on subjects such as children's wellbeing, child poverty, and adolescent neglect.[22] During the 1990s it began focusing on social justice and cycles of disadvantage, lobbying to change legislation and to improve welfare provision. In 2006 it commissioned a research project into modern childhood – *The Good Childhood Inquiry* – to examine unacceptable levels of disadvantage, poverty, and social exclusion.[23] This provided an incentive for the Society develop its 'Good Childhood Index' which measures subjective wellbeing in relation to ten aspects of life for children over the age of eight.

Youth work

In recent years the Society's efforts have focused on vulnerable children and young people aged 10 to 18, including those who have been sexually exploited or in care, and on work with young refugees. Its youth work has sought to encourage the empowerment of, and self-advocacy by, young people.

Save the Children

Founded in the UK by Eglantyne Jebb and Dorothy Buxton in 1919 to improve the lives of children through better education, health care, and economic opportunities – as well as by providing emergency aid in natural disasters, war, and other

22 See, for example, the Children's Society, *Still Running: Children on the Streets in the UK*, 1999.

23 See Layard, R. and Dunn, J., *A Good Childhood: Searching for Values in a Competitive Age*, Penguin Books, 2009.

conflicts – this is one of the leading UK charities and is now also a global movement. It is mainly known for its co-ordination of international emergency relief to protect children from the effects of war and violence, but it also promotes policy changes to gain more rights for young people especially by encouraging enforcement of the UN Declaration of the Rights of the Child.

Agency response to child welfare issues

This international umbrella organisation, with 30 national member organisations serving over 120 countries, works with donors to develop programmes abroad, which are coordinated and delivered by a central body – Save the Children International – via teams on the ground.

Pioneering fund-raising techniques

This agency was the first charity in the United Kingdom to use page-length advertisements in newspapers. It pioneered the strategy of mass advertisement campaigns to generate public awareness of disasters and incentivise donations to enable the rescue and protection of the children affected. It also introduced individual child sponsorship as a way to engage more donors. The many national and global fund-raising campaigns launched by this charity to protect the welfare of children include: *Rewrite the Future*, 2006, focused on obtaining equal and quality education for those children unable to attend school due to conflict or war; the *Every One Campaign*, 2009, aimed to reduce the child mortality rate; *No Child Born To Die*, 2011, designed to combat the more than eight million deaths of children under five from preventable or treatable illnesses; and *Every Beat Matters*, 2012, which aimed to end preventable child deaths.

Contribution to international child welfare law

In 1923 the charity drew up and submitted an initial draft for what would become the UN Declaration of the Rights of the Child. This was the first important assertion of the rights of children, as distinct from the rights of adults, and it began a process that culminated in the UN Convention on the Rights of the Child 1989 which now serves as a touchstone for the work of Save the Children and many other child welfare organisations.

Other contemporary child welfare organisations

A small number of other charities are now also active in this field, some as service providers (e.g. Sure Start), others as advocates for children's rights (e.g. Family Rights Group and the Children's Rights Alliance).

The public sector and child advocacy organisations

As mentioned earlier, there has long been a pattern whereby charities or other voluntary organisations initiate services that are demonstrably effective in meeting a definite social need, responsibility for delivery of which is then assumed by government. This would seem to be what has occurred, to some extent, in relation to advocacy services for children. Reflecting the greater political salience now given to such matters, government ministers and government funded advocacy bodies have been established with a specific brief for children's welfare/rights and services.

Children's Commissioner/Ombudsman/Rapporteur

Towards the end of the twentieth century, a rising human rights awareness – boosted by the United Nations Committee on the Rights of the Child and thereafter by the Council of Europe – led to a number of European countries establishing public offices with responsibility for promoting children's rights in policy, law, and practice. In England, following the example set by Norway in 1981, the post of Children's Commissioner was launched in 2004.[24] Its responsibilities are as stated in the Children Act 2004 'to represent the views and interests of children,' as amended by the Children and Families Act 2014. Essentially, the objective of this independent national public body is to provide a voice for children on issues affecting their welfare and rights and to ensure that the law and practice on such issues conforms to the principles embodied in the UN Convention on the Rights of the Child. Membership of the umbrella organisation – the British and Irish Network of Ombudsman and Children's Commissioners – enables the Commissioner to share experience and promote a consistency of approach on issues across the British Isles.

Conclusion

Arguably the roots of voluntary organisation's contemporary engagement with the welfare of children lie deep in the religious origins of 'charity.' Christianity has been involved in diaconal care for the poor and needy from its apostolic beginnings, and canon laws governing charity were part of the earliest apostolic constitutions and conciliar decrees. Ecclesiastic teachings, perhaps primarily the catechist instruction that only by doing good to another in this life could salvation of the soul of the giver be secured in the next, recognised and established the inherent public/private value of good works. From the outset, one strand of such charitable good works was directed towards protecting and promoting the welfare of children.

This chapter has indicated – but hardly done full justice to – the link between Christianity, charity, and child welfare. Most of the relevant charities – Coram, Barnardos, the Children's Society, and others – were founded by Christians, were expressly grounded on Christian beliefs, at a time when the Christian

24 Established by the Children Act 2004 in response to a recommendation made by Lord Laming in his report on the death of Victoria Climbié (Cmnd 5730), London, HMSO, 2003.

Church was part of the British establishment, and were thus well positioned to exert pressure on that establishment to make the changes to law and policy necessary to further the welfare interests of children. The leverage then gained by charities – with regard to government determination of the law and social policy relating to child welfare – has since been developed by other voluntary organisations and by the sector.

Part II

Shaping the modern welfare principle

3 Domestic influences

Introduction

The transition from the twentieth century to the twenty-first saw the interpretation, role, and functions of the welfare principle in the family law of England and Wales affected quite radically by agents of change, both domestic and international. This chapter considers the former (see Chapter 4 for the influence of international change agents).

Beginning with a brief reflection on the fact that the common law cultural legacy laid the foundations for a shared family law structure, and for the role of the welfare interests of the child within it, this chapter continues to trace developments in the law relating to those interests from a UK perspective. It then examines the nature and depth of influence exercised by social science research and publications on those with a professional engagement with children. It strongly suggests that this influence – both domestic and international – was transformative in the insight it provided to practitioners – lawyers, social workers, and others – regarding the emotional and psychological needs of children at different developmental stages. The pressure for changes in family law at the close of the twentieth century, and the effect of the accompanying official inquiries and reports, are considered. Finally, account is taken of the influence of the Human Rights Act 1998 and its consequences for the welfare and rights of children in this jurisdiction.

The common law cultural context

The common law jurisdictions largely evolved from the same cultural context. This is of course particularly true of those currently being considered – England and Wales and Ireland (see, further, Chapters 5 and 6).[1] As constituent parts of the British Empire, all common law nations grew to share a great deal: language, parliamentary democracy, modes of governance, and cultural and social mores

1 Forthcoming books in this series will examine the role of the welfare principle in the law relating to children in other common law jurisdictions.

DOI: 10.4324/9781003268642-6

were all in the mix; but it was probably their continued adherence to the twin formative influences of Christianity and the common law that proved most binding and enduring. The template then established permitted the development, over centuries, of not dissimilar societies striated by the same Christian beliefs, morality, and values, and structured by the discipline of the common law. In all those jurisdictions the duality of church and state was nowhere clearer than in their shared experience of family law. This evolved in accordance with the structures, principles, and judicial precedents established in England and Wales, including a shared respect for the principle of the welfare interests of the child.[2]

A background of shared social values and legal principles

The shared cultural heritage of the common law nations was one in which the twin governing influences of church and state provided the framework for developing, nurturing, and protecting much the same set of social mores and for evolving related legislation. This proved to be a durable frame of reference, facilitating the growth of civil society and providing space for an independent voluntary sector (see, further, Chapter 2), throughout the common law world.

Similar social infrastructure

The shared experience has been evident in the modes of governance, in the laws, procedures, administrative measures, and in certain legal doctrines – such as case law precedent, *habeas corpus*, and *stare decis* – and was evident also in their social infrastructure – health, social care, and education – as it relates to general public benefit provision.

In England, a succession of Poor Laws[3] provided a legal framework designating the state as 'carer of last resort' for those most in need. The modern concern of the state for the welfare of children – as well as for the poor, the ill, and the disabled – was legislatively introduced in England at the beginning of the seventeenth century with the Act for the Relief of the Poor 1601. Always at best rudimentary, state provision then largely took the form of harsh institutional care for the desperate. In practice this meant the poor house, work house, or asylum for adults and orphanages for abandoned or orphaned children. This harshness was offset, to some extent, by the many religious organisations, designated charities under the

2 They also shared rules which constrained the principle of the welfare of the child. One such rule – traditionally honoured throughout the common law nations – was the sentencing of a juvenile, convicted of a grave offence, to be detained 'for the duration of Her Majesty's Pleasure'. This was found to be in breach of the ECHR in *Hussain and Prem Singh v. United Kingdom*, 22 EHRR 1 (1996).

3 In England, these were first codified in 1597–98, followed by a series of Poor Laws, including the Poor Law Amendment Act 1834, until the Poor Law system was abolished in 1948. See, further, Book 1, chapter 1, in this series.

1601 Act,[4] providing succour for the ill and needy in furtherance of beliefs that required the performance of good works in this life in order to ensure everlasting salvation of the soul in the next. The Poor Laws provided a base from which the state and the church significantly extended their reach into family affairs: a model subsequently transferred to its colonies and reinforced by the practice of transporting to those colonies the many tens of thousands of children unwanted in their homeland.[5]

As explained in the previous chapter, it would be difficult to overstate the important contribution made by Christian organisations in terms of putting in place the physical infrastructure of schools, hospitals, and other institutions that came to form the basis of public benefit services in the common law nations. A model of church/state public benefit partnership, initially forged in England, travelled with its armies to Ireland, Australia, New Zealand, the United States, and Canada. These were among the many countries much indebted to the religious organisations that laid the foundations for their present health and education systems – often providing the staff and resources for their functioning and maintenance – and indeed, faith-based educational facilities and hospitals continue to play a role in those countries. Equally difficult to overstate would be the less tangible influence of the Christian values and beliefs, the perception of the family, and the roles of its members – as modelled on the 'Nazarene family'[6] – which permeated the common law culture, providing a shared understanding of related social constructs.

Family law

Family law, perhaps more so than any other branch of law, is deeply embedded in, and continues to evolve from, that shared traditional Christian, common law, cultural context. As Lord Finlay LC commented in *Bowman v. Secular Society Ltd.*, when reflecting on previous centuries of case law:[7]

> It has been repeatedly laid down by the Courts that Christianity is part of the law of the land, and it is the fact that our civil polity is to a large extent based upon the Christian religion. This is notably so with regard to the law of marriage and the law affecting the family.[8]

4 That being the Statute of Charitable Uses 1601, the Preamble to which introduced a legal framework for voluntary organisations and their purposes.

5 See, for example, Bean, P. and Melville, J., *Lost Children of the Empire*, London, Unwin Hyman Ltd., 1989.

6 A reference to the first Christian family, founded in Nazareth.

7 [1917] AC 406 (H.L.).

8 Ibid, citing: *Briggs v. Hartley* (1850) 19 L. J. (Ch.) 416; *Cowan v. Milbourn* (1867) L. R. 2 Ex. 230; *De Costa v. De Paz* (1754) 2 Swans, 487; and *In re Bedford Charity* (Part II1819) 2 Swans. 470, 527.

Throughout the nineteenth century, and for a good part of the twentieth, the influence of Christianity on the legislators and judiciary of the common law jurisdictions was unmistakable. The jurisprudence of that era reveals how much the social construct of 'family' was determined by Christian beliefs and reinforced by the concept of 'sin.' This was most graphically apparent in the categorisation of those who were defined-out of the legal status of 'family.' So, and most invidiously, unmarried couples and their 'illegitimate' children were denied that status, as were those whose marriage was found to be bigamous and it could be removed from marital couples where one alleged that the other was homosexual or had sexual relationships with someone other than their spouse. Indeed, a characteristic of the common law is the emphasis on legal status, accompanied by the corollary that the formal authority of court proceedings is necessary when any question of change to that status arises.

Over the centuries, Christianity and the pooling of case precedents gave the common law nations a shared understanding of what constituted a family and of relationships judged to be sinful or virtuous.[9] This framework continued well into the twentieth century and even now much family law – certainly the basic principles, rules, and concepts – can still be read across those jurisdictions fairly seamlessly. The disengagement of the church from its role as arbitrator and custodian of values in family matters, while legally complete, is far from constituting a complete severance as religious organisations and adherents consider that each and every legal step away from the traditional religious frame of reference for 'family' (from divorce to same-sex marriage) and for 'parenting' (from single to same-sex parenting) is sinful and to be resisted.

Functions of family law

For church as for state, the primary function of family law has traditionally been to provide a mechanism for ordering familial roles and relationships: establishing and maintaining the rules that allow autonomous adults to form families, own and inherit property; and thereby facilitate the continuation and management of the basic units that collectively constitute society.

The state and the parent/child relationship

Family law – that coherent body of principles, procedures, and Christian values envisaged by Lord Finlay LC – that had prevailed for many generations, and more or less replicated throughout the common law world, provided a clear if patriarchal model of the parent/child relationship, which rested legally on whether the

9 A long catalogue of cases beginning with *De Costa v. De Paz* (1754) 2 Swans 487, Chancery, including *Lawrence v. Smith, Murray v. Benbow* (1822) *The Times* 2 Feb. 1822, *Briggs v. Hartley* (1850) 19 L. J. (Ch.) 416, and ending with *Pare v. Clegg* (1861) 29 Beav 589, 54 ER 756, established that 'the Courts will not help in the promotion of objects contrary to the Christian religion.'

child in that relationship could be defined as 'legitimate' or 'illegitimate,' depending on their parents marital status, or was an orphan (see, further, Chapter 1). Not until the introduction of divorce legislation in 1857,[10] and the break then made with ecclesiastical courts, did parenting arrangements become a matter to be judicially appraised in accordance with rules other than those set by Christian values. Nonetheless, more than a century elapsed before the UK courts, along with their counterparts in Ireland as in other common law jurisdictions, were faced with such a volume of cases – at first in private family law then in public – that new rules were required. These reflected a degree of state withdrawal from determining the many adversarial disputes featuring rival parental claims to custody, matched by increased state intrusion into family affairs where standards of parental care were suspect. When that occurred, family law coherence began to unravel.

Family law proceedings

The traditional binary division into public and private family law, in place since at least Victorian times, has been customarily represented by twin sets of proceedings: coercive state intervention, most usually by a local authority, to prosecute parents and/or children for infringement of statute law; and consensual, when state intervention is invited by the parent/s to resolve an inter-relationship issue, most usually one concerning their legal status as spouse or parent. A persistent theme and cause of much controversy for some decades at the turn of the millennium, was the need to consolidate the court structure and proceedings into a streamlined Family Court. While the debate continued the family proceedings courts struggled to cope with an ever increasing workload.

Family Proceedings Court

This court, precursor to the Family Court established in 2014 (see, further, Chapter 5), was a Magistrate's Court – comprising, usually, a panel of two lay magistrates chaired by a district judge – dealing with family matters and deriving its authority from the Magistrates Courts Act 1980 and the ancillary Rules.[11] The family matters brought before the court, from both public and private family law, consisted in the main of proceedings initiated under the Children Act 1989 but also proceedings under the Domestic Proceedings and Magistrates' Courts Act 1978, Family Law Act 1996, Child Support Act 1991, and the Adoption and Children Act 2002. The rationale for consolidation was in large part driven by a realisation that, as the welfare interests of the child had become the common denominator for both public and private family law, it would facilitate overall coherence if the court system was reorganised to enhance consistency in giving effect to this principle.

10 The Matrimonial Causes Act 1857 transferred the jurisdiction of matrimonial proceedings from the ecclesiastical to the civil courts.

11 The Family Procedure Rules 2010 and the Magistrates' Courts Rules 1981 (as amended).

The drive to establish a Family Court was greatly influenced by the prototype models already functioning in countries such as New Zealand.

Private

Characterised as consensual, the traditional type of private family proceedings have always been: matrimonial, divorce, and judicial separation; guardianship; wardship; and adoption.

At times of marriage breakdown, death of a parent, or voluntary relinquishment of a child for adoption, proceedings begin when a parent or guardian invites a court to settle the legal status of the parents and to rule on future care responsibility for any children. The court then exercises its powers in the context of proceedings which involve the welfare interests of a child for whom responsibility will almost always remain vested in their family of origin, most usually with a parent. This consensual frame of reference for the exercise of judicial powers, where parental parties have the *locus standi* of petitioner and/or respondent rather than as defendants, allows the proceedings to be conducted in an enquiring rather than adversarial manner. The threshold for a judicial hearing in relation to welfare matters in a private family law context rests essentially on permissive grounds: an applicant invites the court to formally validate an exercise of their rights as spouse, parent or guardian, etc.; the child concerned is most usually not a party to the proceedings.

Public

Characterised as generally coercive because these proceedings commence at the initiative of the state, rather than the family, in order to provide for the protection of children, in statutorily proscribed circumstances of abuse or neglect at the hands of their parents or third parties (though the provision of services is consensual when intended to promote welfare or is for preventative purposes). Such proceedings are distinct and separate from those similarly initiated in order to protect society from the statutorily proscribed criminal conduct of a child or young person.

Traditionally, when a child was brought before the court, for reasons of a public rather than a private interest in matters affecting his or her welfare, then the exercise of judicial authority was closely circumscribed by statute. Any question of altering the legal status of a child, by vesting future care responsibility outside the family of origin, required judicial attention to focus firstly on a technical legal dissection of the rights and duties of the respective parties. The whole approach to the welfare of a child, in this context, was then treated as subsidiary to the primary issues concerning the legal standing of the adults involved. Now the legal emphasis is reversed: the primary issue will be the welfare of the child who will almost always be made a party to proceedings.

Hybrid

A characteristic feature of modern family law is the shrinking of the binary division. Increasingly, although matters brought before the court are designated as public or private under traditional proceedings – such as matrimonial or care and protection – they will often require a mix of public and private orders to resolve. Moreover, certain orders – such as wardship and adoption – are now equally applicable in both public and private sectors of family law.

Influence of the social sciences

In the latter half of the twentieth century a resurgence of interest in the social sciences impacted upon the childcare professions on both sides of the Atlantic.

The study of society had become well-established by the seventeenth and eighteenth centuries,[12] even if as little more than a derivative of philosophy. By the nineteenth century, it had acquired a more scientific approach, largely due to Emile Durkheim. However, sociology and the range of modern social sciences were a product of the regenerated social sciences that emerged much more recently. When it took hold, in the latter half of the twentieth century, the resulting breadth and intersectionality of the subjects being explored had a particular influence on shaping our current understanding of a child's needs and their welfare interests.

Social science and the needs of the developing child

It was the emergence of disciplines such as developmental psychology, cognitive science, evolutionary biology, and others that fuelled a step change in how a broadening range of professionals understood and engaged with troubled children. Beginning in the mid-1960s, judicial notice was increasingly taken of the work of leading British child psychiatrists and psychologists, together with that of their counterparts in the U.S. (see, further, Chapter 4), and decisions became grounded more on evidence of the child's emotional and psychological welfare as distinct from their material wellbeing.[13]

Child care professionals

By the time the 1989 Act was taking effect, a new cohort of professionals with responsibilities for children had emerged, trained to have insight into family dynamics, an awareness of different forms of abuse, and of the need for professional collaboration. Within a period of two or three decades, attention to the causes and effects of dysfunctional families had been transformed from the traditional community 'welfare officer' – or institutionally based social care worker in hospitals, orphanages, and asylums – to professionally trained staff employed

12 See, for example, the works of Thomas Locke (1588–1679), John Locke (1632–1704), and Jean Jaques Rousseau (1712–78).

13 See evidence of such a trend beginning with the judgment in *Re C(L) (An Infant)* [1965] 2 QB 449 and culminating in the HL judgment in *Re W (An Infant)* [1971] AC 682.

by local authorities and by voluntary organisations. An important aspect of that transformation was the new focus on understanding the complexity of children's welfare interests.

Child psychiatry

While this profession gained recognition, as a distinct branch of mental health, more than a century ago[14] and was practised in the Maudsley Hospital as early as 1930, it probably only gained traction in the UK as a mainstream discipline in the 1970s. This was largely due to the influential research and publications of psychiatrists such as Robin Skynner[15] and Michael Rutter.[16] By the end of the twentieth century child psychiatry clinics were to be found in regional health care settings – hospitals or GP surgeries – across the UK. Working closely with local authority social workers in the community and often involved with them in therapeutic counselling in family centres, this profession brought considerable expertise and positive intervention to local authority engagement with troubled children and their families.

Education psychology

Again, like child psychiatry, this profession is little more than a century old. It owes its origins primarily to U.S. pioneers such as William James (1842–1910), Alfred Binet (1857–1911), and John Dewey (1859–1952). Their research and practice – on understanding human cognition, learning, and social perception – did much to raise awareness of children's learning capacity at different stages of their development. The discipline relies heavily on quantitative methodology, particularly to test and measure children's ability to achieve educational objectives and to assess their cognitive processes. Although initially largely confined to assisting children with special learning needs, or those on the autism spectrum, they now work alongside teachers, social workers, and speech therapists to assist any child with learning difficulties and to constructively mediate on their behalf in institutional environments.

Social work

As has been explained: 'the social work profession originated in volunteer efforts to address the social question, the paradox of increasing poverty in an increasingly productive and prosperous economy, in Europe and North America during the late

14 Due, in part, to the work of Maria Montessorri, among others, and her use of creative play with children as a means of exploring their developmental issues.

15 Skynner, R., *Families and How to Survive Them*, Cedar Books, 1984.

16 Rutter, M., *Maternal Deprivation*, Wiley, 1972.

nineteenth century.'[17] Its origins in the nineteenth century probably lay with the pastoral care provided by voluntary philanthropists and religious organisations, which led into the public service provision delivered by local authority or council workers throughout most of the twentieth. In the 1970s, however, following the Seebohm report[18] and the reorganisation of social service provision, social work began its transformation from an occupation to a professional discipline that required training in child care, the behavioural sciences, and in the social sciences – including sociology, psychology, economics, social policy, law, etc. – and resulted in academic qualifications.[19] At that time most social workers had generic training, were community based, and most usually employed by local authorities, though some had additional specialist qualifications, or experience, and were located in hospitals or assigned to specific health or social care teams such as in mental health, disability, and work with the elderly.

Child care social work

Beginning with the charitable children's organisations – such as the NSPCC and Barnardos – social workers with specialist training in children then started being employed by local authorities in the years following the Seebohm reorganisation. This was an era when the focus, developed by the NSPCC, on the 'battered baby syndrome' (see, further, Chapter 4) strongly influenced all child care professionals, prompting the setting-up of 'care and protection' teams throughout local authorities. That focus on physical abuse triggered research aimed at differentiating between different types of harm which led to the recognition of several distinct forms – most notably, neglect, emotional abuse, and sexual abuse – and led also, arguably, to the 'pathologising' of child care and protection work. As inter-disciplinary teams – including social workers, paediatricians, psychiatrists and psychologists, health visitors, GPs, and teachers – co-ordinated their professional expertise at child protection case conferences, so child care and protection gained increasing media salience, and became more divorced from other work with children and from social services in general.

In fact it is probably not an exaggeration to say that child care and protection, an acutely stressful and uncertain area of social work, has now developed its own rather closed and defensive culture which does not readily accommodate positive and creative engagement with children and their families. This defensive culture may well be linked to the litany of child care failures – as exemplified by the

17 Stuart, P.H., 'Social Work Profession: History', *Encyclopedia of Social Work*, OUP, 2013, at: https://doi.org/10.1093/acrefore/9780199975839.013.623.

18 See Report of the Interdepartmental Committee on Local Authority and Allied Personal Social Services, C(68) 88, 1968.

19 Not until 2001, however, when the General Social Care Council (GSCC) was established, did social work attain the status of a regulated profession.

Victoria Climbié tragedy[20] – but is also due to institutionalised problems associated with staffing and career prospects.

Welfare of the child: new disciplines and theoretical approaches

Strongly associated with the influx of a new range of child care professionals was the emergence of some singular theoretical approaches which continue to play an important role in aspects of child care.

Attachment theory

John Bowlby,[21] a leading exponent of attachment theory, was a psychologist, psychiatrist, and psychoanalyst who specialised in child development in the late 1960s and introduced child care professionals and the judiciary to the importance of preserving the bonding relationship between mother and child. He continued the earlier work of Melanie Klein,[22] a British psychologist, who had researched child anxiety, insecurity, their causes, and the relevance of play therapy. Along with Mary Ainsworth, Bowlby researched and published on the consequences of maternal deprivation for a child's ability to thereafter form the secure emotional attachments essential to his or her welfare interests.[23] He understood attachment as a lasting psychological connectedness between human beings which suggested that a child had an innate need to form an emotional bond with a caregiver. Importantly, Bowlby took the view that the mother was the caregiver best placed to provide the nurture that fostered an emotional bond, though he conceded that the relationship need not be exclusively maternal, other caregivers could share or replace the maternal role and achieve an equivalent bond. Subsequent research by the child psychiatrist Michael Rutter,[24] which focused on maternal deprivation and the consequent effects of privation, challenged the Bowlby thesis by arguing that a child needed to develop multiple attachments rather than be dependent upon a single caregiver such as their mother.

The paediatrician and psychoanalyst Donald Winnicott,[25] a contemporary of Bowlby, also cast a considerable influence on what was then an emergent child care profession. His reassurance as regards 'good enough parenting' is still, if

20 See, further, *The Victoria Climbié Inquiry*, HMSO, 2000.

21 Bowlby, J., *Attachment and Loss*, Pimlico, New York, Basic Books, (1968).

22 Klein, M., *The Psycho-Analysis of Children*, (first published in 1932), Vintage, 1997.

23 A theoretical approach which echoed that of Romilly MR a century earlier in *Austin v. Austin* (1865) 34 Beavan 257:

> The welfare of the child is so intimately connected with its being under the care of the mother that no extent of kindness on the part of any other person can supply that place.

24 See, for example, Rutter, M., *Maternal Deprivation Reassessed*, Penguin, (1972).

25 Winnicott, D., *The Child, the Family, and the Outside World*, (first published, 1964), Penguin Classics, 2021.

with some equivocation, used as a judicial benchmark for questioning whether the 'significant harm' threshold has in fact been breached or breached irreparably.

- **The 'psychological bond'**

It was only after dissemination of Bowlby's research that the judiciary and others began to recognise the importance of preserving the 'psychological bond' which allows a child to develop and sustain a relationship with at least one nurturing adult; the younger the child the more important the bond and the more probable that this is best supplied by a mother or maternal figure. Distinct, but often in practice closely related, was the judicial significance attached to the 'blood-tie.' The preference shown for care arrangements which permit a child to have his or her home with a parent or member of their family of origin became evident, for example, in contests between first and third parties. It could also be seen playing a part in step-parent adoptions where the order made favoured the caring parent in a position to provide the child concerned with continuity of home environment. An extension of the respect for such attachments became evident in the judicial attention given to maintaining for a child those reference points which are demonstrably important to his or her psychological development, such as contact with members of nuclear and extended family, friends, school, neighbours, and neighbourhood. This insight was one reflected in the broadening of the welfare principle – away from the traditional emphasis on care, protection, prevention, and control – to accommodate emotional and psychological needs and an awareness of a child's possible 'attachment issues.'

- **Identity**

As a natural corollary to the importance of 'attachment theory,' there emerged a growing awareness of how essential a secure framework of psychosocial relationships was to forming an authentic and independent personal identity. As Triseliotis expressed it:[26]

> There is a psychosocial need in all people, manifest principally among those who grow up away from their original families, to know about their background, their genealogy and their personal history if they are to grow up feeling complete and whole.

A child's psychosocial context, as a determinant of their evolving identity, was also matter that focused the research of Erik Erikson who defined identity as 'a

26 Triseliotis, J., 'Obtaining Birth Certificates', in Bean, P., (ed), *Adoption: Essays in Social Policy, Law and Sociology*, London, Tavistock, 1984. See, also, Triseliotis, J., *In Search of Origins: The Experience of Adopted People*, London, Routledge & Kegan Paul, 1973.

subjective sense of invigorating sameness and continuity.'[27] His developmental theory – anchored on eight successive stages – had a revolutionary impact upon child care professionals, their training, and on practices such as serial foster care placements.

Cognitive theory

This aspect of psychology surfaced in the 1960s to raise awareness of sensory processes as a counterbalance to the emphasis on, and limitations of, behavioural psychology. It stressed, instead, the importance of reasoning, perception, the use of language, and a capacity for problem solving. Jean Piaget[28] was a leading international exponent of this discipline (see, further, Chapter 4). Closer to home, Kellmer-Pringle,[29] an educational psychologist and the first director of the National Children's Bureau, who became renowned for her work on early childhood development, may also be considered as having applied this approach in her work with children. She recognised the need to ensure that a child's nurturing environment catered for and balanced their emotional, social, and physical needs and provided the context for the four crucial elements required for healthy development: love and security, new experiences, praise and recognition, and responsibility. She emphasised a child's need for positive reinforcement and warned of the risk that a failure to meet a child's needs in the early years may well lead to long-term difficulties.

Pressure for change: government inquiries and other official reports

The appointment of the Seebohm Committee in 1965[30] 'to review the organisation and responsibilities of local authority personal social services in England and Wales, and to consider what changes were desirable to secure an effective family service,' set in train the ensuing change process that was to continue for some decades and which would profoundly affect the ways in which the law relates to children in England and Wales. The Local Authority Social Services Act 1970, which gave effect to many of the recommendations made in the Seebohm report, sought to establish a co-ordinated and comprehensive approach to social care, providing support to families in accordance with the principle that family care was best for children, by requiring every local authority to establish a social services committee to carry out social services functions. Against the background of that structural change to the organisation of

27 Erikson, E., *Identity Youth and Crisis*, London, Faber & Faber, 1968. See, also, Erikson, E., *Identity and the Life-cycle*, New York, Norton, 1980.

28 Piaget, J. and Inhelder, B., *The Psychology of the Child*, London, Routledge & Kegan Paul, 1969.

29 Pringle, M.K., *The Needs of Children*, London, Hutchinson, 1975.

30 See Report of the Interdepartmental Committee on Local Authority and Allied Personal Social Services, C(68) 88, 1968.

local authority services, coupled with the impact of social science research, a sequence of reviews unfolded in which the legal framework relating to children was examined with a view to achieving a better fit with new perspectives on the needs and services of children and their families.

Child care and protection

One of the more powerful forces for legislative change in the child care law of England and Wales in the latter decades of the twentieth century had its roots in a growing public disquiet centred on media portrayal of social workers' conduct in child abuse situations. On the one hand they were criticised for what was perceived to be heavy-handed intervention in family affairs prior to a judicial hearing. On the other, they were condemned for a perceived lack of sufficiently assertive intervention. Either way, the deaths of many children led to public inquiries and to changes in law and policy.[31]

The child abuse public inquiries

During the 1970s and into the 90s, a succession of tragic cases (e.g. the misguided intervention of social workers in Cleveland, Rochdale, and the Orkneys) had been the focus of much media attention and eventual public inquiries.[32] They were accompanied by a series of cases involving the deaths of children,[33] which were attributed to the failure of social workers to act promptly and decisively in giving effect to the powers vested in them by court order and were the subject of much publicised public inquiries.[34] One of the earliest was that conducted in relation to the death of Maria Colwell,[35] who was killed by her step-father after being returned home from foster care. The public inquiry, which found serious failings in the child protection system, led to the introduction of the Children Act 1975. In all, during the 15 year period 1972–87, there were 34 public inquiries into deaths of children known to social workers.[36] Whether associated with too much or too little social work intervention, child abuse had become a matter of great public concern by the mid-1980s. The effect of public childcare scandals, combined with the expense of that care and the influence of the principle that family

31 See Norris, E. and Shepheard, M., 'How Public Inquiries can Lead to Change', Institute of Government, 2017, at: www.instituteforgovernment.org.uk/sites/default/files/publications/Public%20Inquiries%20%28final%29.pdf.

32 See, for example, the *Report of the Inquiry into Child Abuse in Cleveland 1987*, Cmnd 412, (1987).

33 See, for example, the deaths of Jasmine Beckford and Tyra Henry.

34 As in, 'A Child in Mind: Protection of Children in a Responsible Society: Report of the Commission of Enquiry into the Circumstances Surrounding the Death of Kimberley Carlile.'

35 DHSS, 'Report of the Committee of Inquiry into the Care and Supervision Provided in Relation to Maria Colwell,' London, Her Majesty's Stationery Office (HMSO), 1974.

36 See, for example, 'the Waterhouse Inquiry' into the physical and sexual abuse of children in care homes in North Wales between 1974 and 1990.

care is best, led to the outcomes research for looked-after children which, together with attachment theory, suggested that once rehabilitation had been found to be impracticable then a local authority should institute permanency planning and that adoption rather than foster care was more likely to produce long-term beneficial outcomes for the children concerned.

Family law: review processes

The family law reviews conducted in the latter part of the twentieth century, and continuing well into the twenty-first,[37] reflected the perceived binary split between public and private and were duly undertaken separately by different bodies.[38] While child abuse may well have been the main source of pressure for change, it was not the only subject of the many official inquiries conducted into child welfare-related matters.

Review of public family law

The Interdepartmental Committee review, triggered mainly by the death of Jasmine Beckford,[39] commenced in 1984, produced 12 consultation papers, and was solely concerned with aspects of public family law governing statutory child care issues.[40] Its findings were published as a consultative document[41] and formed the basis for a subsequent government White Paper.[42] As Bainham noted, the welfare principle as a basis for taking children into care was then expressly rejected by the Committee. Instead it cautioned that

> grounds which look only to the best interests of the child or are based on a broad criterion, such as 'exceptional circumstances', would provide insufficient protection against unwarranted interventions where parents were 'good

37 See Ministry of Justice, *Family Justice Review: Final Report* (2011). This was followed by the Ministry of Justice and Department for Education, *The Government Response to the Family Justice Review: A System with Children and Families at its Heart*, Cm 8273 (TSO, 2012). Later, the Public Law Working Group, *Recommendations to Achieve Best Practice in the Child Protection and Family Justice Systems*, final report 2021, at: www.judiciary.uk/wpcontent/uploads/2021/03/March-2021-report-final_clickable.pdf.

38 See Bainham, A., 'Private and Public Children Law: An Under-explored Relationship', *Child and Family Law Quarterly*, Vol 25, No 2, at pp 138–58, 2013.

39 Four-year-old Jasmine Beckford, who lived in London, was starved and beaten to death by her step-father in July 1984, despite some 78 home visits by a social worker.

40 The Rt Hon Lady Justice Hale (formerly Professor Brenda Hoggett QC), was the Law Commissioner in charge of the programme of reform in family law from 1984–93.

41 See DHSS, 'Review of Child Care Law: Report to Ministers of an Interdepartmental Working Party', HMSO, 1985.

42 See *The Law on Child Care and Family Services*, Cmnd 62, HMSO, (1987).

enough' but not providing as well for the child as a local authority or foster parent might.[43]

This sentiment seemed to form the starting point for the subsequent 1989 Act. As Baroness Hale reflected, the Act embodied the principle that "it is the bedrock of society that children belong in families and not to the state."[44] The review and the White Paper both exercised a formative influence in determining the content of the Children Act 1989.

Review of private family law

The Law Commission's review formed part of a staged but comprehensive examination of all aspects of private family law governing the care and custody of children in England and Wales. This was ongoing throughout the period of the Committee review. Between 1985 and 1987 the Commission issued a series of papers; the last[45] making a particularly strong contribution to the formulation of principles and content in Parts 1 and 11 of the 1989 Act.

Adoption

Some two decades after the Houghton Committee[46] produced its last report on adoption law and practice (the recommendations of which were incorporated into the Adoption Act 1976), and following introduction of the Children Act 1989, the interdepartmental group commenced its public consultation process on adoption law.[47] The 1992 review of this law, conducted jointly by the Department of Health and the Law Commission,[48] resulted in the Consultation Document[49] which recommended that: adoption should continue to be restricted to married applicants; extended to single persons only in exceptional circumstances; that the consent of

43 Department of Health and Social Security, *Review of Child Care Law: Report to Ministers of an Interdepartmental Working Party* (HMSO, 1985), para 3.27. As cited in Bainham, A., 'Private and Public Children Law: An Under-explored Relationship', op cit, at p 143.

44 See Hale, D.B., 'In Defence of the Children Act', *Archives of Disease in Childhood* 2000; 83: pp 463–7, at p 463.

45 See *Review of Child Law: Guardianship and Custody* (Law Commission Report No 172), HMSO, (1988).

46 See Report of the Departmental Committee on the Adoption of Children (Houghton Committee), Cmnd 5107, London, HMSO, 1974.

47 Issuing a succession of papers: 'The Nature and Effect of Adoption', September 1990; 'Agreement and Freeing', September 1991; 'The Adoption Process', November 1991; and 'Intercountry Adoption', January 1992.

48 The working party, drawn from the two agencies, was established in 1989. Constituted as the Interdepartmental Review of Adoption Law, it published four preliminary discussion papers: The Nature and Effect of Adoption (1990), Agreement and Freeing, The Adoption Process, and Intercountry Adoption; and three background papers: International Perspectives (1990), Review of Research Relating to Adoption (1990), followed by Intercountry Adoption (1991–2).

49 Department of Health, *Adoption Law Review: Consultation Document*, London, HMSO, 1992.

unmarried fathers without parental responsibility should remain unnecessary; and that post-adoption contact and greater openness[50] in accessing information should have a part to play in adoption in the future. It also addressed the long-standing concern that step-adoptions had the effect of legally guillotining the interests of all members of one side of the child's family in maintaining relationships with that child[51] and suggested that other less extreme orders, such as a residence order, would be more appropriate. This led in turn to the publication of the government's White Paper *Adoption – The Future*[52] and its sequel *Adoption – A Service for Children.*[53] However, despite a gestation period of 13 years, it was not until the pressure generated by childcare scandals became acute that the government was finally prompted to consider new legislation.[54] Preparations began with the White Paper, *Adoption: A New Approach* in 2000 which proposed that child care and adoption legislation should be brought into alignment to make the welfare interests of the child, interpreted in the light of the welfare checklist, the matter of paramount importance in all decisions throughout the adoption process, thereby facilitating a linkage between child care and adoption proceedings. It set out the government's expectation that there would be a 40 per cent increase in adoption orders over the next five years in respect of looked-after children. This process concluded with the Adoption and Children Act 2002 which aligned the principles of the 1989 and 2002 Acts and succeeded in mainstreaming adoption into childcare and protection policy, thus creating a new platform for addressing the needs of children failed by their parents.

The paramountcy principle

As embedded in s 1(2) of the 2002 Act, this principle provided for the first time a statutory mechanism to bridge both childcare and adoption proceedings. Although held to govern any decision taken in respect of a child's prospective adoption – whether by an adoption agency (such as a local authority) or court – including dispensing with consent of the birth parent/s, the UN CRC nonetheless had 'regrets that the right of the child to have his or her best interests taken as a primary consideration is still not reflected in all legislative and policy matters and judicial decisions affecting children, especially in the area of alternative care.'[55] It recommended that 'this right is appropriately integrated and consistently interpreted and applied in all legislative, administrative and judicial proceedings and

50 Review of Adoption Law, para 4.2.
51 Ibid., at para 19.2.
52 (Cmnd 2288), 1993.
53 Adoption – A Service for Children, London, HMSO, 1996. Note also the Green Paper, Every Child Matters (2003) and Every Child Matters: Next Steps, Department of Skills and Education, London, HMSO, 2004.
54 See, in particular, the Waterhouse Inquiry.
55 UN CRC, Concluding Observations, para 26.

decisions and in all policies, programmes and projects that are relevant to and have an impact on children.'[56]

Use of wardship in private and in public family law matters

During the 1970s and 80s, the spate of wardship orders – very largely issued in relation to child care and protection issues gave the High Court judiciary, other lawyers, and social workers an opportunity to experience the many points of similarity between public and private aspects of family law when dealing with issues concerning the welfare interests of a child. Ultimately, however, in relation to both sectors of family law, government policy concluded that, notwithstanding the much greater flexibility offered by wardship in reaching a solution favouring the welfare of a child, where Parliament had provided a statutory procedure this must be used.

Private

In England and Wales, the exercise of the inherent jurisdiction in the context of private family law was constrained by the passing of the Family Law Reform Act 1969 which in effect superimposed a statutory framework on the management of wards of court.

Public

In public family law, the urgency, complexity, and volume of child care cases had become such that they could no longer be readily processed through statutory proceedings. The discretionary powers of the wardship jurisdiction allowed local authorities to avoid the restrictive technical grounds of statutory child care law and permitted the judiciary to take almost any action they deemed necessary to safeguard the welfare of a child. Local authorities resorted to wardship to secure either a more effective alternative or to supplement their statutory powers. The judiciary granted wardship orders only when convinced that the statutory grounds did not provide the local authority with sufficient powers to appropriately secure the welfare of the children concerned. In effect this practice of using the powers of wardship alongside statutory powers to deal with certain child care issues was steadily consolidating into a dual approach by the legal system to such matters; one approach attaching a significantly greater weight to the welfare of the child than the other. There was increasing concern that this practice disadvantaged the birth parent/s and would lead to great uncertainty in the application of the law to child care matters.

Prior to the introduction of the Children Act 1989, if a child was made a ward of court and committed to care, the court exercised its powers under the inherent

56 Ibid, at paras 26–7.

jurisdiction and under s 7 of the Family Law Reform Act 1969. The child as ward was committed, in effect, to the care of a local authority under that section.

The use of wardship by local authorities was inequitable as parents did not enjoy an equal right of access to that jurisdiction. This inequity, compounded by the relative immunity from judicial scrutiny enjoyed by local authorities as a result of the ruling in *Liverpool*,[57] caused considerable professional concern and frequent parental applications for judicial review (see, further, Chapter 5). In 1987, the Law Commission's review of wardship found 'that the universal character of wardship and the restrictions on its use create anomalies and make it inconsistent with the statutory codes relating to custody and to the care of children by local authorities.'[58]A reduction in the discretionary powers of social workers at the point of initial intervention in family affairs, which had been greatly facilitated by their use of wardship, was among the primary objectives of the 1989 Act. This statute, as intended, placed the wardship jurisdiction for most purposes outside the reach of local authorities, though it continued to have a marginal relevance for the protection and promotion of legal interests of children. As regards private law cases, however, the volume of wardship orders increased following the introduction of the 1989 Act and the High Court will still, occasionally, exercise its wardship jurisdiction to assist a local authority in circumstances where no statutory remedy is readily available.

Family law: legislative change

The Children Act 1989 was a formative statute that introduced some fundamental changes to family law, particularly to private proceedings. Important as it was, however, it was just one in a succession of statutes that changed that body of law in the latter part of the twentieth century.

Private family law

In the UK, the Divorce Act 1969, followed by the Matrimonial Causes Act 1973, ushered in the present era in which family breakdown – marital or not – is a wholly accepted aspect of contemporary social life, as is the need to then provide for the living arrangements and parental responsibilities for the children concerned. It has become a feature of the grounds for these proceedings that they are broadly framed, entitling an applicant to be heard by the court on a matter which may change the status of family member/s without having to first satisfy rigorous eligibility criteria. Objectively stated grounds, such as those requiring proof of fault, have been displaced by grounds such as 'mutual consent.' The significance of a public interest in defending the legal integrity of the marital family unit (evident in the long-standing influence of the fault based grounds in

57 See *A v. Liverpool City Council* [1982] AC 363.

58 See Law Commission, *Wards of Court*, Working Paper No 101, (1987)

matrimonial proceedings) or the permanency of adoption (evident in the non-use of conditions and the secrecy requirements) has greatly diminished. The initial importance attached to formal status in private family law has faded and been replaced by a policy of facilitating autonomous action by family members whose decisions to enter and exit marital and other family relationships now encounter minimum legal hindrance. Further, freed from the constraints of what traditionally has been an adversarial process, the judicial role in private family law proceedings has shifted from being adjudicative, where issues were determined on a 'win-or-lose' basis – particularly evident in matrimonial proceedings – to reserving that approach to the small minority of contested proceedings, leaving all others to be resolved in accordance with an approach now resting more on mediation and adjustment of the parties legal interests and an assurance that they have reached a satisfactory agreement regarding future care arrangements for their children. In this context, several developments have occurred in relation to the resolution of issues affecting the welfare interests of a child.

Welfare interests

This era is one in which birth parents have in the main been the litigants. The core statutory proceedings, from the outset, have been those concerning parental responsibility for, or access to, children following a breakdown in their birth parents relationship. Increasingly, parental disputes have taken the form of actions relating to custody, education, religious upbringing, and maintenance following separation; and long-term or permanent alternative care in proceedings for guardianship, wardship, and adoption. Section 25 of the 1973 Act required the court, in the course of proceedings for separation or divorce, to give first consideration to the welfare of a child. Subsequently, the Children Act 1989 introduced the paramountcy principle and the welfare 'checklist' as the basis for settling civil disputes in relation to the future upbringing of a child whether in the context of public or private family law proceedings.

In contested proceedings, identifying the welfare interests of each individual child has now acquired a higher priority and the court may be advised by a number of professionals making representations about or on behalf of a child. The court is more likely than formerly to hear the views of a child directly from him or her on matters believed to constitute their welfare interests. When such interests arise for judicial consideration, or where they are in conflict with the legal interests of other parties, the judiciary will now accord them a paramount weighting. Finally, judicial determination in private family law proceedings is now primarily characterised by exercises of discretion rather than the simple fixed choice between order, no order, or a set package of orders that typified earlier determinations. In keeping with the trend towards compromise, the preferred judicial disposal option will be one that achieves a balance between the legal interests of the adult parties while affording optimal recognition and protection for the welfare interests of a child. Judicial discretion and flexibility, rather than adjudication, will be employed to adjust the respective legal interests of the parties and provide the most suitable and secure care arrangements for the child or children concerned.

Public family law

The Children Act 1989 radically adjusted the role and weighting given to the principle of the welfare of the child in public family law. This has affected the responsibilities of both court and local authority.

The core statutory proceedings constituting coercive state intervention remain as traditionally defined and concern the care, protection, and control of children. However, these blanket proceedings now include issues that have grown to become separate proceedings in their own right: training; supervision; access; non-consensual adoption placement; secure accommodation, and others. In this public family law context, the use of authority as provided for by statute and judicially applied, has changed since the proceedings were first introduced. The 'discovery' of child sexual abuse and the increase in child protection measures, brought ever widening permutations of care and protection issues before the courts. But, as with private family law, the fundamental distinguishing characteristics of the use of authority have remained relatively intact.

Welfare interests

The distinguishing legal hallmarks of public family proceedings, in relation to the welfare principle, may be generally and crudely summarised as: coercive; resting on threshold criteria of prescriptive grounds; determined by adjudication; and disposed of by relatively fixed disposal options in relation to which judicial discretion is restricted.

First, coercive intervention is the means by which welfare-related issues are brought before the court in a public family law context. Criminal proceedings for injuries caused to a child and civil proceedings in respect of care, protection, or control issues are a consequence of state initiated intervention in the family. The instigation of such proceedings is mandatory by police or local authority, respectively, on receipt of relevant information. Consent of the family is immaterial, the alleged offender or person suspected of being in breach of a duty of care has the *locus standi* of defendant in proceedings which are conducted in prosecutory manner.

Second, the intervention threshold is set by prescriptive grounds which identify, directly and objectively, the circumstances and conduct held to endanger a child's welfare interests. The grounds for both criminal and care and protection proceedings share the common feature that they are largely retrospective in effect; they provide mainly for circumstances in which a child's welfare has already been breached. The criminal law is used to proscribe certain types of behaviour construed to be so detrimental to a child's welfare, or to that of others, as to justify criminal sanctions. The civil law of care and protection is used to proscribe situations of risk to children (e.g. parental inadequacy or incapacity) from which they need protection. The grounds in both sets of laws create the threshold for access to measures which may safeguard a child's welfare interests; but in civil law these are identified in broad terms which are capable of some degree of subjective interpretation in relation to an individual child's particular needs. The law has slowly changed from resting on grounds proscribing specific indicators of welfare needs to employing less precise more generalised terms such as 'unreasonable,' 'unfit,' or 'moral danger.' With the introduction of the 1989 Act this trend has been further refined by the substitution of 'significant harm' for the 'avoidable prevention of proper development and need of care and control' in the 1969 Act. Also, a prospective dimension is now more often present in the grounds; intervention to prevent a likelihood of welfare being damaged is often authorised.

Third, public family law proceedings have a definite adversarial nature. Under the 1989 Act, such proceedings are required to be conducted as enquiries rather than prosecutions but in fact they more often closely resemble the latter. Extending full party status to children has also brought in train the use of representatives and expert witnesses, the practice of cross-examination, and many other features typical of adversarial prosecutions. In this context, the first stage of judicial decision-making is an adjudication of the issues. This concludes with a determination that the significant harm threshold – representing the welfare interests of the child before the court – has or has not been damaged, or placed at risk, in relation to the statutorily specified grounds.

Fourth and finally, the second stage of judicial decision-making deals with disposal options. Once the threshold criteria have been met, the adjudicative role exercised and all legal issues fully addressed in the course of proceedings conducted in an adversarial manner then the function of the court changes to focus on welfare interests. The judicial role at the disposal stage of public family law proceedings changed significantly during the latter half of the twentieth century. The fact that welfare has been accorded paramountcy status throughout the proceedings, and is reinforced by the checklist at the point of case disposal, would itself have transformed the judicial role by placing a responsibility and power on the court to subordinate all other factors to welfare considerations when determining disposal. But the ambit of judicial discretion at point of disposal in public family law proceedings was also significantly broadened under the 1989 Act to permit use of private law orders. At the final stage the court may now creatively employ discretionary powers to address the subjective position of a particular child's welfare interests rather than be constrained by the objective specifications of traditional public law proceedings.

The authority of the court ends with the conclusion of proceedings. Any uncertainty regarding the availability of a residual power of judicial review in relation to local authority decisions in respect of children subject to public law orders, existing prior to the ruling in *Liverpool*,[59] and to some extent subsequently in the wardship jurisdiction, has been removed. The 1989 Act specifically confines

59 *A v. Liverpool City Council*, op cit.

judicial use of authority to the duration of proceedings; though judicial juggling with interim orders and care plans has tempered that finality.

New approaches to welfare

The common law legacy facilitated cultural reciprocity between the beneficiary nations. The traffic was not always one way. Some of the changes to established domestic law and practice in the UK resulted from the example set by other common law nations.

Influences from the common law world on domestic law and practice

Reciprococity was illustrated, for example, by the transfer to the UK of child welfare oriented practices developed in New Zealand. The initiatives that evolved there, with open adoption, kinship foster care arrangements, family conferences, etc. and, more recently in relation to same-sex adopters, also attracted the attention of legislators, judiciary, and social workers in the UK. Influences from U.S. law and practice were also important. The 'freeing' of children in state care for third party adoption was a policy initiative first established in the U.S. Kinship foster care as the preferred placement and the debate around mixed race placements were also absorbed into UK practice following transfer from the U.S. These more relaxed approaches to meeting the welfare interests of children by broadening the placement parameters for those needing long-term care outside their family of origin, did much to loosen the rather rigid and 'closed' models of child care that had become accepted as good practice in the UK.

One reason why such initiatives influenced developments in this jurisdiction was its timing. Coincidentally, as mentioned above, the law relating to children in the UK was undergoing its most intense and comprehensive period of review since its statutory origins, with reports being published of challenging new developments in other common law jurisdictions. One initiative, successfully developed in such common law jurisdictions as Australia, New Zealand, parts of Canada, and in some U.S. states, but to which this jurisdiction had remained impervious, was the forming of unified family courts.

Influence of domestic human rights law

As the structured homogeneity of late-Victorian England gave way to a more fluid, multicultural society with permeable boundaries so family life became much less likely to be based on marriage, more impermanent, with serial parenting and shared care arrangements increasingly common. The modern self-reliant fairly mobile nuclear unit was less likely to be reinforced by an extended kinship network or by community links and became more transient as families relocated in pursuit of employment opportunities. Moreover, these changes were accompanied by improvements in family planning, welfare benefits, housing, and perceptions of stigma that transformed the social circumstances of unmarried mothers.

Against this background the welfare interests and indeed the rights of the child steadily acquired a raised and more defined salience. This was partly a consequence of the above-mentioned increased knowledge of child development: a product of research in the new fields of child psychiatry and developmental psychology; and to the resulting theories of attachment, bonding, and the 'psychological parent'; all of which did much to bring more depth to the professional understanding of what, for any particular child, might constitute their 'welfare,' thereby helping to correct the tendency towards reification.[60] It was also due to the general withdrawal throughout family law from a defence of the status determined obligations of adults (e.g. marriage) to upholding the principle that the welfare interests of children must prevail in any set of circumstances. Also very relevant, however, was the Human Rights Act 1998, which incorporated the ECHR into UK domestic law. This greatly strengthened the position of children and inaugurated an era which has seen the gradual transformation of some of their welfare interests into rights.

The Human Rights Act 1998

The 1998 Act, incorporating 16 ECHR rights, together with the Equality Act 2010, constitute for most purposes the relevant domestic human rights framework. Article 1 of the ECHR directing that it is unlawful for a public authority to act in a way which is incompatible with any Convention right, has resulted mainly in local authorities rewriting procedures and adjusting practice so as to forestall a human rights challenge in court. The courts, for their part, now reflexively cross-check with ECtHR rulings, in order to achieve such compliance. The domestic framework is supplemented by certain international treaties, conventions, protocols, etc. including the Universal Declaration of Human Rights (UDHR), the European Convention on Human Rights (ECHR), and the United Nations Convention on the Rights of the Child (UN CRC).[61]

Rights relating to child welfare

While the rights embodied in the 1998 Act are clearly not child specific, some have been applied in the context of proceedings involving children and their overall effect on the practice of local authorities and courts has been considerable. By the end of the twentieth century, the related principles and case law were beginning to make their influence felt. This became apparent, for example: in the switch from defending parental rights to an emphasis upon parental responsibilities;[62] in

60 See, for example, Sutton, A., 'Science in Court', in King, M., ed. *Childhood, Welfare & Justice*, Billing & Son Ltd., 1981 at p 55.

61 See, further, O'Halloran, K., Children, the Law, and the Welfare Principle: Perspectives from Europe, , Routledge, (forthcoming).

62 Baroness Hale "[t]here is no question of a parental right," in *Re G (Children)* [2006] UKHL 43, at para 30.

a central focus on the welfare interests of the child; and in a changed approach to unmarried fathers without parental responsibility whose involvement in decision-making was now to be sought.[63] While some rights are absolute, the exercise of a right must otherwise be balanced against the rights of others. Of particular significance is their latent effect: domestic law and practice must be 'proofed' against the possibility of being in breach of the 1998 Act; as the ECHR rights are now embedded in domestic law, and in the professional culture of those engaged with the welfare of children, they have come to serve as benchmarks for practice and, in so doing, largely obviate the need for their assertion in court.

Right to life

Article 2, the absolute right to life, implies that government will protect life and provide the means to ensure that it does not end prematurely. However, a considerable body of research testifies both to the enduring level of poverty in the UK,[64] which might well affect a child's normal life expectancy, and the strength of the correlation between it and family breakdown.[65] In so doing it also highlights the inability of government to satisfy its obligation to safeguard the welfare of children in need and promote their upbringing by their families through a range of support services: under the Children Act 1989, s 17(1).

It is to be noted that a considerable weight of case law has accumulated in this jurisdiction testifying to the principle that there can be no justification for denying lifesaving medical assistance to children. Most often such cases concern Jehovah's Witnesses and blood products.[66]

Right to a fair trial

Article 6 of the 1998 Act – the due process provision – reiterates the corresponding ECHR provision and establishes the right to a fair and public hearing. This requires that a trial or hearing: is held within a reasonable time; heard by an independent and impartial decision-maker; provides all relevant information; is open to the public; allows representation; and concludes with a public decision.

63 See, for example, *Re B (Adoption Order)* [2001] EWCA Civ. 347 [2001] 2 FLR 26.

64 UN Committee on the Rights of the Child, Concluding Observations on the Fifth Periodic Report of the United Kingdom of Great Britain and Northern Ireland (CRC/C/GBR/CO/5), 2016, para 70; see also UNICEF 2017 report which found that one in three British children were in 'multi-dimensional poverty' at: www.theguardian. com/society/2017/jun/15/levels-of-child-hunger-and-deprivation-in-uk-among-highest-of-rich-nations.

65 See, for example, the HBAI (Households Below Average Income) report which concluded that 3.8 million children – one in three – are currently living in poverty in the UK, one of the highest rates in Western Europe. Also, see, Bywaters, P., 'Inequalities in Child Welfare: Towards a New Policy, Research and Action Agenda', *British Journal of Social Work*, Vol 45, No 1, 2015, at pp 6–23.

66 See, for example, *Birmingham Children's NHS Trust v. B & C* [2014] EWHC 531 (Fam); *Re S (A Minor) (Medical Treatment)* [1993] 1 FLR 376; and *Re R (A Minor) (Blood Transfusion)* [1993] 2 FCR 544.

The requirement that decisions be taken without undue delay has given rise to a good deal of concern. In 2012, for example, the Department for Education noted in *An Action Plan for Adoption*[67] that delays in the adoption system were causing lasting harm for vulnerable children. In 2019, the Court of Appeal held that an 18-month adjournment of care proceedings concerning a baby, who was 7 months old at the time of the judgment, to allow time for the parents to make sustained changes, was prejudicial to the child's welfare.[68]

The basic human right, that a person whose interests are at stake in any decision-making process must be afforded every opportunity to fully engage in that process, was illustrated in *H v. Kingston upon Hull City Council*[69] when the court warned that a child should not be removed from the family "unless and until there has been due and proper consultation and an opportunity to challenge the proposal." Such consultation must consist of more than mere information giving; the parent/s must be listened to and their views taken into account. In *Re B-S*,[70] Sir James Munby, the president of the High Court (FD), in a ruling deeply critical of social work practice, urged his colleagues in the lower courts to explore all possible options in cases of adoptions from state care and stressed the need for proper evidence, warning that current "sloppy practice must stop. It is simply unacceptable in a forensic context where the issues are so grave and the stakes, for both child and parent, so high."[71] Again, 'sloppy practice' was revealed in the inquiry into the brutal torture and murder of eight-year-old Victoria Climbié.[72] Led by Laming LJ, this inquiry excoriated the 'blinding incompetence' of the professionals from many statutory and voluntary agencies involved with the relatives responsible for her death. Indeed, arguably the right to representation is also endangered by 'sloppy practice' when left to the cursory oversight of a solicitor in uncontested matrimonial proceedings, which account for by far the majority of judicial case regarding the welfare of children following family breakdown. Similarly, the fact that prospective adoption applications from relatives of the child concerned are viewed as a matter of private family law – and therefore not subject to scrutiny by the local Adoption Panel (unless the child is in care) in effect – means that perhaps the most important quality control mechanism in the adoption process has no relevance for a considerable proportion of UK adoptions.

Article 5 of the 1998 Act, reiterating the corresponding ECHR provision, declares that no one shall be deprived of his liberty save ... in accordance with a procedure prescribed by law. *In the Matter of T (A Child)(Appellant)*[73] the UKSC considered the position of children who the local authority consider required to

67 *An Action Plan for Adoption: Tackling Delay*, London, HMSO, 2012.

68 *Re H (A Child) (Refusal of Placement Order)* [2019] EWCA Civ 1557.

69 [2013] EWHC 388 (Admin.), para 54.

70 (Children) [2013] EWCA Civ. 1146.

71 Ibid, at para 40.

72 *The Victoria Climbié Inquiry*, HMSO, 2000, at: https://lx.iriss.org.uk/sites/default/files/resources/113A.%20The%20Victoria%20Climbie%20Inquiry%20-%20Summary-Report.pdf.

73 [2021] UKSC 35.

be deprived of their liberty, and in relation to whom the statutory criteria for the making of a secure accommodation order under s 25 of the Children Act 1989 were satisfied, but in respect of whom the local authority proposed to use wardship as a means to place elsewhere than in a secure children's home approved for that purpose. In relation to Article 5, the court considered the question: was the use of wardship to authorise the deprivation of liberty in such a case 'in accordance with a procedure prescribed by law' as required by that Article? The UKSC found no obstacle to the use of wardship: "there is nothing in Article 5, or in the case law of the European Court of Human Rights, that requires that the domestic law and procedure should be set out in statute and/or regulations, rather than being common law based."[74] The court also considered whether the consent of the child concerned prevented the confinement constituting a deprivation of liberty within the meaning of Article 5 and, in an inconclusive judgment, took the view that, given the circumstances, there would be doubt as to the validity of that child's consent[75] (see, further, Chapter 5).

A more structural problem with the legal system as it relates to children's interests is the restricted availability of legal aid. The CRC drew attention to this in its 2016 report, when it expressed concern that 'the reduction of legal aid in all four jurisdictions appear to have a negative impact on the right of children to be heard in judicial and administrative proceedings affecting them.'[76]

Right to respect for family life

Article 8, the right most heavily relied upon in proceedings affecting the welfare interests of children, declares that 'everyone has the right to respect for his private and family life, his home and his correspondence' and that 'there shall be no interference by a public authority with the exercise of this right except such as is in accordance with the law and is necessary in a democratic society.' It has been interpreted very broadly to include matters such as: personal privacy and autonomy; personal identity (e.g. sexual orientation and gender transition), cultural identity (e.g. to belong to culture of birth); and the right to access the information necessary to preserve that identity.[77] In at least one respect – the right to confidential pregnancy advice and access to contraception – Article 8 has firmly established the right to such services, independent of parental knowledge or permission.

Most importantly, in this context, Article 8 refers to a child's right to protection from interventions that may threaten their family links (whether their birth family, or one acquired by fostering or adoption) and if removed from their family,

74 Ibid at para 91.

75 Compliant, that is, with the test in *Storck v. Germany* (2005) 43 EHRR 6.

76 UN CRC, Concluding Observations, op cit, at para 30(b).

77 Arguably, this right has been compromised by the removal of the statutory requirement to give consideration to the birth parent/s racial and cultural background from adoption legislation.

it affirms the right to maintain contact and to be reunited with that family. As the ECtHR stressed in its criticism of local authority practice in *YC v. the United Kingdom*:[78] 'family ties may only be severed in very exceptional circumstances and that everything must be done to preserve personal relations and, where appropriate, to "rebuild" the family.'

The freedoms of religion, expression, and association/assembly

These rights – 9, 10, and 11 of the 1998 Act, respectively – clearly have most relevance for older children and youths, with perhaps particular implications for lifestyle choices, and for conduct in settings such as school. In the latter context, the rights of children and their parents are reinforced by Protocol 1, Article 2 which establishes a right to education.

The tension between the freedoms of religion and expression – as they affect schoolchildren – have given rise to some issues and a few important cases in England and Wales. For example, because religious education is mandatory for pupils of all ages throughout the state education system, regardless of the pupils beliefs or lack of them, the interests of children from irreligious families are necessarily compromised.[79] All state funded schools must provide opportunities for pupils between the ages of three and 19 to engage in daily acts of collective worship.[80] Moreover, the requirement is that schools engage in daily acts of collective prayer or worship of 'a wholly or mainly ... Christian character,'[81] and in schools with such character, worship should be in keeping with it.[82] The interests of children from religious, but not Christian, families are clearly compromised. This is the case if only because of the perceived stigma that accompanies being set apart from their class when religious education or worship takes place.

Pupil admission or rejection, on religious grounds, clearly has the potential to damage welfare interests. This was the case in *Mandla (Sewa Singh) and another v. Dowell Lee and others*[83] when a Sikh boy was denied admittance to a private school, because he refused to comply with the school uniform requirement to cut his hair and remove his turban: a turban being emblematic of his religious/cultural identity, he could not remove it without sacrificing that identity. The House of Lords held that it was unlawful indirect discrimination for a headmaster of an

78 (2012) 55 EHRR 33.

79 The Education Act 1944, as amended by the Education Reform Act 1988 and the School Standards and Framework Act 1998, accompanied by the 1994 Act, requires religious education to be provided for all children between the ages of three and 19 in state funded schools which must provide opportunities for pupils to engage in daily acts of collective worship.

80 See, further, AHRC Network report, *Collective Worship and Religious Observance in Schools: An Evaluation of Law and Policy in the UK*, 2015 at: http://collectiveschoolworship.com/documents/CollectiveWorshipReligiousObservanceAHRCNetworkReport13November2015.pdf.

81 Schools Standards and Framework Act 1998, Schedule 20, para 3(2).

82 Ibid, at para 5.

83 [1983] 2 AC 548.

independent school to impose a universal uniform requirement of short hair and caps for boys, thus unfairly burdening a religious group, Sikhs; a ruling subsequently echoed in *R (Watkins-Singh)*[84] where the issue concerned the wearing of Sikh jewellery. Generally, however, the wearing of religion-specific clothing by children or adults – including turbans or burqas – to express religious identity does not give rise to issues.[85]

The right to protection from discrimination

Article 14 provides protection against discrimination experienced in respect of any of the rights and freedoms enumerated in the 1998 Act, as reinforced and extended by the Equality Act 2010. The prohibition includes discrimination on the basis of 'other status' which includes sexual orientation and gender identity, or non-marital status. Traditional theological precepts are clearly not readily reconcilable with principles of equality and nondiscrimination. Most Christian organisations are fundamentally unable, for example, to reconcile the precept of marriage as a lifelong monogamous and heterosexual union with the contemporary human rights recognition of it as a union that may encompass same-sex relationships. This has led to many confrontations, some of which have compromised the welfare interests of the children involved. One such instance was a case concerning the Catholic Care adoption agency[86] which argued, unsuccessfully, that its non-compliance with equality legislation was justified because providing adoption services to same-sex cohabiting couples or civil partners would require it to violate the tenets of the Roman Catholic Church. On its failure to demonstrate that the less favourable treatment it proposed to offer same-sex couples would constitute a proportionate means of achieving its legitimate aim of providing suitable adoptive parents for a significant number of 'hard to place' children, and consequent dismissal of its argument, the agency closed its doors to same-sex couples to the considerable detriment of the welfare interests of the children in need of family care.[87]

Again, in *R (L and others) v. Manchester City Council*[88] a local authority practice of paying kinship foster parents less than foster parents caring for children unrelated to them was found to be discriminatory and prejudicial to the welfare interests of children, because family members would be relatively disadvantaged should they offer to undertake care responsibility. The court found the practice

84 *R (Watkins-Singh) v. Aberdale Girls' High School* [2008] EWHC 1865; [2008] 3 FCR 203. See, also, *R(E) v. Governing Body of JFS* [2010] IRLR 136; [2009] UKSC 15.

85 See *R (On the Application of Begum (by her litigation friend, Rahman) v. Headteacher and Governors of Denbigh High School* [2006] UKHL 15 (HL).

86 *Catholic Care (Diocese of Leeds) v. The Charity Commission for England and Wales* [2011] EqLR 597.

87 See, also, *St Margaret's Children and Family Care Society v. OSCR* [2014] SCAP App 02/13 which found in favour of the Society on very similar facts.

88 [2001] EWHC Admin 707.

breached Article 8 which obliged the local authority to take 'all appropriate positive steps' to enable children to live with their families.

Conclusion

Traditionally, and for most of the twentieth century, the welfare principle was interpreted and applied quite differently in the public and private sectors of family law, differing even within each. Public law was characterised by a weak, non-proactive role for the principle in respect of its preventative and promotional functions with a broad latitude for interpretation, but by an assertive role and narrowly interpreted, compartmentalised functions in respect of child care, protection, and control. In relation to the criminal dimension of public law, the principle initially had little if any bearing but then, following the failed experiment with an equal application for all young children under the 1969 Act, the welfare differential between the civil and criminal dimensions was restored by the 1989 Act. Private law saw the welfare principle bearing most heavily and with the widest latitude on decisions taken in the wardship jurisdiction, with rather less weight in guardianship and adoption, while having a restricted role – secondary to parental rights – in matrimonial and associated custody and contact proceedings.

By the end of the twentieth century, much had changed. While this was due in large part to the fundamental adjustments induced by the Acts of 1989 and 1998, these domestic legislative initiatives were very much influenced by international human rights instruments and by ECtHR case law; though undeniably the internal pressures resulting from the failings in the local authority child protection system, the obsolescent structuring of family law proceedings, and the sheer volume of child welfare cases coming before the courts, were combining to generate a momentum that would have brought about radical change anyway. The scale of the resulting restructuring of the law relating to the welfare interests of children has, perhaps, overshadowed a full appreciation of the important changes wrought to a professional understanding of what constitutes that welfare.

4 International influences

Introduction

International convergence in the recognition of key family law principles gained momentum in the last decades of the twentieth century. A strategy of facilitating the harmonisation of principles and procedures between the nations of the European Union was by then well underway. Countries sharing common and relatively 'open' borders, such as the United States of America and Canada, the two jurisdictions on the island of Ireland, and those comprising Scandinavia also had to at least explore areas of commonality and difference. It was a time when international treaties, conventions, and protocols were designed explicitly to promote a common recognition of principles, to co-ordinate procedures, and to effect agreed joint action.

It is, however, necessary to distinguish between the effects of international influence directed specifically towards child welfare considerations from those directed towards all persons but also affecting children. This is most obviously the case with human rights in general but perhaps particularly in relation to equality and non-discrimination. It is also necessary to bear in mind that while, from a UK perspective, international influence has been and is exercised most directly from Europe, it has also been generated from other sources. A great deal of it has come from the U.S.

This chapter examines the source, nature, and effect of international influences that have, historically, contributed to shaping the role of the welfare principle as it related to children in the UK at the end of the twentieth century. The chapter is in three parts. The first chronicles the history of the formal European instruments which have impinged on this role. The second considers the effect of these influences on family law in general and on a child's welfare interests/rights in particular. The final part focuses on how the welfare principle has been impacted by advances in medicine – most notably by child psychiatry and developmental psychology – and in relation to women's reproductive rights. The origins, application, and importance of concepts such as 'attachment' and 'psychological parent' are considered. In short, this chapter counterbalances its predecessor by demonstrating that the principle of the welfare interests of the child was by no means derived wholly from UK jurisprudence but was very much shaped by international

DOI: 10.4324/9781003268642-7

influences such as the ECHR and the UN CRC together with the contribution of U.S. researchers such as Goldstein, Freud, and Solnit.

Influences from Europe

The Geneva Convention of 1924 is the accepted starting point for any review of international influence on the development of domestic law relating specifically to the welfare of children. The fifth Assembly of the League of Nations then adopted a declaration emphasising children's material needs. Responding to the deprivations which followed the First World War, it proclaimed that children 'must have' the necessary means for their normal development – including food for the hungry, nursing for the sick, help for the handicapped, and shelter and succour for the orphan and waif. Essentially, this was an aspirational document.

International instruments

The body of international human rights treaties, conventions, and protocols is steadily growing: some are binding on all nations, and all are binding on a few; the accompanying body of related jurisprudence binds some but provides a common point of reference for all. Their internationalism is evidenced not only by signed treaties and agreements between countries but also by the adoption of those same provisions into the domestic law of many nations including that of England and Wales. While there may be a degree of uncertainty, in the immediate post-BREXIT years, as to the extent of that binding, nonetheless for the foreseeable future domestic proceedings will continue to take place within a context of rights and principles set by international and regional legislation.[1]

European Convention for the Protection of Human Rights and Fundamental Freedoms (ECHR)

In 1948, the General Assembly of the United Nations unanimously adopted this formative Convention which addressed the fundamental rights of all persons and declared that an infringement by court or by tribunal would be actionable. A procedure for enforcement was eventually established in 1959 when the European Court of Human Rights was set up. The Convention made no specific reference to children but, in its Preamble, referred instead to 'the inherent dignity and…equal and inalienable rights of all members of the human family.' The rights pronounced did eventually come to be viewed as applicable also to children.[2] In 1979, the Parliamentary Assembly to the Committee of Ministers to the Council of Ministers recommended steps to create a

1 Children, the Law and the Welfare Principle: Perspectives from Europe (Routledge, forthcoming).

2 In the period 1984–9, 14 judgments concerning its application to minors were passed at the European Court of Human Rights in Strasbourg; five in 1976–84.

European Charter on the rights of the child "which should among other considerations take account of 'the new concept of parental responsibility.'" In 1984 it further recommended that parental responsibilities be defined

> as a collection of duties and powers which aim at insuring the moral and material welfare of the child, in particular by taking care of the person of the child, by maintaining personal relationships with him and by providing for his education, his maintenance, his legal representation and the administration of his property.

This recommendation takes account of the views of children by stating that when decisions are to be taken relating to parental responsibilities and applying to the legal interests of children then the children 'should be consulted if their degree of maturity with regard to the decision so permits.' In 1988, at a conference in Lisbon, the European Ministers of Justice upheld a resolution on the principle that the interests of the child should be paramount.

In the UK, the relevance of the ECHR to children's welfare interests and legal rights began in 1966 when this country declared its recognition of the Commission's jurisdiction. It acquired a more direct immediacy when it became incorporated into UK law with the introduction of the Human Rights Act 1998. This 'gifted' UK jurisprudence with the body of caselaw accumulated by the ECtHR and required existing domestic law to be revised to ensure conformity with standards set by the ECHR. Until then it had been necessary for a litigant, having first exhausted all domestic appeal procedures, to petition the European Commission for leave to appeal to the ECtHR. Thereafter, instead of seeking redress before the ECtHR, a UK litigant could have 'Convention rights' directly enforced by the UK courts.

Because the ECHR was so emphatically focused on rights, it had great potential for exercising leverage on behalf of children's independent legal interests – their rights – as opposed to their welfare interests. It positively represented rights, did so in a prescriptive manner, provided an adversarial forum for adjudication, and was directly and wholly embedded in the UK body of law by the 1998 Act. This distinguished its influence on domestic law from such other international instruments as the 1989 Convention which represented welfare interests in a negative manner, was somewhat ambivalent in the balance it struck between rights and welfare, was not wholly and directly incorporated by statute and did not have any formal enforcement mechanism (see, further, below).

The UN Declaration of the Rights of the Child

This declaration, issued in 1959, was based on the premise first articulated in the 1924 Geneva Convention, that 'mankind owes to the Child the best it has to give,' and addressed the needs of children particularly for service provision in the areas of health, housing, and education. It contained an implicit emphasis on duties to children. However, although going further than the orthodox protection function, to recognise an entitlement to some rights, it succeeded in little more than proclaiming ten general principles.

Both this declaration and the 1924 League of Nations Declaration emphasised child protection, particularly from discrimination, rather than rights. Each declaration called for state assistance to ensure a child's normal development,[3] protection from exploitation,[4] and abandonment,[5] and to receive relief in times of disaster.[6] Of the two, the 1959 Declaration was more comprehensive and covered standards for play and recreation,[7] parental care,[8] name and nationality,[9] social security,[10] education,[11] and care of the handicapped.[12]

The significance of the 1959 Declaration lies in the fact that it laid down the foundations of principle and subject matter upon which the 1989 Convention was later to build. Of particular importance was that it articulated, for the first time, the paramountcy principle:

Principle 1 –

> The child shall enjoy special protection, and shall be given opportunities and facilities, by law and by other means, to enable him to develop physically, mentally, morally, spiritually and socially in a healthy and normal manner and in conditions of freedom and dignity. In the enactment of laws for this purpose, the best interests of the child shall be the paramount consideration.

This resolute statement of the standard to be set in relation to specified aspects of a child's development provided an important international benchmark prompting the UK to subsequently adopt a prescriptive legislative approach to child welfare rather than continuing to rely on judicial discretion. However, the provisions of the 1959 provisions may now be taken to have been superseded by those of the 1989 UN Convention on the Rights of the Child.[13]

The Council of Europe (CoE)

By the end of the twentieth century, the work of the Council of Europe (CoE) had been somewhat overshadowed, particularly by the UN Declaration of the

3 The League of Nations Declaration 1924: para 1. The UN Declaration of the Rights of the Child 1959: principle 2.
4 1924: para 4 1959: principle 9.
5 1924: para 2 1959: principle 6.
6 1924: para 3 1959: principle 8.
7 1959: principle 7.
8 1959: principle 6.
9 1959: principle 3.
10 1959: principle 4.
11 1959: principle 7.
12 1959: principle 5.
13 See *Re A (Children: 1959 UN Declaration)* [1998] 1 FLR 354 where the Court of Appeal questioned the current relevance of the 1959 Declaration.

Rights of the Child in 1959, and by the 1989 Convention. The Council was responsible for producing some influential Conventions including the European Convention on the Legal Status of Children Born Out of Wedlock which was ratified by the UK in 1981. It had also issued the European Convention on the Adoption of Children 1967, and the European Convention on Recognition and Enforcement of Decisions Concerning Custody of Children and on Restoration of Custody of Children 1980. The profile of the CoE was raised by the launching of the International Year of the Child in 1979, that being the twentieth anniversary of the 1959 Declaration, which provided an important child oriented landmark in legal and social recognition of child welfare.[14] To mark the occasion, a draft update of the Declaration was drawn up by the government of Poland as a proposed template for a new international law on the rights of children. Having been found to be inadequate, this was overtaken by preparations for the UN Convention on the Rights of the Child which was formally adopted by the General Assembly of the UN in 1989, on the thirtieth anniversary of the 1959 Declaration. In 2007 it issued the Convention on the Protection of Children against Sexual Exploitation and Sexual Abuse (the 'Lanzarotte Convention') with effect from 2010, requiring states to ensure the criminalisation of certain forms of sexual abuse against children.

The United Nations Standard Minimum Rules for the Administration of Juvenile Justice (The Beijing Rules) 1985

The 'Beijing Rules,' dealing exclusively with juvenile justice and adopted by the General Assembly in 1985, outlined a framework for relating the needs of juveniles to the requirements of the legal system. Although not legally binding on the signatory states, the Rules put in place a platform of principles to govern the minimum requirements for any legal system administering juvenile justice. Among such principles is that of respect for the wellbeing – if not the welfare interests – of juveniles: the proceedings and their outcome must not be solely concerned with punishment; rehabilitative measures should also be considered. It also stresses the importance of the principle of proportionality: proceedings must take into account the particular circumstances of the juvenile, his or her remorse for the damage caused, and the relative significance of the offence and its consequences. It enumerates a list of basic rights – such as a presumption of innocence and a right to representation in court proceedings – which should always play a part in any juvenile justice system.[15]

14 The provisions of the International Covenant on Civil and Political Rights and the International Covenant on Economic, Social and Cultural Rights, both ratified by the UK in 1976, were essentially assimilated into the 1989 Convention.

15 See, further, at: www.ohchr.org/sites/default/files/Documents/ProfessionalInterest/beijingrules.pdf.

The UN Convention on the Rights of the Child 1989

This Convention, launched in 1989, was ratified by the UK[16] on 16 December 1991 and it took effect from 15 January 1992.[17] Applicable to all children below the age of 18, it provided the first positive assertion of their entitlement to rights as opposed to being merely recipients of welfare. In so doing, it purported to represent a change of approach from the concern with 'special protection' of children which characterised the 1959 Declaration. Of its 38 articles devoted to substantive rights, at least ten had never been recognised as rights for children in any other international instrument.[18] They all related to the child's 'individual personality': the right to be heard (Article 12), freedom of expression and information (Article 13), freedom of thought, conscience, and religion (Article 14), freedom of association and assembly (Article 15), and the right to privacy (Article 16). The emphasis on rights was, however, balanced by reference to the more familiar need to assure protection of welfare interests. This ideological compromise is well illustrated in the wording of the two key provisions. In Article 12, states were required to

> assure to the child who is capable of forming his or her own views the right to express those views freely, on all matters affecting the child, the views of the child being given due consideration in accordance with the age and maturity of the child … For this purpose, the child shall in particular be provided the opportunity to be heard in any judicial and administrative proceedings affecting the child.

Although giving a child the opportunity to participate in proceedings and the right to express views and for those views to be taken into account, it stopped short of giving a right to separate representation. While in Article 3, para 1, this tendency to favour welfare rather than rights when faced with a choice between the two is evident in the directive that:

> In all actions concerning children, whether undertaken by public or private social welfare institutions, courts of law, administrative authorities or legislative bodies, the best interests of the child shall be a primary consideration.

16 Currently ratified by 196 nations. The only nation to have failed to become a party to the Convention is the U.S. For an analysis of the former's reasons for non-ratification see, for example, 'The Wayward Americans – Why the USA has Not Ratified the UN Convention on the Rights of the Child' in *Child and Family Law Quarterly*, Vol 10, No 3, 1998.

17 The provisions of the International Covenant on Civil and Political Rights and the International Covenant on Economic, Social and Cultural Rights, both ratified by the UK in 1976, were essentially assimilated into the 1989 Convention.

18 Articles 8, 10, 12, 13, 14, 15, 16, 25, 37, and 40, among others.

The compromises embodied in this Convention are not restricted to the welfare/rights dilemma. It also equivocated on the separation of parental and child interests. In its Preamble, it states:

> that the family, as the fundamental group of society and the natural environment for the growth and well-being of all its members and particularly children, should be afforded the necessary protection and assistance so that it can fully assume its responsibilities within the community.

So, the family is given full recognition as a vehicle for achieving the wellbeing of children and state interference could be a violation both of it and of the child's right to a secure and private family life.

Status of the welfare principle

The fact that a majority of countries subscribed to the 1989 Convention meant that the welfare principle as expressed in this provision was, for the first time, elevated to the status of a truly international legal standard in 'all actions concerning children.' The corollary being that it also, thereby, made it internationally permissible for a welfare rather than a rights approach to be sufficient in such actions. Then there was the question of the precise weighting to be attached to the welfare standard. The wording used clearly avoided any suggestion that a child's welfare was to be treated as the matter of paramount importance, instead it inferred that it may be only one of a number of primary considerations.

Article 3, para 1, gave rise to three distinct implications for the role and functions of the welfare principle in UK law. First, the uniform application of the 'primary consideration' standard, across the range of legal and administrative decision-making bodies, was a most significant extension of its role. Instead of being confined by the 1989 Act to judicial decisions taken in the context of matters concerning upbringing, welfare interests were required to be the primary consideration for social workers, social security officers, and for just about everyone involved in the formal decision-making processes of an agency on any matter concerning a child. A matter could, presumably, be quite tangential to the main business in hand but if it concerned a child then the welfare principle would have to come into play. The business of very many agencies then had to be routinely 'welfare proofed'; not only those with a statutory child care, health, or education remit but also agencies such as planning bodies, leisure centres, housing, and libraries. Second, the fact that the international requirement was for a welfare weighting less than that already demanded under the 1989 Act raised questions as to which was more appropriate. While unquestionably welfare in this jurisdiction was to be treated as 'the paramount' rather than as 'a primary' consideration in the judicial determination of upbringing issues, it could be queried whether this weighting was appropriate. Arguably, by imposing relative disadvantages on the interests of others, most notably parents, the Children Act 1989 did not conform with the balance between the interests of family members required by the 1989 Convention. Third, and paradoxically, this provision stamped a welfare rather than a rights ethos on the decision-making *modus operandi* of all relevant bodies. Just when the 1989 Act and the *Gillick*[19] line of precedents had made room for a distinct children's rights focus in UK law, the Convention had introduced a requirement that all relevant judicial and administrative forums should be infused with a welfare orientation. Given the title of the 1989 Convention and the fact that it does address so many rights, it is striking that this particular provision is so unequivocal in its welfare focus. The 1989 Convention, like the public law provisions of the 1989 Act, can be seen to be juggling the two different approaches of legal rights and welfare interests.

Enforceability

If its implications for family law in the UK were to be of more than academic interest then the provisions of the 1989 Convention had to meet an enforceability test. It sought to provide for this and consolidate its impact on domestic law by establishing, under Article 43, a Committee on the Rights of the Child. This was to enable the progress of member states to be monitored and periodically reviewed to assess the extent which each had complied with the provisions of the Convention. When, for example, the Committee reviewed and reported on UK progress in 1995 it recorded its concern about matters such as 'the extent of child poverty, the law permitting corporal punishment, the low age of criminal responsibility and the lack of children's rights in the educational sphere.'[20] The government responded by making some concessions – largely due to pressure resulting from ECHR rulings – in relation to corporal punishment in schools, but the remaining matters did not improve; indeed legislative change regarding criminal responsibility increased the number of younger children being drawn into the criminal justice system. Given that ratification occurred in 1991, a lack of haste has been notable in the measures taken to ensure that domestic legislation and administration is made Convention compliant (see, further, at 'Conclusion').

The Hague Conventions

In addition to the broad sweep of the 1989 Convention, there have been a number of Hague Conventions focused on particular aspects of children's welfare interests.

Abduction was the first in what was to become a series of specific issue child welfare matters addressed at The Hague. The need to end the practice of 'forum shopping' and restore some semblance of comity between nations in private family law disputes had become increasingly urgent by 1980. This prompted the

19 *Gillick v. West Norfolk and Wisbech Area Health Authority* [1986] AC 112.

20 See Concluding Observations of the Committee on the Rights of the Child: United Kingdom Of Great Britain And Northern Ireland C RC/C 15Add34 (1995).

making of both the Hague Convention on the Civil Aspects of International Child Abduction and the European Convention on Recognition and Enforcement of Decisions Concerning Custody of Children. These were incorporated into UK law by the Child Care and Custody Act 1985 to become the basis for regulating the wrongful removal of children to or from the UK. Both in effect placed considerations of comity before those of welfare by directing the prompt return of any wrongfully removed child to the country with jurisdiction, where all matters – including those affecting welfare interests – must be addressed. Both also made concessions to the welfare principle. Article 13 of the Hague Convention allowed a court to refuse to order a child's return in circumstances:

> where the child objects to being returned and has attained an age and degree of maturity at which it is appropriate to take account of its views.

Usually the court declined to accord a child's views sufficient weight to prevent his or her return, holding that to do so would be to defeat the central purpose of the Convention. Article 10 of the European Convention provided the basis for a similar court refusal in circumstances:

> where it is found by reason of a change of circumstances including the passage of time but not including a mere change in the residence of the child after an improper removal, the effects of the original decision are manifestly no longer in accordance with the welfare of the child.

This provision required the central purpose of the European Convention to be submitted to a frank application of the welfare test; more so than Article 13 in relation to that of the Hague Convention.

Intercountry adoption was the next specific issue addressed at The Hague, by the standing Hague Conference on Private International Law, drawing from the principles established in Article 21 of the 1989 Convention. In 1993 the Hague Convention on Intercountry Adoption was issued and although the UK subsequently became a signatory, it did not proceed to full ratification until 2003. This Convention declared in Article 1 its intent to influence the welfare interests of children by establishing:

> safeguards to ensure that intercountry adoptions take place in the best interests of the child and with respect for his or her fundamental rights as recognised in international law.

This it endeavoured to do, in the first instance, by promoting the development of professional adoption services in 'donor' countries, i.e. countries which for reasons of poverty and/or social instability are allowing children to be adopted by non-nationals. This was a significant moral stand with long-term implications for the international role of the welfare principle. The 'child rescue' approach, with its attendant dislocation for human relationships and cultural identity, was to be rejected as the preferred means of safeguarding welfare interests either locally or internationally. Giving priority to retaining a child in need within his or her family and social context of origin was an important milestone in the interpretation of the welfare principle, common to both the 1993 Convention and the Children Act 1989. The convergence between the two was evident also in circumstances where consensually based retention of a child was not feasible: both then favoured the provision of foster care services which would permit a child to be placed as close as possible, in terms of geography and relationships, to his or her family/culture/community of origin. Only when these options are not possible did both then facilitate adoption and then again preference was given to maintaining the child within the cultural norms of his or her family of origin. The Convention viewed intercountry adoption as the final step in a continuum, to be taken when all others have been tried, and only then if all the professional filters were in place and the adoption process regulated to ensure the safeguarding of a child's welfare interests.

The protection of children was the specific issue addressed by the Hague Child Protection Convention 1996. This was based on its predecessor the Hague Convention on the Protection of Minors 1961 and dealt with matters of jurisdictional conflict arising in relation to child protection proceedings. It outlined the inter-jurisdictional rules and procedures for taking protective measures in relation to a child's property and physical integrity. It established that the primary jurisdiction for dealing with issues relating to such matters was the child's country of habitual residence. This Convention, of fundamental importance to children's welfare interests, remained unratified by the UK until 2012.

In the European Convention on the Exercise of Children's Rights 1996, the Council of Europe sought to strengthen the mechanisms for enforcing the provisions of the 1989 Convention. In keeping with the latter, it continued the equivocal balance between legal rights and welfare interests. Its central objective being, as stated in Article 1(2):

> in the best interests of children, to promote their rights, to grant them procedural rights and to facilitate the exercise of these rights by ensuring that children are, themselves or through other persons or bodies, informed and allowed to participate in the proceedings affecting them before a judicial authority.

A statement which would seem to make the exercise of legal rights conditional upon this being compatible with the welfare interests of the child concerned, while also confining the assurance of participatory rights to judicial proceedings. Article 3 of the Convention requires signatory states to ensure that a child 'considered by internal law as having sufficient understanding' has the right

> to receive all relevant information;
> to be consulted and express his or her views; and
> to be informed of the possible consequences of his or her wishes and the possible consequences of any decision.

Article 4 required separate representation to be provided for a child in cases where a conflict of interest arises between him or her and a party with parental responsibility. Article 7 imposed a 'no-delay' principle.

Family law, welfare interests, and international influences

From about the late 1960s onwards, the welfare principle became a potent force for leveraging the interests of children relative to those of parents and others. The correlation between the rise of the principle and the decline of the traditional nuclear marital family unit is clearly not coincidental. This dynamic became a characteristic of all affluent western societies at much the same time. The indicators of decline were also similar and contemporaneous: a fall in numbers of marital families; a rise in serial parenting; developments in artificial methods of human reproduction; an increase in forms of substitute parenthood and in a reliance on a range of third party carer arrangements, etc. Against this background the welfare interests and indeed the rights of the child have steadily acquired a more defined salience. This has been partly a consequence of increased knowledge of child development, particularly in relation to theories of attachment and bonding as attested to by a considerable body of research. It is also attributable to the general withdrawal throughout family law from a defence of the status determined obligations of adults (e.g. marriage) to upholding the principle that the welfare interests of children must prevail in any set of circumstances.

It would have been surprising if the UK had managed to insulate its domestic legislative and judicial response to this international pattern of change from the similar experiences of other western societies. The evidence is that changes in UK family law were heavily influenced by international changes in social mores and by the example of legislators and judiciary in other countries as they responded to the same set of resulting issues.

Private family law in general

By the closing decades of the twentieth century, the boundaries of private family law in the UK had been redrawn, most notably by the Children Act 1989 and the impact of rulings by the ECtHR. In relation to the latter, it is important to bear in mind that though such rulings were obviously important and directly influential, the indirect effect of domestic rulings being required to be compliant with ECtHR jurisprudence – particularly as regards Article 8 parameters – was far more pervasive in its influence, though more discrete. While it is also certain that seminal international academic publications contributed towards forming the domestic legislative intent to restrict state interference in family affairs, it is more difficult to estimate the significance of that contribution, though it fitted well with traditional Christian beliefs (see, Chapter 3) and with contemporary political UK policies, the latter being demonstrated by the general privatisation objectives of the Thatcher government and its particular concern to restrict state intervention in family affairs. Their work may well have influenced the legislative intent which formulated the no-order, parental responsibility, and family-based care principles underpinning the 1989 Act. It may also have contributed towards the preference placed on family based care, parental responsibility, and non-interference by the state in Article 5 of the Convention:

> State parties shall respect the responsibilities, rights and duties of parents or, where applicable, the members of the extended family or community as provided for by the local custom, legal guardians or other persons legally responsible for the child, to provide, in a manner consistent with the evolving capacities of the child, appropriate direction and guidance in the exercise by the child of the rights recognised in the present Convention.

This Article and the provisions of the 1989 Act are too close in time and substance to each other and to the approach advocated by the American writing team for the legislative initiative in this jurisdiction not to have been heavily influenced by both.

The family

The influence of European instruments challenged, and ultimately contributed significantly towards broadening, the traditional definition of 'family' in the UK.

Non-marital family

Article 8 guarantees the right to respect for family life but the definition of 'family' is not restricted to one based on marriage, it includes unmarried couples, non-marital children, and homosexual relationships. As the European Court of Human Rights has pointed out:[21]

> the notion of 'the family' ... is not confined solely to marriage-based relationships and may encompass other de facto 'family' where the parties are living together outside of marriage. A child born out of such a relationship is *ipso iure* part of that 'family' unit from the moment of his birth and by the very fact of it.

Article 8 makes no distinction between the 'legitimate' and 'illegitimate' family:[22]

> 'family life' within the meaning of Article 8 includes at least the ties between near relatives, for instance, those between grandparents and grandchildren, since such relatives may play a considerable part in family life.

21 See *Keegan v. Ireland* 18 EHRR 342 at para 44.
22 See *Marckx v Belgium* 2 EHRR 330.

The incentive to eliminate the remaining difference between the legal position of marital and non-marital families in the UK was provided by such judgments delivered against other European countries. As Bainham at the time noted:[23]

> Belgium[24] and the Republic of Ireland[25] have, for example, both fallen foul of the Convention in failing to give adequate recognition to the principle that 'family life' can be constituted outside marriage, can arise from the moment of a child's birth and can give rise to positive obligations on the part of States to foster it, as well as the more obvious negative obligations not to interfere with it.

Arguably, these rulings of the ECtHR, to the effect that the definition of 'family' was not to be determined by marital status, led directly to the reform of the UK relating to 'illegitimacy.'[26]

Unmarried father

UK legislation continued for some years to overtly discriminate against the legal standing of unmarried fathers[27] while at the same time the presumption favouring family life was extended to include the role of an unmarried father by rulings of the ECtHR, though this was something of an evolutionary process.[28]

Article 18(1) of the 1989 Convention, with its emphasis on 'the principle that both parents have common responsibilities for the upbringing and development of the child,' provided a clear challenge to the inequitable UK approach towards unmarried fathers. In *McMichael v. UK*[29] the difference in treatment in UK law for married and unmarried fathers was found to be justified on the basis that it was intended to thereby provide a means of identifying 'meritorious' fathers. However, in subsequent rulings the ECtHR firmly held that an unmarried father involved in direct care of his child or children would meet the definition of 'family' for the purposes of the ECHR, Article 8.[30]

Privacy of family life

Article 8(2) declares that a public authority shall not interfere with the right to respect for family life, the existence or otherwise of which can be determined

23 See Bainham, A., *Children: The Modern Law*, (2nd ed) 1998, at p 598.

24 *Marckx v. Belgium* (1979) 2 EHRR 330.

25 *Johnston v. Ireland* (1986) 9 EHRR 203 and *Keegan v. Ireland* (1994) 18 EHRR 342.

26 See Law Commission No 118, *Family Law Report on Illegitimacy* HMSO 1982. The recommendations of which led to the Family Law Reform Act 1987.

27 See ss 2, 4, and 12(1) of the Children Act 1989.

28 See *Soderback v. Sweden*, 28 October 1998 ECHR. Also, see, *Johansen v. Norway* (1997) 23 EHRR 33 and *Rieme v. Sweden* (1993) 16 EHRR 155.

29 (1995) Fam Law 478. Also, see, *B v. UK* 2000 1 FLR 1.

30 *Elsholz v. Germany* [2000] 2 FLR 486.

as a matter of fact. As observed in *Re C and B (Children) (Care Order; Future Harm)*[31] a state can only legitimately interfere with this right if it satisfies three requirements: that it be in accordance with the law; that it be for a legitimate aim (in this case of the protection of the welfare and interests of the children); and that 'it is necessary in a democratic society.' In *X, Y and Z v. UK*, it was held that in determining whether a relationship can be defined as 'family life' the following factors are relevant:[32]

> including whether the couple live together, the length of their relationship and whether they have demonstrated their commitment to each other by having children together or by other means.

Gender identity and family life

By the end of the twentieth century, the orthodox model of UK family relationships was being further challenged by rulings upholding the rights of transsexuals.[33] The fact that UK law prevented a marriage involving a transsexual did not mean that the law should deny the capacity of such a person, their partner, and child to enjoy 'family life.' Moreover, in *Salgueiro da Silva Mouta v. Portugal*,[34] the ECtHR laid the ground for an acceptance of same-sex family life in domestic law in its ruling that there had been a breach of Article 8 when a court awarded a mother custody on the grounds that the father's homosexuality was an abnormality and the children should not have to grow up in its shadow. This ruling followed on from, and in all likelihood was influenced by, the example set in New Zealand regarding the required gender identity of a marital couple.[35] The Court of Appeal, in *Quilter v. Attorney-General*,[36] then took a significant step towards broadening the legal interpretation of 'marriage' when it accepted the argument of the plaintiffs, three lesbian couples seeking marriage licences, that[37]

> the traditional common law does not actually address the question of same-sex marriages and it may be that it does not reflect current social realities and values ... Community attitudes in 1996 are much more relaxed to lesbian and gay couples as a result of social change

31 See (2000) 2 FCR 614 at p 625.

32 [1997] 2 FLR 892.

33 See, for example, *X, Y and Z v. United Kingdom* Application No. 21830/93. European Commission of Human Rights, and *B v. France* Series A, No 232 (1993); 16 EHRR 1. However, the decisions in *J v. ST* [1997] 1 FLR 402 and *Sheffield and Horsham v. UK* [1998] 2 FLR 928 demonstrate continued UK resistance to recognising the legal validity of a marriage where one partner is a transsexual.

34 [2001] 1 FCR 653.

35 See Atkin, B., 'New Zealand: Challenging Conventional Understandings' in *The International Survey of Family Law, 1996*, Martinus Nijhoff Publishers, 1998.

36 [1996] NZFLR 481.

37 Ibid at 491 and 494.

The eventual ruling against the plaintiffs was based on a finding that legislation, if not specifically the common law, operated on an assumption that only heterosexual partnerships met the definition of 'marriage.'

The discrepancies between UK and Convention interpretations of legally constituted family units were important. They disclosed the extent to which legal status in the UK endured as the test of defensible parental relationships. Endorsing the validity of forms of family life and parental relationships other than those based on marital union, gave legal and social security to the children involved and confirmed the need to safeguard their welfare interests in that context.

Rights and duties of parents

The 1989 Convention, despite its focus on children, made several clear statements about the need for states to protect the standing of the family and to respect the rights and responsibilities of parents when attending to the interests of children.[38] This need to balance the welfare interests of children against the rights of parents, and to weigh any conflict between them against the threat this might present to the sustainability of the family unit, had become more evident in the caselaw than in the legislation of the UK by the end of the twentieth century.[39] To that extent, the ambivalence in the 1989 Convention between giving priority to rights or welfare, to children or parents, to family unity or to unilateral action by its members, influenced domestic law by confirming the appropriateness of the judicial approach. The most significant point of difference being, that whereas the 1989 Act firmly assigned a paramountcy weighting to a child's welfare interests the 1989 Convention did not.

Chastisement

One issue of prominence at that time was the well-established common law right of a UK parent to administer or authorise reasonable chastisement to their child. This was scrutinised by the EHRR which, in two significant rulings, held that if there was such a right it was personal to parents and should not be available to public bodies. This led directly to the abolition of corporal punishment in UK state schools[40] and was followed by a case concerning the administration of corporal punishment to a seven-year-old boy in preparatory school.[41] Subsequently, recognition of this parental right was further narrowed by the ruling of the ECtHR

38 See, for example, the Preamble, Articles 3(2), 5, 14(2), and 29.

39 See, in particular, the Children Act 1989 and cases such as *Re C (A Minor) (Leave to Seek Section 8 Orders)* [1994] 1 FLR 26.

40 See *Campbell and Cozans v. United Kingdom* (1982) 4 EHRR 293. See, also, *Tyrer v. United Kingdom* (1979–80) 2 EHRR 1 where the court had warned that "such injury to a teenage boy is unacceptable whoever were to inflict the punishment, be it parent or teacher."

41 See *Costello-Roberts v. United Kingdom* [1994] ELR 1.

in *A v. United Kingdom (Human Rights: Punishment of Child)*[42] where it was held that the acquittal by an English court of a stepfather who had beaten a nine-year-old boy with a stick did not comply with Convention requirements to respect human rights. However, in the long run, the greater influence on discontinuing this UK practice will probably come from an awareness that it has been prohibited in a number of European countries.[43]

To be involved in decision-making processes

Article 8 requires that parents be involved in relevant decision-making processes to a degree sufficient to provide them with the requisite protection of their interests. If they are not, there will have been a failure to respect their family life. As was illustrated by the ruling in *Airey v. Ireland*,[44] Article 8 places an obligation on the court to ensure that the rights of an individual are properly secured and are protected against infringements by other individuals. It also inherently requires procedural fairness.

To access information

Within the right to privacy and to family life, Article 8 arguably also provides a right to information about ancillary matters such as family of origin or genetic background. In *Gaskin v. UK (Access to Personal Files)*[45] the ECHR endorsed the view of the Commission that

> respect for private life requires that everyone should be able to establish details of their identity as human beings and that in principle they should not be obstructed by the authorities from obtaining such very basic information without specific justification.

That the right to establish the 'details of their identity as human beings' included the right to information about a biological parent was established by the decision in *Rose v. Secretary of State for Health and Human Fertilisation and Embryology Authority*.[46]

Rights and duties of children

In the U.S., the Constitution and Bill of Rights provided both a legal framework for articulating the rights of minority groups, such as those disadvantaged by race,

42 [1998] 2 FLR 959.
43 Then prohibited in Sweden, Finland, Denmark, Norway, Austria, and Cyprus.
44 See 2 EHRR 305.
45 (1990) 12 EHRR 36.
46 [2002] EWHC 1593 (Admin) [2002] 2 FLR 962.

gender, or disability, and a basis for 'class actions' to remedy those legal inequities. The anti-discriminatory and equal opportunities jurisprudence, assembled in the context of campaigns to gain leverage for the socially disadvantaged, when applied to the welfare interests of children in the 1960s, began to yield caselaw with a relevance for the UK.

From welfare to rights: a beginning

The principles forged during the course of the 'social movement' litigation in the U.S. during the 1960s, began to form a platform for children's rights jurisprudence by the end of that decade. Civil liberties for minors – as much as for other minority groups – and the positioning of the children's rights debate in the context of the civil rights campaign, was directly attributable to writers such as Foster and Freed.[47] This ethos generated a certain amount of caselaw and related publications which aroused interest and stimulated controversy in this jurisdiction. The U.S. judiciary recognised that children possessed rights under the 14th Amendment and under the Bill of Rights,[48] that prohibitions on the sale of obscene materials to minors could be constitutional (though unconstitutional if imposed on adults),[49] that a child had a right to freedom of speech,[50] and a right to a hearing in school discipline cases where suspension was threatened.[51] Subsequently, cases concerning children purporting to 'divorce their parents,'[52] also attracted considerable UK media attention.

The welfare interests of a child are clearly contingent upon a basic right to life. Perhaps because it is so basic it has never been stated as such in UK domestic law; it has been left to the criminal law to frame penalties for breach of an implied right to life and to the civil law of tort to identify the circumstances and liability for endangering life. This negative approach was evident also in Article 6(2) of the 1989 Convention (see, below). Not until the incorporation of the ECHR into domestic law, with the passing of the Human Rights Act 1998, did Article 2 finally establish a child's positive right to life. As J Fortin then pointed out, Article 2 would force UK courts "to justify the merit of decisions to withhold life-saving treatment."[53]

Article 12 of the 1989 Convention (see, above), recognised that children of an age to do so should be given the right to express their views freely in all matters affecting them and the right to have those views taken into account. These very

47 See Foster and Freed, 'A Bill of Rights for Children', *Family Law Quarterly*, Vol 6, No 4, 1972.
48 See *Re Gault* 387 US 1, 13 (1967).
49 See *Ginsberg v. New York* 390 US 629 (1968).
50 See *Tinker v. Des Moines Independent Community School District* 393 US 503 (1969).
51 See *Goss v. Lopez* 419 US 565 (1975).
52 See *Kingsley v. Kingsley* 623 So. 2d 780 (Fla. Dist. Ct. App. 1993) and *Polovchak v. Meese* 774 F. 2d 731 (1985). Note, also, that by 1986 some 20 states had in place legislation which permitted children to petition the courts for a declaration of independence.
53 See Fortin, J., '*Re C (Medical Treatment)* A Baby's Right to Die', in *Child and Family Law Quarterly*, Vol 10, No 4, 1998, at p 413.

significant rights were made applicable to any relevant judicial or administrative proceedings. However, the influence of this particular provision has not always been felt in private family law in the UK, as statute law does not necessitate that the views of a child should be heard by the court, though its influence has since been asserted in judicial rulings.[54] Articles 3, 4, 13, and 17 supplement this provision by giving a child the right to access relevant information and to be represented independently from any adult where there may be a conflict of interests.

Articles 7 and 8 of the 1989 Convention recognise the rights of a child 'to know and be cared for by their parents' and 'to preserve his or her identity,' respectively. However, these provisions failed to have much influence on UK laws relating to assisted or substitute parenthood whether this takes the form of artificial insemination by donor (AID), in vitro fertilisation (IVF), gamete intra-fallopian transfer (GIFT), surrogacy, or adoption. There is no right, exercisable during childhood, enabling a child: to access information regarding the identity of their genetic parents (should such information exist); to be brought up by genetic parents; or to have an identity other than that provided by the legal rather than the genetic parent. These are difficult matters to resolve to the satisfaction of the parties concerned but the Convention provisions require that they be addressed by the UK and the role played by the welfare principle, as defined by Article 3 of the 1989 Convention, might be expected to have a crucial influence in determining the parameters for the exercise of the parties rights in this context.[55] That the UK judiciary recognised, and were prepared to act to rectify, legislative omission became apparent in caselaw. In at least two cases the requirements of Article 7 were cited to justify overturning previous decisions in support of a parental veto and to instead direct that blood tests be conducted so as to ensure that children had access to accurate information regarding their parentage.[56]

The recognition of a child's independent rights is constrained by Article 5 of the 1989 Convention which requires states to respect the parental right to give 'appropriate direction and guidance in the exercise by the child of the rights recognised in the present Convention.' A child's exercise of a particular right may also be constrained by the court's ruling that this would be detrimental to his or her welfare interests.

Uncontested proceedings

There was a significant discrepancy between the provisions of the Family Law Act 1996 and the 1989 Convention in relation to the legal standing of a child in the context of divorce proceedings; a problem which was, and remains, particularly

54 See, for example, *Re D (A Child) (International Recognition)* [2016] EWCA Civ 12, per Lady Hale at para 44.

55 See *Gaskin v. UK* (1980) 12 EHRR 36 where a person who had been in care sought identity information.

56 See *Re H (Paternity: Blood Test)* [1996] 2 FLR 65 and *Re G (Parentage: Blood Sample)* [1997] 1 FLR 360.

acute when the proceedings are uncontested. The requirement in Article 9(1) that 'a child shall not be parted from his or her parents against their will' was not provided for within the 1996 Act. In by far the majority of all divorce proceedings – now as then – there is little possibility of the court taking into account the will of the child concerned and every probability, should it do so, that the will of such a child will not determine his or her future care arrangements. Parental decisions and procedural requirements effectively nullify opportunities for a child's exercise of the right promised under Article 9(1).

Contested proceedings

In the UK, the paramountcy principle must be applied in the context of contested proceedings. This places domestic law at variance with the lesser demands made under the 1989 Convention. By so doing UK legislation imposes a corresponding disadvantage on other parties and ascribes a lesser weighting to other considerations, relative to the balance struck in the Convention. The influence of the 1989 Convention has, so far, not been brought to bear to challenge this overriding advantage conferred on UK children's welfare interests nor to address the resulting discrepancy in the treatment of children's welfare interests in contested and uncontested private family law proceedings (see, further, Chapter 5).

Divorce, nullity, and separation

The continuing lack of statutory provision for children to be independently represented in such contested proceedings is an indicator of the limits of UN CRC influence. The amendment to s 41 of the Matrimonial Causes Act 1973 by the 1989 Act, has left UK divorce law at variance with the requirements of Articles 9(2) and 12 of the 1989 Convention; the latter in particular requires that a child be given 'the opportunity to be heard in *any* judicial and administrative proceedings affecting the child.'

- Contact

Most contested private family law procedures concern rights of access or contact between a child and other adults after family breakdown; proceedings being instigated by parents after their divorce, by unmarried parents after their relationship has broken down, by grandparents or foster parents, etc. Articles 7, 8, and 9(3) of the 1989 Convention may be invoked to lend weight to any claim that a UK child's right to contact with a parent or significant other should be restored but are unlikely to be needed given the substantial body of domestic statutory and caselaw material already available to support such a claim. In this context, the ruling of the ECHR in *Hokkanen v. Finland*[57] is significant because, while acknowledging the

57 [1996] 1 FLR 289.

justice of the father's custody claim, the court ruled that the removal of a ten-year-old child from grandparents who had provided care for the previous eight years was not an option when this would be against the child's express wishes.

Abduction

The Hague Convention on the Civil Aspects of International Child Abduction and the European Convention on Recognition and Enforcement of Decisions Concerning Custody of Children 1983 have directly influenced UK law and practice, both Conventions now govern the legal response to international child abduction in this jurisdiction. They have also served to place the welfare interests of the child concerned at the forefront of related decision-making by the authorities. Article 10 submits attainment of the Convention's central purpose to a frank application of the welfare test.[58] Article 13 provides for judicial discretion to endorse the decision of a child who is of an age and maturity to refuse to return. In recent years there have been indications of a growing judicial willingness to permit the views of children to have the effect of vetoing a return to jurisdiction of habitual residence.[59] In contrast, while the UK judiciary have often sought and given a determining weighting to the opinions of quite young children[60] this has not always been their approach.[61] However, in circumstances where neither Convention applies then the UK courts have no hesitation in applying the welfare test to determine this particular issue[62] (see, further, Chapter 5).

Adoption

Again, the Hague Convention on Intercountry Adoption has radically influenced law and practice in this as in many other jurisdictions.

The main significance of this Convention for welfare interests lies in the stand it takes for preserving the 'identity' of children, within the broad meaning of Article 8 of the 1989 Convention. By placing an emphasis on the expectation that 'donor' countries will provide the professional supports necessary to retain children within their

58 See, for example, *F v. F (Minors) (Custody: Foreign Order)* [1989] Fam 1; *Re G (A Minor) (Child Abduction: Enforcement)* [1990] 2 FLR 325; and *Re R (Abduction: Hague and European Conventions)* [1997] 1 FLR 663.

59 See, for example, *The Ontario Court v. M and M (Abduction: Children's Objections)* [1997] 1 FLR 475 and *Re B (Abduction: Children's Objections)* [1998] 1 FLR 667.

60 Non-return, in compliance with the objections of the children concerned, was ordered in: *S v. S (Child Abduction: Child's Views)* [1992] 2 FLR 492, where the child was aged 9; *B v. B (Child Abduction)* [1993] 1 FCR 382, where they were aged 9 and 7; and *Re R (A Minor: Abduction)* [1992] 1 FLR 105, in respect of a 14-year-old child.

61 See *Re HB (Abduction: Children's Objections)* [1997] 1 FLR 392, where Hale J held that in the absence of firm evidence that the Hague Convention requirements could not be met the children, aged 13 and 11, should be returned not withstanding their objections.

62 See, for example, *Re P (A Minor) (Child Abduction: Non-Convention Country)* [1997] 1 FLR 780 and *Re JA (Child Abduction: Non-Convention Country)* [1998] 1 FLR 231.

countries of origin, wherever possible, the numbers of children becoming available for intercountry adoption was suddenly and radically reduced. By encouraging the good practice in some 'receiving' nations, such as the UK, of ensuring that adopted children are provided with information about their culture of origin, the Convention gave such children the opportunity to maintain a sense of cultural identity.

There are instances when the influence of an international initiative is to turn a spotlight upon an aspect of UK law and reveal the extent of its incompatibility with a required welfare standard. For example, the provision in the 1993 Convention that intercountry adoption requires the consent of the child serves as a reminder that there is no comparable consent requirement in UK adoption law, nor in most of its family law proceedings. The setting of this requirement as an international standard places considerable pressure on the UK to review its position in relation to proceedings which require the views, rather than the consent, of the child concerned. Also, the provision in Article 2 of the same Convention gives equal and separate recognition to two forms of adoption: 'full' which permanently ends legal ties between child and parent/s of origin; and 'simple' which allows for retention of some level of legal relationship. UK legislation, however, has always restricted legal recognition to the most absolute or 'full' model of adoption. Consequently, intercountry adoptions arranged in 'donor' countries on a 'simple' adoption basis must, on entering the UK, be converted automatically to 'full' status, with parental agreement. If, on entry, that agreement proves to be unavailable this could have serious implications for the child's welfare interests. Even if available, it could be contrary to initial parental intentions.[63]

In relation to stepfather adoptions, the ruling of the ECtHR, in *Soderback v. Sweden*,[64] established a benchmark against which UK judicial practice of accommodating step-parent adoption applications can be measured. Again, the development of an 'open' model of adoption in New Zealand fundamentally challenged the exclusiveness of the UK approach. The widespread media and academic attention given to the positive outcomes in New Zealand, of this more relaxed approach to the legal boundaries of adopting families, served to challenge the orthodox view in the UK that a 'closed,' unconditional and permanent model was necessary to secure a child's welfare interests.[65] These are just further instances of international influence calling into question established UK practice.

Public family law, welfare interests, and international influences

The influence of the ECHR and the UN CRC on the law relating to the welfare interests of children in UK law has been considerable, perhaps particularly as regards improving the position of children within public family law.

63 See, further, Duncan, W., 'Children's Rights, Cultural Diversity and Private International Law' in *Children's Rights and Traditional Values*, op cit.

64 [1999] 1 FLR 250.

65 See, for example, Dominick, *Early Contact in Adoption*. Research series No 10 (Wellington, New Zealand, 1988).

The UN Convention on the Rights of the Child 1989 is having a growing influence upon the law relating to local authority child care practice while the caselaw and academic publications of other jurisdictions have also proved influential.

Public law in general

The requirement in Article 12 of the 1989 Convention that the views of a child shall be heard 'in any judicial and administrative proceedings affecting the child' has certainly influenced policy but has yet to be fully addressed by local authorities. Involvement of children in case conferences, for example, is patchy: a child may be present at the beginning or end or not at all, he or she may or may not be supported by a representative of a child advocacy organisation, there is no uniformity of practice. Again, children have virtually no rights in an educational setting and there would not appear to be any plans for a legislative initiative to give them a place on relevant administrative forums.

The balance struck between the interests of parents and children in the public law provisions of the 1989 Act was also different from that required by the Convention; children's interests in the UK were accorded a paramount weighting not required by the Convention. Both differed from the U.S. where welfare interests had been given important recognition and protection in law, since the early 1960s, by the mandatory reporting requirement where child abuse or neglect was suspected.[66] A legislative initiative that failed to influence child care law in the UK.

Consensual state intervention

There is a considerable emphasis in the 1989 Convention on the need for states to provide support services for vulnerable families. The influence of this approach may be seen in certain provisions in the 1989 Act such as those relating to children in need, family based care, and partnership with parents. Article 6(2) of the 1989 Convention requires states to 'ensure to the maximum extent possible the survival and development of the child.' Article 18(2) and (3) require states to assist parents to provide for their children.

Prevention and promotion

Fortin has drawn attention to the preventative emphasis in the 1989 Convention:

> children must also be provided with the resources to develop their full potential.[67] The Convention acknowledges that a child cannot do so without a

66 Children's Bureau, U.S. Dept. of Health, Education and Welfare, *The Abused Child–Principles and Suggested Language for the Reporting of the Physically Abused Child* (1963). As cited in Katz, S.N., in Probert, R. and Barton, C., (eds), *Fifty Years in Family Law*, Intersentia, Cambridge, 2012, at p 309.

67 Article 6(2).

> standard of living adequate for her 'physical, mental, spiritual, moral and social development,'[68] social security benefits,[69] and the right to the 'highest attainable standard of health and to facilities for the treatment of illness and rehabilitation of health.'[70]

However the numbers of children living in poverty in this jurisdiction has been a constant source of concern to international observers. Moreover, it is not enough to provide protection for a child's welfare interests. States are also required to go further and, as she then noted, they must 'promote positively children's civil, economic, social, and cultural rights in order to enjoy a full life, with the ability to mature into healthy adulthood.'[71]

Coercive state intervention: civil

Again, the example from New Zealand has had its influence on broadening an established UK approach to welfare interests. In addition to innovation in foster care practice, New Zealand pioneered the 'family group conference' which has operated on a statutory basis since 1989. Convening a meeting of relevant family members, together with the professionals concerned, is the preferred means of planning an appropriate response to the needs and deeds of children who have become the subject of coercive intervention in either a care or an offence context. This approach of shared responsibility between family and state and making room in decision-making for family members can be seen in the principles of the Children Act 1989, in local authority practice in some areas, and in the more recent juvenile justice legislation.

The balance to be struck between private and public family law was a central issue for UK legislators at the end of the twentieth century and was influenced by the ECtHR decision in *Johansen v. Norway*.[72] The court then considered the extent to which a state's coercive intervention powers, enabling a child to be taken into care, were 'necessary in a democratic society' as required by Article 8(2) of the European Convention on Human Rights. It determined that the appropriate balance could not be prescribed by the court but must be left to individual states, provided they took into account the crucial importance of children's welfare interests.

Care

The capacity of the ECHR to influence the welfare interests of UK children was perhaps most clearly demonstrated in cases[73] where the ECtHR ruled that the

68 Article 27.
69 Article 26.
70 Article 24.
71 See Fortin, J., *Children's Rights and the Developing Law*, Butterworths, 1998, p 38.
72 See (1997) 23 EHRR 33.
73 See *W, O, B and R v. United Kingdom* (1987) 10 EHRR 29, ECHR and *R v. United Kingdom* [1988] 2 FLR 445.

power of local authorities, to coercively assume full parental responsibilities in respect of children consensually placed in care, contravened the Convention. This led directly to the abolition of that domestic power. Subsequently, the rights of UK children, or more specifically those subject to proceedings under the Scottish hearing system, were found to be inadequately protected by the proceedings for lodging preliminary documents in care proceedings.[74] The welfare interests of children were the incidental beneficiaries of ECtHR rulings that the procedural rights of parents in relation to public child care proceedings were unsatisfactory[75] and that disclosure should be made of confidential records relating to children in care.[76]

Fortin, at the end of the twentieth century, drew attention to a trend she had detected in the approach taken by the ECtHR towards cases where the rights infringed concerned children.[77] Instead of simply ruling on whether or not a state party is in breach of a duty owed to a child, or in respect of a child, the court had seemed to be developing a more flexible and discretionary approach in its interpretation of the weighting to be given to the welfare interests of a child relative to other considerations. She then saw the court adopting an approach which was more mediatory than adjudicatory; demonstrating a concern to reach a balanced resolution between parental rights and child welfare; and taking into account the value system of the society in question when doing so. At that time this resonated with practice in the UK which was driven by a policy, enshrined in the 1989 Act, of 'partnership with parents.' In retrospect it has to be said that such influence as the ECtHR rulings might have had on similar UK practice has since dissipated. Instead, local authority practice has tended to become less mediatory, tipping the balance against parental rights and responsibilities; an approach that has encountered some resistance from the judiciary.

Adoption from care

The interface between the public child protection system and human rights can be problematic, particularly in relation to adoption from care. The UK practice of permitting coercive state intervention on care and protection grounds to lead to the permanent transfer of care of a child from the birth parent/s to others, has been a matter of concern to international bodies: a concern reinforced by a suspicion that public service cuts in this jurisdiction can translate into less preventative family support services but more funding for childcare adopters. As the UN Committee on the Rights of the Child pointed out in its 2016 UK report, the state removal of

74 *McMichael v. United Kingdom* (1995) Series A, No 307 which concerned procedures under the Scottish 'children's hearings' system.

75 Influenced in part by *W, O, B and R v. United Kingdom* (1987) 10 EHRR 29 and *R v. United Kingdom* [1988] 2 FLR 445.

76 See *Gaskin v. United Kingdom* (1989) 12 EHRR 36.

77 See, for example, *Johansen v. Norway* (1997) 23 EHRR 33, *Olsson v. Sweden (No 2)* (1994) 17 EHRR 134, and *Hokkanen v. Finland* [1996] 1 FLR 289.

children 'from their biological families owing to the family's economic situation or because a foster family may provide a more beneficial environment for the child'[78] is to be deplored, not least because once in foster care the next step can be towards non-consensual adoption.

Protection

Article 19(1) of the 1989 Convention requires states to provide the necessary coercive intervention powers to ensure that children are protected from all forms of neglect and abuse while in the care of parents, guardian, or other authorised carer. At the end of the twentieth century, the fact that local authorities could exercise a discretion available under s 47(8) of the 1989 Act not to do so, called into question whether the statutory definition of their duties was wholly in compliance with Convention requirements. Possibly such an exercise of discretion, resulting in avoidable harm to a child, would fall foul of the ruling in *Osman v. UK*[79] when the ECtHR held that a public body (the police) was not immune from challenge for negligence in its duty to afford protection to the plaintiff. The claim to immunity on the grounds of public policy was held to be in breach of Article 6. It is notable that, two decades later, there is little evidence that local authorities have been sufficiently influenced by this decision to forego their discretionary rights. However, in future, a local authority's claim not to be judicially accountable for negligence in respect of an exercise or non-exercise of its statutory powers would leave it open to a similar challenge; one which would now be more viable following implementation of the 1998 Act.

Control

There has probably always been a form of 'secure accommodation' within local authority residential provision for children and young persons who are not guilty of criminal offences but are considered to be a danger to themselves or others, or likely to abscond if placed in other settings. Such control measures are currently available in respect of 'looked after' children under the 1989 Act, s 25. While it is accepted that the deprivation of liberty imposes a severe constraint upon the welfare interests of a confined child, and as such may breach Article 5 of the ECHR, these measures are viewed as compatible with the principle and a proportionate response in certain circumstances. Nonetheless, the influence of the ECtHR in establishing parameters for such circumstances can be seen, for example, in *Koniarska v. United Kingdom*.[80]

78 UN Committee on the Rights of the Child, Concluding observations on the fifth periodic report of the United Kingdom of Great Britain and Northern Ireland (CRC/ C/GBR/CO/5), 2016, para 52(b).

79 [1999] 1 FLR 193.

80 (2000) 30 EHRR CD 139.

Coercive state intervention: criminal

The influence of the 1989 Convention may be seen in the establishing of Youth Courts in the UK which comply with the requirement in Article 37 that states ensure the separation of juvenile and adult detainees and keep deprivation of liberty to a minimum. However, the application of Crown Court procedures to children as young as ten is clearly not compatible with Article 40 of the 1989 Convention nor is the practice of remanding children to prisons while awaiting trial,[81] nor that of failing to provide opportunities for representation for a child or for independent review, after a secure accommodation is made. Article 39 requires the promotion of rehabilitation for offenders in the community but the use of special care orders and secure accommodation for child offenders is increasing. The fact that the welfare interests of UK child offenders are disadvantaged relative to those elsewhere in Europe, because the age of criminal responsibility is so much lower in this jurisdiction, has attracted repeated criticism from the United Nations and is frequently mentioned in the UN CRC reports.

The latter half of the twentieth century was also a period when, in the aftermath of the civil rights movement, the U.S. courts were sensitised to minority rights, and this was occasionally reflected in their response to issues affecting the welfare and liberties of children. So, for example, the USSC in *Application of Gault*[82] found that a juvenile was entitled to the five basic constitutional rights accorded to adults at the adjudicatory phase of a hearing: notice, counsel, confrontation, self-incrimination, and appeal. As Sanford Katz has noted, this was a period 'where, for example, family law doctrines, like the best interests of the child … were once left to judicial discretion for definition,' but now became increasingly the subject of statute law. Unquestionably, the initiatives of U.S. legislators and rulings of their judiciary on such matters would have influenced their UK counterparts.

The severity of court directed restrictions on the liberty of UK children have also given rise to concern in Europe. For example, the indeterminate nature of sentences to be served 'for the duration of Her Majesty's pleasure' have been challenged for being in breach of Article 5(4) of the European Convention on Human Rights, as has the introduction of a penal 'tariff' to be determined at the discretion of the Home Secretary before the Parole Board can consider setting a date for release. The fact that these and other such practices have persisted, despite decades of criticism, indicates the very real limitations on the extent to which this jurisdiction is amenable to influence from Europe. It would seem that legislative trend in the UK towards accentuating punitive and custodial measures instead of

81 See the criticism of this practice in 'Children, Crime and Society: Perspectives of the UN Convention on the Rights of the Child' in *Child Offenders: UK and International Practice*, the Howard League, 1995, at p 20.

82 387 U.S. 3 (1967). Cited by Katz, S.N., in Probert, R. and Barton, C., (eds), *Fifty Years in Family Law*, op cit, at p 304.

emphasising diversion and rehabilitation, is distancing the domestic response to youth crime from that advocated in the 1989 Convention[83] and the Beijing Rules.[84]

Advances in medicine and the social sciences

For most of history, children and childhood have been peripheral to the law. Not until towards the end of the nineteenth century and into the early decades of the twentieth, did the child begin to emerge as a legal entity that represented more than their parents proprietary interests. Even then a further stage was necessary before children were treated not merely as the objects of legal proceedings but as subjects, though this was little more than recognition of children as small adults, with a 'legal personality,' in jurisprudential terms, but without any special distinguishing characteristics. The transition to an 'object of concern' in early child protection law or to a 'social problem' in juvenile justice law did not allow for a focus on any needs particular to childhood. The further step towards judicial recognition in the UK that 'the child is a person and not an object of concern'[85] was essentially a mid-to-late twentieth-century development that owed much to insights generated in the U.S. by a new cohort of professionals.

Emergence of the social sciences and a body of child care professionals

Although the core social sciences are long established, it was not until the mid-twentieth century that certain branches – sociology, psychology, social work, social policy, etc. – seemed to suddenly become more relevant and vibrant. Whether as cause or effect of the rebirth of the social sciences, a cluster of new professionals – social workers, child psychologists, behavioural psychologists, therapists, health visitors, etc. – joined with lawyers, probation officers, and others – to focus on child development and protection issues, resulting in the welfare interests of the child acquiring a raised social profile and heightened scrutiny from the mid-1960s. This capacity of law to absorb and use information from other sources is a well-established characteristic. As Saunders J noted in 1553: "If matters arise in our law which concerns other sciences or facilities we commonly apply to the aid of that service or facility which it concerns. This is a commendable thing in our law."[86]

83 See Article 40(3)(b) of the UN Convention on the Rights of the Child 1989.

84 See Rules 11.1–11.4 of the UN Standard Minimum Rules for the Administration of Juvenile Justice 1985.

85 See the *Report of the Inquiry into Child Abuse in Cleveland, 1987*, Cmnd. 412 (1988), per Butler-Sloss LJ at p 245.

86 Quoted by Hammelman, 1947 at p 32 (cited by Sutton, A., 'Science in Court', in King, M., (ed), *Childhood, Welfare & Justice*, ibid, at p 47).

Child psychiatry and developmental psychology

The grounds for insight into what constitutes the modern welfare interests of children in the UK was laid by U.S. child care experts in the 1950s such as Dr Spock, a paediatrician and psychoanalyst, whose book *Baby and Childcare*[87] was the first to generate widespread public interest in child rearing, though his focus was more on supporting confident parenting than on children. Somewhat later, Bruno Bettelheim,[88] an Austrian-born psychologist and leading U.S. Freudian psychoanalyst, led research into emotionally disturbed children. His book, *Love Is Not Enough*, became very influential for a generation of child care workers in the U.S. and subsequently in the UK. Jean Piaget,[89] a Swiss developmental psychologist, was less interested in parenting and more specifically focused on understanding the cognitive development of children at different stages in their maturation; he viewed children not as 'small adults' but rather as complex individuals whose experience of life differed depending upon which of the four successive phases of cognitive development they happened to be in. In the later decades of the twentieth century, the work of the American partnership Goldstein, Freud, and Solnit[90] gained wide circulation and credibility among UK academics and professionals. Their powerfully argued case that the welfare interests of children would be enhanced if the state increased its respect for the legal integrity, autonomy, and privacy of the family, found general acceptance on this side of the Atlantic. Later still, and also influential on both sides of the Atlantic, was the research and publications of Robert Mnookin,[91] a child care lawyer who studied and published on effective advocacy on behalf of children's interests.

Consequently, in the UK since the mid-1960s, judicial notice was increasingly taken of the work of leading U.S. child psychiatrists and psychologists and decisions have been grounded on evidence of the child's emotional and psychological welfare – even if, at times, this has strayed into a tendency to pathologise their behaviour – as distinct from their material wellbeing.[92]

Attachment theory

Whereas the law in the late nineteenth and early twentieth centuries had held fast to the principle that maternal care, particularly for young children, was *de*

87 Spock, B., *The Commonsense Book of Baby and Childcare,* Duell, Sloan and Pearce, New York, 1946.

88 Bettelheim, B., *Love Is Not Enough*, Free Press, 1950.

89 Piaget, J., *The Psychology of the Child*, New York, Basic Books, 1972.

90 See Goldstein, J., Freud, A., and Solnit, A. *Beyond the Best Interests of the Child*, New York, Free Press, 1974; *Before the Best Interests of the Child*, New York, Free Press, 1979; and *The Best Interests of the Child: The Least Detrimental Alternative*, Simon and Schuster, 1996. Also, Goldstein, J., *In the Best Interests of the Child: Professional Boundaries*, New York, Free Press, 1986.

91 Mnookin, R.H., *In the Interest of Children*, WH Freeman & Co, 1985 and *Child, Family and State* (7th ed.), Walters Kluwer, 2014.

92 See evidence of such a trend beginning with the judgment in *Re C(L) (An Infant)* [1965] 2 QB 449 and culminating in the HL judgment in *Re W (An Infant)* [1971] AC 682.

rigueur for child development, this approach wilted in the face of U.S. equality jurisprudence in the aftermath of the civil rights movement. As Katz observes, 'the maternal preference role, long adhered to both in fact and in law, was basically abandoned'[93] in favour of the security derived from the attachment formed between a child and their primary caregiver. Equality claims, together with evidence of attachment, greatly strengthened the position of fathers – including unmarried fathers[94] – and weakened the traditional presumption favouring mothers, as prospective custodians in divorce and custody proceedings.

Attachment theory suggests that the future psychological wellbeing of every child is dependent upon their experiencing an intimate one-to-one relationship with a caring adult for a crucial period during their formative early years. The corollary being that this opportunity can be missed, as when a child moves through a series of short-term care arrangements, leaving him or her psychologically stranded or in limbo. As Wilkes notes:[95]

> The unfortunate outcome for many children in limbo is that they become 'attachment resistant'. Such children pose significant problems for their caregivers, and they consume an inordinate amount of professional time and expertise.

It was attachment theory, bringing with it an acute awareness of the costs for the emotional wellbeing of each child and for the child care system as a whole, that fuelled the drive to make adoption available for children in that system, first in the U.S. and then in the UK.

As the volume of family breakdown cases escalated, from the 1960s onwards, bringing with them a wave of child custody disputes, so the courts became more familiar with expert witness testimony from child care professionals.

Emotional bonding

The concept of a 'psychological parent,' which emerged from the work of U.S. developmental psychologists, was based on research showing that not only was the gender of the primary caregiver unimportant but so also was the fact that caregiver was not a parent. What was important, and crucial to the welfare of every child, was that he or she had a sufficiently close and trusting relationship with a caregiver that would allow an emotional bond to develop between them.[96]

93 See Katz, S.N., in Probert, R. and Barton, C., (eds), *Fifty Years in Family Law*, Intersentia, Cambridge, 2012 at p 305.

94 See *Stanley v. Illinois*, 405 U.S. 645 (1972).

95 See Wilkes, J.R., 'Introduction', in *Permanency Planning in the Child Welfare System*, Ottawa, Sparrow Lake Alliance: Children in Limbo Task Force, 2002 at p 6.

96 See Goldstein, J., et al, *Beyond the Best Interests of the Child*, op cit.

The importance of an emotional bond did much to raise awareness regarding the limitations of residential care, to legitimate foster care, to strengthen the case for those who believed that every child should have a family and, by extension, to strengthen also the argument for making the adoption option available to children in long-term state care. It was an approach that having gained widespread judicial approval in the U.S. was subsequently adopted by UK child care professionals and then by the judiciary.

The 'battered baby syndrome'

A particularly influential area of childcare research, with repercussions on relevant professions on both sides of the Atlantic, was that of the paediatrician Henry Kempe on the 'battered child.'[97] The suggestion that a child could be diagnosed as suffering from such a syndrome by a clinical assessment to determine whether he or she presents with specific symptoms seemed at the time, and for some years later, to provide a valuable tool for identifying children in need of protection.

Women's reproductive rights

Procreation, a woman's right in relation to – commencing, terminating, or otherwise regulating – her conception/pregnancy, did not first surface as a legal issue in the 1960s but, in the wake of the civil rights movement, it was then that it became most forcefully asserted and ultimately established in the U.S. courts.[98] The advances in medical science that allowed procreation to become a matter subject to female choice was, of course, a transformative development for society as a whole, for women in general, and for the welfare interests of children. Such advances also greatly improved the survival rate for babies born with complex health and social care needs, which brought with it a more intense paediatric focus on what might constitute the welfare of a child; a focus that with increased frequency required forensic analysis in the wardship jurisdiction of the High Court.

Family planning

Again, the influence from the U.S. was instrumental in establishing family planning services in the UK. Beginning with the birth control advice from Margaret Sanger and Emma Goldman in 1916 and continuing with the Planned Parenthood Federation of America which influenced the work of Maria Stopes in England, there has been constant collaboration in research and dissemination on both sides

97 See Kempe, C.H., et al, 'The "Battered-Child Syndrome,"' *Child Abuse & Neglect*, Vol. 9, 1985, at pp 143–54.

98 Probably beginning with the USSC ruling in *Griswold v. Connecticut*, 381 U.S. 479 (1965) and continuing with its decisions in *Roe v. Wade*, 410 U.S. 113 (1973) and *Planned Parenthood v. Casey*, 505 U.S. 833 (1992).

of the Atlantic. The fact that for women in the 1960s and onwards, though not for all and perhaps not even for the majority in either the U.S. or the UK, childbirth meant the arrival of a planned and wanted child must necessarily have boosted the welfare interests of those children.

IVF

In vitro fertilisation treatment (IVF) emerged in the 1970s and, since then, some seven million children have been born as a consequence of such treatment, but it was only in 2010 that the Nobel Prize was awarded to Robert Edwards for his work in this area, though. Over the years, any research conducted as regards the welfare interests of the many children conceived by means of IVF, or assisted reproductive technology (ART) as it is sometimes known, has been rather inconclusive.[99] It perhaps can at least be fairly said that as children born by such means are clearly very much wanted, the parenting they experience is likely to be of a high standard and their welfare interests will benefit accordingly.

Surrogacy

Surrogacy has been judicially defined as 'an arrangement whereby a woman (the "surrogate mother") agrees to conceive and bear a child, which she intends to give to another or others (the "commissioning couple" or the "commissioning husband" and "commissioning wife") upon the child's birth.'[100] This arrangement may proceed either on a commercial basis which includes a fee, or on an altruistic basis where any payment is restricted to the reimbursement of medical and other expenses.

It is probable that the current law and practice relating to surrogacy in the UK owes a good deal to the 1988 New Jersey case of *In re Baby M*[101] as consolidated in the 1993 Californian Supreme Court decision in *Johnson v. Calvert.*[102] The latter case essentially determined that the surrogate – who had no genetic link with the baby – was therefore unrelated to the child and instead the commissioning woman, who was genetically linked to the baby, could be construed as the legal mother. This decision seemed to clear the way for non-altruistic surrogacy arrangements in the U.S. Surrogacy 'tourism' is now becoming something of a moral issue as prospective parents shop among the less developed nations and among the socially disadvantaged in the developed western nations for the best deal available.

99 See, for example, de Lacey et al, 'Child Interests in Assisted Reproductive Technology: How is the Welfare Principle Applied in Practice?', *Human Reproduction*, Vol 30, No 3, 2015, at pp 616–24.

100 *Lowe & Barry and Anor* [2011] FamCA 625 at para 5.

101 537 A.2d 1227 (NJ 1988).

102 851 P.2d 776 (Cal. 1993).

For the most part, surrogacy results in a child much wanted by those who will thereafter be his or her parents and therefore works to the positive advantage of a child's welfare interests. However, there can be a downside. Among the problems associated with surrogacy is that the information the child receives will be entirely at parental discretion with resulting crucial implications for the development of his or her identity and cultural affiliation: due to the anonymity surrounding the use of genetic material a child may never know their true genetic origins. More immediately, as has been pointed out, there may be questions as to the child's parentage and nationality:[103]

> Often commissioning parents may not be recorded on the birth certificate of the surrogate child. This can create difficulties in obtaining passports and travel documents for the child, to enable him or her to accompany the commissioning parents home. If parentage and nationality cannot be established there is the potential that the child may be left 'marooned, stateless and parentless'.[104]

Conclusion

While the extent to which the law relating to the welfare interests of children in the UK has been influenced by international instruments and by principles developed in the caselaw and academic research of other jurisdictions is difficult to judge, it is certain to be very considerable. The many and frequent judicial references made in the course of everyday family proceedings cases to the provisions of international instruments – particularly the ECHR and the UN CRC – testifies to an increased awareness of the relevance of this additional tier of law. But it is highly probable that UK legislators and judiciary have for many decades been conducting low profile adjustments to the law relating to children in order to take account of principles developed elsewhere. As this chapter has shown, the source of such influence has very often been the U.S.

103 See Pascoe, CJ., 'Issues of Forced Adoption and International Commercial Surrogacy, Federal Court of Australia, Melbourne (2nd October, 2013)' at: www.law.monash.edu.au/about-us/events /chie-judge-pascoe-dpeech-notes.pdf.

104 See *Re X & Y (Foreign Surrogacy)* [2009] Fam 71 at 76C.

Part III

Profiling contemporary jurisdictional experiences of welfare

5 England and Wales

Introduction

As the twentieth century drew to a close, it was apparent that both public and private sectors of family law were no longer aligned with contemporary social pressures and had become steadily less able to respond appropriately to the emerging patterns of child care needs being generated by the volume and variety of family breakdowns. In particular, the primary function of adoption had become one of repairing boundaries for reformed family units while many thousands of children, admitted to state care and denied permanent families, were being shuttled between foster homes in over-stretched local authority resources.

This chapter continues the narrative outlined in Book I,[1] Chapters 1–3. It begins with a brief introduction to the developing policy, principles, and legislation before considering the welfare interests in the context of fundamental human rights. It then examines the role of the welfare principle with many references to evolving case law: first in contemporary public family law, both civil and criminal; then in its private counterpart; and finally as it transects both sectors. In so doing, it sets out a thematic structure – together with indicators of the role played by the welfare principle and picks out key benchmarks of the principle's effectiveness – to be loosely replicated in the following jurisdiction specific chapters.

Policy, principles, legislation, and the legal system

Public family law was adjusted to make a clear distinction between the criminal justice system (for youth offenders) and the public child care and protection system, though both clearly impact upon the welfare interests of children.[2] Similarly, although for many generations a firm distinction had been maintained between entry to the latter system and to the adoption process, rigorously policed by the

1 O'Halloran, K., *The Principle of the Welfare of the Child: A History*, Routledge, 2022.

2 See, for example, Utting, D., Bright, J., and Henricson, C., *Crime and the Family: Improving Child-Rearing and Preventing Delinquency*, Family Policy Studies Centre, London, 1993.

DOI: 10.4324/9781003268642-9

judiciary, this gap was bridged by legislation. Furthermore, certain hybrid court orders were introduced to apply across the public/private sectors of family law.

Policy

The crosscutting principles, procedures, and court orders that have come to increasingly bind public and private sectors of family law, reflect a policy which recognises the instability of modern families and has refocused on the common strand of securing the future welfare of children placed at risk by parental choice, fault, or default.

Public family law relating to children: civil jurisdiction

The Children Act 1989 introduced the paramountcy principle, the welfare 'checklist,' a menu of orders (any one, none, or combination of which may be made), together with the parental responsibility concept and court order. In recent years this has been supplemented and amended by the provisions of the Children Act 2004 and the Children and Social Work Act 2017[3] but not sufficiently to offset what the UN CRC perceives as 'the "intolerance of childhood" and general negative public attitude towards children, especially adolescents, within society.'[4] Although the criminal jurisdiction cannot be wholly discounted, in relation to the principle of the welfare of the child, its application within the remit of the Youth Court is secondary to considerations of justice and public policy.

The prevention/protection balance

At a time of tight budgetary constraints on all public services, the resources that might otherwise have been allocated to preventative intervention with vulnerable families have instead been targeted towards children for whom the standard of parental care places them at risk of significant harm.

'Diagnostic inflation' – as identified by Dingwall[5] – resulted in a trend that over time has distorted the thresholds for state intervention: 'children in need,' the consensual threshold has been raised and the coercive 'significant harm' threshold lowered to permit resources of social workers and attendant facilities to be redirected from the former group to the latter. Family centres, respite care foster parents, home helps, etc. are among the supportive modes of intervention that are now seldom available unless the children concerned are on the 'at risk' register or are at home under care or supervision orders. Nonetheless, the significant

3 As Julie Doughty comments: local authority responsibilities to children in need and their families have, since 2016, been governed in Wales by the Social Services and Wellbeing (Wales) Act 2014 (note to author, 21.05.2022).

4 See the UN Committee on the Rights of the Child, *Concluding Observations: United Kingdom Of Great Britain And Northern Ireland*, United Nations (2016) at para 22.

5 Eekelaar, J. and Dingwall, R., *The Reform of Child Care Law: A Practical Guide to the Children Act 1989*, Routledge, 1990, at p 129.

impact of early intervention programmes such as Sure Start should not be underestimated. Further, under s 20 of the 1989 Act, children may still be admitted to care on a voluntary basis in circumstances where there are resources available and if: this is necessary to safeguard their welfare interests; the child's welfare cannot be adequately ensured by the parent/s or others with parental responsibility; and with the latter's consent or absence of dissent.

Another very contentious issue, relating mainly to adolescents, has been the need to formulate a restraint and seclusion policy to address the legal predicament of those whose behaviour presents a real risk to their own welfare and that of others. This problem has for many years been acutely felt by staff in children's homes and by foster carers when responding to recalcitrant adolescent girls whose insistence on exercising rights of independence often places them at risk of sexual abuse. This prevalent issue was acutely manifested in the prolonged sexual abuse of some 1,400 girls in the Rotherham area over a period of 16 years.[6] Again, the problem is also one faced by teachers exposed to the disruptive and possibly damaging behaviour of pupils (neither necessarily adolescent nor wilful, as autistic children and others with complex needs can present management issues) in the classroom. How to intervene in a manner and with methods that balance the welfare interests of a disruptive pupil against the duty of care and protection owed by teachers to all others in the classroom, is an ongoing challenge in many schools.

Foster care

Family based care, for out of home or 'looked after' children, has been a cornerstone of government policy for many years. It has been estimated that four out of every five children who now come into care in England are fostered.[7] There is some hard evidence that local authorities are diverting funds towards supporting children in care instead of towards preventing that necessity arising. In *R & L v. Manchester City Council*,[8] for example, the practice of a local authority was found to be in breach of Article 14 of the ECHR because it discriminated between payments for family based care and foster care to the disadvantage of the former.

Kinship care

The placing of a looked after child – whether for foster care or adoption purposes – with approved members of their extended family has become standard practice over the past decade or two. Indeed, s 1(2)(f) of the 2002 Act directs the agency/court specifically to have regard to relationships with relatives (which, in

6 See Jay, A., *Independent Inquiry into Child Sexual Exploitation in Rotherham (1997–2013)*, 2014, at: www.rotherham.gov.uk/downloads/file/279/independent-inquiry-into-child-sexual-exploitation-in-rotherham.

7 See *Fostering Network* at www.fostering.net/.
In 2019, of the 78,150 children in the public care system some 56,160 were in foster care.

8 [2001] 1 FLR 43.

this context, under s 22C(2)), includes parents) such as grandparents.[9] Arguably, by placing a duty on the local authority to look first to family members as potential adopters for a child in care, s 22C thereby implies that such a child has a corresponding right to expect the authority to prioritise an adoption placement within their extended family of origin.

Adoption from care

By the early decades of the twenty-first century the annual number of judicially issued care orders was rapidly increasing while adoption orders were in steep decline: for decades the proportion of looked after children voluntarily relinquished for adoption had been shrinking; almost all adoptions from care were resisted by parents who did not consent to the state enforced adoption of their children. The consequent lack of permanent family based care for growing numbers of children had become a serious policy concern.[10]

In keeping with the long-established U.S. precedent, a clear government policy had been growing to accelerate the number and pace of nonconsensual adoptions: an option viewed as preferable to allowing children to 'drift' in the care system; and one that in effect demolished the principle of 'partnership with parents' that had been such a cornerstone of the 1989 Act. In 2019 of the 78,150 children in the care system, 3,570 exited by way of adoption (compared with 5,360 in 2015); many being adopted by their foster parents with assistance from the 'Adoption Passport' scheme which provides two years of post-adoption financial support: viewed by some as another of the many government initiatives to privatise a public service. This policy was expedited by the introduction of 'concurrent placements' whereby a child would be placed with carers, dually approved as foster parents and as prospective adopters, while the local authority embarked on a rehabilitative programme with the child's birth parent/s. If the programme was unsuccessful then the child would remain in their placement and be adopted; but time clearly worked to the disadvantage of the parent/s as it allowed attachments to form that could ultimately determine where the child's best interests lay. This was a policy that caused some concern. For example, in *H v. UK*[11] the parent complained of the 'deplorable delay' of almost two years in court proceedings concerning her contact application in relation to her child in local authority care. By the time the matter was brought before the court almost three-and-a-half years had elapsed since she had last seen her child who was by then well settled with prospective adopters. The court stressed that:

> In cases of this kind the authorities are under a duty to exercise exceptional diligence since … there is always the danger that any procedural delay will

9 *Re W (A Child)* [2016] EWCA Civ 793.

10 See, for example, Bilson, A., *Suffer the Little Children*, London, Legal Action for Women, 2017.

11 (1988) 10 EHRR 95.

result in the *de facto* determination of the issue submitted to the court before it has held the hearing.

Aligning the principles of the 1989 and 2002 Acts succeeded in mainstreaming adoption into child care and protection policy and created a new platform for addressing the needs of children failed by their parents. The paramountcy principle was embedded in s 1(2) of the Adoption and Children Act 2002 – the paramount consideration of the court or adoption agency must be the child's welfare, throughout his life – to govern all decisions, whether taken by court or adoption agency, affecting a child's upbringing throughout his or her life including dispensing with parental consent for adoption (complying with Article 21 of the UN CRC). A bridge was thus strategically placed to directly link the private family law role of adoption with the public child care system. But this was a policy that generated controversy. The CRC, for example, expressed concern that 'parents have not been provided with adequate family support' and that 'children have reportedly been removed from their biological families owing to the family's economic situation or because a foster family may provide a more beneficial environment for the child.'[12] While the British Association of Social Workers expressed misgivings in its 2018 report 'The role of the social worker in adoption – ethics and human rights: An enquiry' which likened the current use of adoption by local authorities to a 'runaway train' which had become impossible for individual social workers to stop[13] (see, further, below).

Residential care

In recent years, following a succession of inquiries concerning abuse and neglect in children's homes,[14] there has been a sharp change in government policy towards prioritising family based care and a consequent fall in the number of residential care places available for looked after children. From a position where most children in care were accommodated in such homes, now only few tend to be so and they are often children with complex needs, likely to be there on a long-term basis. Otherwise, in keeping with research findings that family based care is more conducive to promoting a child's welfare interests, government policy is firmly directed towards foster or adoption placements in preference to residential care.

Whereas previously it could have been anticipated that children with a degree of physical or learning impairment would have remained in residential care, this is no longer necessarily the case. New levels of investment in ongoing support services and financial allowances, together with careful preparation for placement,

12 See UN Committee on the Rights of the Child, 2016, op cit, at para 52.

13 See, further, at: www.basw.co.uk/media/news/2018/jan/basw-unveils-adoption-enquiry-report-and-key-findings.

14 See, for example, Waterhouse, *Lost in Care: Report of the Tribunal of Inquiry into the Abuse of Children in Care in the Former County Council Areas of Gwynedd and Clwyd since 1974*, The Stationery Office, London, 2000.

have facilitated the successful foster care or adoption of a small number of children with special needs. Professional expertise, more relevant support services and the encouragement offered to foster carers and prospective adopters have served to widen their expectations as regards the challenges and satisfactions involved in such parenting. In addition, the influence of equality and non-discrimination legislation has prompted local authorities to extend opportunities for the promotion of welfare interests, through permanent family care, to children with more complex needs.

Public family law relating to children: criminal jurisdiction

While the Children Act 1989 had made provision for children on remand or ordered to serve a custodial sentence – becoming 'looked after children' – it was the Youth Custody Service, established in 2017, that had become designated as provider of custodial facilities for those on remand and for all convicted child offenders.

The welfare/justice balance

This balance was marked out, respectively, by: the Children Act 1989 and the Criminal Justice Act 1991; and the twin pathways of Family Courts and Youth Courts. Policy, however, continued to equivocate[15] until with a neat sleight of hand 'welfare' became subsumed into 'justice..' As the Home Office stated in 1997:

> The Government does not accept that there is any conflict between protecting the welfare of a young offender and preventing that individual from offending again. Preventing offending promotes the welfare of the individual young offender and protects the public.

This elision was completed by the early years of the twenty-first century when official policy firmed up around the clearly identified purpose of preventing offending, even if the courts would also be required to have regard to such other factors as public protection, welfare, punishment, and reparation. In short, welfare in a justice context had lost the paramountcy status assigned to it under the 1989 Act and indeed had little relevance as a threshold criterion at points of either entry or exit in criminal proceedings even if, as Julie Doughty notes, provision in the Children and Young Persons Act 1933 that courts have regard to children's welfare remained in place.[16]

15 So, for example, in *J.M. v. Runeckles* (1984) 79 Cr.App.R.255 it was held that in addition to the conduct, it must be shown that the child knew what they were doing was seriously wrong.

16 Note to author (21.05.2022).

Private family law relating to children

For the most part, matters affecting the welfare interests of children in a private family law context come before the court in matrimonial (i.e. divorce, nullity, and judicial separation) or adoption proceedings with wardship and guardianship continuing to provide their traditional supplementary roles (see, further, below). They may also do so when issues arise relating to aspects of parental responsibility, and in surrogacy or abduction disputes.

Matrimonial

State retreat from intervention continues to be the most characteristic aspect of policy governing this area of family law.[17] The law removed an essentially fault based approach to sanctioning the decisions of spouses to terminate their relationship in 2022 as it was clear that policy had shifted towards a preference for a simple finding of irretrievable breakdown and on safeguarding the welfare interests of any children involved. The latter concern was evident in the Matrimonial Causes Act 1973: s 25, requiring the court to give first consideration to the welfare of a child; and s 42, allowing the court in any proceedings for divorce, nullity of marriage, or judicial separation to 'make such order as it thinks fit with respect to the custody of any child of the family.' More importantly, however, as mentioned above, the subsequent Children Act 1989 introduced the paramountcy principle, the welfare 'checklist,' a menu of child custody and access orders, and the parental responsibility order, all with equal application to private and to public family law proceedings.

Guardianship and wardship

Guardianship, is now most usually restricted for use by court or testator to appoint someone to undertake parental responsibilities for an orphan. In giving effect to a legislative intent to divert applicants away from a perceived misuse of adoption proceedings, the 'special guardianship' order has been introduced. This allows courts to appoint foster parents and step-parents as 'special guardians' where the child concerned has already formed a sense of identity and/or strong attachments to members of their birth family, but where adoption is seen as inappropriate.

Wardship, that most ancient of court orders,[18] like guardianship, is now governed by provisions of the Children Act 1989. It has an even more restricted

17 Evident, for example, in the repeal of the discretionary court power to commit, on its own motion, a child into local authority care.

18 Earliest recorded case being a decision of the Exchequer Chamber in *Calvin's Case* (1608) 77 ER 377 when the rights of a Scottish child's property in England were preserved by the court. The proactive nature of wardship was attested to by Lord Eldon LC, in *Wellesley v. Duke of Beaufort* (1827) 2 Russ 1, who stated:

> It has always been the principle of this court, not to risk the incurring of damage to children which it can repair, but rather to prevent the damage being done.

application: wardship proceedings may not be commenced in circumstances where an alternative statutory order is available and deemed more appropriate. Essentially, the use of wardship is confined to situations of urgency, where only the *parens patriae* powers of the High Court are sufficient to direct intervention on behalf of a child (see, further, below).

Adoption

The policy of exercising caution when choosing adoption for a looked after child, where a less draconian option is available, has also been applied to family adoptions. For many decades judicial equivocation has facilitated the continuing sanctioning of adoption by step-parents; even though alternatives were available. Now the judiciary are specifically required to consider the relative merits of a 'special guardianship' order, in relation to the particular needs of the child concerned, when responding to a step-parent adoption application.

The statutory removal of the previous requirement that such an application should be made jointly with the child's birth parent finally dispenses with the curious anomaly – reversing legislative intent –whereby a parent was obliged to adopt her own child. A further statutory amendment removed the requirement in England of s 1(5) of the Adoption and Children Act 2002 that 'due consideration be given to religious persuasion, racial origin and cultural and linguistic background' when placing a child for adoption which was designed to counter public concern regarding 'politically correct' adoption placements.

Intercountry adoption

This has never been as popular a social phenomenon in England and Wales as elsewhere in Europe which is largely due to a firm government policy of redirecting prospective adopters towards children in the domestic public care system. This policy has in recent years been considerably reinforced by financial support. ICA is now declining as a proportion of annual adoption orders as a consequence of a reversal of government policy in previously well established 'donor' countries such as China, Korea, Romania, and Russia.

Family planning, abortion, surrogacy, IVF, etc.

By increasing the proportion of children who are 'wanted,' family planning services correspondingly increase the probability of successful parenting and lower the threshold of risk to the welfare interests of the children concerned. These services are well established and generally readily accessible as part of public service provision. The introduction of legal abortion under the Abortion Act 1967, which continues to be the governing legislation,[19] has generated a steady

19 Modified by the Human Embryology and Human Fertilisation Act 1990 which reduced the legal time limit for abortions from 28 to 24 weeks.

growth in annual procedures: in 2006 a total of 193,700 abortions were conducted in respect of women resident in England and Wales, compared with 186,400 in 2005; rising to 205, 295 in 2018.[20] The Human Fertilisation and Embryology Act 1990 and the consequent developments in fertility treatment (AID, GIFT, etc.) offer an important and improving route for childless couples who want the opportunity to become parents. As has been pointed out, 'IVF used to be around 7% successful and now it's around 30%.'[21]

Safeguarding the welfare interests of children has been an ongoing issue for England's only Gender Identity Clinic (providing a Gender and Identity Development Service) for young people which was launched as part of England's only Gender Identity Clinic (providing a Gender and Identity Development Service) for young people which was launched as part of the Tavistock in 1989 and attracted growing controversy in recent years. In the course of a decade there had been a sudden sharp increase in referrals (from 250 to 5,000 resulting in a two-year waiting list) generating concerns regarding the sufficiency of available counselling and the capacity of many 16-year-old children – some with autism or other mental health issues – to give an informed consent for puberty blocking drug treatment (see, further, below).

- Surrogacy

Government policy on surrogacy has been at best conflicted. For the past couple of decades or so, expressions of concern for the status of the children involved and their rights to origins information has been balanced by an absence of any initiative to introduce regulatory measures. Currently the law favours surrogate mothers: agreements are unenforceable, and create insecurity for commissioning couples by allowing surrogate mothers to choose to keep the child after birth; the courts ensure that surrogacy arrangements are altruistic and that no improper payments have been made; while the insertion of s 1(2A) into the 1989 Act established a presumption that the involvement of a birth parent in the life of the child concerned would further that child's welfare.[22] The welfare interests of the several thousand children born by surrogate arrangements, and those who may be so in the future, need protection.

An allied complication is the possibility of genetic editing – whether involving an embryo implanted in a surrogate or birth mother – which may be conducted to eliminate a genetic pre-disposition towards particular diseases or to enhance an innate attribute. This has given rise to a concern that we could be on the verge of entering an era of 'designer babies.' In order to safeguard the welfare interests of

20 See, further, at: https://assets.publishing.service.gov.uk/government/uploads/system/uploads/attachment_data/file/808556/Abortion_Statistics__England_and_Wales_2018__1._

21 See, further, at: www.theguardian.com/society/2018/nov/03/england-adoption-rates-falling-as-ivf-improves-says-senior-official.

22 See *in Re H (A Child) (Surrogacy Breakdown)* [2017] EWCA Civ 1798.

the children involved, regulatory procedures providing rights of access to identity-related information, to the security of legal status, and to clear and firmly differentiated legal relationships with birth parent/s and those with parental responsibility, are long overdue.

Principles

The role of certain crosscutting principles, particularly 'parental responsibility' and 'paramountcy' together with the welfare 'checklist,' have contributed greatly to promoting judicial consistency in decisions relating to child welfare interests and to the overall coherence of family law.

Paramountcy principle

This principle, drawn initially from case law[23] and first statutorily stated[24] in s 1 of the Guardianship of Minors Act 1971, was asserted to govern judicial determination of all issues affecting a child's upbringing and administration of his or her property. Initially it was resolutely confined to judicial decisions (unavailable to other decision makers, like local authority social workers) in child care and wardship proceedings and was specifically prevented from having any application to decisions relating to adoption, which resulted in the policy and principles governing the two contexts becoming increasingly conflicted. Moreover this was a time when the failings of state care were becoming only too apparent. The effect of public child care scandals, combined with the expense of that care and the influence of the principle that family care is best, led to the outcomes research[25] for looked after children. The comprehensively negative findings of that research, together with attachment theory[26] and 'permanency planning,' suggested that once rehabilitation had been found to be impracticable then a local authority should secure family based permanent care arrangements that would allow a child to optimise their potential for emotional, psychological, and physical growth. As adoption had long been viewed by child care professionals as the gold standard of the permanency planning options, there was professional consensus that it, rather than foster care, was more likely to produce long-term beneficial outcomes for the children concerned.

In addition to matters statutorily excluded as not constituting 'upbringing' or administration of property, case law established some further limitations

23 See *J v. C* [1970] AC 668.

24 Although it had previously appeared in the UN Declaration of the Rights of the Child 1959.

25 The 'outcomes research,' analysing and evaluating the care careers of looked after children, comprises many different reports compiled in the main from within the social work and allied professions.

26 See Bowlby, J., *Attachment and Loss*, Hogarth Press, London, 1973.

to the principle's applicability. It has been held[27] that the principle does not apply to the issue of whether leave should be granted to allow application to be made for a 'section 8' order under s 10 of the 1989 Act. The principle is expressly excluded from having any bearing on certain statutory procedures where the main issues affect adult interests: for example, on applications for secure accommodation orders, for child maintenance, or for ouster orders or on matters falling within the scope of Part III of the 1989 Act. The UN CRC has expressed regret that

> the right of the child to have his or her best interests taken as a primary consideration is still not reflected in all legislative and policy matters and judicial decisions affecting children, especially in the area of alternative care, child welfare, immigration, asylum and refugee status, criminal justice, and in the armed forces.[28]

Paramountcy: child consent

There are virtually no statutory provisions that require the consent of a child. The only definite exception is provided for in the Sexual Offences Act 2003 which expressly recognises that a child, aged between 16 and 18 years of age, can give a valid legal consent to a sexual relationship (see, further, below).

Paramountcy: extension to adoption and other matters

The paramountcy principle is now operationalised through application of the checklist of welfare indicators specified in s 1(3).

Parental responsibility principle

The 1989 Act replaced the concepts of 'parental rights' and 'parental duties,' which for centuries formed the basic constructs of family law in this jurisdiction, with the composite term 'parental responsibility,' defined in s 3(1) as all the rights, duties, powers, responsibilities, and authority that by law a parent of a child has in relation to the child and their property.[29] The change signalled a profound difference of approach from a proprietal frame of reference to one which implied that parental use of authority was valid only if employed for the benefit of the child. Only those attributes with a functional bearing upon the nurture needs of

27 See *Re A & W (Minors) (Residence Order: Leave to Apply)* [1992] 2 FLR 154. Also, see, *Re SC (A Minor) (Leave to Seek Residence Order)* [1995] 1 FLR 96 and *Re C (Residence: Child's Application for Leave)* [1995] 1 FLR 927 which both concerned adolescent girls.

28 See the UN Committee on the Rights of the Child, *Concluding Observations: United Kingdom Of Great Britain And Northern Ireland*, United Nations (2016) at para 25.

29 See, further, Lowe, N.V., 'The Allocation of Parental Rights and Responsibilities: The Position in England and Wales', *Family Law Quarterly*, Vol 39, 2005, at pp 267–8.

the child, rather than those traditionally associated with the status of parent, were in future to comprise such responsibilities. The reframing of this concept allowed it to play a more consistent role in both public and private family law.

Parental responsibility and corporal punishment

This ill-defined traditional parental right to administer reasonable chastisement was criticised by the UN Committee on the Rights of the Child two decades ago.[30] However, it continues to be asserted under the Children Act 2004, s 58, though the presumption of lawfulness may be rebutted[31] by evidence of harm – bruising, swelling, broken skin – constituting a criminal assault.[32]

Sharing parental responsibilities

The exact nature of parental responsibilities will clearly depend on the age and circumstances of the child concerned. Broadly speaking, however, 'the effect of having parental responsibility is to empower a person to take most decisions in the child's life.'[33] Bromley, more specifically, suggests that this composite term comprises at least 16 separate areas of responsibility including: providing a home; having contact; determining and providing for education; determining religion; discipline; consent to treatment, marriage, adoption, emigration, and change of surname; vetoing the issue of a passport; taking the child outside the jurisdiction; administering property; protection and maintenance; representing the child in legal proceedings; burial or cremation and; appointing a guardian for the child.[34] More than one person may bear such responsibility in respect of the same child at the same time. Having parental responsibility does not entitle the bearer to act in any way which is incompatible with a court order made under the 1989 Act in respect of the child. The mother does not lose parental responsibility merely because the father has it or because he later acquires it. Nor do either or both parents lose it when the court grants a care order to a local authority.

30 The Committee, in its 2002 report, then condemned the UK parental right to physically chastise a child as 'a serious violation of the dignity of the child.' It repeated its recommendation in 2016 that the authorities 'prohibit as a matter of priority all corporal punishment in the family, including through the repeal of all legal defences, such as "reasonable chastisement"' (*Concluding Observations: United Kingdom Of Great Britain And Northern Ireland*, United Nations, op cit, at para 40(a)).

31 The 'reasonable punishment' defence was abolished in Wales with effect from March 2022 (comment from Julie Doughty in note to author, 21.05.2022).

32 Although this parental 'right' continues to find legislative protection in England, as in Northern Ireland, it was abolished in Scotland in 2020 and in Wales in March 2022.

33 See Introduction to the Children Act 1989, DoH, (para 2.4).

34 *Bromley's Family Law* (8th ed), at p 301.

Parental accountability

As a corollary to the principle of parental responsibility, state intervention – e.g. by way of Parenting Orders and Acceptable Behaviour Contracts – was introduced in a youth justice context.

Consanguinity principle

Re G (Children)[35] can be seen as establishing something of a milestone in UK jurisprudence dealing with welfare interests in the context of a parent-child relationship. On the face of it the case concerned a disputed shared residence order made in favour of two women whose lesbian partnership had broken down, in relation to two children born by artificial insemination to the parent who now had primary care responsibility. However, it in fact led the court into an examination of 'what is a parent?' and 'how much does the blood tie matter?' Overturning the decisions of the court at first instance and the Court of Appeal, the House of Lords ruled that insufficient weight had been given to the 'important and significant factor'[36] of the biological link between the birth parent and children. In a judgment that claimed to be 'raising no presumption in her favour,'[37] the birth mother, argued Baroness Hale, could not be viewed as being on the same footing in relation to the two children as the other 'parent' because she was "both their biological and their psychological parent … in the overall welfare judgment that must count for something in the vast majority of cases." This resurgence of judicial interest in the 'blood tie' as the rationale for preferring first party to third party care arrangements for a child resonates with earlier decisions.[38] These important rulings – in keeping with ECtHR case law – would seem to establish the blood-link as a factor of some legal weight in differentiating between the rival claims of birth parents and others, whether in a same sex context, a child care and protection context, or otherwise.

No presumption favouring consanguinity

On the other hand, in *Seddon v. Oldham MBC*[39] Jackson J considered and dismissed the appellant birth mother's claim that "the significance of the blood-tie cannot be denied"[40] and with it the implication that residual traces of 'family

35 [2006] UKHL 43 [2006] FLR 629.
36 Ibid at para 44.
37 Op cit, at para 44.
38 See, for example: *Re W (A Minor) (Residence Order)* [1993] 2 FLR 625; *Re B (Adoption: Child's Welfare)* [1995] 1 FLR 895; and *Re M (Child's Upbringing)* [1996] 2 FLR 441.
39 [2015] EWHC 2609 (Fam).
40 Ibid, at para 55.

life' as defined in Article 8 of the ECHR persisted after adoption. Subsequently Lindblom LJ warned that:[41]

> The repeated reference to a 'right' for a child to be brought up by his or her natural family, or the assumption that there is a presumption to that effect, needs to be firmly and clearly laid to rest. No such 'right' or presumption exists.

This refrain has been reiterated more recently by McFarlane LJ and others. In *Re W (A Child)*,[42] for example, the Court of Appeal heard an appeal by prospective adopters against the granting of a special guardianship order (SGO) in favour of grandparents of the child placed with them for a year – shortly after birth – and in respect of whom they had lodged an adoption application. The SGO application had been supported by the Child's Guardian and an independent social worker. The Court of Appeal, rejecting any such presumption and granting the appeal, warned against an automatic reliance on the phrase 'nothing else will do' from *Re B* as "some sort of hyperlink … to bypass the need for a full, comprehensive welfare evaluation of all the pros and cons."

Proportionality principle

In child care adoption cases the Court of Appeal[43] has stressed that the proper test for dispensing with parental agreement is whether the child's welfare requires adoption as opposed to something less interventionist. As Wall LJ put it:[44]

> A child's circumstances may 'require' statutory intervention, perhaps may even 'require' the indefinite or long-term removal of the child from the family and his or her placement with strangers, but that is not to say that the same circumstances will necessarily 'require' that the child be adopted. They may or they may not. The question, at the end of the day, is whether what is 'required' is adoption.

The same judge had earlier noted:[45]

> Inevitably, however, every order made under Section 8 of the Children Order 1989 represents in some measure interference by a public authority (the court)

41 *Re W (A Child)* [2016] EWCA Civ 793 at para 71. See, also, *Re H (A Child)* [2015] EWCA Civ 1284, per McFarlane LJ at paras 89–94.

42 [2016] EWCA Civ 793. See, also, [2014] EWFC 47.

43 See *SB v. A County Council; Re P* [2008] EWCA Civ 535.

44 *Re P (Placement Orders: Parental Consent)* [2008] EWCA Civ 535, [2008] 2 FLR 625 at para 126.

45 *Re H (Contact Order)* [2002] 1 FLR 22 at 37. See also comments of Hale LJ in *Re C & B (Care Order: Future Harm)* [2001] 1 FLR 611, at paras 33–4 and 620–1 and in *Re O. (Supervision Order)* [2001] 1 FLR 923 at paras 24–8.

> in the right to respect for family life contended in Article 8. The court's interference must, of course, be in accordance with the powers given to that court under the Children Act 1989 and be proportionate. Every application involves a court balancing the rights of the participants to the application (including the children who are the subject of it) and arriving at a result which is in the interest of those children…and proportionate to the legitimate aim being pursued.

Sir James Munby, in *Re B-S*, subsequently reinforced this message in a ruling that was to restrain child care adoptions for several years. He warned that:[46]

> The local authority cannot press for a more drastic form of order, least of all press for adoption, because it is unable or unwilling to support a less interventionist form of order. Judges must be alert to the point and must be rigorous in exploring and probing local authority thinking in cases where there is any reason to suspect that resource issues may be affecting the local authority's thinking.

He urged his colleagues in the lower courts to explore all possible alternative options in such cases.

More recently, in an important case, the UKSC considered the proportionality of final care orders in *Re H-W (Children)*[47] where such orders had been made in relation to three children with care plans for their removal from their mother's care into separate long term foster placements. The threshold criteria centred around one of the children having been sexually abused by an adult half sibling, a risk of future sexual harm and a failure to protect the children by their parents. The appeal did not turn on any issue regarding whether the judge at first instance had made a mistake in law, or had been wrong in assessing the facts, but whether the making of care orders removing the children from their mother's care and placing them in separate placements, with limited contact and against their wishes, was a proportionate response to the established risk. In granting the appeal, the court explained:

> The judge does not state why the emotional damage that each of the very different subject children would suffer under a care plan which separated them from their mother, from their stepfather and no less importantly from their siblings, was proportionate to and necessitated by the identified risk of sexual harm.

Legal system: legislation, courts, welfare/rights, and representation

This jurisdiction has, in recent years, finally undertaken the long promised reform of its court structure in order to ensure a more efficient alignment of the court

46 [2013] EWCA Civ 1146 at para 29.
47 (No 2) [2022] UKSC 17.

hierarchy and family law proceedings. This, most notably for child welfare, has included the introduction of CAFCASS.

Legislative framework

Although remaining a signatory state to many international treaties, conventions, and protocols it is probable that, following Brexit, England and Wales will become even further distanced from most European countries in terms of legislation relating to linkages between child care and adoption.

International law

The main components of the international legal framework as it relates to children in England and Wales are the Universal Declaration of Human Rights (UDHR), the European Convention on Human Rights (ECHR), the UN Convention on the Rights of the Child (UN CRC), and the Hague Convention and the International Covenant on Civil and Political Rights (ICCPR). Also relevant are: the International Covenant on Economic, Social and Cultural Rights (ICESCR), ratified in 1976; the UN Convention on the Elimination of all forms of Discrimination Against Women (CEDAW) with its Optional Protocol, ratified in 1986; the Convention on the Rights of Persons with Disabilities (CRPD), ratified in 2009; the United Nations Declaration on Social and Legal Principles relating to the Protection and Welfare of Children with Special Reference to Foster Placement and Adoption Nationally and Internationally.

Domestic legislation

Since the introduction of the 1989 Act, the sequence of subsequent legislation tracks government policies that lean increasingly towards coercive child protection measures and a steady withdrawal from private parental decision making where there has been no notice of child welfare issues.

- Divorce, Dissolution and Separation Act 2020

Entering into effect in April 2022, this legislation ended the ‘blame game’ in divorce proceedings by introducing ‘no fault’ divorce. Proceedings may be commenced by one or both parties giving notice that their relationship has broken down irretrievably. Following commencement of proceedings a 20 week period of reflection is mandated after which a Conditional Order is granted – replacing the decree nisi – then a Final Order – replacing the decree absolute – is issued.

- The Civil Partnerships, Marriages and Deaths (Registration etc.) Act 2019

This Act makes provision for the registration of marriages including for the extension of civil partnerships to couples not of the same sex. In so doing it provides greater security for children being parented by same-sex couples.

- The Children and Social Work Act 2017

Intended to improve support for looked after children and care leavers, promote the welfare and safeguarding of children, and make provisions to regulate social workers and their standards of practice, this Act strengthens a policy emphasis on promoting the welfare interests of children failed by parental care.

- The Serious Crimes Act 2015

Enabling courts to issue protection orders to protect potential or actual child victims of female genital mutilation.

- The Care Act 2014

Although primarily directed towards reforming the law relating to the care and support for adults in the community, and to clarify and strengthen the law relating to support for their carers, this statute also (in ss 58–66) addressed the local authority support responsibilities for children and young persons on their discharge from care. It states six principles that should govern care of the vulnerable: accountability, empowerment, partnership, prevention, proportionality, and protection.[48]

- The Children and Families Act 2014

This legislation, which came into effect in April 2014, introduced reforms relating to adoption and children in care. Section 11 introduced the concept of continued parental involvement into the 1989 Act (*s 1(2A)*). It also amended the 2002 Act to allow a contact order to be issued, at the making of the adoption order or at any time afterwards – and also to prohibit any contact – between a child and member/s of their birth family. Before granting an adoption order, the court must consider whether there should be arrangements for allowing any person contact with the child, must consider any existing or proposed arrangements, and must take account of the views of the parties; such contact may be direct or indirect. Section 14 requires care proceedings to conclude as soon as possible or, in any event, to take no longer than 26 weeks.[49] Other important provisions include the

48 Note that the Social Services and Wellbeing (Wales) Act 2014 also reformed the law relating to care services, but unlike the Care Act 2014 in England, applies to children in need of care and support, as well as adults. Its provisions replace Part 3 of the Children Act 1989 in Wales (comment from Julie Doughty in note to author, 21.05.2022).

49 The Court of Appeal warned in *Re B-S Children* [2013] EWCA Civ 114 that:

> where the proposal before the court is for non-consensual adoption, the issues are too grave, the stakes for all are too high, for the outcome to be determined by rigorous adherence to an inflexible timetable and justice thereby potentially denied.

Approved and re-stated by the President in *Re S (A Child)* [2014] EWCC B44 (Fam).

repeal of the requirement under the 2002 Act to give consideration to religion and cultural matters when placing for adoption.

- The Children and Young Persons Act 2008

This statute introduced provisions to safeguard children in private fostering arrangements by preventing looked after children being moved to such placements from foster care or children's homes without a formal review chaired by an Independent Reviewing Officer to confirm that the setting would meet their needs.

- The Children and Adoption Act 2006

The legislative intent of this statute, which came into effect on 21 June 2006, was to[50]

> make provision as regards contact with children; to make provision as regards family assistance orders; to make provision about risk assessments; to make provision as regards adoptions with a foreign element; and for connected purposes.

The Act gave courts a wider range of powers for use in dealing with contact disputes after parents separate, and also contained measures on intercountry adoption, including a statutory framework for the suspension of adoptions from countries where there are concerns about practices. It also introduced a procedure enabling a step-parent to be a sole adoption applicant in respect of their partner's child.

- The Children Act 2004

This Act addressed recommendations made in the Laming Report[51] and provided authority for implementing the government's strategy as expressed in *Every Child Matters*.[52] Key provisions included: the creation of the post of Children's Commissioner for England; provision for better regulation of children's services; creation of adoption review panels; mandatory joint working and information sharing between agencies involved with children; and a duty on local authorities to promote the educational achievement of looked after children.

- The Adoption and Children Act 2002

This formative legislation, introducing a wide range of provisions to update and co-ordinate child care and adoption practice, came into effect in December 2005,

50 See Preamble to statute.

51 See Laming L.J., *The Victoria Climbié Inquiry* (the 'Laming Report'), D.o.H., London, 2003.

52 See the consultation process in relation to the Children Bill: The Green Paper *Every Child Matters*, 2003; and *Every Child Matters: Next Steps* published by the Dept. of Skills and Education, 2004.

repealing the Adoption Act 1976 and amending the Children Act 1989. It introduced provisions allowing allowed civil partners, same sex couples, and unmarried couples to adopt. Most importantly, it provided that the paramountcy principle must govern all decisions, whether taken by court or agency, affecting a child's upbringing throughout his or her life including dispensing with parental consent for adoption. Provision was made for the introduction of placement orders and special guardianship orders,[53] for single applicant adopters and for post-adoption information disclosure. It also continued the practice of not making provision for automatic representation by a solicitor in private family law proceedings.

- The Human Rights Act 1998

This Act incorporates the European Convention on Human Rights (ECHR), thereby directly importing into UK law all Convention fundamental rights and freedoms and accompanying jurisprudence.

- The Family Law Act 1996

Although providing generally for divorce, separation, related legal aid entitlement, and for mediation in disputes relating to family matters, this legislation was notable mainly for the adjustments made to divorce proceedings. The two main changes in that respect were: retention of irretrievable breakdown as the sole ground but this to be established by reference a period of time rather than to specific facts; and the introduction of a mandatory 11 month 'cooling off' period when mediation would allow the parties to resolve issues, particularly as regards child care arrangements.

- The Children Act 1989

This cornerstone of contemporary UK child care law has been subject to considerable amendment. Among its more significant statements of principle were: that in children's proceedings the welfare of the child is paramount; children should be brought up and cared for within their own families and services should be provided to families in need; the state should work in partnership with such families; children should be protected by effective intervention if they are at risk of significant harm; and that parental responsibility may need to be shared with the state.

- Matrimonial Causes Act 1973

Self-described as 'An Act to consolidate certain enactments relating to matrimonial proceedings, maintenance agreements, and declarations of legitimacy,

53 They have increased by 122 per cent since 2009; 58 per cent of all orders are made in favour of foster parents.

validity of marriage and British nationality, with amendments to give effect to recommendations of the Law Commission,' this is essentially the statute governing divorce. The sole ground for divorce, as stated in s 1(1) was that 'the marriage has irretrievably broken down' but this had to be proven by reference to one or more of the of five factors listed in s 1(2): adultery; unreasonable behaviour; desertion; 2 years separation with consent; and 5 years separation with or without consent. These 'five facts' were removed by the Divorce Dissolution and Separation Act 2020, with effect from April 2022.

Other relevant legislation

The provisions of the Human Rights Act 1998 and the Equality Act 2010 necessarily have a bearing on family law matters.

Courts and regulatory framework

Traditionally, the law relating to children was administered through the courts: legal decisions affecting their upbringing, welfare interests, or property were matters reserved exclusively for judicial determination. This is no longer the case.

International judicial and regulatory bodies

The domestic law of this jurisdiction has been and will continue, post-Brexit, to be influenced by judgments of the ECtHR, though those of the ECJ remain somewhat uncertain. The decisions of other bodies such as the UN CRC will continue to be relevant. The impact of special rapporteurs are also important as is the influence of the many national Children's Commissioners (see, further, Chapter 1).

Domestic judicial and regulatory bodies

The primary forum for determining issues relating to the welfare interests of children is the Family Court which now exercises jurisdiction in respect of most family proceedings, both public law cases (care orders, supervision orders, and emergency protection orders) and private law (matrimonial disputes, etc.); and hybrid domestic violence proceedings (non-molestation and occupation orders).

- Regulatory bodies

The welfare interests of children are now afforded a great deal more protection than formerly by the office of the Children's Commissioner and the existence of a tier of domestic regulatory bodies that set benchmarks for establishing and operating facilities involving children. The health and safety standards and child protection procedures that must be met by adoption agencies, creches, child minders, etc. are all subject to registration and ongoing monitoring by government agencies.

Family Court and family proceedings

In 2014, the Family Proceedings Court was replaced by a single unified Family Court established by s 31A of the Matrimonial and Family Proceedings Act 1984 (inserted by Part 2 of the Crime and Courts Act 2013). Since 2018, proceedings and cases have been transferable within the Family Court to High Court level.

Although reorganised, the court system as it relates to the care and protection of children continues to function in a context framed 40 years ago by the decision in *A v. Liverpool City Council*,[54] when the court ruled that the exercise of powers entrusted by Parliament to statutory bodies was not amenable to judicial supervision; the court cannot take decisions on matters affecting the welfare of children when statute has assigned responsibility for such decisions to the local authority. This demarcation between powers, reinforced by the 1989 Act, has since withstood repeated challenges and probes in many cases. Moreover, that legislation greatly changed the judicial role. The fact that welfare has been accorded paramountcy status throughout the proceedings – reinforced by the 'no delay and no unnecessary litigation rules – and underpinned by the welfare checklist at the point of case disposal, would itself have transformed that role by placing responsibility and power on the court to subordinate all other factors to welfare considerations when determining disposal. But the ambit of judicial discretion at point of disposal in public family law proceedings has also been significantly broadened under the 1989 Act to permit use of private law orders. At the final stage it may now creatively employ discretionary powers to address the subjective position of a particular child's welfare interests rather than the objective specifications of the public law proceedings.

The authority of the court ends with the conclusion of proceedings.

- Specialist court system

Most issues are now resolved by magistrates sitting in a Family Court but many are adjudicated by appointed judiciary (district and circuit judges) or the High Court. The Family Division of the High Court has a quite separate jurisdiction dedicated to family matters, and will often hear complex child care and adoption applications. Cases may be appealed from the Family Court to the Court of Appeal and possibly on to the Supreme Court (UKSC, formerly the House of Lords).

Youth Court and criminal proceedings

Youth Courts are specialist courts, presided over by a district judge or three lay magistrates, for hearing cases of criminal offences allegedly committed by children aged between 10 and 17 years of age. Those aged 16 or less must be accompanied by a parent or guardian.[55] Most alleged offences involving children

54 [1982] AC 363.
55 Children and Young Persons Act 1933, s 34A.

are adjudicated in Youth Courts but more serious charges may be remanded to a Crown Court.

Representation for children

While the child is a party in public law proceedings, and the appointment of a children's guardian is the norm,[56] in private law proceedings they are rarely parties but may be made so,[57] though usually only where there is 'an issue of significant difficulty.' The CRC has registered its concern regarding representation:

> Many children feel that they are not listened to by their social workers, reviewing officers, paid carers, judges, personnel working with children in conflict with the law, or other professionals, in matters affecting them, including in family proceedings.[58]

The Children and Family Court Advisory and Support Service (CAFCASS)

Established in 2000, CAFCASS supplements the judicial role by bringing together the role, functions, and staff of the Probation Service in private law proceedings, the Guardian *ad Litem* Panels in public law proceedings and the child section of the Official Solicitor's Department. A non-departmental body, it provides welfare reports and other support services in contested family proceedings at judicial request, throughout the three tiers of the court system, and is accountable to the Lord Chancellor. This marks a significant change to long established practice under the 1976 Act whereby the appointment of a guardian *ad litem* – to safeguard the interests of the child – was mandatory in all divorce and adoption proceedings. Now that divorce proceedings are uncontested, CAFCASS is not involved unless the court is put on notice of issues affecting the welfare of any child involved. In consensual adoptions, the CAFCASS officer acts as a Reporting Officer, only in non-consensual adoptions does the officer then act as the children's guardian *ad litem*.

This agency has a statutory duty to safeguard and promote the welfare of children who become the subjects of family proceedings and will provide representation in Family Court cases.[59] On referral from the court, a CAFCASS officer will contact all parties, interview the child concerned, make such additional enquiries as are appropriate, and then compile and submit a report to the court which will contain an assessment of matters constituting the welfare interests of the child. Where appropriate, CAFCASS will instruct a solicitor to provide independent representation for that child.

56 A guardian must be appointed for the child unless the court is 'satisfied that it is not necessary to do so in order to safeguard his interests' (Children Act 1989, s 41(1)).

57 The Family Procedure Rules 2010, Practice Direction 16A.

58 See the UN Committee on the Rights of the Child, *Concluding Observations: United Kingdom Of Great Britain And Northern Ireland, United Nations* (2016) at para 29(d).

59 The Parliament (Criminal Justice and Court Services Act 2000).

- The child in court

A child's views, his or her evidence, and how these are brought before the court, have been the subject of a range of judicial rulings[60] and guidance[61] over the last decade or two perhaps most firmly in *Re D (A Child) (International Recognition)*[62] when Lady Hale observed that[63]

> the rule of law in England and Wales includes the right of the child to participate in the process that is about him or her. That is the fundamental principle that is reflected in our legislation, our rules and practice directions and jurisprudence. At its most basic level it involves asking at an early stage in family proceedings whether and how that child is going to be given the opportunity to be heard. The qualification in section 1(3)(a) [of the Children Act 1989] like that in article 12(1) [of the United Nations Convention on the Rights of the Child 1989] relates to the weight to be put upon a child's wishes and feelings, not their participation.

While this continues to attract attention, much depends on the child and the nature of the presenting issue. There is little in the way of hard and fast rules governing the role of a child as witness in court.

- Consent of child

There are virtually no statutory provisions that provide a child – someone under the age of 18 years – with a right to give or withhold a legal consent. Nevertheless, it is generally accepted that the consent of a child aged 16 or older should be sought on any decision affecting him or her; and that consent will be legally binding. Further, since the landmark decision *Gillick v. West Norfolk and Wisbech Area Health Authority*,[64] while a child below the age of 16 continues to be treated in law as non-competent this may be rebutted by evidence based on age and understanding; a child over that age will be presumed to have the necessary competence. As Lord Scarman then explained:

> a minor's capacity to make his or her decision depends upon the minor having sufficient understanding and intelligence to make the decision and is not to be determined by reference to any judicially fixed age limit.

60 See, for example, *Re D (A Child) (Abduction: Rights of Custody)* [2006] UKHL 51, [2007] 1 FLR 961, per Lady Hale and *Re D (A Child) (International Recognition)* [2016] EWCA Civ 12; [2016] 2 FLR 347, per Ryder LJ.

61 See the Family Justice Council, *Guidelines for Judges Meeting Children who are Subject to Family Proceedings*, April 2010, [2010] 2 FLR 1872 and *Guidelines in Relation to Children Giving Evidence in Family Proceedings*, December 2011, [2012] Fam Law 70.

62 [2016] EWCA Civ 12.

63 Ibid, at para 44.

64 [1986] 1 AC 112, HL.

Consequently, where a child is aged 16, or though younger is deemed to be '*Gillick* competent,' the law now requires that his or her consent is sought in relation to the matter at issue (see, further, below).

Other domestic fora

The landscape of official agencies bearing responsibility for aspects of child welfare/rights has changed in recent years as a direct result of international influence.

- Equality and Human Rights Commission

This regulatory agency, with responsibility for enforcing equality legislation and anti-discrimination law, also has a brief for human rights issues that impact upon children.

- Children's Commissioner

Established under the Children Act 2004, and further strengthened by the Children and Families Act 2014, the Children's Commissioner is a public body which operates independently of government and parliament with a mandate to protect and promote – and advocate on behalf of – the interests of children and young people. It has conducted significant research projects and published reports with potential to influence government policy in relation to the rights and welfare interests of children.[65] The Commissioner is positioned to be a powerful champion of children's welfare interests by monitoring domestic law and practice against benchmarks established by the UN CRC[66] and by exercising direct leverage on behalf of children with government bodies and other decision-making agencies.[67]

- Special Rapporteur

This UN appointee is required to 'examine, monitor, advise, and publicly report' on human rights issues. Most often they address thematic problems like 'the sale of children, child prostitution and child pornography' but may also be appointed with a country specific remit. Of the approximately 80 currently serving rapporteurs, some few have a brief which includes gathering information on law and

65 See, for example, Children's Commissioner, *Family Review*, 2022, at: www.childrenscommissioner.gov.uk/family/family-review/.

66 See the UN Committee on the Rights of the Child, *Concluding Observations: United Kingdom Of Great Britain And Northern Ireland*, United Nations (2016) at para 15 where the Committee recommends that measures be taken to 'further strengthen the independence of established Children's Commissioners, in line with the Paris Principles, and enable them, inter alia, to receive and investigate complaints from or on behalf of children concerning violations of their rights.'

67 See, further, at: www.childrenscommissioner.gov.uk/about-us/the-childrens-commissioner-for-england/.

practice affecting children in this jurisdiction. One such is the United Nations Special Rapporteur on extreme poverty and human rights.

The welfare principle in contemporary practice: public family law: civil jurisdiction

While the Children Act 1989 remains the basic statute for child care and protection it has since been joined by the Adoption and Children Act 2002, which repealed the Adoption Act 1976 and significantly amended the 1989 Act. Together with the Children Act 2004, the Children and Adoption Act 2006, the Children and Families Act 2014, and the Children and Social Work Act 2017,[68] these statutes now provide the policy, principles, and law relating to the same hierarchy of functions that has given effect to the law relating to the welfare interests of children for generations: prevention; protection; state care; supervision; and control. In effect, the role of a local authority in relation to families within its area is governed by the two intervention thresholds identified in the 1989 Act: the consensual threshold, which requires it to offer services to support parents and reinforce their capacity to give effect to their parental responsibilities and provide other services aimed more directly at 'children in need', and the coercive threshold of 'significant harm' requiring it to ensure that those children suffering or at risk of suffering significant harm are safeguarded and protected.

A parallel criminal jurisdiction, governed primarily by the Children and Young Persons Act 1933 and the Crime and Disorder Act 1998, now regulates a limited role for the welfare principle in respect of those children amenable to the jurisdiction of the Youth Court (see, further, below).

Prevention

Preventative local authority duties in relation to the welfare interests of children begin with the requirement in Schedule 2 of the 1989 Act that every local authority shall take reasonable steps to identify the extent to which there are children in need within its area (see, further, Chapter 3).

State duties to support families and children in need

The 1989 Act imposes a general duty upon local authorities in England 'to safeguard and promote the welfare of children within their area who are in need,' and 'so far as is consistent with that duty, to promote the upbringing of such children by their families' (s 17(1)). Similar provisions apply in Wales. The local authorities are required to take reasonable steps to protect children from abuse

68 The legislative framework is supplemented by the provisions of the Children & Social Work Act 2017, the Education and Adoption Act 2016, and the Children and Young Persons Act 2008. The Adoption Support Services Regulations 2005 are also important.

and neglect and to reduce the need to bring children into care and to expose them to other proceedings (Sched 2, paras 4 and 7). It also imposes nine separate and quite specific preventative duties upon a local authority in relation to children identified as being in need. These are mostly permissive, only a few are mandatory, and they include provision of: assistance which may be a cash grant, a loan, or as a grant of 'necessities'; such family centres as it considers appropriate within its area; such resources as may be necessary to reduce the need to bring proceedings in respect of children, encourage them not to commit criminal offences, and avoid the need to place them in secure accommodation; and resources to prevent children within their area suffering ill-treatment or neglect. Sched 2(9) places a duty on a local authority to provide an explicit programme of services to support children in need who are living with their families. Sched 2(5) gives a local authority a discretionary power to provide financial assistance to enable a person who may be causing a child to suffer, or who may do so in the future, to find alternative accommodation away from that child. The prescriptive directives are those with a more marginal bearing on welfare such as the strict duty to publish information. Of considerable significance to the modern role of the welfare principle is the legislative definition of 'family,' which the 1989 Act interprets as virtually any enduring care relationship which opens up the range of persons whom a local authority should consider when assessing possible service provision to children in need.

Service provision

In *AG (ex rel Tiley) v. London Borough of Wandsworth*[69] the local authority pleaded insufficient finance in defence to the charge that it had failed to meet the claimant's statutory entitlement to support services. The court determined that this was an inadequate justification. Subsequently, however, the court rulings have demonstrated a steady retreat from this position.[70] In *R v. Cambridge District Health Authority ex parte B (No 2)*,[71] the Court of Appeal acknowledged that it was not empowered to review the basis upon which a local authority elected to use its resources; the latter was entitled to prioritise the services it was prepared to fund as it saw fit. Nor did the court have any power to direct a local authority to recognise a child as being in need within the definition of s 17 for the purposes of ensuring a service entitlement.[72]

69 [1981] 1 WLR 854.

70 See, for example, *Re C (Family Assistance Order)* [1996] 1 FLR 424 where the court was forced to discharge the order on being informed that the local authority lacked the resources to comply with it.

71 [1995] 1 FLR 1055.

72 See *Re J (Specific Issue Order: Leave to Apply)* [1995] 1 FLR 699.

State intervention: consensual

The more emphatic child protection effects of the 2002 Act (see, further, below) were moderated to some extent by the introduction of the Children and Social Work Act 2017 which, among other objectives, sought to promote the welfare and safeguarding of children, and the Care Act 2014 requiring local authorities to carry out an assessment of anyone appearing to require care and support, regardless of their likely eligibility for state-funded care. Nonetheless, despite this additional pressure to provide services, on top of local authority family support duties, the increased volume of child care and protection cases coming before the courts testified to the inadequacy of that family support. The President of the Family Division drew attention to this, in his speech to the Association of Lawyers for Children in October 2018, when he referred to the[73]

> very significant and sudden rise in the number of cases coming to court, these "new" cases must, almost by definition, be drawn from the cohort of cases which, in earlier times, would simply have been held by the social services with the families being supported in the community without a court order.

Thereby directly attributing the increase in child protection cases to a lack of local authority investment in preventative services.

Specific support services

Accessing family support services is at the discretion of local authorities. In respect of most services listed in the body or schedules of the 1989 Act, a claimant may clear the first hurdle, by satisfying the threshold criteria and being designated a 'child in need,' only to fall at the second when their claim is nullified by a local authority's considered decision not to exercise a discretionary duty in favour of that claimant. The two main sets of specific support services relate to day care and accommodation.

Day care or 'supervised activity' 'means an activity supervised by a responsible person.' A local authority's basic preventative strategy will rest on the range of services it has available to help and support those children in need resident in its area and their families. Most usually this involves providing direct financial assistance, or it may involve a local authority paying for places with childminders, playgroups, or family centres. Section 18 places on a local authority a strict duty to provide appropriate day care for pre-school children in need but only a power to provide day care for other children of that age who are not in need. In relation to school aged children the duty similarly placed is to provide day care outside school hours and during school

73 As cited by Keehan, J. in 'Introduction' to the Public Law Working Group, 'Recommendations to Achieve Best Practice in the Child Protection and Family Justice Systems', final report 2021, at 'Introduction': www.judiciary.uk/wp-content/uploads/2021/03/March-2021-report-final_clickable.pdf.

holidays for those in need and attending school while it may also do so for those who are attending school but are not in need. Section 19 makes elaborate provision for reviews and review procedures in relation to day care services. However, childcare services are not financially accessible to many families with children in need. This prompted the UN CRC, in 2016, to recommend

> that the State party and the devolved governments conduct a rigorous child rights impact assessment of the recent reduction of funding for childcare and family support and adjust the family support policy in order to make childcare services available to all those who need it.[74]

The duty to provide accommodation, placed on a local authority by s 20 of the 1989 Act, is one of the most tangible expressions of the partnership principle between parents and local authority and one which represents the considerable potential of the welfare principle. However, as it is a duty that rests unequivocally on the voluntary consent of all parties, an objection from a parent or from someone with parental responsibility will relieve a local authority of its obligation to provide accommodation. The use of this provision has given rise to a great deal of contention: a child admitted voluntarily nonetheless acquires the status of a 'looked after child'; such a child may be allowed to 'drift in care' because either or both parents are unable/unwilling to resume responsibility, or are considered not ready to do so by the local authority; consequently the foster placement may be transformed over time into one that gives foster parents a claim to consider adoption. The uncertainty surrounding use of s 20 was of concern to Lady Hale in *Williams & Anor v. London Borough of Hackney*[75] and has aroused similar judicial unease in other cases.[76]

A discretionary power exists under s 20(5) enabling a local authority to provide accommodation for a person between the ages of 16 and 21 where it considers that to do so would safeguard or promote his or her welfare. Under s 20(6) a duty is placed on a local authority, insofar as is reasonably practicable and consistent with the child's welfare, to ascertain and give due consideration (having regard to his age and understanding) to the latter's wishes before providing accommodation. If that child is aged 16 or more and consents to being accommodated (and this is judged to be necessary on welfare grounds), or to being discharged from accommodation, then a local authority is obliged to give effect to that consent regardless of any opposition from a parent or from elsewhere.

In practice the provision of housing for homeless youths has been a particularly contentious issue and one for which, until the ruling in *R (On the application*

74 See CRC/C/GBR/CO/5: Concluding Observations on the Sixth Periodic Report Of The United Kingdom Of Great Britain And Northern Ireland, (2016), at para 50.

75 [2018] UKSC 37 at para 34.

76 See, for example: *Re CA (A Baby)* [2012] EWHC 2190 (Fam); *Wiliams and Another v. London Borough of Hackney* [2015] EWHC 2629 (QB); and *Medway Council v. M and T* [2015] EWFC B164.

of G) v. London Borough of Southwark,[77] local authorities had largely avoided responsibility. In that respect, it is clear that since the Children (Leaving Care) Act 2000 inserted sections 23A, 23B, 23C, and 24A and 24B into the 1989 Act, a local authority must provide accommodation for those 'looked after children' who need it following their discharge from care.[78]

Further, case law[79] has established that a housing authority has no duty to provide accommodation for a homeless family under housing legislation. However, it is clear that such a duty does arise under child care legislation if the application comes, not from a family, but from a local authority on behalf of that family. The housing authority must then consider the request and must comply with it unless compliance would be incompatible with its own obligations and/or it would unduly prejudice the discharge of any of its functions.

Parents, if they satisfy eligibility criteria, are to be provided with respite care as of right without any implication that they have been in any way deficient or at fault (evidenced also by the phrase 'for whatever reason') in the execution of their parental duties. The accommodation must now be the subject of a written and signed agreement between the parties. At no time do the parents lose, nor the local authority acquire, any parental responsibilities. The child is not 'in care' and may be removed by the parent/s, or by someone with parental responsibility (under s 20(8)), from local authority accommodation at any time; subject to the authority being satisfied that such discharge would not be exposing the child to a risk of significant harm. If the child has reached the age of 16 then, under s 20(11), he or she may not be removed from such accommodation without his or her consent.

- Children with disabilities

A family with a child that has a disability is defined as a 'family in need' for the purposes of the 1989 Act. This requires a local authority to undertake a needs assessment in respect of family and child and is then specifically required to provide appropriate social care support services. This obligation is often met by funding local voluntary organisations – like Disability Helpline – and by channelling support services through designated 'child disability' teams which typically comprise social workers, occupational therapists, and physiotherapists.

Promotion

At a time of tightly constrained government spending on public services, leaving local authorities struggling to maintain a basic level of provision, it is perhaps

77 [2009] UKHL 26.

78 *R(A) v. London Borough of Lambeth* [2010] EWHC 1652; [2010] 2 FCR 539, Admin.

79 See the House of Lords decision in *R v. Oldham Metropolitan Borough Council ex parte Garlick and Related Appeals* [1993] 2 FLR 194 when the court held that a local housing authority had no duty to a homeless dependant child under Part 111 of the Housing Act 1985.

fanciful to imagine that they would have the capacity or willingness to devote the extra resources needed to promote, as opposed to salvage, the welfare interests of children. Nonetheless, some steps in that direction have been taken; more often as a result of a raised threshold of protection being imposed by legislation than initiated by local authority. One such has been the removal of any discretion to impose physical chastisement on pupils in schools, together with new protocols governing bullying and the introduction of lunch clubs and after-school supervised activities.

Protection

The 2002 Act, with the paramountcy principle bridging child protection and adoption law, was an attempt to bring domestic law into closer alignment with the requirement in Article 8 of the ECHR that state authorities respect the right of a child to 'family life.' As indicated by Hale LJ in *Re W and B; Re W*,[80] this right could be viewed as presenting an opportunity and a challenge to authorities requiring them to think positively rather than negatively: the adoption option should be considered for children failed by parental care.

State intervention: coercive

In part, the rationale for the Adoption and Children Act 2002 was to address the consequences of failure in preventative intervention as mandated by the 1989 Act: it marked a policy shift from consensual state intervention in support of families in need to coercive intervention to protect children at risk of significant harm.

Coercive state intervention in family affairs is authorised by care and supervision orders. These are available under Part IV of the 1989 Act if the two stages of the application process are completed: the threshold criteria of s 31 have been met; and the court is satisfied that the order, if made, would be compatible with the child's welfare interests and would be preferable to not making any order. This is ascertained by the court applying s 1(2), (3), and (5). Court determination of that which is held to constitute a child's welfare is in accordance with statutorily prescribed indicators together with certain judicial and agency criteria as interpreted and applied by those professionals with a duty to advise the court. There must be clear evidence substantiating the statutory grounds. As Baronness Hale has warned:[81]

> It is not enough that the social workers, the experts or the court think that a child would be better off living with another family. That would be social engineering of a kind which is not permitted in a democratic society.

80 [2001] EWCA Civ 757, [2001] 2 FLR 582. See, also, *Re C and B (Children) (Care Order; Future Harm)* [2000] 2 FCR 614 at 625.

81 *Re SB (Children)* [2009] UKSC 17, [2010] 1 FLR 1161, at para 7.

A statutory weighting is given to the wishes of the child in determining his or her welfare. The selection of the most appropriate disposal option is accompanied by a degree of judicial discretion.

The House of Lords, in a leading case[82] on the standard of evidence applicable in cases warranting a care order, determined that the correct approach was to apply the simple balance of probabilities test. This was a case which rested on the single issue of whether the elder of four sisters had been sexually abused by her step-father who had been acquitted of rape on that issue. The court, subsequently, had to consider an application for care orders in respect of the other three sisters on the grounds that they were 'likely to suffer significant harm' (as per s 31(2)) if the orders were not made. Having considered possible different interpretations of the requisite standard and reviewed related case law, the House confirmed the balance of probabilities test; a ruling subsequently endorsed 'loud and clear' by Baroness Hale.[83] This ruling also served to underline the basic obligation of applicants in such cases to discharge the burden of proof on them to show that the child concerned is likely to suffer significant harm, which requires actual evidence.

It should be noted that there is an alternative school of thought[84] which holds that the *Re H and R* ruling has raised the threshold of proof by requiring a somewhat higher standard of evidence in sexual abuse cases than in others and that this therefore works to the disadvantage of children's welfare interests. Nonetheless, the ruling has exercised a persuasive influence in determining many child abuse and neglect cases on the basis that – on a balance of probabilities – there was a risk of sexual abuse such as would breach the significant harm threshold.

Mandatory reporting

There is no general UK mandatory requirement that members of the public report to the appropriate authorities any instance of child abuse or neglect that comes to their attention. However, since 2016 there has been such a mandatory reporting requirement in respect of: 'a reasonable cause to suspect' child abuse and neglect in Wales under the Social Services and Wellbeing (Wales) Act 2013, s 130; and in respect of female genital mutilation – a form of female child abuse – under the Female Genital Mutilation Act 2003, s 5B, which came into force for England and Wales in 2015. Further, local authority staff have a duty to report suspicions of abuse or neglect and under the Children Act 1989, s 47, there is a duty on such staff to make enquiries, and, if need be, to take action to safeguard or promote the child's welfare, where there is reasonable cause to suspect that a child is suffering, or is likely to suffer, significant harm.

82 See *Re H and R (Minors) (Sexual Abuse: Standard of Proof)*, [1996] 1 ALL ER 1.
83 *Re B* [2008] UKHL 35, at para 70.
84 See Fortin, J., *Children's Rights and the Developing Law*, Butterworths, 1998, at pp 383–7.

Emergency child protection order

Issued under s 44 of the 1989 Act, this order empowers a local authority to protect a child from ongoing or imminent risk of physical, mental, or emotional harm by removing him or her to a place of safety. The fact that local authorities have a duty to protect – by promptly investigating when alerted to the possibility that a child may be at risk – was stressed by the ECtHR in *E v. United Kingdom*,[85] when it found that they "should have been aware that the children remained at potential risk" and had "failed to take steps which would have enabled them to discover the exact extent of the problem and, potentially, to prevent further abuse taking place,"[86] which was held to have violated Article 3.

The court, however, must be satisfied by evidence demonstrating that there is reasonable cause to believe the child is likely to suffer significant harm unless so removed. The order is valid for a maximum period of eight days though extensions are possible.

Care proceedings

Coercive state intervention in family affairs is authorised by care and supervision orders. These are available under Part IV of the 1989 Act if the two stages of the application process are completed: the threshold criteria of s 31 have been met; and the court is satisfied that the order, if made, would be compatible with the child's welfare interests and would be preferable to not making any order. This is ascertained by the court applying ss 1(2), (3), and (5). Court determination of that which is held to constitute a child's welfare is in accordance with statutorily prescribed indicators together with certain judicial and agency criteria as interpreted and applied by those professionals with a duty to advise the court. There must be clear evidence substantiating the statutory grounds. As Baroness Hale has warned:[87]

> It is not enough that the social workers, the experts or the court think that a child would be better off living with another family. That would be social engineering of a kind which is not permitted in a democratic society.

A statutory weighting is given to the wishes of child in determining his or her welfare. The selection of the most appropriate disposal option is accompanied by a degree of judicial discretion.

Care plan

This is a document prepared for the court which explains, justifies, and identifies the intended outcomes of, a local authority's proposed plan of action – tailored to

85 Application No. 33218/96, (2002).

86 Ibid at [96] to [97].

87 *Re SB (Children)* [2009] UKSC 17, [2010] 1 FLR 1161, at para 7.

meet the specified needs of a particular child – should the court grant its application for a care order. It will include an account of the extent to which the wishes and views of the child have been obtained and acted upon.

Care order

A care order is only available on evidence of: the significant harm threshold, as set out in s 31(2) and (9) of the 1989 Act, having been breached or of a likelihood of such; the level of harm being due to either the care the child is receiving or is likely to receive if the care order is not made, or to the child being beyond parental control; 'harm' meaning ill-treatment or the impairment of health and development; and that making an order would be better for the child than making no order. Essentially, the threshold consists of two arms, the court must be satisfied: (a) that the child is suffering – or is at risk of – significant harm; and (b) that that harm is attributable to the care given not being what it would be reasonable to expect a parent to give.

What may constitute 'significant harm' has been examined in a number of cases[88] and Lady Hale, *In the matter of J (children)*,[89] reviewed the interpretation given to the term in six of them.[90] She noted that in two the court stressed that it had to be satisfied on the balance of probabilities that the named person did actually did harm a named child and in both it was not established that the child had been harmed at all.[91] The issue *In the matter of J* – as in *In Re H*,[92] *In Re B*,[93] and *In Re S-B*[94] – concerned the likelihood of other children suffering significant harm when one child in the family was known to have been abused by an unidentifiable perpetrator; though it is of course possible to find that the threshold has been breached without confirming the identity of the perpetrator.[95] She drew attention to the determination in *In Re H*, as confirmed in *In Re O*, that a prediction of future harm has to be based upon findings of actual fact made on the balance of probabilities and admonished those tempted to rush to judgment:[96]

> Time and again, the cases have stressed that the threshold conditions are there to protect both the child and his family from unwarranted interference by the

88 See, for example, *Re MA (Care Threshold)* [2009] EWCA Civ 853.
89 [2013] UKSC 9.
90 *In Re M (A Minor) (Care Orders: Threshold Conditions)* [1994] 2 AC 424; *In Re H (Minors) (Sexual Abuse: Standard of Proof)* [1996] AC 563; *Lancashire County Council v. B* [2000] 2 AC 147; *In Re O (Minors) (Care: Preliminary Hearing)* [2003] UKHL 18, [2004] 1 AC 523; *In Re B (Children) (Care Proceedings: Standard of Proof)* (CAFCASS intervening) [2008] UKHL 35, [2009] AC 11; and *In Re S-B (Children) (Care Proceedings: Standard of Proof)* [2009] UKSC 17, [2010] 1 AC 678.
91 Citing *In Re H* [1996] AC 563 and *In Re B* [2009] AC 11.
92 Ibid.
93 Ibid.
94 [2010] 1 AC 678.
95 *Lancashire County Council v. B* [2002] 2 AC 147.
96 *In the matter of J (Children)*, op cit, at para 44.

> state. There must be a clearly established objective basis for such interference. Without it, there would be no 'pressing social need' for the state to interfere in the family life enjoyed by the child and his parents which is protected by Article 8 of the ECHR.

Once granted, the order places a duty on the named local authority to take the child concerned into its care. Thereafter, the local authority gives effect to its duty to promote the welfare interests of the child by carrying out the agreed care plan, though it has discretion to deviate from it.

These cases represent only a small fraction of the considerable volume of judicial deliberations dedicated to a forensic examination of the significant harm threshold. Together they stand as a reminder that the simple currency of a 'good enough' standard of parenting, sufficient for earlier generations, would seem to have become irretrievably devalued. It seems much longer than 40 years ago since Templeman LJ's confident assertion that:[97]

> The best person to bring up a child is the natural parent. It matters not whether the parent is wise or foolish, rich or poor, educated or illiterate, provided the child's moral and physical health are not in danger.

An opinion cited with approval by Hedley J, some 15 years ago, when he added that "basically it is the tradition of the UK, recognised in law, that children are best brought up within natural families"[98] and "society must be willing to tolerate very diverse standards of parenting, including the eccentric, the barely adequate and the inconsistent"[99] while taking into account that "it is not the provenance of the state to spare children all the consequences of defective parenting … it simply could not be done."[100] Such sentiments have not worn well and to some now seem to be bordering on the naive. Seemingly more appropriate to contemporary watchful society is the recent judicial warning that there can be no right or presumption that a child should be brought up by their natural family.[101]

There is no more specific statement of what in law now constitutes the welfare interests of a child and of the responsibility to safeguard it, than the checklist as set out in s 1 of the 1989 Act:

> (1) When a court determines any question with respect to—
> (a) the upbringing of a child; or
> (b) the administration of a child's property or the application of any income arising from it,
> the child's welfare shall be the court's paramount consideration.

97 *Re KD (A Minor Ward) (Termination of Access)* [1988] 1 AC 806, [1988] 2 FLR 139.
98 *Re L (Care: Threshold Criteria)* [2007] 1 FLR 1050.
99 See *Re L (Care: Threshold Criteria)* [2007] 1 FLR 2050 at para 50.
100 Ibid.
101 *Re E-R (A Child)* 2015 EWCA Civ 405, per Vincent J.

(2) In any proceedings in which any question with respect to the upbringing of a child arises, the court shall have regard to the general principle that any delay in determining the question is likely to prejudice the welfare of the child.

(2A) A court, in the circumstances mentioned in subsection (4)(a) or (7), is as respects each parent within subsection (6)(a) to presume, unless the contrary is shown, that involvement of that parent in the life of the child concerned will further the child's welfare.

(2B) In subsection (2A) "involvement" means involvement of some kind, either direct or indirect, but not any particular division of a child's time.

(3) In the circumstances mentioned in subsection (4), a court shall have regard in particular to—

- (a) the ascertainable wishes and feelings of the child concerned (considered in the light of his age and understanding);
- (b) his physical, emotional and educational needs;
- (c) the likely effect on him of any change in his circumstances;
- (d) his age, sex, background and any characteristics of his which the court considers relevant;
- (e) any harm which he has suffered or is at risk of suffering;
- (f) how capable each of his parents, and any other person in relation to whom the court considers the question to be relevant, is of meeting his needs;
- (g) the range of powers available to the court under this Act in the proceedings in question.

(4) The circumstances are that—

- (a) the court is considering whether to make, vary or discharge a section 8 order, and the making, variation or discharge of the order is opposed by any party to the proceedings; or
- (b) the court is considering whether to make, vary or discharge [**F2**a special guardianship order or] an order under Part IV.

(5) Where a court is considering whether or not to make one or more orders under this Act with respect to a child, it shall not make the order or any of the orders unless it considers that doing so would be better for the child than making no order at all.

(6) In subsection (2A) "parent" means parent of the child concerned; and, for the purposes of that subsection, a parent of the child concerned—

- (a) is within this paragraph if that parent can be involved in the child's life in a way that does not put the child at risk of suffering harm; and
- (b) is to be treated as being within paragraph (a) unless there is some evidence before the court in the particular proceedings to suggest that involvement of that parent in the child's life would put the child at risk of suffering harm whatever the form of the involvement.

(7) The circumstances referred to are that the court is considering whether to make an order under section 4(1)(c) or (2A) or 4ZA(1)(c) or (5) (parental responsibility of parent other than mother).

The court, being satisfied that the significant harm threshold has been breached, having applied this checklist (see, further, Chapter 3), considered the bearing of Article 8 of the ECHR must also be convinced that making an order would be better for the child than making no order. On this last point there is clear authority that a care order should only be made if it is necessary: the aim of the court must be to make the least interventionist order possible.[102] It may then issue a care order assigning a local authority legal responsibility for safeguarding and promoting the welfare interests of the child.

Supervision order

Alternatively, having completed the above steps, the court may instead issue a supervision order (see, further, Chapter 3). This order imposes a duty on a local authority to 'advise, assist and befriend' the child and may include directions such as that the child live in a specified place, does certain activities, and reports to a supervisor in a particular place at a set time. Unlike a care order, it does not vest parental responsibility in a local authority, only lasts for one year, and may be extended annually for a total of three years. Under Schedule 3 of the 1989 Act, it may also impose obligations on a responsible person – someone with parental responsibility for the child or a person with whom the child is living – at a minimum requiring the supervisor reasonable contact with the child. The limitations of this order, as a means for a local authority to safeguard the welfare interests of a child, were examined in *Re FC (A Child: Care or Supervision Order)*[103] which concerned an 18-month-old child in the care of a mother with learning difficulties. The court, determining that it provided insufficient control and could not guarantee adequate local authority support, substituted a care order, a decision endorsed on appeal.

Interim orders

The interim care order requires a slightly lower threshold – 'reasonable grounds' – than that needed for a full care order.[104] It has evolved well beyond a legislative intent that had designated it as functionally restricted to providing a time limited breathing space, securing a measure of safety for a child, enabling local authority evidence gathering to be completed.

In practice, an interim care order allows the court, for a time limited period – but a period that may be extended by an unlimited sequence of orders – to impose its own care plan on a local authority instead of granting a care order application by that authority. It has a proven capacity to act as a judicial bridgehead into local

102 *Re B (A Child) (Care Proceedings: Threshold Criteria)* [2013] UKSC 33 and *Re B-S (Children) (Adoption Order: Leave to Oppose)* [2013] EWCA Civ 1146. See, most recently *Re H-W (Children) (No 2)* [2022] UKSC 17.

103 [2016] EWFC B90.

104 See, for example, *Re C* [2019] EWCA Civ 1998 per Jackson LJ at [2].

authority decision making affecting the welfare interests of the child concerned. This is achieved by the court making the order subject to directions designed to provide the information necessary for a judicially approved care plan to be compiled. The court is thereby placed in a position to decide, when the interim care order has run its course, whether the making of a full care order would be in the child's best interests.[105] This discretionary judicial power, to make the order considered by the court rather than the applicant to be most appropriate to the welfare of a child, has also been used to give preference to interim care orders instead of child assessment orders at the early stages of coercive intervention. It offers the court a final opportunity to require a professional evaluation of the welfare interests of a child, the submission of evidence that such interests are being, or are in danger of being, so impaired as to justify a care order and to test agency commitment to its declared objectives before full responsibility for decisions relating to those interests passes to a local authority with the issue of a care order.

Numerous repeat interim care orders in respect of the same child have become a feature of child protection proceedings, making it a very powerful exercise of authority in respect of a child's welfare interests.

State care

A child, whether the subject of a care order or voluntarily admitted with parental consent, on entry to local authority care becomes a 'looked after child.' The Children Act 1989, s 22(3) obliges the local authority to safeguard and promote the welfare of any child they are looking after, which includes, under s 22(3A), a duty to promote the child's educational achievement.

Foster care: partnership, rehabilitation, and concurrent planning

A 'looked after child' requires a placement.[106] In keeping with its policy of prioritising family based care for a looked after child, by far the majority of children subject to care orders are placed in foster care; at least four out of every five are fostered.[107]

Foster care

This, the preferred form of state care, is now exercised in favour of extended family placements. Section 1(2)(f) of the 2002 Act directs that a kinship placement

105 This was the course of action approved by the Court of Appeal in *Buckingham County Council v. M* [1994] 2 FLR 506 when the court rejected a care plan which had as its objective the placing of a child for adoption and instead substituted a phased rehabilitation programme underpinned by an interim care order.

106 See the Care Planning, Placement and Case Review (England) Regulations 2010 and the Care Planning, Placement and Case Review (England) (Amendment) Regulations 2021.

107 See *Fostering Network* at www.fostering.net/.

should be the preferred option for the agency/court: they are specifically required to have regard to relationships with relatives (which, in this context, includes parents) such as grandparents.[108]

The Children Act 1989 and subsequent legal developments, as influenced by ECtHR case law, has adjusted child care policy to make adoption more readily available as an alternative to long-term fostering. Not until that Act was amended by s 118 of the 2002 Act, however, was a system of independent review inserted to safeguard children in local authority placements from being allowed to 'drift in care.'

- Partnership and rehabilitation

The viability of the 'partnership with parents' principle that was such a cornerstone of the 1989 Act, and underpinned the Children Act 2004, though never wholly embraced by the under resourced local authorities and regarded with some scepticism by parents of children in need, became even less so in relation to 'looked after' children. However the law if not the principle requires local authorities to work with parents towards the return home of such a child.

Arguably, child welfare interests cannot be easily separated from parental welfare: the younger the child the stronger the assumption that – save in exceptional circumstances – this symbiotic relationship of mutual attachment should be the primary vehicle that determines his or her welfare interests. Pauffley J drew attention to the importance of the mother-baby bond in *Re: NL*[109] when he asserted that "there is, after all, an elemental as well as a physiological need to keep mothers and new born babies together wherever possible, so long as the child will not be endangered." Accordingly, as was previously stated in *Re B*,[110] the court must consider that a child's welfare includes the interest of that child in being brought up by his or her family of origin, and must therefore assess the possibility of that family meeting the child's needs with appropriate support services from the state. However, this would seem to contrast sharply with the above mentioned contemporary judicial view[111] that there is no right or presumption that a child should be brought up by their birth family.

Effectively, the birth parent/s of a child in state care should be offered a rehabilitation training programme, bearing in mind that Article 8 of the ECHR will always be engaged in such issues and the younger the child the stronger that engagement (see, further, Book IV in this series).[112] Indeed there have been

108 *Re W (A Child)* [2016] EWCA Civ 793. Indeed, grandparents are treated favourably as prospective carers in public law proceedings, though not so much in private proceedings.

109 [2014] EWHC 270 at [53].

110 [2013] UKSC 33, at paras 26–8.

111 See *Seddon v. Oldham MBC* [2015] EWHC 2609 (Fam) and *Re W (A Child)* [2016] EWCA Civ 793.

112 O'Halloran, K., *Child Welfare and Rights: Perspectives from European Nations*, Routledge (forthcoming).

repeated reminders to that effect from the ECtHR[113] and, as it admonished in *Kutzner v. Germany*,[114] it was:

> questionable whether the domestic administrative and judicial authorities [had] given sufficient consideration to additional measures of support as an alternative to what is by far the most extreme measure, namely separating the children from their parents.[115]

However, it must first be made clear to such parent/s what exactly is required of them: they need to be fully part of that decision-making process; as was pointed out in the *Re C* case.[116]

An opportunity for rehabilitation can be authorised under s 38(6) of the 1989 Act, which allows the court to direct assessments in respect of the child's best interests, usually accompanied by an interim care order.

- Termination of parental rights

The joint and equal parental responsibility vested in both married parents, or inherently in the mother but acquired by a cohabiting unmarried father or by civil partners, may only be voluntarily relinquished or, in rare instances, terminated by the court if this is deemed necessary to protect the welfare interests of a child.

An unmarried father will forfeit his rights as a parent if convicted of causing serious injury to a child,[117] or to other children,[118] or of inflicting grievous domestic violence[119] or of repeated abusive and intimidating interference in a child's health and education.[120] In those few circumstances the court has applied the paramountcy principle and ordered the permanent and absolute removal of his parental responsibilities.

The parental responsibilities of an unmarried mother or a married couple will be terminated should they voluntarily relinquish their child for adoption or if the court should determine – on grounds of the welfare interests of the child – that adoption proceedings may be concluded without their consent. As a preliminary to adoption, the court may dispense with the need for parental consent for placement and issue a 'placement order' which effectively transfers authority to exercise parental responsibility from the birth parent/s and vests it jointly in the placing agency and the prospective adopters – but it must be shared with the birth

113 See, for example: *Eriksson v. Sweden*, Application No. 11373/85, (1989); *Johansen v. Norway*, (1996) 23 EHRR 33; and *Scozzari and Giunta v. Italy*, 2000] ECHR 372.

114 (2002) 35 EHRR 25.

115 Ibid at para 75.

116 *Care Proceedings: Disclosure of Local Authority's Decision Making Process* [2002] 2 FCR 673.

117 *Re P (Terminating Parental Responsibility)* [1995] 3 FCR 753.

118 *CW v. SG* [2013] All ER (D) 117.

119 *A v. D (Parental Responsibility)* [2013] EWHC 2963 (Fam).

120 *C v. D & Another* [2018] EWHC 3312 (Fam).

parent/s – until such time as an adoption order permanently terminates the latter's parental responsibilities. The Court of Appeal[121] has stressed that the proper test for dispensing with parental agreement to the making of a placement order, under Adoption and Children Act 2002, s 52(1)(b), is whether the welfare interests of the child require his or her adoption as opposed to something short of adoption.

- Concurrent placements

In order to reduce the number of placement changes, local authorities have developed a practice of initiating a rehabilitation programme designed to return a child to safe parental care while also putting in place a parallel permanent placement plan.[122] It relies upon foster parents chosen for their capacity to engage directly with the birth parents and facilitate the rehabilitation plan but who, in the event of that plan failing, are also approved and willing to adopt the children concerned. These two options will then be played out in tandem with emphasis given to rehabilitation but the fallback position of adoption is kept alive and preparations for utilising it are attended to constantly. In very many cases, where the rehabilitation option has demonstrably failed, children have then been successfully and relatively swiftly adopted by their carers.[123] This approach avoids the traditional care career of serial placements and 'drift' in long-term foster care.

Arguably, however, there is cause for some concern as to whether such a practice is wholly Convention compliant: specifically, there are grounds for considering that, by allowing alternative attachments to form over a considerable period, concurrent placements[124] may in effect prejudice the long-term welfare interests of the child concerned, reduce the likelihood of a return to parental care, and preempt the court's decision making, thereby possibly breaching Articles 6 and 8.[125] Much will turn on the birth parent/child contact arrangements and rehabilitation programme, particularly in relation to young children. As Munby J warned in *Re: MR*:[126]

> It is a dreadful thing to take a baby away from his mother: dreadful for mother, dreadful for father and dreadful for the baby. If the state, in the guise of a local authority, seeks to intervene so drastically in a family's life – and at a time when, *ex hypothesi*, its case against the parents has not yet even been established – then the very least the state can do is to make generous arrangements for contact.

121 *SB v. A County Council; Re P* [2008] EWCA Civ 535. Also, see, *Re P (Placement Orders: Parental Consent)* [2008] EWCA Civ 535, [2008] 2 FLR 625, per Wall LJ at para 126.

122 See, for example, Wolfson, R., 'Concurrent Planning: A Route to Earlier Permanence for Young Children', *Seen and Heard*, Vol 23, No 2, 2012, at pp 46–58.

123 *Re M'P-P (Children)* [2015] EWCA Civ 584. Accelerated by provisions of the 2014 Act.

124 First introduced in the U.S. by the Adoption and Safe Families Act 1997.

125 Though note *YC v. the United Kingdom* (2012) 55 EHRR 33.

126 [2003] 2 FLR 171, [2003] EWHC 850 (Admin) at [44].

Residential care

A small minority of 'looked after' children, mostly those with complex health or social care needs, live in residential children's homes. A small proportion of those are in secure accommodation. The governing statutory provisions are to be found in the Care Standards Act 2000 which, amongst other things, makes provision for the registration and regulation of children's homes. Also relevant are the Care Standards Act (Registration) (England) Regulations 2010 and the Children's Homes (England) Regulations 2015.

The Children's Commissioner has published a set of reports expressing concern that, as presently constituted, residential care provision for children is not safeguarding the welfare interests of the 8,000 children currently being accommodated. The Commissioner's reports show how the children's residential social care system is broken and is failing many of the most vulnerable children, in particular those who are most at risk of falling through gaps in the system and becoming victims of criminal or sexual exploitation.[127]

Secure accommodation

Under s 25 of the 1989 Act, this form of residential care is provided for children and young persons of less than 16 years of age[128] who are likely to abscond if in any other form of accommodation and in which case are then likely to suffer significant harm or may injure themselves or others. While a child's welfare is not the court's paramount consideration it is plainly an important element in the court's analysis and therefore one of the relevant criteria to be considered.[129] As was stated *In the Matter of Child J*: "the secure accommodation procedures provide important protections for children confined in such institutions."[130] Currently, the need for such accommodation far outstrips capacity[131] as was noted by Baker LJ "the absence of sufficient resources in such cases means that local authorities are frequently prevented from complying with their statutory obligations to meet the welfare needs of a cohort of vulnerable young people who are at the greatest risk of harm."[132] Indeed, the forceful advocacy of the judiciary, in lamenting the lack of appropriate resources, should not be overlooked as a factor that has over the years played a role in shaping the modern application of the welfare principle. So, for example, Sir James Munby's lambasted the lack of local authority secure

127 See, further, 'The Children No One Knows What to Do With', 'Private Provision in Children's Social Care', and 'Stability Index 2020' at: www.childrenscommissioner.gov.uk/report/the-children-who-no-one-knows-what-to-do-with/.

128 Note that in *Re P (Application for Secure Accommodation Order)* [2015] EWHC 2971 (Fam) the court sanctioned such accommodation for a girl aged slightly older than 16.

129 See *In the Matter of B (Secure Accommodation Order)* [2019] EWCA Civ 2025, per Baker LJ.

130 [2020] EWHC 2395 (Fam).

131 See, further, at: www.localgovernmentlawyer.co.uk/child-protection/309-children-protection-features/45690-the-courts-and-the-lack-of-secure-accommodation-for-children.

132 *A Local Authority v. B's Mother; et al*, [2019] EWCA Civ 2025, at para 6.

accommodation provision when he referred to what he termed "a well-known scandal," namely:[133]

> the disgraceful and utterly shaming lack of proper provision in this country of the clinical, residential and other support services so desperately needed by the increasing numbers of children and young people afflicted with the same kind of difficulties as X is burdened with.

Such judicial challenges are intended to provoke government at all levels to remedy service deficits and very probably make an important contribution towards the introduction of welfare compliant change.

Secure accommodation and wardship

In the Matter of T (A Child)(Appellant)[134] the UKSC noted that while the 1989 Act provided powers for the use of secure accommodation, nonetheless over recent years, the High Court had found itself faced with a significant number of applications by local authorities seeking orders under the inherent jurisdiction authorising alternative restrictive placements of children; very many applications were being made to place children in secure accommodation by using wardship instead of utilising the statutory proceedings.[135] One of the appeal grounds considered by the court rested on the claim that such local authority recourse to wardship was barred by s 100 of the 1989 Act. Lady Black, on behalf of the court, rejected that claim:[136]

> it seems to me, that it is unthinkable that the High Court, with its long-established role in protecting children, should have no means to keep these unfortunate children (and others who may be at risk from them) safe from extreme harm, in some cases death. If the local authority cannot apply for an order under section 25 because there is no section 25 compliant secure accommodation available, I would accept that the inherent jurisdiction can, and will have to be, used to fill that gap, without clashing impermissibly with the statutory scheme.

Clearly, where there is no statutory process available to effectively give effect to the welfare principle, then the wardship jurisdiction may – and should – be used in its traditional safety net role (see, further, below).

133 *In Re X (A Child) (No 3)* [2017] EWHC 2036 (Fam), at para 37.

134 [2021] UKSC 35.

135 See, for example: *In rRe B (A Child)* [2020] Fam 221 which noted the 'crisis in the provision of secure accommodation in England and Wales'; and *Lancashire County Council v. G and N* [2020] EWHC 2828 (Fam).

136 Op cit, at para 141.

Secure accommodation and child's consent

In the Matter of T (A Child)(Appellant)[137] the UKSC considered the question – what bearing did the 15-year-old child's consent to secure accommodation have on the issue of whether an order should be made? As the court noted:

> consent is highly relevant to the evaluation of whether it is in the child's best interests to make the orders sought, she submits, and on the facts of this case, it was contrary to her best interests to make the order, given that she consented to the regime arranged for her.[138]

However, the Children's Commissioner made the important point that a child in any such stressful position may be perceived as having given agreement – thereby waiving her ECHR rights under Article 5 – but in fact be unable to give and sustain an authentic and valid consent to care arrangements. The Commissioner invited the court to consider an appropriate way in which to secure the voice of the child in such a context. [139]

Lady Black's opinion on this difficult question – one which goes to the heart of the welfare/rights of a child – may be viewed as being, at best, circumspect:[140]

> When the court considers the local authority's application, any consent on the part of the child will form part of the circumstances that it evaluates in deciding upon its order ... His or her personal autonomy will be respected by being fully involved in those proceedings, and able to express views about the care that is being proposed.

Ultimately, the UKSC upheld the ruling in the lower court that T's consent was not authentic and unlikely to endure and therefore took the view that the consent was not *Gillick*-compliant. This decision, while in this instance negative, clearly acknowledges that in such circumstances it is wholly possible that a child could give a valid consent.

Adoption

Adoption is the primary means available to a local authority for directly securing the paramount welfare interests of a child on a lifetime basis. It may do so with or without parental consent.

A local authority may also contribute to safeguarding and promoting welfare interests by assessing and training prospective adopters, maintaining a waiting list, and by supervising placements. Section 4 of the 2002 Act places upon all local authorities: a duty to respond to any request for assistance from a party to an adoption by carrying out a needs assessment; but a discretion as to whether or not

137 [2021] UKSC 35 at para 120. Also, see, *In Re D (A Child)* [2019] UKSC 42; [2019] 1 WLR 5403.
138 Ibid at para 94.
139 Ibid at para 104.
140 Ibid at para 162.

they provide any related services.[141] Subsequently, the Adoption Support Services Regulations for England (SI 2003) and its successor the Adoption Support Services Regulations 2005 (SI 2005 No 691) gave adopters, adopted children, and birth relatives the right to request an assessment of need regarding contact arrangements and it requires agencies to maintain services to assist such contact arrangements.[142] The Regulations require local authorities to appoint an adoption support services adviser, to be responsible for the provision of advice and information to all persons affected by an adoption or proposed adoption.

Domestic voluntary adoption

Married or not, any parent with full parental responsibility is entitled to voluntarily relinquish a child for adoption and, following the introduction of the 2002 Act, such consent may be given on an 'advanced' basis. The consent of the other parent, if he or she has parental responsibility, must be obtained or the need for it dispensed with. A local authority has the duty to receive into its care any child so relinquished and must then secure for him or her an appropriate adoption placement. Nevertheless, this does provide a local authority with an opportunity to select and match the needs of the child with the particular strengths of approved adopters on its waiting list. In accordance with the Children Act 1989, s 22C, the authority will look first to family members as potential adopters but it has a free hand to make the arrangements which offer the best likelihood of advancing a child's welfare interests.

Unaccompanied migrant minors

The migrant crisis of 2015/16 triggered a significant increase in unaccompanied migrant children coming into Europe, including England and Wales, from countries such as Vietnam, Afghanistan, the Middle East, and north Africa. Most recently this phenomenon has been exacerbated by the war in Ukraine. Between January and June 2020 some 3,455 unaccompanied migrant children were registered as such in the UK.[143] While the intensity of the flow has abated somewhat, there are reports that many unaccompanied minors – some trafficked – are still entering this jurisdiction.[144] By far the majority are male adolescents and on arrival, if they have no UK relatives, they become the responsibility of the nearest local authority which will seek to house them with approved foster parents.

141 See Adoption Support Services Regulations 2005 (SI 2005 No 691).

142 Also, see, the Adoption Support Services Regulations 2005.

143 See, further, at: www.unicef.org/eca/emergencies/latest-statistics-and-graphics-refugee-and-migrant-children.

144 See, for example, Every Child Protected Against Trafficking, '**Child Trafficking in the UK 2021: a Snapshot**', at: www.ecpat.org.uk/Handlers/Download.ashx?IDMF=23b51868-f257-49bc-b779-a5059bd65a04.

The European Economic and Social Committee recommends that the response of national authorities to this phenomenon should be governed by the principle of 'the best interests of the child' which should take precedence over all other national and international law.[145]

Trafficking

In 2019, the Committee against Torture stated that

> the Committee remains concerned about reports that law enforcement officers are not adequately trained in identifying victims of trafficking; that the specialist care and support for trafficked children provided for in the Modern Slavery Act 2015 has not been put into place in practice.[146]

In the so-called 'county lines' cases in the United Kingdom, traffickers target children of separated parents or those looked after by social services, including those with behavioural or developmental disorders. Trafficked children, as well as victims emotionally attached to their traffickers, can also be incited to use drugs or alcohol, thereby increasing the control the traffickers have over them.[147]

The welfare principle in contemporary practice: public family law: criminal jurisdiction

Criminal proceedings in relation to children are largely governed by a combination of the Children and Young Persons Act 1933, the Crime and Disorder Act 1998, and the Youth Justice and Criminal Evidence Act 1999, which allow for a limited overlap with the Children Act 1989.[148] The primary aim of the system is not welfare oriented but is firmly focused on the prevention of further offences.

The Youth Custody Service

This government body (part of HM Prison and Probation Service) determines whether a child on remand or convicted of an offence is placed in either a Young Offender Institution, a Secure Training Centre, or a Secure Children's Home. Only the latter option is a local authority facility and is designated as suitable

145 See, further, at: .www.eesc.europa.eu/en/our-work/opinions-information-reports/opinions/protection-unaccompanied-migrant-minors-europe-own-initiative-opinion.

146 See Concluding Observations on the Sixth Periodic Report of the United Kingdom Of Great Britain And Northern Ireland, (2019), at para 58. See, further, at: https://documents-dds-ny.un.org/doc/UNDOC/GEN/G19/154/71/PDF/G1915471.pdf?OpenElement.

147 See, the 2020 UNODC report Trafficking in Persons' at p 91, at: https://www.unodc.org/documents/data-and-analysis/tip/2021/GLOTiP_2020_15jan_web.pdf.

148 See, also, the Powers of Criminal Courts (Sentencing) Act 2000, the Criminal Justice and Immigration Act 2008, and the Legal Aid, Sentencing and Punishment of Offenders Act 2012.

accommodation for young offenders aged 12 to 14, girls up to the age of 16, and 15- to 16-year-old boys, who are assessed as particularly vulnerable. Safeguarding the welfare of the child is always a relevant factor – if only to the extent that their rehabilitation is a declared YCS outcomes objective.

Children who pose a threat to the welfare of self or others

While the welfare interests of the child play a part determining the court disposal option, following conviction of an offence, so also do factors such as the risk of harm to self or others. In recent years the numbers of children involved in the murder of other children (particularly due to knife crime in the greater London area) has risen sharply.

Age of criminal responsibility

Ten years of age is still the prescribed age of criminal responsibility; the law permits the arrest, detention, and criminal prosecution of children between 10 and 17 years of age. This has long been a matter of concern to the UN CRC which, in 2016 and again in 2019, expressed concern regarding the fact that 'the Children and Young Persons Act 1933 defines a child as a person under the age of 16 for the purpose of the criminal law on child abuse and neglect' and recommended that consideration be given to 'the possibility of expanding legislation to provide protection of all children under 18 years of age against discrimination on the grounds of their age.'[149]

Where a child has committed a minor offence, admits to having done so but has no previous convictions, then a police officer may exercise discretion and issue an official caution rather than instigate proceedings, and indeed most such transgressions are dealt with in that manner. The relevant age for the purposes of determining court disposal options is the age of the child at the time of trial rather than when the offence was committed.

Prevention

The welfare principle is given effect through the preventative duty under the Children Act 1989, Sched 2, para 7, requiring local authorities to take reasonable steps to reduce the need to bring criminal proceedings against children and to encourage them not to commit criminal offences. The Crime and Disorder Act 1998 placed further preventative duties on local authorities: s 39 requiring every

149 See the UN Committee on the Rights of the Child, *Concluding Observations: United Kingdom Of Great Britain And Northern Ireland*, United Nations (2016) at paras 41(b) and 21, respectively. Also, see, Committee against Torture Concluding Observations on the Sixth Periodic Report of the United Kingdom Of Great Britain And Northern Ireland (2019) at para 23.

local authority to set up at least one 'youth offending team' in its area; while under s 38–41 youth justice services must be made available.

Youth Court

This is a magistrates' court, consisting of either three magistrates or a district judge, designated to adjudicate on offences – such as theft, burglary, anti-social behaviour, and involvement with drugs – allegedly committed by children aged between 10 and 17; more severe crimes, or offences in which there is a public interest, are referred to the Crown Court where proceedings are conducted in a similar manner as for adult offenders. In what may be interpreted as concessions to welfare: a child aged under 16, or between 16 and 17 and liable to be given a court order, must be accompanied by a parent; and proceedings are held 'in camera.' A further such concession may be noted: the traditional sentence for grave crimes of detention "for the duration of Her Majesty's Pleasure" has been abolished following the ruling of the ECtHR that such wording could not permit wholly punitive life-long detention.[150]

There have been criticisms of non-welfare oriented practices in the Youth Court such as handcuffing children and locking them in secure docks, even though they are being charged with minor offences, and leaving some without legal representation.[151]

Role of the welfare principle

The 1933 Act, s 44, requires the court to 'have regard to the welfare of the child' but nonetheless the fact remains that – despite legal aid being available for legal representation since 1960 – many children find themselves in court without the benefit of it.[152] The court does have discretion, when merited by the circumstances, to grant legal aid for the purposes of providing representation. A 'home study' report will be submitted by a local authority social worker or probation officer and any mitigating family issues may influence the court towards electing a non-custodial disposal option. Section 44(1) of the 1933 Act requires the court not only to 'have regard to the welfare of the child' but 'in a proper case {to} take steps for removing him from undesirable surroundings, and for securing that proper provision is made for his education and training.' This, as Brenda Hoggett

150 See, *Hussain and Prem Singh v. United Kingdom*, 22 EHRR 1 (1996) which found that it breached Articles 3 and 5(4) of the ECHR which required that changes in the character, personality and mental state of a young offender serving a long sentence be considered during mandatory and repeated parole reviews.

151 See Children's Commissioner 2019 report at: www.theguardian.com/society/2019/nov/03/youth-court-system-in-chaos-says-childrens-commissioner.

152 It is reported that between 1969 and 1976 the proportion of children legally represented in the juvenile court in England and Wales rose from 3 per cent to 21 per cent: Criminal Statistics, HMSO; as cited in King, M., *Childhood, Welfare & Justice*, Billing & Son Ltd, 1981, at p 118.

has noted, 'stops short of making his welfare the first, let alone the paramount consideration.'[153]

Community sentences

The Youth Court does not provide any specific 'welfare' court disposal option on conviction for an offence, the use of care orders for offenders was abolished by the 1989 Act, s 90(2), but it may issue fines, impose a Supervision Order, a Probation Order, or make a Reparation Order, an Attendance Centre Order, or a Youth Community Order. In some circumstances orders imposing a curfew, or excluding a child from being in the vicinity of specified persons or places, or providing for their supervision order, may be made.

Custodial sentences

A Detention and Training Order, the maximum sentence issued by a Youth Court, is only imposed in respect of persistent offenders. It combines detention with a training component and may last for two years. A detention order may also be issued by the Crown Court under the Criminal Courts (Sentencing) Act 2000, s 91, in respect of serious offences. The CRC has expressed concern regarding the use of restraint measures in custodial facilities and recommends that the authorities 'abolish all methods of restraint against children for disciplinary purposes in all institutional settings, both residential and non-residential, and ban the use of any technique designed to inflict pain on children.'[154]

The welfare principle in contemporary practice: private family law

If there ever was any legal substance in the adage that 'a man's home is his castle' this has wholly disappeared under a barrage of state intervention measures usually associated with a general concern for public health and safety and for ensuring child protection.

Children and re-constituted families

Unmarried parents and their children currently constitute 20.7 per cent of all family units, their married counterparts comprise 79 per cent, while some 0.3 per cent are in same sex relationships.[155] In 2020, some 21.8 per cent of all families were

153 Hoggett, B., *Parents and Children* (4th ed), Sweet & Maxwell, 1993 at p 224–5.

154 See the UN Committee on the Rights of the Child, *Concluding Observations: United Kingdom Of Great Britain And Northern Ireland*, United Nations (2016) at para 39(b).

155 See ONS data at: www.ons.gov.uk/peoplepopulationandcommunity/birthsdeathsandmarriages/families/bulletins/familiesandhouseholds/2020.

led by single parents.[156] The annual divorce rate is approximately 42 per cent.[157] Given such statistics it may be that family instability in this jurisdiction places the welfare of children at particular risk.

Matrimonial

The welfare interests of children affected by the breakdown of their parent's marriage remain governed by the Matrimonial Causes Act 1973[158] and the Civil Partnership Act 2004 as supplemented by the Children Act 1989; as adjusted by the recently introduced Divorce, Dissolution and Separation Act 2020. Also relevant are the Marriage Act 1949, the Family Law Act 1996, the Matrimonial and Family Proceedings Act 1984, the Marriage (Same Sex Couples) Act 2013, the Children and Families Act 2014, and the Civil Partnerships, Marriages and Deaths (Registration, etc.) Act 2019.

Divorce, nullity, and judicial separation

The right of a couple to divorce, separate, or annul their marriage is conditional upon their first satisfying the court that satisfactory care arrangements have been made to safeguard the welfare interests of any 'child of the family' under the age of 16 years. Before the 2020 Act this rule applied with some rigour in contested proceedings, when it was the subject of CAFCASS inquiries and judicial examination, but was not judicially examined in the majority of divorce proceedings which were by mutual consent. The court then simply needed to be assured that the couple had made appropriate care arrangements for their children: if solicitors representing the parties could provide details of agreed arrangements and affirm that they were satisfactory then they would not be judicially examined. Following the introduction of the 2020 Act and the removal of any possibility of contested divorce proceedings, the welfare interests of all dependent children will presumably be similarly cursorily affirmed, unless the court is put on notice of issues likely to compromise those interests.

The welfare checklist

Matrimonial proceedings being 'family proceedings' the welfare checklist as set out above applies. The court is required, under s 1(3) Children Act 1989 to be satisfied as to: the ascertainable wishes and feelings of the child concerned; the child's physical, emotional, and educational needs; the likely effect on the child if circumstances changed as a result of the court's decision; the child's age, sex,

156 See, further, at: https://care.org.uk/news/2021/03/dramatic-reduction-in-family-breakdown-thanks-to-stronger-marriages-new-evidence-shows.

157 See, further, ONS data, op cit.

158 Previously, the Matrimonial Proceedings (Children) Act 1958 and the Divorce Reform Act 1969.

backgrounds and any other characteristics which will be relevant to the court's decision; any harm the child has suffered or may be at risk of suffering; the capability of the child's parents (or any other person the courts find relevant) at meeting the child's needs; and the powers available to the court in the given proceedings.

Court orders

The court has wide powers in matrimonial proceedings – whether for divorce, separation, or dissolution – to make such orders as it deems appropriate, subject to any child support scheme to be made under the Child Support Act 1991, for the distribution of such assets, lump sums, or periodical payments as may be needed for the maintenance of children. A 'child arrangements' order is available. When deciding such financial arrangements, the court is required to treat the welfare interests of any child under the age of 18 years not as a matter of paramount importance but as a matter of the first consideration.

In cases of cohabitation, an unmarried parent may apply to court for financial provision by way of a lump sum, regular maintenance payments, or a transfer of property for a child – perhaps to meet housing needs[159] – from the other parent under Sched 1 of the 1989 Act. Whether married or not, following a relationship breakdown the parents may either agree their children's future living arrangements and contact times in respect of their children or disagree and apply to the court, under s 8 of the 1989 Act, for a child arrangements order. The Children and Families Act 2014, s 11, introduced the concept of continued parental involvement into the 1989 Act (s 1(2A)) requiring the court, when considering a parental application regarding a child's living and contact arrangements, to presume (unless the contrary is shown) that involvement of the applicant parent in the life of the child will further his or her welfare.[160] Accordingly, the court may now order that the child lives with one or both parents or spends time with a parent or someone named in the order. Where the order provides for the child to live with both parents in their respective homes, time in each home will not necessarily be equal. The order may be adjusted by adding such conditions and directions as may be appropriate to meet the particular needs of a child, including specifying indirect contact, and it may accommodate arrangements between the child and wider family members such as grandparents and siblings. This important addition to the welfare principle projects protection for a child's relationship with a parent, and/ or significant others, for the duration of their childhood.

159 See, for example, *DN v. UD (Schedule 1 Children Act: Capital Provision)* [2020] EWHC 627 (Fam).

160 Note that the Ministry of Justice launched a review of this presumption in 2020 to assess whether the right balance is being struck in private law cases between the risk of harm to a child and their right to have a relationship with both parents.

Guardianship

Rooted in the feudal system, and then initially largely concerned with safeguarding the property of a child heir, guardianship is one of the oldest legal procedures associated with substitute parental care and the protection of children. Developed by the Court of Chancery and eventually incorporated into statute law – the Guardianship of Infants Act 1925, the Guardianship Act 1973 – the governing legislation as applicable to children is now to be found in the Children Act 1989, as amended. It has, however, shrunk considerably in terms of its former role in private family law.

Court appointment

Now more commonly associated with court orders relating to adults, usually with mental health issues, guardianship orders are also occasionally issued by Family Proceedings Courts where no alternative is appropriate. In contemporary practice, guardianship has become either an implied component of the responsibilities of a parent or someone in *loco parentis* to a child, or is incorporated into orders such as a child arrangement order, or it takes the form of a 'special guardianship order' (see, further, below). As with all measures governed by the 1989 Act, when determining whether to make a guardianship order, s 1(1) requires that 'the child's welfare shall be the court's paramount consideration.'

Adoption

The governing legislative framework is a loose amalgam of the Adoption Act 1976, the Children Act 1989, the Adoption and Children Act 2002, and the Children and Families Act 2014. In recent years the welfare interests of children have been greatly facilitated and strengthened, relative to other considerations, by changes in the law which include extending: the paramountcy principle for dispensing with parental consent; adoption eligibility to include same sex couples; the relevant period for welfare interests, when considering the appropriateness of adoption, to throughout the lifetime of the child concerned; and the entitlement to post-adoption support.

Step-parent adoption

For many years step-parent adoptions constituted the largest category of adopters in England and Wales, despite the long-standing concern that they had the effect of: legally guillotining the interests of all members of one side of the child's family in maintaining relationships with that child; distorting his or her legal relationships with family members; and, by obscuring actual blood relationships, could obstruct the adoptee's capacity to develop an authentic and independent sense of identity.[161] Step-adoptions are now steadily decreasing both in number and as a

161 See the Department of Health, *Adoption Law Review: Consultation Document*, 1992, at para 19.2.

proportion of annual orders due to recent and more concerted legislative and judicial efforts to guide such applicants towards alternative orders.

Since 2005 the Children Act, s 8(1)(a), has allowed a step-parent married to, or the civil partner of, a birth parent to apply for an order for a 'parental responsibility' order or to enter into a parental responsibility agreement, in respect of the latter's child;[162] and under the Children Act 1989, s 14C(1) as inserted by s 115 of the Adoption and Children Act 2002, 'special guardianship' orders are now available.[163] Such constraints require the court to give precedence to promoting the long-term welfare interests of the child rather than to strengthening the familial role of a step-parent.

Cultural/religious affinity

The Children and Families Act 2014, s 3, deleted s 1(5) of the 2002 Act requiring that 'due consideration be given to religious persuasion, racial origin and cultural and linguistic background' when an adoption agency in England places a child for adoption.[164] The significance of this repeal was demonstrated in the *Manders* case[165] when the court discounted the importance that the local authority and adoption agency had placed on race and culture when matching prospective adopters and children. Similarly, a parent's views and wishes as to their child's religious upbringing, though still taken into account – as are the wishes of the child in this regard – have become wholly subject to the paramountcy principle. As Munby LJ explained, in *Re S; Newcastle City Council v. Z*,[166]

> whilst the court will no doubt be slow to conclude that a parent faithfully striving to follow the teachings of one of the great religions of the world is acting unreasonably, there is nothing to prevent the court coming to that conclusion in an appropriate case … context is everything.[167]

On the other hand, however, the deletion could arguably impair welfare interests by licensing a potentially serious infringement of a child's right to have the opportunity to develop an authentic culturally contextualised identity.

162 See, for example, *S (A Child), Re (Rev 1)* [2013] EWHC 1295 (Fam), [2013] All ER (D) 76 (Jun).

163 But note *Re P (A Child)* [2014] EWCA Civ 1174 on inappropriateness of special guardianship as an alternative to step-parent adoption.

164 Section 1(5). There was no equivalent requirement regarding racial considerations in the 1976 Act.

165 See *Sandeep and Reena Mander v. RBWM Adoption Berkshire* [2019], CO1RG 184.

166 [2005] EWHC 1490 (Fam), [2007] 1 FLR 861. Also, see, *Re T (Minors) (Custody: Religious Upbringing)* (1981) 2 FLR 239, per Scarman LJ at paras 244–5.

167 Ibid, at para 56.

Post-adoption contact, information disclosure, and state support services

In almost all domestic adoptions there is now some form of ongoing contact between an adopted child and their birth parent and/or with other members of the family of origin. In the latter context, the recent case of *XY*[168] highlighted the importance of sibling relationships as a determinant of children's welfare interests. As Lady Hale pointed out: "it is important to recognise that there are differences between the relationship of a parent and a child and the relationship between a sibling and a child."[169] Recourse to a combination of adoption and contact orders accelerated in the wake of the 2002 Act because of the requirement in s 46(6) that the court consider the necessity for post-adoption contact arrangements. The National Adoption Standards also contain provisions explicitly addressing the need for possible post-adoption contact to be explored with the child, his or her birth parent/s, and other members of the birth family. Further reinforcement for post-adoption contact was made by the insertion through the Children and Families Act 2014, s 9, of sections 51A and 51B into the Adoption and Children Act 2002 permitting the making of a contact order at any time, including any time after an adoption order. The court may make an order, under s 51A, prohibiting contact.

The 2002 Act introduced the concept of local authority support services, made them more comprehensive, and with wider applicability than previously available. These are to be provided at any time (i.e. both pre- and post-adoption) and for all parties or others involved in any type of adoption.[170]

A characteristic of the adoption process in this jurisdiction is the presumption, prevailing since 1975, that on reaching the age of 18, every adopted person has had the right to access their original birth certificate and any information held by the relevant adoption agency. This entitlement distinguishes the adoption process from that of the U.S. and other jurisdictions. Adoptees have the further right to specify, in the Adoption Contact Register, those birth relatives with whom they do or do not wish to have contact: they may enter an absolute or a qualified veto.[171]

Intercountry adoption

For children who are orphans, have been abandoned in poorly resourced institutional care, and/or have complex health needs, their removal into the homes of

168 *[2020] UKSC 26. Though not an adoption case, it is significant because it recognises that sibling relationships are particularly long lasting and their* importance should be reflected in court proceedings.

169 Ibid, at para 46.

170 Following the 2002 Act, the Dept of Health issued a consultation paper entitled the Draft Adoption Support Services (Local Authorities) (Transitory and Transitional Provisions) (England) Regulations and Draft Accompanying Guidance, December 2002. See, also, Dept of Health, Providing Effective Adoption Support.

171 See, further, the Adopted Children and Adoption Contact Registers 2005.

western adopters most often results in an unqualified promotion of their welfare interests. It must be added that for the very many children in those developed nations who are left in state institutions or in long-term foster care, due to being unadoptable for various reasons, the fact that others have been adopted in their place is disastrous.

The Adoption (Intercountry Aspects) Act 1999 gave effect to the Hague Convention 1993 and introduced a new framework to govern the adoption of overseas children by UK. citizens. It requires prospective adopters to be assessed, approved, and authorised in the UK before children are brought into the jurisdiction;[172] reinforced by the Adoption of Children from Overseas Regulations 2001. It also requires all local authorities to include services to intercountry adopters within the general duty to provide an adoption service; a provision reinforced by s 2(8) of the 2002 Act. The English court has jurisdiction to make an adoption order in respect of a foreign national child and to dispense with the consent of a foreign national parent.[173]

Surrogacy

The governing legislative framework essentially consists of the Surrogacy Arrangements Act 1985, the Adoption & Children Act 2002, and the Human Fertilisation and Embryology Act 2008.

This jurisdiction does have some legal provisions governing the type of arrangements that can be made and preparations are underway for introducing new laws.[174] Currently, commercial surrogacy is prohibited and it is illegal to recruit mothers or to advertise or negotiate contracts on a commercial basis. However, under the Human Fertilisation and Embryology Act 2008, s 54, there is legal provision enabling the transfer of parental status as married or unmarried commissioning parents (including single persons[175] and same sex couples) can obtain a 'parental order,' providing them with parental rights and responsibilities, with the birth mother's consent. The latter caveat clearly creates considerable insecurity for commissioning couples as surrogate mothers remain free to choose to keep the child after birth. In such circumstances, the surrogate is the legal mother of the child and any husband of hers is the legal father. If she is in a civil partnership, her partner will be a legal parent. If the woman is unmarried at the time of the surrogacy, the intended father can be named as the legal father.

172 See *Re C* [1998] 2 FCR 641 and the case of 'the internet twins.'

173 *Re N (Adoption: Jurisdiction)* 2015 EWCA Civ 1112.

174 See Law Commission consultation paper 'Building Families Through Surrogacy: A New Law', (2019), at: https://s3-eu-west-2.amazonaws.com/lawcom-prod-storage-11jsxou24uy7q/uploads/2019/06/Surrogacy-consultation-paper.pdf.

175 The Human Fertilisation and Embryology Act 2008, s 54(A).

Surrogate, child, and the commissioning parents

Surrogates may only claim 'reasonable expenses' (though the courts will now usually approve almost any level of expenses). Once the child is born, legal parenthood can be transferred from the surrogate (and her husband or partner) to the commissioning parent/s who must acquire a parental order within six months of the child's birth, although late applications may be accepted.[176] Case law has determined that while most applications for a parental order are from couples – who must be either married, civil partners of each other, or living as partners in an enduring family relationship – a sole applicant is also eligible.[177] The courts examine surrogacy arrangements to ensure that they are altruistic in nature and that no improper payments have been made.[178]

For those who can afford it, surrogacy offers an attractive alternative to adoption and possibly the only route for acquiring a healthy baby. It may also provide a genetic link between parents and child, with many cases[179] resulting from the hundreds of UK commissioning parents making arrangements with overseas surrogates.[180]

Abduction

Welfare interests also have a role to play – if of uncertain nature and weight – alongside justice, in the somewhat atavistic context of child abduction; cases in which the future care of a 'snatched' child are now most often governed by the Hague Convention on the Civil Aspects of Child Abduction (see, further, Chapter 4).

The leading case of *Re J (A Child) (Return to Foreign Jurisdiction: Convention Rights)*[181] concerned parents married under shariah law who left the U.S. to return to Saudi Arabia – the father's home country – where they parted, the mother bringing their son to England against the father's wishes and in breach of an agreement. The mother refused an order requiring the child to be returned to Saudi Arabia, claiming that his human rights would be breached there. Baroness Hale then said:

> In all non-Convention cases the courts have consistently held that they must act in accordance with the welfare of the individual child. If they did decide to return the child, that is because it is in the best interests to do so not because the welfare principle has been superseded by some other consideration.

176 See *Re X (A Child) (Surrogacy: Time Limit)* [2014] EWHC 3135 (Fam).

177 *In the matter of Z (A Child) (No 2)* [2016] 2 FLR 327.

178 See, also, the Brazier Committee report which pointed out that any argument that payment is for the surrogacy and not for the baby is specious.

179 See, for example, *Re C* 2013, *Re IJ (A Child)* 2011, *Re L (A Minor)* 2010, *and Re X and Y (Foreign Surrogacy)* 2008.

180 It is estimated that the number of parental orders made following a surrogate birth tripled from 121 in 2011 to 368 in 2018. See, further, at: https://surrogacyuk.org/2018/12/31/surrogacy-survey-2018-results/.

181 [2005] UKHL 40.

This is in contrast to Convention cases when the court must bear in mind that Hague contains no express requirement to make the best interests of the child its primary consideration. In an important statement, she went on to draw attention to the need to interpret what constitutes 'welfare' in accordance with its cultural context:

> In a world which values difference, one culture is not inevitably to be preferred to another. Indeed we do not have any fixed concept of what will be in the best interests of the individual child ... We are not so arrogant as to think that we know best ... Hence our law does not start from any a priori assumptions about what is best for any individual child. It looks at the child and weighs a number of factors in the balance, now set out in the well known checklist in section 1(3) of the Children Act 1989: These include his own wishes and feelings, his physical and emotional and educational needs, and the relative capacities of the adults around him to meet those needs, the effect of change, his own characteristics and background, including his ethnicity, culture and religion, and any harm he has suffered or risks suffering in the future. There is nothing in those principles which prevents a court from giving great weight to the culture in which a child has been brought up when deciding how and where he will fare best in the future.

An opinion that offers an interesting contrast with that of six judges who grounded their joint minority dissent, in *A, B and C v. Ireland*,[182] on the rationale that where national or regional cultural norms conflict with a prevailing international moral consensus, the former should give way to the latter[183] (see, further, Chapter 1). It would also seem to be at variance with the policy that resulted in the removal from statute law of the clause requiring that 'due consideration be given to religious persuasion, racial origin and cultural and linguistic background.'[184]

Returning an abducted child

In *Re J (A Child)*,[185] on similar facts to the above 2005 case, the UKSC again found that the child should be returned to the non-Convention jurisdiction from which he had been wrongfully removed. The law governing such cases is as stated in *Re F (A Child) (International Relocation Cases)*[186] that the court must undertake a 'global holistic evaluation' by weighing up all the relevant factors, look at

182 [2010] ECtHR (GC) Application No. 25579/05, (2010).

183 Ibid, per Judges Rozakis, Tulkiens, Fura, Hirvea, Malinverni, and Poalelungi, at para 9.

184 This clause, in s 1(5) of the Adoption and Children Act 2002, was removed by s 3 of the Children and Families Act 2014. See, also, UN Committee on the Rights of the Child, General Comment No. 7 'Implementing Child Rights in Early Childhood', (2005).

185 [UKSC] 70.

186 [2015] EWCA Civ 882.

the case as a whole, and determine the course that best meets the need to protect the child's welfare.

Article 13(b) of the Convention provides that an abducted child should not be returned if this would expose him/her to a grave risk of harm or otherwise place him/her in an intolerable situation. This defence has been considered in cases such as *Re M (Abduction: Zimbabwe)*,[187] *Re E (Children)*,[188] and most recently in *Re K (A Child: Hague Convention: Child Abduction)(REV 1)*.[189] In the latter, the court was clear that the gravity of the risk must have reached a level of demonstrable seriousness and that 'intolerable' must be such as the particular child placed in the particular circumstances could not be expected to tolerate.[190]

Proportionality

The above cases draw attention to the difficulty inherent in holding a balance between the Hague requirement to expeditiously return an abducted child, Article 8 of the ECHR, and the paramountcy principle in s 3 of the 1989 Act. This was underlined in *Re E (Children)*[191] when the UKSC reiterated its view that while the best interests of the child must be a primary consideration it is not of paramount importance and, in summary proceedings, should not deflect from the purpose of expeditiously returning an abducted child. The Hague Conference on Private International Law, in its guide to implementation of the Convention, similarly advises that 'where safeguards or guarantees are applied which place limits or restraints on the exercise of contact, these should be proportionate to the risks of abuse and no more than are necessary to achieve the protection of the child.' It suggests that 'the principle expressed here is one of proportionality, reminding authorities that limits on parental contact should be justifiable in terms of the child's interests.'[192]

Child's wishes

The objection of a child to his/her return to their country of origin, even if no more than six years of age, will be taken into account when determining abduction proceedings.[193] Where a *Gillick* competent child objects, the court may well refuse to order their return. As mentioned earlier, this was a landmark decision for children's welfare/rights. The *Gillick* ruling was the first step away from the

187 [2007] 3 WLR 975.
188 FC [2011] UKSC 27.
189 [2020] NIFam 9.
190 Citing *Re D* [2007] 1 AC 619 at para 52.
191 Op cit.
192 The Hague Conference on Private International Law, 'Transfrontier Contact Concerning Children', *Family Law*, (2008) at para 1.2.
193 *W v. W (Abduction: Acquiescence: Children's Objections)* [2010] England and Wales High Court 332 (Family Division).

objectification of the child within a paternalistic welfare philosophy and a step towards welfare as a matter capable of subjective interpretation, and of justifying action as a right, by the child concerned. However, the objection must be a forceful rejection as 'the word "objects" imports a strength of feeling which goes far beyond the usual ascertainment of the wishes of the child in a custody dispute.'[194] Moreover, as Baroness Hale explained in *Re D (A Child) (Abduction; Rights of Custody)*:[195]

> Although strictly this only applies to cases within the European Union (over half of the applications coming before the High Court), the principle [that a child should be heard] is in my view of universal application and consistent with our international obligations under Article 12 of the United Nations Convention on the Rights of the Child. It applies, not only when a 'defence' under Article 13 has been raised, but also in any case in which the court is being asked to apply Article 12 and direct the summary return of the child - in effect in every Hague Convention case. It erects a presumption that the child will be heard unless this appears inappropriate. Hearing the child is, as already stated, not to be confused with giving effect to his views.

In January 2015, the Court of Appeal set out a two-part test for the assessment of a child's objections to returning. At the 'gateway stage,' it is necessary to establish that the child objects to a return and is of an age and degree of maturity at which it is appropriate to take account of his or her views. If these factual matters are established, the court will then proceed to the discretionary stage of assessing whether the child's objections to a return should prevail.[196]

The welfare principle in contemporary practice: public/private family law

The traditional cohesion of family law jurisprudence, its divisions into sets of proceedings that had seemed fixed at the end of the nineteenth century began to unravel at the end of the twentieth. Partly this was associated with the growing proportion of non-marital families coupled with an escalating rate of family breakdown. Partly it was necessitated by the volume of child protection cases coming before the courts. In response to such pressures, family law developed a central focus on the welfare interests of children separated from parental care for whatever reason.

194 *Re R (A Minor: Abduction)*, [1992] 1 FLR 105 *per* Bracewell J at 107–8.

195 [2007] IAC 619.

196 *Re MC (Republic of Ireland) (Child's Objections) (Joinder of Children as Parties to Appeal)* [2015] EWCA Civ 26.

Public/private family law

The binary split between the public and private sectors of family law is becoming progressively less clearcut as crossover issues relating to children – their wellbeing and upringing, their needs and deeds – forces the law to adjust and to accommodate principles and facilitate practices that can promote consistency in society's approach to children.

Public service matters

The private right of parents to conduct family life as they see fit has for some generations been subject to the requirement that they do so in ways that protect the welfare of their children and comply with public regulatory requirements governing developmental needs. This is counterbalanced by an understanding that government will provide a social environment – by managing an effective and sufficient framework of public services – enabling at least 'good enough parenting'. Arguably, the second half of the equation is failing as poverty levels increase. The Rowntree Foundation estimates that currently one in five (22%) of the UK population are in poverty and that poverty levels are rising. It adds:[197]

> Children have had the highest poverty rates throughout the last 25 years. Twenty five years ago, a third of children lived in poverty. This fell to 28% by 2004/05 and reached its lowest level of 27% in 2010/11 to 2013/14. Since then, child poverty has been rising, reaching 31% in 2019/20.

Much international law is devoted to establishing children's rights to avail of core public services – and to setting benchmarks for standards of service provision – as such are deemed essential to their welfare.[198] The correlation between levels of public service provision and levels of poverty is inescapable and it suggests that currently not enough children and their parents are able to access sufficient public services.

Employment

From at least the Dickensian era, there have been laws to protect children from exploitation and from risk of injury in the workplace: from 1802, maximum time limits began to be legally prescribed for children working in factories, etc. Currently, their employment is conditional upon factors such as parental permission, their age, hours of working, wages, and safety of working environment. There is also a long-running argument that mothers who work outside the family

197 See, Joseph Rowntree Foundation, 'UK Poverty 2022' at: https://www.jrf.org.uk/report/uk-poverty-2022.

198 See, for example, Articles 24, 28/29, and 32 in respect of health, education, and employment, respectively.

home are, by so doing, adversely affecting the developmental welfare of their children.[199]

Health

In this jurisdiction, the availability of a state funded National Health Service – delivering needs based services, free to all at point of delivery – has entitled very many failing parents to avail of non-stigmatising services and thereby continue to provide safe care for their children.

Local authorities are legally required to intervene when parental neglect in relation to health and safety matters jeopardises the life of their child; an issue which most usually involves Jehovah's Witnesses and blood products.[200] In both *Re R*[201] and *Re W*[202] the court suggested that the power of parents to authorize treatment co-existed with the child until he or she reached the age of majority, entitling parents to consent to treatment that the child did not want, even where the child was '*Gillick*-competent'. This interpretation would seem to undermine the Gillick ruling: 'mature minors' can consent to treatment, and parents cannot veto that consent; but minors cannot *refuse* treatment against the wishes of their parents because the parents can consent on the mature child's behalf.[203]

The capacity of minors to give a valid consent has also been challenged in the context of gender transition treatment. Following whistleblower disclosures, a High court case,[204] and an NHS commissioned review of the service in 2021 – led by Dr Cass[205] – the Tavistock Clinic was closed in 2022 because of the weight of concern regarding the ability of the Clinic to ensure a holistic treatment response to the increasing numbers of 16-year-old adolescents presenting with gender identity issues and ostensibly consenting to irreversible puberty blocking treatment.

More recently such health and safety concerns have tended to focus on parental supervision of their child's access to social media platforms. At the beginning of the second decade of the twenty-first century, the concern – and shared parent/local authority responsibilities – was illustrated on a nationwide basis by the requirement to ensure testing, social distancing and, where necessary, quarantining for children in the context of the COVID-19 pandemic.

199 See, for example, www.theguardian.com/money/2003/nov/14/workandcareers.

200 See, for example, *Birmingham Children's NHS Trust v. B & C* [2014] EWHC 531 (Fam); *Re S (A Minor) (Medical Treatment)* [1993] 1 FLR 376; and *Re R (A Minor) (Blood Transfusion)* [1993] 2 FCR 544.

201 *Re R (a minor) (wardship: medical treatment)*, [1991] 4 All E.R. 177.

202 *Re W (a minor) (medical treatment)*, [1992] 4 All E.R. 627.

203 See, for example, Douglas, G., 'The Retreat from *Gillick*' (1992), 55 *Mod. L. Rev.* 569 and Freeman, M., "Removing rights from adolescents" (1993), 17 *Adoption & Fostering* 14.

204 *Bell v. Tavistock* [2020] EWHC 3274 (Admin).

205 See, further, at: https://cass.independent-review.uk/publications/interim-report/.

Education

Every child of compulsory school age is required to be enrolled in, and to attend, an authorised school,[206] except in special circumstances or where a parent has opted for, and been approved to provide, home schooling. Most often difficulties arise when parents, usually with strong religious beliefs, claim that curriculum content is prejudicial to their child's welfare. Failure to comply with this duty, without good reason, can result in local authority intervention which may lead to prosecution and a School Attendance Order, an Education Supervision Order, or a Parenting Order to enforce parental compliance.

Legal proceedings

The dominance of the welfare principle has had the functional effect of virtually erasing some of the boundaries that traditionally separated private and public family law procedures.

Adoption from state care

The uniform application of the paramountcy principle across both the 1989 and 2002 Acts was a change of fundamental importance to both child care law and adoption law: its application to override the withholding of parental consent being a watershed development; giving legal recognition to the primacy of the welfare principle; even if this meant severing all legal ties between the child and his or her family of origin. In the light of its draconian effect on parent/child relationships, the UN CRC expressed concern that, in this jurisdiction, 'parents have not been provided with adequate family support' and that 'children have reportedly been removed from their biological families owing to the family's economic situation or because a foster family may provide a more beneficial environment for the child.'[207]

These sentiments were supported by Sumner J, in *Birmingham City Council v. S*,[208] when he described adoption as "a last resort for any child" to be invoked only "when neither of the parents nor the wider family and friends can reasonably be considered as potential carers for the child," and then – touching on a recurring theme – went on to recognise a child's "right to be brought up by her own family."[209] This advice was reiterated by Munby LJ who stressed that[210] "the judge must keep at the forefront of his mind the teaching of *Re B*"[211] this being that "orders contemplating non-consensual adoption – care orders with a plan for

206 Education Act 1996, s 444.
207 As noted in UN CRC, Concluding Observations, op cit at para 52.
208 [2007] 1 FLR 1223.
209 See, also, the ruling in *Re B-S* [2013] EWCA Civ 1146, [2014] 1 FLR 1035.
210 *Re R (Children)*, [2013] EWCA Civ 1018 at para 22.
211 *In Re B (A Child) (Care Proceedings: Threshold Criteria)* [2013] UKSC 33, [2013] 1 WLR 1911.

adoption, placement orders, and adoption orders – are "a very extreme thing, a last resort," only to be made where "nothing else will do," where "no other course [is] possible in [the child's] interests," they are "the most extreme option," a "last resort – when all else fails," to be made "only in exceptional circumstances and where motivated by *overriding requirements* pertaining to the child's welfare." Over the following few years, this admonition had a chastening effect on child care adoptions,[212] sharply reducing the number of annual applications submitted.

A non-consensual adoption from state care requires the court to: bear in mind that it is generally in every child's best interests to be brought up by their birth parents;[213] examine all possible alternatives including provision of additional state support; consider whether any delay in making an order would adversely affect the child's welfare; and to apply the welfare checklist. As regards the latter, a customised version of the welfare checklist in the 1989 Act was embodied in the 2002 Act;[214] some items being deliberately calibrated across both statutes to ensure consistency of interpretation.[215] This list, crucial to identifying the particular welfare interests of a child in care who may be considered for adoption, is as follows:

(a) *The child's ascertainable wishes and feelings regarding the decision (considered in the light of the child's age and understanding).* This conservative restating of the law relating to the capacity of a child to influence decisions taken concerning their welfare clearly avoids addressing consent issues.

(b) *The child's particular needs.* This clause implicitly refers to the 'physical, emotional and educational needs' in s 1(3)(b) of the 1989 Act and its associated case law which must be interpreted in relation to the particular circumstances of the child concerned. The need to retain the child in the care context in which he or she has formed safe attachments and which offers the best chance of permanency will be crucial to addressing their emotional needs.

(c) *The likely effect on the child (throughout his life) of having ceased to be a member of the original family and become an adopted person.* This requirement imposes on the court the duty to take a long-term view of whether adoption will continue to meet the needs of the subject throughout their adult life and as such constitutes a most significant extension of the welfare principle's application. Established case law indicates that

212 The same judge, in *Re D (A Child) (No 3)* [2016] EWFC 1, noted that parents with learning difficulties could often be "good enough" parents as long as they were provided with emotional and practical support.

213 See *Birmingham City Council v. S* [2007] 1 FLR 1223.

214 Section 1(4).

215 For example, provisions s 1(3)(a), (d), and (c) of the 1989 Act are replicated in s 1(4)(a), (d), and (e), respectively, of the 2002 Act.

even if adoption could only promote welfare in adulthood, this would be sufficient justification for making the order.[216]

(d) *The child's age, sex, background and any of the child's characteristics which the court or agency considers relevant.* This catchall provision gives the court absolute discretion to determine the welfare factor most relevant to the circumstances of the child concerned.

(e) *Any harm (within the meaning of the Children's Act 1989) which the child has suffered or is at risk of suffering.* Again, correlating the provisions of the 1989 and 2002 Acts strategically strengthens the child care context of modern adoption practice and maximises consistency of interpretation. It is to be noted that the definition of 'harm' in the 1989 Act has been broadened by the 2002 Act to include 'impairment suffered from seeing or hearing the ill-treatment of another'[217] to, in effect, allow for the possible non-consensual adoption of children who have suffered harm from witnessing domestic violence.

(f) *The relationship which the child has with relatives, and with any other person in relation to whom the court or agency considers the question to be relevant, including—*

   i. the likelihood of any such relationship continuing and the value to the child of its doing so;
   ii. the ability and willingness of any of the child's relatives, or of any such person, to provide the child with a secure environment in which the child can develop, and otherwise to meet the child's needs;
   iii. the wishes and feelings of any of the child's relatives, or of any such person, regarding the child.

The last provision places a statutory duty on court and local authority to assess the ability and willingness of relatives to undertake care responsibility for a child, requiring an assessment be made of the value to that child of any ongoing relationship with a relative, which can be particularly useful in safeguarding established sibling relationships.

Moreover, as has been judicially emphasised "the checklist demands consideration of the likely effect on the child *throughout her life* of having ceased to be a member of her original family. Mere lip service to such matters is not enough."[218] The judiciary have been at pains to stress that the statutory checklists in s 1(3) of the 1989 Act, in respect of a care order, and s 1(4) of the 2002 Act, in respect of placement and adoption orders must be considered in conjunction with Article

216 See *Re D (A Minor) (Adoption Order: Validity)* [1991] 2 FLR 66.

217 Section 31(9) of the 1989 Act as amended by s 120 of the 2002 Act.

218 See *In the Matter of N (Children) (Adoption: Jurisdiction)* [2015] EWCA Civ 1112, per Sir James Munby, President of the Family Division, at para 105.

8 of the Convention when a court is determining whether or not the adoption order is in the best interests of a child despite the absence of parental consent.

Subsequently, the Children and Families Act 2014 inserted new subsections 9A, 9B, and 9C into s 22C of the 1989 Act, the effect of which was to statutorily endorse 'concurrent planning' and thereby position the paramountcy principle at the placement stage of the adoption process.

Post-adoption support

The 2002 Act introduced the concept of local authority support services: more comprehensive and with wider applicability than previously available; to be provided at any time (i.e. both pre- and post-adoption) and for all parties or others involved in any type of adoption; and in relation to looked after children, additional service specification was provided by the National Standards. This was followed by the Children and Families Act 2014 which introduced statutory rights to employment leave and pay for parents and adopters. The Adoption Passport scheme together with the Adoption Support Fund also play an important role in easing the financial costs of adoption from the state care system.

Wardship

A local authority is for most purposes prohibited from using wardship. Under s 100(2)(d) of the 1989 Act it can only make application with prior leave of the court, which will be granted if the court is satisfied that the result 'could not be achieved through the making of any order' which could be made otherwise than in the exercise of the inherent jurisdiction and which the local authority is entitled to apply for and there is 'reasonable cause to believe that if the court's inherent jurisdiction is not exercised with respect to the child he is likely to suffer significant harm.'[219] MacDonald J in *A City Council v. LS*[220] usefully explained the extent and limitations of the jurisdiction as follows:[221]

> The inherent jurisdiction with respect to children is exercised by reference to the child's best interests, which are the court's paramount concern. Whilst under its inherent jurisdiction, the court may make any order or determine any issue in respect of a child and whilst, therefore, the jurisdiction of the court under the inherent jurisdiction is theoretically unlimited, there are, in fact, far-reaching limitations on the exercise of the jurisdiction (see *Re X (A Minor) (Wardship: Restriction on Publication)* [1975] All ER 697 at 706G). The boundaries of the inherent jurisdiction, whilst malleable and moveable in response to changing societal values, are not unconstrained.

219 Children Act 1989, ss 100(4) and (5).
220 [2019] EWHC 1384.
221 Ibid, at paras 35-37.

> Prior to the implementation of the Children Act 1989, the most frequent example of the exercise by the High Court of its inherent jurisdiction over children was in wardship. However, wardship is only one manifestation of the inherent jurisdiction with respect to children. Subject to the distinguishing characteristics of wardship being that custody of the child is vested in the court and that, although day to day control is vested in the individual or local authority, no important step can be taken in the child's life without the court's consent, the jurisdiction in wardship and the inherent jurisdiction of the High Court are the same (see *Re Z (a minor) (freedom of publication)* [1997] Fam 1). In the circumstances, the inherent jurisdiction in respect of children can be invoked without the use of wardship (see *Re W (A Minor) (Medical Treatment: Court's Jurisdiction)* [1993] Fam 64). This is sometimes known, for convenience, as the 'residual' inherent jurisdiction of the High Court.
>
> Article 173 of the Children Order] imposes specific prohibitions on the use of the inherent jurisdiction where the applicant for relief under the inherent jurisdiction is a local authority.

However, as Keehan J stated in *Birmingham City Council v. Riaz*[222] 'none of the statutory or the "self-imposed limits" on the exercise of the jurisdiction prevent the court from making the orders sought by the local authority in this case'. It remains the case, as McFarlane J has pointed out, that 'a primary justification for the continued use of the inherent jurisdiction with respect to children in modern times is to provide protection for young people when their welfare demands it'.[223]

Recently, as mentioned above, the UKSC reviewed local authority use of wardship in *In the Matter of T (A Child)(Appellant)*[224] when it considered the question of whether it was a permissible exercise of the High Court's inherent jurisdiction to make an order authorising a local authority to deprive a child of his or her liberty and place the child in a facility not registered as secure accommodation. It concluded that there was nothing in s 100 that presented an obstacle to the local authority's application under the inherent jurisdiction.[225]

From time to time wardship orders are issued in a private family law context, most often in a context where a child's need for lifesaving medical treatment is being obstructed by a lack of consent.[226] In such circumstances – where a child under the age of 16 refuses his or her consent to such treatment – the courts have consistently over-ruled the child: either on the ground that the *Gillick* competence test had not been met;[227] or on the ground that even though the test was satisfied,

222 EWHC 4247 at para 46.

223 *In the Matter of T (A Child) (Appellant)* [2018] EWCA Civ 2136 at para 6.

224 [2021] UKSC 35.

225 Ibid at para 121.

226 See, for example, *Re KH (A Child)* [2012] EWHC B18 (Fam).

227 See, for example, *Re E (a minor) (wardship: medical treatment)*, [1993] 1 F.L.R. 386 (Fam. Div.); *Re S (a minor) (consent to medical treatment)*, [1994] 2 F.L.R. 1065 (Fam. Div.); *Re L (medical treatment: Gillick competency)*, [1998] 2 F.L.R. 810 (Fam. Div.).

the court in applying the welfare principle determined that treatment was in the child's best interests.[228]

Court orders

In all public and private family law proceedings, the judiciary now have both a legislative duty to consider the full range of orders available and a discretion to choose – the order, or combination of orders, or no order – most appropriate to further the welfare interests of the child concerned and to do so expeditiously. This is provided for in s 1(6) of the 2002 Act in reference to the powers and orders under both that legislation and the 1989 Act. The 'no-delay' and the 'no-order' principles are further reinforced by s 109 which requires a timetable to be drawn up and specified steps taken to expedite it. These provisions build in a wide ambit of flexibility and discretion enabling the court to tailor outcomes to address welfare interests in a way not formerly available. It must also consider the bearing of Article 8 of the ECHR and related rulings of the ECtHR.[229]

Parental responsibility order

Available under s 4A of the 1989 Act (as inserted by the 2002 Act), this order may be made in favour of a step-parent – married to the birth parent – as an alternative to the more informal means of acquiring parental responsibility through agreement with the birth parent/s and provides for an ongoing sharing of parental responsibilities with them. It also provides the means whereby an unmarried father, who is unable or unwilling to acquire parental responsibility for his child by making a voluntary agreement with the mother, may be vested with such responsibility by the court, or may acquire it as a consequence of being issued with a child arrangements order, a special guardianship order, or through adoption. It also now similarly provides for someone who is registered as a parent under the Human Fertilisation and Embryology Act 2008.

The making of an order is clearly a matter of judicial discretion to be exercised according to the welfare interests of the child concerned. The order vests parental responsibility in the bearer; though not necessarily to the exclusion of others. It lasts until terminated by the court on the application of any person with parental responsibility or, with the leave of the court, the application of the child concerned. The court has decided[230] that where the following tests are satisfied then it would *prima facie* be in the child's best interests for a parental responsibility order to be made: (a) the degree of commitment which the father had shown to the child; (b) the degree of attachment which existed between them;

228 See, for example, *Re M (medical treatment: consent)*, [1999] 2 F.L.R. 1097 (Fam. Div.).
229 Particularly the judgments in *K and T v. Finland* (2001) 36 EHRR 255, *R and H v. United Kingdom* (2012) 54 EHRR 2, [2011] 2 FLR 1236, and *YC v. United Kingdom* (2012) 55 EHRR 967.
230 See *Re H (Illegitimate Children: Father: Parental Rights) (No 2)* [1991] 1 FLR 214.

and (c) the reasons of the father for applying for the order.[231] Where a father has been previously convicted of violence against the mother and of cruel behaviour towards the child[232] or where he is in prison and there is little evidence of attachment[233] then the court will refuse his application.

In terms of the welfare interests of a child, this order has the clear advantage over adoption in that it does not remove parental responsibility from the other birth parent and does not legally separate the child from the family of the other birth parent.

Child arrangements order

Available under s 12 of the 1989 Act (as amended by s 114 of the 2002 Act), this order – a combination of the previous residence and contact orders – may be made in favour of any person who is not a parent or guardian of the child concerned and may continue until the latter attains adulthood. The court has a power, under s 10(1)(b) of the 1989 Act, to intervene and on its own initiative make a s 8 order in 'any family proceedings in which a question arises with respect to the welfare of a child.' Before making a child arrangements order it must apply the welfare checklist, the 'no order' principle, and the presumption that a parent's involvement will further the child's welfare. In theory this provides a powerful safety net to ensure that private law proceedings are concluded in a manner compatible with the welfare interests of the children involved. However, the opportunity for such intervention is dependent upon information being placed before the court alerting it to the existence of grounds for concern regarding welfare matters. This may not happen, if for no other reason than that it will delay proceedings.

Even the full formal divorce process offers no guarantee that the court will scrutinise care arrangements for children. Under s 41 of the Matrimonial Causes Act 1973[234] (as substituted by the Children Act 1989, Sched 12, para 31) the court is prevented from making a final order for divorce, nullity, or separation unless satisfied that: there are no children of the family, or; the arrangements for the welfare of the children that have been made, are satisfactory or are the best that can be made in the circumstances, or; it is impracticable for the party or parties appearing before the court to make any such arrangements for the children. Following the introduction in 2022 of the Divorce, Dissolution and Separation Act 2020, and the replacement of the fault based grounds with the simple 'irretrievable breakdown' declaration, the parties and the court are freed from the previous focus on 'laying blame' and able to concentrate dispassionately on the welfare interests of any children affected by the family breakdown.

231 This approach was later endorsed by the court in *Re G (A Minor) (Parental Responsibility Order)* [1994] 1 FLR 504.

232 As in *Re T (A Minor) (Parental Responsibility: Contact)* [1993] 2 FLR 450.

233 See *Re P (Parental Responsibility Order)* [1997] 2 FLR No 5.

234 Amended by the Divorce (Religious Marriages) Act 2002.

As before the 2020 Act, the court will initiate enquiries regarding the children only where a disclosure of information obviously calls into question the adequacy of proposed arrangements. If the court is able to make a finding of satisfaction it may then issue an order to that effect and need not be concerned about the possible bearing of the provisions available under the 1989 Act. The judge will usually only see the applicant's 'statement of arrangements for children.' As previously, this statement will frequently be perfunctory with few details and no means whereby the court can check the accuracy of the facts presented therein. Even where the facts give rise to some judicial disquiet in relation to proposed care arrangements, the no-order presumption of s 1(5) and the presumption that involvement of a birth parent in the life of the child concerned would further that child's welfare will militate against any initiative by the court to exercise its discretionary power under s 10(1)(b) to issue a s 8 order. There will very seldom be any opportunity for the court to hear the views of the children concerned.

Child consent order

This, an alternative to the above child arrangement order, is applicable in circumstances where the parents agree on living arrangements for their child but wish to convert that informal agreement into a formal legally binding document. It generally requires court confirmation, which will only be forthcoming if the court is satisfied that the arrangements are compliant with the welfare interests of the child concerned. It is not without irony that, despite its title, the one consent that is not legally necessary to obtain this order – is that of the child.

Placement order

The Adoption and Children Act 2002, s 21(1), enables a court to issue a placement order on the application of a local authority. This may be made: where 'the welfare of the child requires the consent to be dispensed with'; having had regard to the welfare checklist in s 1(4); the paramount consideration, under s 1(2), being the welfare of the child *throughout his life*. This crucial change to the law enables a local authority to promptly operationalise a decision that adoption offers the best means for promoting the welfare interests of a child in its care. The Court of Appeal[235] has stressed that the test for dispensing with parental agreement to the making of a placement order is whether the child's welfare requires adoption as opposed to something short of adoption; and whether the child's welfare throughout his life was the paramount consideration. In *LC (Placement Order)*[236] the Court of Appeal remained unconvinced and confirmed the decision of the

235 *SB v. A County Council; Re P* [2008] EWCA Civ 535. Also, see, *Re P (Placement Orders: Parental Consent)* [2008] EWCA Civ 535, [2008] 2 FLR 625, per Wall LJ at para 126.
236 [2020] EWCA Civ 787.

court at first instance that the child's strong ties with her two brothers and with her mother outweighed the welfare benefits of 'stranger' adoption.

Special guardianship order

The Children Act 1989, s 14C(I), as inserted by s 115 of the Adoption and Children Act 2002, provides that a named person may be appointed the 'special guardian' of a child and that such an order may be made by a judge on his or her own motion.[237] A further amendment introduced s 14(f) requiring local authorities to assess whether any of the parties were in need of support services. The legislative intent being that this order should be used to safeguard the welfare interests of a child in circumstances where an adoption order would be too draconian. It may be accompanied by a 'child arrangements' order or a prohibited steps order.

Wall LJ, noting that the legislation does not prescribe different sets of circumstances in which an SGO would be appropriate, stated that the White Paper gave the following helpful illustrations of some circumstances in which SGO's would be useful: where older children do not wish to be legally separated from their birth families; where a child is being cared for on a permanent basis by members of the child's wider family; where a child is from a particular ethnic or religious community and cultural difficulties make an adoption order less likely to be honoured; and where an unaccompanied asylum-seeking child needs a secure, permanent home, but maintains strong attachments to a family abroad.[238]

A special guardianship order does not provide a secure lifelong legal relationship between parents and child, nor does it grant inheritance or citizenship rights. It has been noted that

> it is a material feature of the special guardianship regime that it is 'less intrusive' than adoption ... it involves a less fundamental interference with existing legal relationships ... in some cases, the fact that the welfare objective can be achieved with less disruption of existing family relationships can properly be regarded as helping to tip the balance.[239]

Nonetheless, as Julie Doughty has pointed out 'the use of special guardianship has increased to the extent that more children now leave care under these orders than are adopted by non-kinship carers.'[240]

237 See, also, Special Guardianship Regulations 2005, SI 2005 No. 1109.

238 See *Re S (Special Guardianship Order)* [2007] EWCA Civ 54. See, also, *Re M-J* [2007] EWCA Civ 56.

239 *Re S (Adoption Order or Special Guardianship Order)* [2007] 1 FLR 819, at para 49.

240 Note to author: 21.05.2022.

Other

Arguably, a non-molestation order (prohibiting particular behaviour or general molestation), an occupation order (defining or regulating rights of occupation of the home), and an exclusion order (barring entry to the family home) are also hybrid orders, equally applicable to both private and public family law and play an important role in providing a safe, secure, environment that affords protection for a child's welfare interests. So, also, with secure accommodation orders which have applicability to children from both the youth justice and the care and protection systems.

Conclusion

This jurisdiction has seen a recalibration of family law to prioritise the welfare interests of children which, to that extent, has resulted in a degree of convergence between the public and private divisions. The convergence has been driven primarily by the pervasive statutory leverage of the paramountcy principle together with welfare 'checklists' and a range of 'across the board' court orders functionally tailored to address specific issues. It is a trend most starkly represented by the bridging of child protection and adoption proceedings. Overall coherence has been greatly assisted by the restructuring of the court system from which the Family Court and CAFCASS have emerged, which has provided an opportunity to build expertise focused on children, regardless of which particular set of family law proceedings give rise to issues regarding their welfare interests and rights.

6 Ireland

Introduction

As the current *Taoiseach* Micheál Martin once remarked, "the concept of the child as a separate individual with rights came late to this country."[1]

Family law in Ireland, perhaps in particular as it relates to children, remained relatively static throughout most of the twentieth century. This, in large part, was due to the tenacious hold of the Constitution on all family matters and the widespread acceptance of that state of affairs as signifying an appropriate affirmation of national culture. By the latter decades of that century, however, the family and social mores generally were rapidly changing in Ireland as elsewhere, and the tensions were such that a wave of constitutional amendments began to clear the way for legislative adaptations to realign family law with contemporary social issues. New legislation was necessarily influenced, if not benchmarked against, the principles established by the ECHR, of which Ireland was an original signatory nation.[2] The consequences – for family law and for the welfare interests of children – of Ireland becoming a member state of the EU and being signatory to a raft of international treaties, conventions, and protocols (see, further, Chapter 4) have been, and continue to be, transformative.

This chapter unfolds in much the same way as its predecessor. Beginning with a brief overview of the policy, principles, and practice that shaped the law relating to children in the latter half of the twentieth century, it then outlines the national and international framework of legislation and courts most relevant to children's welfare interests and rights. It considers such welfare/rights in the context of the core fundamental human rights before going on to do so in relation to contemporary law and practice by examining: first, public family law, civil and criminal; second, the private sector; and finally how such welfare/rights are increasingly crosscutting both sectors. The greater part of the chapter is concerned

1 See, Arnold, B., *The Irish Gulag*, Gill & Macmillan, Dublin 2009, at p 4, citing Micheál Martin as so stating on 13 May 1999.

2 Though not until the introduction of the European Convention on Human Rights Act 2003 was the ECHR actually formally incorporated into Ireland's domestic law.

DOI: 10.4324/9781003268642-10

with identifying and analysing key cases in order to track and trace how judicial interpretation of children's welfare interests and rights has evolved in Ireland.

Policy, principles, legislation, and the legal system

The law and policy relating to children has been modernised within a relatively brief period. By a process that has involved acceptance of key ECHR and UN CRC principles and an almost continuous programme of constitutional amendments, Ireland has leapfrogged from a largely inherited nineteenth-century legislative platform to one that – though still patchy – is now comparable to that of any modern western nation. The court system, however, as it relates to children, has in the main escaped modernisation.

Policy

State policy for safeguarding the welfare interests of Irish children was set by the First Dáil on 21 January 1919. In a proclamation that placed those interests at the heart of its aspirations, it declared:[3]

> It shall be the first duty of the Government of the Republic to make provision for the physical, mental and spiritual well-being of the children, to secure that no child shall suffer hunger or cold from lack of food, clothing, or shelter, but that all shall be provided with the means and facilities requisite for their proper education and training as Citizens of a Free and Gaelic Ireland.

The experience throughout the following century – as detailed in many official reports – provide a record of the extent of the state's shortfall in achieving its laudable aspirations.[4]

For most of the twentieth century, it was the Children's Act 1908 that provided the legal framework for implementing government policy. That legislation, essentially a legacy from the Poor Laws era, designated responsibility for the care, maintenance, and housing of children – whether abandoned, in need of protection, or out of control – to religious organisations, in practice the Catholic Church, which established a national network of government funded Industrial and Reformatory residential school facilities. These provided containment,

3 See, further, at: www.oireachtas.ie/en/visit-and-learn/history-and-buildings/history-of-parliament-in-ireland/.

4 See, for example: Justice Eileen Kennedy, 'Report on Industrial Schools and Reformatories' (the 'Kennedy Report'), Dublin, the Stationery Office, 1970; inquiry into the allegations of clerical sexual abuse in the Roman Catholic Diocese of Ferns in County Wexford (the 'Ferns Report'); the Commission to Inquire into Child Abuse (the 'Ryan Report'), 2009; and the Department of Justice and Equality, *Report by the Commission of Investigation into Catholic Archdiocese of Dublin* (the 'Murphy Report'), 2009; and Mother and Baby Homes Commission of Investigation, *Fifth Interim Report* (March 2019).

discipline, and a rudimentary form of education and training. Not until 1970, with the publication of the Kennedy Report[5] and its revelations of the systemic abuse to which many thousands of children had been subjected, did government policy begin to consider alternatives to institutional care, to question the appropriateness of religious organisations as caregivers for children, and to establish national Health Boards to take over responsibility for child health and welfare. The European Committee of Social Rights (ECSR) has noted the failure to implement 'safeguarding policies and procedures in practice" as well as a "culture of silence around issues of childhood sexual abuse and exploitation in Ireland.'[6]

Public family law relating to children: civil jurisdiction

The principles governing the state/family relationship are as set out in the Constitution, as subsequently judicially interpreted. Under Article 40.3.1, 'the State guarantees in its laws to respect and as far as practicable by its laws to defend and vindicate the personal rights of the citizen.' Article 40, as Hardiman J stated in *N v. H.S.E.*[7] is "one of the great bulwarks of personal liberty and of a free society." Further, as O'Higgins CJ pointed out in *G v. An Bord Uchtála*,[8] the child also had natural rights which must be equally protected and vindicated by the state. Hamilton CJ, in *D.G. v. Eastern Health Board*,[9] added that no one could with impunity set these rights at naught or circumvent them and the court's powers in this regard were as ample as the defence of the constitution required.

Until 2015 and the introduction of Article 42A into the Constitution (see, further, below), Article 42.5 provided that

> [i]n exceptional cases, where the parents for physical and moral reasons fail in their duty towards their children, the state as guardian of the common good, by appropriate means shall endeavour to supply the place of the parents, but always with due regard for the natural and imprescriptible rights of the child.

The balancing of parental failure and the 'rights' of the child (then a concept that lacked substance) by the state 'as guardian of the common good' was thus, from the outset and for many generations, the established axis around which rotated the public family law relating to children.[10]

In the latter half of the twentieth century, considerable economic and other social changes occurred in this country as elsewhere in the western world, leading

5 See the 'Kennedy report,' ibid.

6 European Committee of Social Rights, *Conclusions 2019: Ireland*, at: https://rm.coe.int/rapport-irl- en/16809cfbc0.

7 [2006] 4 IR 374 at p 534.

8 [1980] IR 32 at p 55.

9 [1998] ILRM 241, citing O'Dalaigh CJ in *The State (Quinn) v. Ryan* [1965] IR 70 at p 122.

10 See, for example, Nolan, A., 'The Battle(s) over Children's Rights in the Irish Constitution', *Irish Political Studies*, Vol 22, No 4, 2007, at pp 495–516.

to a loosening of the legal relationship between family and state. This was to prove more challenging in Ireland due to a deeply embedded Catholic morality, reinforced by the Constitution, which nurtured a culture adverse to any interference with traditional religious values centred on the marital family unit, on stereotype gender roles, and on church/state control of sexuality. However, an increased awareness of the prevalence of child abuse in Ireland was being generated by reports from the Committee on Non-Accidental Injury, the Law Reform Commission report on Child Sexual Abuse,[11] academic research,[12] and some high-profile media coverage of court cases.[13]

In a first response to the growing level of public and professional concern, the government introduced the Child Care Act 1991.[14] This formative piece of legislation, arguably, owed a great deal to the protracted policy debates which had presaged the introduction of the Children Act 1989 in the neighbouring island two years earlier.

The prevention/protection balance

The Child Care Act 1991 introduced several fundamental themes that laid the statutory foundations of modern Irish childcare policy, intended to reduce the reliance on constitutional provisions, and established the basic principles determining the balance to be struck between prevention and protection as grounds for state intervention.

First, legal responsibility for ensuring the health and welfare of children in general, but particularly those in need of care and protection, was statutorily vested in a national government body, the Health Boards. The guiding principle for their role in that respect was, as stated in s 3, that 'it is generally in the best interests of a child to be brought up in his own family' while s 3(1) placed upon them a specific duty to promote the welfare interests of those children not receiving adequate care and protection. The remit of the Health Boards included a duty to identify children at risk of being failed by parental care and to provide the supportive services necessary to prevent the need for alternative care arrangements. Unfortunately, as was demonstrated in cases such as *D. G.* v. *Eastern Health Board & Ors.*[15] (see, further, below), this duty was unaccompanied by the funding necessary to allow the relevant bodies to provide the supportive services needed for preventative intervention to fulfil its potential.

11 Law Reform Commission, 'Report on Child Sexual Abuse', Dublin, 1990.

12 Gilligan, R., *Irish Child Care Services: Policy, Practice and Provision*, Dublin, Institute of Public Administration, 1991.

13 McGuinness, C., 'Report of the Kilkenny Incest Investigation', Dublin, the Stationery Office, 1993.

14 See, further, Buckley, H., Skehill, C., and O'Sullivan, E., *Child Protection Services in Ireland*, Oak Tree Press, Dublin, 1997, at: www.lenus.ie/bitstream/handle/10147/250811/ChildProtectionPracticesinIrelandaCaseStudy.pdf?sequence=1.

15 [1997] 3 IR 511.

Second, under s 4 of the 1991 Act, parents had the right to voluntarily place their child into state care to relieve family stress in circumstances of parental death, illness, etc. and the Health Board had a corresponding duty to accept and to return the child at parental request. This important concession to parental rights – and an acknowledgement of the state duty to safeguard the welfare of children – is indicative of a strong consensual theme in the state/family relationship, and continued to underpin Irish childcare policy until somewhat overtaken in recent years by child protection concerns.

Third, under s 20 of the 1991 Act, the courts as ultimate arbiters in balancing the welfare interests of children against parental rights, were granted new powers. In cases of contested custody, the relevant Health Board would be required to appoint a social worker to undertake an independent assessment and report their findings to the court.

Foster care

Dating back to at least the Irish Poor Law Amendment Act 1862, which enabled young children who would previously have been consigned to the workhouse to instead be 'boarded-out' with state approved caring families, foster care has long been relied upon as the preferred setting for children needing alternative accommodation.

The Child Care Act 1991, s 4, states:

> nothing in this section shall authorise (the Health Service Executive) to take a child into its care without the wishes of a parent having custody of him or of any other person acting in *loco parentis* or to maintain him in its care under this section if that parent or any such person wishes to resume care of him.

This provision anchored childcare services on a long-term family support basis: where parental care was compromised by difficult circumstances (e.g. parental illness) then the welfare interests of any children involved could be safeguarded by respite care with foster parents. In addition, foster care was the preferential placement choice in respect of children the subject of care orders.

Kinship care

Kinship care has a long history in Ireland. A thousand years ago, under the Brehon laws, this well established practice enabled members of a child's extended family or clan to rear him or her as a means of binding the clan group into a stronger more cohesive unit. Much the same ends were achieved by reciprocal placements of children between clans as a demonstration of mutual allegiance. More recently, under the Irish Poor Law Amendment Act 1862, kinship fostering – where a family would take in its own rather than let, or be seen to let, relatives go to the workhouse – was both common and encouraged by the Poor Law authorities.[16] This continued to be accepted practice under the statutes of 1908 and 1991, and into contemporary times.

Adoption from state care

Adoption as a statutory process began – late relative to other nations – on 1 January 1954 when the Adoption Act 1952 came into effect. This was a time when the social stigma associated with the role of a single mother was acutely felt in Catholic Ireland and resulted in considerable pressure on those in that position to surrender their children for adoption. It was an era when government in Ireland – perhaps more so than elsewhere – colluded with religious bodies to provide residential care for pregnant unmarried women and girls as a precursor to the 'enforced' adoption of their babies. Countless mothers, as depicted in the film 'Philomena,'[17] were induced to relinquish babies that were then 'trafficked' for adoption overseas – at least 2,000 going to Catholic adopters in the U.S.[18] The still unfolding scandal of the role played by the Catholic Church agency St Patrick's Guild in the 1960s – when hundreds of birth certificates and baptismal records were fraudulently altered to permit the illegal adoption of Irish infants in the U.S. – provides one indicator of the scale of church abetted trafficking that occurred in that era.[19] Unmarried mothers were then viewed as a threat to marriage and the family, institutions venerated and assured of protection in the Constitution, to public morality, and more generally to the integrity of civic values jointly upheld by church and state.[20] An 'illegitimate' child was treated by the state as *sui juris* (outside the law) and by the church as 'lost to God.' Consequently, by far the majority of non-marital births resulted in adoptions; as was the case with some 96.9 per cent of such births in 1967.

16 See O'Halloran, .K., *The Politics of Adoption* (4th ed.), Springer, 2021 at p 290. Also, Eekelaar, J., *Family Law and Social Policy*, 1984.

17 See the 2013 Oscar-nominated film 'Philomena,' about an Irish mother forced to give up her son for adoption. Ms Philomena Lee, a teenager in 1952, was consigned to the care of Catholic nuns in Ireland after she became pregnant and, like an estimated 60,000 other young Irish women, had her baby removed and adopted and was thereafter required to repent for the shame of having had an 'out-of-wedlock' child.

18 In February 2014, a report by the UN Committee on the Rights of the Child urged the Vatican to conduct an investigation into the Magdalene laundries. At least one priest facilitating the U.S. adoptions of Irish children was later found to have been a paedophile.

19 See, further, O'Rourke, M., et al, 'CLANN: Ireland's Unmarried Mothers and their Children: Gathering the Data: Principal Submission to the Commission of Investigation into Mother and Baby Homes' Dublin: Justice For Magdalenes Research, Adoption Rights Alliance, Hogan Lovells, 2018. It would seem probable that that as many as 150,000 Irish adoptions might need to be investigated to determine the scale of this human rights abuse, see, further, at: www.nytimes.com/2018/05/30/world/europe/ireland-illegal-adoptions-apology.html.

20 See, for example, Redmond, P., *The Adoption Machine: The Dark History of Ireland's Mother & Baby Homes*, Merrion Press, Dublin, 2018.

Paradoxically, given the above record of government collusion with religious organisations to divert into the adoption process those children who would otherwise have been admitted to the public care system, adoption from that system has not subsequently been an actively pursued policy objective (perhaps, a wholly understandable reaction to the earlier misuse of that process). To the extent that legislators and the judiciary resisted, for many decades, allowing adoption to be available for children failed by parental care – particularly when the parents were married – government policy, arguably, constrained the welfare interests of those children thereby excluded from consideration for that option (see, further, below).

Residential care

This form of care is tarnished with a well-documented history of abuse by the religious orders that provided government funded accommodation: for single women and their children; and for children and youths deemed by the courts to be out of parental control. In the former instance, this is now a matter of official record following the 2021 publication of the Commission of Investigation into Mother and Baby Homes established by the Irish Government in 2015 to provide a full account of what happened in such facilities during the period 1922 to 1998.[21] It was an era that included the disgrace of the 'Magdalene laundries,'[22] the proliferation of private nursing homes in which very many babies died, to be buried in unmarked graves,[23] and from which many others were spirited away to new homes overseas.[24]

Industrial schools and reformatories were established in the late nineteenth century – under the Industrial Schools Act 1888 and the Reformatory Schools (Ireland) Act 1858 – for orphans/abandoned children and for those convicted of criminal offences, respectively. This form of residential care earned the comment from a government commissioned inquiry in 1960 that 'the Child Care system has evolved in a haphazard and amateurish way and has not altered radically down

21 See, further, at: www.gov.ie/en/publication/d693a-report-of-the-confidential-committee-to-the-commission-of-investigation-into-mother-and-baby-homes-october-2020/.

22 In June 2013, the Irish government offered a public apology – and agreed to pay €34.5 million in compensation – for the years of unpaid labour and public shame endured by the estimated 770 survivors of more than 10,000 young mothers who lived in a dozen such facilities from the 1920s to 1996.

23 See Harrington, K., 'New BBC series to look at Irish mothers forced to give up their babies', *The Irish Post*, which reports that the bodies of some 800 babies and infants were found in one burial pit at one mother and baby home in Tuam. See, further, at: www.irishpost.co.uk/news/philomena-journalist-lands-new-bbc-series-irelands-lost-babies.

24 See Milotte, M., *Banished Babies: The Secret History of Ireland's Baby Export Business*, New Island Press, 2014.

the years.'[25] It was also a system that perpetrated systemic child abuse.[26] As the ISPCC pointed out:[27]

> the most striking feature of the child care scene in Ireland was the alarming complacency and indifference of both the general public and various government departments and statutory bodies responsible for the welfare of children. This state of affairs illustrated clearly the use by a society of residential establishments to divest itself of responsibility for deprived children and delinquent children.

Not until the 1970s did residential care services for children cease to be provided by voluntary organisations, most often the Catholic Church, and become the Health Boards' responsibility. Finally, the Child Care Act 1991, s 69, introduced regulations for the registration, monitoring, and inspection of residential facilities for children.[28]

Public family law relating to children: criminal jurisdiction

In Ireland the law relating to the criminal offences of children is still largely to be found in vestiges of British colonial law including: the Criminal Law Amendment Act 1885 and the Guardianship of Infants Act 1886, which are still in effect; the Probation of Offenders Act 1907 which also continues to operate; and the Children's Act 1908, now repealed.[29] It was a regime that entailed a reliance on the Children Act 1908, and the institutional network of state funded reformatories or industrial schools run by Catholic organisations, which continued well into the second half of the twentieth century.

The justice/welfare balance

Given that the *doli incapax* rule – with its legal presumption that children aged between 7 and 14 years of age lacked the capacity to understand the consequences of their actions and were therefore exempt from criminal liability – continued until repealed by the Criminal Justice Act 2006, it is unsurprising that a welfare oriented approach to the anti-social deeds of children in that age group prevailed throughout the twentieth century. Nonetheless, that approach allowed for court

25 The Kennedy Report, op cit.

26 See *Report of the Commission to Inquire into Child Abuse*, (the 'Ryan Report'), 2009 at: www.dcya.gov.ie/viewdoc.asp?fn=/documents/Child_Welfare_Protection/RyanImplementation.htm. Also, see, the 'Murphy Report' at: www.justice.ie/en/JELR/Pages/PB09000504.

27 Irish Society for the Prevention of Cruelty to Children report, *A Task Force on Child Care Services*, 1980 at p 182.

28 See the National Standards for Residential Care.

29 See for example, Sargent, P., *Wild Arabs and Savages: A History of Juvenile Justice in Ireland*, Manchester University Press, 2013.

hearings in adult courts and for the incarceration of children in industrial schools located far from, and generally inaccessible to, their families of origin. In practice, and in the absence of any genuinely therapeutic or rehabilitative facilities, the justice/welfare balance in the Irish state response towards the criminal activities of children, in the twentieth century, always tended to prioritise criminal over civil law and lean towards justice and punishment.

Private family law relating to children

Article 41.2 of the Constitution declares:–

1. In particular, the State recognises that by her life within the home, woman gives to the State a support without which the common good cannot be achieved.
2. The State shall, therefore, endeavour to ensure that mothers shall not be obliged by economic necessity to engage in labour to the neglect of their duties in the home.

Such traditional gender stereotyping, particularly in relation to the maternal role, provided a constitutionally enshrined frame of reference that for generations impeded any gender parity aspirations. Article 41.2.2, which places a positive – if uncertain – obligation on the state to 'endeavour to ensure that mothers shall not be obliged by economic necessity to engage in labour' outside the home, has attracted a degree of judicial endorsement: as in *Sinott v. Ireland*[30] when Denham J described it as "a recognition of the work performed by women in the home." This constitutional exhortation might be interpreted as conducive to supporting the welfare interests of children. However, in the absence of any government policy or legislative initiative indicative of an intention to so 'endeavour,' the clause would seem wholly redundant.

Matrimonial

The Irish family unit, as envisaged in the Constitution, is one based on marriage though not necessarily dependent upon the presence of children of that marriage.[31] For several generations, this constitutional affirmation of marriage as the appropriate framework for family life – in accordance with Catholic Church values and beliefs – was wholly endorsed by the majority of citizens. It set public policy parameters for alternative relationships, and for managing family breakdown: cohabitation being neither socially acceptable nor providing any mutuality of legal rights for the parties involved; and single mothers being denied state welfare benefits until the 1970s when their circumstances were transformed by

30 [2001] IESC 63.
31 *Murray v. Ireland* [1985] IR 532, 537.

government provision of an unmarried woman's allowance and preferential status for public housing.

Until the introduction of the Family Law (Divorce) Act 1996, family breakdown – and by far the majority of the families concerned were marital – was resolved through separation (by legal proceedings if not by agreement) under the provisions of the Family Law (Maintenance of Spouses and Children) Act 1976, which provided six separate grounds for obtaining a separation decree, as eventually replaced by the Judicial Separation & Family Law Reform Act 1989. Annullment – on grounds of either non-consummation or inability to enter into and sustain a full marital relationship – provided an alternative and often more socially acceptable legal route for terminating a marital relationship. Other grounds which rendered a marriage voidable included: impotence; failure to satisfy legal requirements; absence of consent; mental incapacity; duress; intimidation; and mistake. Under canon law a marriage could be annulled due to lack of capacity, for example involving homosexuality, fraud or emotional immaturity.[32] In short, for most of the twentieth century, the welfare interests of the many children outside the constitutionally approved marital family unit – or trapped within it, victims of their parents' unhappy marital relationship – were insecure and relatively disadvantaged. Currently, the Family Law Act 2019 (amending the 1996 Act) provides three essential criteria for divorce: living apart for more than two out of the previous three years; no reasonable prospect of reconciliation; and appropriate arrangements having been made for the other spouse and for any dependents. The 2019 Act also made some changes to judicial separations: there is now an entitlement to a judicial separation, with or without the consent of the other spouse, if living apart for one year.

The post-family breakdown arrangements for the children concerned were legally addressed through the traditional court orders for guardianship, custody, access, and child maintenance which had not changed significantly since the Custody of Infants Act 1873.

Guardianship and wardship

These ancient common law procedures were developed in feudal England, subsequently recognised as applicable in Ireland,[33] and assimilated into Irish law following independence.

Guardianship entrusted a legally appointed guardian with the custody and maintenance of a child, including the right to make decisions as to their religious and secular education, health, and general welfare. Traditionally it functioned at the heart of private family law alongside the right to custody.

Wardship proceedings, initiated in respect of an adult or child, in practice were mostly undertaken in relation to adults with mental incapacity; when used

32 Canon 1095 of the revised Code of Canon Law 1983.

33 See, for example, *In Re Mesdes, Minors* (1871) 51 IR Eq 98.

in relation to a minor this has usually been in order to protect their property rather than their welfare interests.[34] The wardship jurisdiction is judicially acknowledged to derive from the *parens patriae* powers of the Sovereign, then exercised by the Lord Chancellor[35] until transferred to the High Court under the Supreme Court of Judicature Act (Ireland) 1877. It has been described as 'special' or 'unique' and as 'set … in a place apart.'[36] It encompasses and is much broader than the statutory powers available under either guardianship or child care legislation.[37] There is some unresolved debate as to whether *parens patriae* powers could have survived the birth of an independent state and adoption of the Constitution: Finlay CJ would seem to have been of the view that such powers were absorbed by the Constitution and are now to be found in Article 40.3.2.[38] Although there is no doubt as to its discretionary nature,[39] wardship has not attracted the same intensity of use as it did in England where for some years it became an alternative to statutory proceedings – mainly in public family law – as it offered an immediate, expedient, and flexible mechanism for social workers and judiciary to manage complex child care issues.

Adoption

Adoption in Ireland has been, and very largely remains, a consensual process. The latter part of the twentieth century was a period when adoption changed from being a means of regulating the non-kinship placements of voluntarily relinquished illegitimate babies and became more a means of sanctioning the private family arrangements of birth parents, almost always mothers, in respect of their own children. By the early decades of the twenty-first century the adoption process, governed by the Adoption Act 2010, mainly attracted step-parent, foster parent, and intercountry applicants; whereas in 1960 it was comprised almost entirely of third party applicants adopting voluntarily relinquished infants.

Intercountry adoption

Social changes in Ireland in the 1980s led to the introduction of the Foreign Adoption Acts 1991–1998 and facilitated the adoption of many children, originally largely from Romania and Russia, although countries such as Guatemala,

34 See *Re J.S. (An Infant)* [1976] 111 ILTR 146.

35 *Re a Ward of Court (Withholding Medical Treatment) (No. 2)* [1996] 2 IR 79 and *J.M. v. Board of Management of St Vincent's Hospital* [2003] 1 IR 321.

36 *Eastern Health Board v. M.K.* [1999] 2 IR 99, per Denham J at paras 110 and 111.

37 As Geoffrey Shannon points out, the wardship jurisdiction will be re-defined to some extent when the Assisted Decision Making (Capacity) Act 2015 takes effect in June 2022 (note to author: 25.05.2022).

38 *Re D* [1987] IR 449.

39 See, for example, *Re D*, ibid, per Finlay CJ at p 456 and *A.M. v. HSE* [2019] IESC 3 per MacMenamin J at para 30.

China, Thailand, Belarus, the Philippines, and India have also at times been popular.[40] In recent years ICA has been proportionately more significant in Ireland than in neighbouring jurisdictions.[41] This may well be due to the relative difficulty in adopting from the public care system in Ireland: the jurisdictional difference in recourse to ICA may be seen as a measure of the corresponding benefit to the welfare interests of adoptable children in domestic public care. Although, as Geoffrey Shannon points out, there was a sharp decline in ICA in Ireland 'following the ratification of the 1993 Hague Convention in the Adoption Act 2010.'[42]

Family planning, abortion, surrogacy, IVF, etc.

Family planning has only very relatively recently become a genuine reality for Irish women: helped by the introduction of abortion services, however limited (as of 2021, nine of the nation's 19 hospitals did not provide such procedures), and by improved and more accessible contraceptives.[43] Ireland is one of six out of 43 European countries that have failed to introduce specific legislative provisions to regulate assisted reproduction techniques.[44] Donor assisted human reproduction (DAHR) services are accessed by married couples – including female couples – and by single women but are fraught with legal complications.[45] The introduction of the Children and Family Relationships Act 2015[46] has contributed to improving the situation: although not all relevant provisions have yet been activated. As yet there is no specific legislation governing surrogacy[47] which has led to the CRC expressing concern that insufficient attention is being given 'to the rights and interests of children born as a result of assisted reproduction technologies.'[48] It remains the case that under the Guardianship of Infants Acts 1964 to 1997 (pending activation of relevant provisions in the Children and Family Relationships Act 2015) the mother of any child born outside marriage is in law that child's sole guardian (see, further, below).

40 See the website at www.hse.ie/eng/Find_a_Service/Children_and_Family_Services/Adoption_and_Tracing/Intercountry_adoption/.

41 For example, in 2004 the Adoption Board made 648 adoption orders, of which 375 (58 per cent) were entries in the Register of Foreign Adoptions; a high rate of foreign adoptions by international standards.

42 Note to author: 25.05.2022.

43 *McGee v. Attorney General* [1974] IR 284.

44 See, further, at: www.eurekalert.org/pub_releases/2020-02/esoh-emt020320.php.

45 See, for example, *Roche v. Roche* [2010] 2 IR 321.

46 See, also, the Children and Family Relationships (Amendment) Bill 2018 and the General Scheme of the Assisted Human Reproduction Bill.

47 See, further, at: www.citizensinformation.ie/en/birth_family_relationships/adoption_and_fostering/surrogacy.html.

48 UN Committee on the Rights of the Child, Concluding Observations of the Committee on the Combined Third and Fourth Periodic Reports of Ireland, 2016, at para 33.

Principles

It was the 'children's referendum' in 2012 – an iconic moment in Irish law relating to children – that marked the point at which Ireland, perhaps in a spirit of atonement for the litany of reports documenting church/state complicity in historical child abuse, resolved to establish a constitutionally embedded threshold of children's rights as the best means of ensuring future legal protection for their welfare interests. The outcome of this, the 31st Amendment to the Constitution, resulted in the replacement of Article 42.5 with Article 42A and was finally given legislative effect in 2015. It sought to reset the core principles of family law around a new central focus on children's welfare/rights.

The paramountcy principle

Article 42A, among other things, declared that 'the State recognises and affirms the natural and imprescriptible rights of all children and shall, as far as practicable, by its laws protect and vindicate those rights.' It goes on, in Article 42A.4.1(ii), to assert the principle that 'the best interests of the child shall be the paramount consideration' in application to public law proceedings relating to the 'safety and welfare of any child' and private law proceedings 'concerning the adoption, guardianship or custody of, or access to, any child.' While this provision now serves to counterbalance those that have traditionally given constitutional primacy to parental rights and to the *locus standi* of 'the family' it leaves open to question the point at which the paramountcy principle comes into play. The constitutional amendment achieves a balancing of principles but leaves to statute law and the judiciary the tricky bit of translating this into functionality.[49]

Paramountcy: child consent

There is no requirement in any Irish legislation for a child's consent on a matter affecting his or her welfare. Nonetheless, the consent of a child aged 16 or over will most usually be sought in respect of a surgical, medical, or dental procedure.

Paramountcy: extension to adoption and other matters

The requirement that a child's welfare must be the paramount consideration in any decision taken regarding his or her upbringing was first statutorily stated in the Guardianship Act 1964 but has always been judicially applied by the High Court in wardship proceedings. In recent years, following its constitutional recognition, this principle is now incorporated into: the Adoption Act 2010, s 19; the Children First Act 2015, s 7; the Children and Family Relationships Act 2015, s

49 See, further, Aspell, J., 'Children's Best Interests? A Constitutional Question', *Trinity College Law Review*, (2018), at: https://trinitycollegelawreview.org/childrens-best-interests/#_ftnref21.

45; and the Adoption (Amendment) Act 2017, s 9. Nonetheless, in 2016 the CRC registered its concern that 'the right of the child to have his or her best interests taken as a primary consideration has yet to be fully implemented as a positive obligation in all relevant legislation and administrative procedures and decision-making processes.'[50]

The principle of parental rights/responsibilities

The constitutional guarantees in Articles 41 and 42 that the state would protect 'the inalienable and imprescriptible rights' of the family and the 'inalienable right and duty of parents' set the legal context for relationships between state and family for several generations. These clauses, together with the recognition given to the family as 'the primary and fundamental group of society,' placed the state on a footing of respectful support for the marital family and established constraints on its readiness to coercively intervene on grounds of child protection. The effect of such a constitutional preferencing of family unity was alluded to in the Kilkenny Incest Investigation which noted that 'the very high emphasis on the right of the family in the Constitution may consciously or unconsciously be interpreted as giving a higher value to the rights of parents than to the rights of children.'[51] Article 42A was a legislative attempt to reconcile the inherent conflict between the constitutional assurances that the state would ensure the integrity and autonomy of the family unit and the provisions of the Child Care Act 1991 which required state bodies to intervene in families when put on notice that a child was in need of protection.

However, although Article 42A replaced Article 42.5 it left in place Articles 41 and 42.1–42.4 together with the case law and ethos which had established and continues to assert the state's special protection for the status of parents and family. As the legislators chose to retain these basic constitutional building blocks of family law and the associated body of jurisprudence, the paramountcy principle is now left to function alongside entrenched conservative precedents. Much now depends on the introduction of the legislation necessary to give effect to Article 42A and on how the judiciary interpret and balance what are competing constitutional principles.

Parental responsibility and corporal punishment

The common law parental right to administer 'reasonable chastisement' – recognised in the Children Act 2004, s 58 – was repealed in 2015. While such chastisement is no longer permitted it will only constitute an offence if it causes actual

50 UN Committee on the Rights of the Child, Concluding Observations of the Committee on the Combined Third and Fourth Periodic Reports of Ireland, 2016, at para 29.

51 McGuinness, C., 'Report of the Kilkenny Incest Investigation', Dublin, the Stationery Office, 1993.

harm under the Offences against the Person Act 1861, ss 18 and 20, or amounts to cruelty under the Children and Young Persons Act 1933, s 1.

Marital and non-marital families

Irish law, complying with constitutional precepts, traditionally differentiated between the *locus standi* of marital and non-marital families and between the corresponding responsibilities of married and unmarried parents. The distinction was highlighted in *The State (Nicolaou) v. An Bord Uchtála*[52] when the IESC found that Article 41 applied only to marital families: unmarried parents were unable to rely on the 'inalienable and imprescriptible rights' vested in parents by Article 41.1. As Henchy J then trenchantly proclaimed

> for the state to award equal constitutional protection to the family founded on marriage and to the "family" founded on an extramarital union would in effect be a disregard of the pledge … in Article 41.3.1 to guard with special care the institution of marriage.

The Guardianship of Infants Act 1964, s 61, has long provided that spouses are joint guardians of their child, thereby establishing that both parents are jointly and equally entitled to rights of custody and required to share the duties of parental responsibility. In contrast, s 6(4), for many decades declared unambiguously that an unmarried mother was to be regarded in law as the sole guardian of her child. The legal complexities resulting from these provisions – and the accompanying minimal judicial regard for developing a focus on the welfare interests of the children involved – were illustrated in several cases but perhaps highlighted in the pivotal 'Baby Ann' case.[53] This concerned a baby relinquished for adoption by her unmarried parents within a week of her birth and four months later placed with a married couple, the prospective adopters, with whom she formed a close attachment and where she remained for almost two years. Her parents subsequently married and initiated proceedings for her return which were ultimately heard by the IESC. The marital status of the birth parents then became the determining factor. The court found no evidence of sufficient 'compelling reasons' and/or of 'a physical or moral failure of the parents' – as required under the above-mentioned Article 42.5 – such as would warrant depriving them of custody of their child. Fennelly J – holding that she be returned to the birth parents – referred to a "primordial constitutional principle that a child's welfare is best served in the heart of its natural family. It is well established and widely known."[54] Had the birth

52 [1966] IR 567. See, also, *G v. An Bord Uchtála* [1980] IR 32.

53 *N v. HSE* [2006] 4 IR 375 and *Re JH* [1985] IR 375, similar facts and similarly decided. See, also, *M v. An Bord Uchtála* [1975] IR 81.

54 *N v. HSE*, op cit at p 592.

parents remained unmarried, however, the court would not then have found in favour of such a family.

This distinction between marital and non-marital families, and the children thereof – at least in a private family law adoption context – was ostensibly addressed by the insertion of Article 42A.2.2 which states that

> provision shall be made by law for the adoption of any child where the parents have failed for such a period of time as may be prescribed by law in their duty towards the child and where the best interests of the child so require.

However, given as mentioned above that Articles 41 and 42.1–42.4 remain in place, it is again uncertain how this additional constitutional provision will work in conjunction with established principles such as the 'inalienable right' of parents (see, further, below).

Unmarried father

Traditionally the legal presumption was that an unmarried mother was the sole guardian of her child. As Finlay CJ stated in *Keegan*, "although there may be rights of interest or concern arising from the blood link between the father and the child, no constitutional right to guardianship in the father of the child exists."[55] However, the law has since been amended allowing the father to become a guardian of their child if: the mother makes a legal declaration to that effect; or the father is so appointed by the court under s 6A of the 1964 Act (as amended); or, when s 49 of the Children and Family Relationships Act 2015 takes effect (inserting ss 6B and 6F into the 1964 Act) and automatically vesting the father with guardianship if he has cohabited with the mother for at least 12 months, 3 being post-birth.

Sharing parental responsibilities

The Constitution enshrines the principle of state respect for the integrity and autonomy of the family, requiring it to exercise a benign influence on family life. Arguably, from the time of independence, there has been a legal presumption that the state had a duty to maintain the special status of the family and to direct such resources as may be needed to ensure that families functioned as 'the primary and fundamental group of society.' To that extent, the law relating to the responsibilities for the welfare interests of children developed from a different baseline in Ireland in comparison with England and Wales.

55 See *Keegan v. Ireland*, 16/1993/411/490, Council of Europe: European Court of Human Rights, at para 12.

Consanguinity principle

In *N. v. HSE*[56] as in *J. McD. v. P.L. and B.M.*,[57] the court stressed the importance of blood or genetic links between a parent and child and intimated, at the very least, that these relationships or links were of paramount importance in deciding parenthood.[58] In the latter case it was stated that "the blood-link, as a matter of almost universal experience, exerts a powerful influence on people."[59] Subsequently, in *M.R. and D.R. & Others v. An t-Ard- Chlaraitheoir & Others*,[60] the IESC reaffirmed the principle (*mater semper certa est*) that the birth mother is the legal mother of a child (see, further, below).

Proportionality principle

Since the implementation of the European Convention on Human Rights Act 2003 the Irish courts have been required, under s 2, to interpret and apply statutory law in a manner compatible with ECHR provisions and with due cognisance of ECtHR rulings, which may also inform interpretation of constitutional rights. Over the past several decades, the principle of proportionality has played a prominent role in ECtHR jurisprudence.

The principle in the Irish courts

The proportionality principle was probably first referenced by Costello J in *Heaney v. Ireland*[61] which, as subsequently restated in the IRSC, essentially declared that the means used in any legislative provision must be proportionate to the aim sought to be achieved, they must:[62]

(a) be rationally connected to the objective and not be arbitrary, unfair or based on irrational considerations;
(b) impair the right as little as possible; and
(c) be such that their effects on rights are proportional to the objective.

This formulation of the proportionality test has been consistently referred to ever since,[63] across a range of different areas of law[64] and is currently most frequently

56 [2006] 1 I.R. 374.

57 [2008] 1 I.R. 417.

58 See, also, *Roche v. Roche*, [2010] 2 I.R. 321 when the Supreme Court considered whether a frozen embryo could constitute an 'unborn' within the meaning of Article 40.3.3.

59 Op cit, at para 81.

60 [2014] IESC 60.

61 [1994] 3 IR 593.

62 *In Re Article 26 and the Employment Equality Bill 1996* [1997] 2 I.R. 321.

63 See Brady, A., '*Meadows* and proportionality in judicial review – Where are we now?' at: www.lawlibrary.ie/News/CPD-JR-Update-Alan-DP-Brady-27-Feb-2017.aspx.

64 *The State (Keegan) v. Stardust Compensation Tribunal* [1986] I.R. 642, and *O'Keeffe v. An Bord Pleanála* [1993] 1 I.R.

deployed in deportation cases.[65] Most recently, *In the Matter of JJ (Unapproved),* the IESC noted that "Article 42A requires that the means by which the place of the parents is supplied by the state should be proportionate."[66]

In reference to the need to ensure that a statutory discretionary power is exercised constitutionally, it has been explained that this "in turn means that the court must act proportionately with regard to the particular transgression in respect of which sanction is being sought."[67]

Legal system: legislation, courts, welfare/ rights, and representation

From a structural perspective, the framework of legislation and courts, the responsibilities of various agencies and the role played by the parties involved are crucial to determining the welfare interests of any child subject to legal proceedings.

Legislative framework

The overshadowing influence of the Constitution on evolving family law legislation in Ireland has been profound. In recent decades this has been offset, to some extent, by case law benchmarks emerging from the ECtHR, particularly in relation to Article 8 of the ECHR.

International law

The main constituent parts of this framework are as in England and Wales (see, further, Chapters 4 and 5). Of particular importance are the United Nations Convention on the Rights of the Child 1989,[68] and the European Convention for the Protection of Human Rights and Fundamental Freedoms 1950. The latter was given effect by the European Convention on Human Rights Act 2003.[69] Other international treaties, conventions, and protocols[70] and certain EU Directives[71] are also relevant, including the Brussels II Regulation (see, further, Chapter 4).

65 *Meadows v. the Minister for Justice, Equality and Law Reform* [2010] 2 I.R. 701.

66 [2021] IESC 1, at para 177(xiii).

67 *Wicklow County Council v. Kinsella* [2015] IEHC 229, per Kearns P citing *Meadows*, op cit.

68 In Ireland the United Nations Convention on the Rights of the Child (UN CRC) is given effect by the National Children's Strategy, launched in 2000, responsibility for the implementation of which rests with the National Children's Office. However, although ratified, this Convention has not yet been incorporated into domestic law. See, further, Horgan, 'The United Nations Convention on the Rights of the Child and Irish Family Law' (1991) 9 ILT 162.

69 This became part of Irish law on 31 December 2003.

70 In particular: the UN Convention on the Elimination of all forms of Discrimination Against Women (CEDAW) with its Optional Protocol; and the International Convention on the Elimination of Race Discrimination (ICERD).

71 See, in particular, the Equal Pay Directive (75/117/EEC), the Equal Treatment Directive (76/207/EEC), and the General Framework Directive (2000/78/EC).

These, together with decisions of the ECtHR, the UN HR Committee and the European Court of Justice are applied, or referred to, as required to align domestic law with that of the EU.

Constitution and domestic legislation

Bunreacht na hÉireann, the Irish Constitution, was enacted by parliament – the *Oireachtas* – in 1937. Articles 40–4 specifically provide protection for fundamental rights: Article 41.1.1 'recognises the Family as the natural primary and fundamental unit group of Society, and as a moral institution possessing inalienable and imprescriptible rights, antecedent and superior to all positive law,' and guarantees its protection by the state. These constitutional assurances of recognition and protection for the special status conferred on the 'family' imply that the welfare interests of children should be protected and promoted in that setting.

- Article 42A

In 2015, in a development marking an important milestone for the evolving welfare interests and rights of a child, the above provisions were counterbalanced by the insertion of Article 42A:

---

1 The State recognises and affirms the natural and imprescriptible rights of all children and shall, as far as practicable, by its laws protect and vindicate those rights.

2 1° In exceptional cases, where the parents, regardless of their marital status, fail in their duty towards their children to such extent that the safety or welfare of any of their children is likely to be prejudicially affected, the State as guardian of the common good shall, by proportionate means as provided by law, endeavour to supply the place of the parents, but always with due regard for the natural and imprescriptible rights of the child.
2° Provision shall be made by law for the adoption of any child where the parents have failed for such a period of time as may be prescribed by law in their duty towards the child and where the best interests of the child so require.

3 Provision shall be made by law for the voluntary placement for adoption and the adoption of any child.

4 1° Provision shall be made by law that in the resolution of all proceedings—
  i brought by the State, as guardian of the common good, for the purpose of preventing the safety and welfare of any child from being prejudicially affected, or
  ii concerning the adoption, guardianship or custody of, or access to, any child,
  the best interests of the child shall be the paramount consideration.
2° Provision shall be made by law for securing, as far as practicable, that in all proceedings referred to in subsection 1° of this section in respect of any child who is capable of forming his or her own views, the views of the child shall be ascertained and given due weight having regard to the age and maturity of the child.

It should be noted, however, that the all-important Article 42A.4 – embodying the paramountcy principle and the requirement to ascertain and take account of a child's wishes – is not a freestanding constitutional right, but only a requirement to legislate.

- Family Law Act 2019

Introduced after the 38th Amendment of the Constitution, this legislation reduced the waiting time for divorce.

- Adoption (Amendment) Act 2017

This amendment brought about a number of key changes to domestic adoptions, including: recognising the best interests of the child as the most important consideration in any adoption application; removing a restriction on the adoption of children born to married parents or who were adopted previously; allowing couples living together in a civil partnership or co-habiting to adopt; and establishing separate provisions for step-parent adoptions.

- Children First Act 2015

This legislation was fully enacted in December 2017. The Children First Guidelines from 2011 have been updated to the Children First National Guidance for the Protection and Welfare of Children 2017. Together they require every 'relevant organisation' to ensure that children are safe from harm while using their services. Under this statute, the Department of Justice and all associated agencies are also required to safeguard children from harm. Section 14 imposes a mandatory duty to report knowledge of actual or suspected child abuse:

> (1). : ... where a mandated person knows, believes or has reasonable grounds to suspect, on the basis of information that he or she has received, acquired or becomes aware of in the course of his or her employment or profession as such a mandated person, that a child
>
> (a) has been harmed,
> (b) is being harmed, or
> (c) is at risk of being harmed, he or she shall, as soon as practicable, report that knowledge, belief or suspicion, as the case may be, to the Agency.

- Child Care (Amendment) Act 2015

This repeals provisions permitting the detention of children in adult prison facilities and provides for aftercare plans to assist those being discharged from state care. It also provides for the inspection of premises in which it is proposed to provide early years service.

- Children and Family Relationships Act 2015

This legislation, following on from the children's rights referendum in 2012, effected some significant changes to the law relating to children. For example, it gave the courts the power to make orders for procuring two types of report: one relating to an expert determining and conveying a child's views on family law matters; the other where a court orders an expert to procure a report on any question affecting the welfare of a child. It introduced guardianship as an alternative to adoption for stepparents, enabled a wider range of unmarried fathers to become guardians of their child automatically, and extended the range of other persons entitled to become guardians. It also imposed more onerous requirements on the Adoption Authority in respect of birth father consultation. cohabiting couples, who have lived together for three years, and civil partners can be considered for adoption. Application must be made to the District Court. In addition, there are provisions relating to surrogacy arrangements.

- Irish Human Rights and Equality Commission Act 2014

Established the Irish Human Rights and Equality Commission and introduced a positive duty on public bodies regarding human rights and equality.

- Child and Family Agency Act 2013

This established Tusla, the national government agency (successor to the Health Boards) with statutory responsibilities for the health and welfare of children, to consolidate and manage services relating to child protection, family support, and education welfare.

- Adoption Act 2010

The 2010 Act repealed and replaced the 1952 Act (the 'principal Act') together with its subsequent amending statutes (in 1964, 1974, 1976, 1988, 1991, and 1998) and together with the ancillary Adoption Rules they now constitute the core domestic legislative framework for adoption law. This has been since been supplemented by further legislation: the Adoption Act 2010 (Revised)[72] which consolidates all Acts up to and including the Judicial Council Act 2019.[73]

- European Convention on Human Rights Act 2003[74]

This legislation partially incorporates the European Convention, together with several of its Protocols, into domestic law. Irish courts are consequently instructed in s 2, that:

> in interpreting and applying any statutory provision or rule of law, a court shall, in so far as is possible, subject to the rules of law relating to such

72 Number 21 of 2010. See, further, at: http://revisedacts.lawreform.ie/eli/2010/act/21/front/revised/en/html.

73 (33/2019), enacted 23 July 2019.

74 (Commencement) Order 2003 (S.I. No. 483 of 2003).

interpretation and application, do so in a manner compatible with the State's obligations under the Convention provisions.[75]

Further, in s 4, it is required that 'judicial notice' be taken of the Convention provisions and of judgments of the ECtHR or any decision of the Committee of Ministers established under the Statute of the Council of Europe on any question in respect of which it has jurisdiction; and they must also, when interpreting and applying the Convention provisions, take due account of the principles laid down in such judgments or decisions.

- Children Act 2001

This legislation deals with the protection, care, and control of children including provision for family welfare conferences. It replaces the Children Act 1908, together with other acts relating to juvenile offenders, and it amends the Child Care Act 1991.

- The Child Trafficking and Pornography Act 1998

Described as an Act to prohibit trafficking in, or the use of, children for the purposes of their sexual exploitation and the production, dissemination, handling, or possession of child pornography, and to provide for related matters.

- Family Law (Divorce) Act 1996

As the title suggests, this statute makes provision for the courts to grant decrees of divorce and enables them to make certain preliminary and ancillary orders in or after proceedings for divorce, regarding transfers of property and other related matters.

- Family Law Act 1995

Where marriages are annulled, or the spouses become judicially separated, this legislation enables the courts to make such orders, regarding maintenance and related matters, as may be necessary.

- Child Care Acts 1991–2011

Since amended by the Child and Family Agency Act 2013, this legislation imposes on Tusla – the Child and Family Agency – a statutory duty to promote the welfare of children who are not receiving adequate care and protection. It states as

75 See *Foy v. An t-Ard Chlaraitheoir & Others* [2007] IEHC 470 when a declaration of incompatibility was made concerning the lack of legal recognition for transgender people under Irish law.

fundamental principles that: it is generally in the best interests of the child to be brought up in their own family; having regard to the rights and duties of the parents, the welfare of the child is the first and paramount consideration; and, as far as is practicable, the wishes of the child should be considered.

- Judicial Separation and Family Law Reform Act 1989

Provision for judicial separation was first introduced by this Act, together with ancillary relief orders. It was subsequently amended and enhanced by the Family Law Act 1995.

- The Status of Children Act 1987

The rights and status of all children were equalised for the purposes of Irish law by this statute. It abolished all residual distinctions between 'legitimate' and 'illegitimate' children that had survived the Legitimacy Act 1931, and amended the Guardianship of Infants Act 1964 to permit an unmarried father to be appointed guardian of his child with maternal consent.

- The Guardianship of Infants Act 1964

This Act, amended in 1997, sets out the legal position of married and unmarried parents in relation to guardianship, custody, and access to children. It was further amended and extended by the Children and Family Relationships Act 2015.

- Other

The Criminal Justice (Victims of Crime) Act 2017 requires state authorities to mitigate the trauma of the criminal justice process for victims of crime, including children, by providing support and specialist services, using video link, and excluding the public from hearings where appropriate. The currently pending Child Care (Amendment) Bill 2019 contains proposals for reform of the law governing guardians *ad litem* (GALs) which will strengthen the rights of a child to be heard in child care proceedings.

The Irish government has a ministerial department dedicated to children-related matters – the Department of Children and Youth Affairs (DCYA) – led by the Children's Minister.

Courts and regulatory framework

The Irish court system, as it relates to children, has not been modernised and currently functions in a manner non-compliant with contemporary standards of child welfare. In 2016, the CRC expressed concern 'that judges in family law cases are not provided with systematic training for dealing with cases concerning children and that there are long delays in such cases, to the detriment of the children involved.'[76] Indeed a recent survey of international practice noted that Ireland was the only jurisdiction identified in which child care proceedings are held in a general, non-specialist court, which the report described as an 'outlier of poor practice.'[77]

International courts

Ireland, unlike England and Wales, is to continue its EU membership for the foreseeable future and will therefore continue to accept the superior appellate jurisdiction of the ECJ and the ECtHR as well as remaining accountable to various international committees for progressing the implementation of convention provisions.

- The European Court of Human Rights (ECtHR)

The ECtHR, initially established in 1959 (permanently in 1998) and replacing the European Commission of Human Rights in 1998, hears complaints alleging that one of the 47 member states has violated rights enshrined in the Convention and its protocols. Under s 4 of the European Convention on Human Rights Act 2003 'judicial notice' is required to be taken of ECtHR judgments. In making its determinations, the court is guided by principles such as: 'proportionality' and 'compatibility with democracy.'[78] Its decisions are reached in the light of 'a margin of appreciation' which permits states a degree of latitude in their interpretation of human rights obligations.[79]

Other international fora

The relevance of European and other international fora for Irish affairs is much the same as for England and Wales. For present purposes, the European Court of Justice (CJEU), the UN Committee on the Rights of the Child, and various other committees and Special Rapporteurs established by their respective international

76 UN Committee on the Rights of the Child, Concluding Observations of the Committee on the Combined Third and Fourth Periodic Reports of Ireland, 2016, at para 41.

77 See Corbett, M. and Coulter, C., *Child Care Proceedings: A Thematic Review of Irish and International Practice* (Department of Children and Youth Affairs, 2019), as cited in Annual Report of the Special Rapporteur on Child Protection 2020 at p 144. See, further, at: www.gov.ie/pdf/?file =https://assets.gov.ie/27780/ a770243297774574af9171c5226fdf74.pdf#page=1.

78 See *Refah Partisi v. Turkey* (2003) 37 EHRR 1, [2003] ECHR 87 when the ECtHR ruled that Shar'ia law is not consistent with democracy and therefore the Turkish government was justified in banning a political party seeking to introduce such law.

79 See, for example, *Lithgow v. United Kingdom* (1986) 8 EHRR 329, *Fredin v. Sweden* (1991) 13 EHRR 784, *Abdulaziz, Cabales and Balkandali v. United Kingdom* (1985) 7 EHRR 471.

treaties and conventions to monitor implementation, will have intermittent relevance.

Domestic courts

The District court is the main 'workhorse' of the court system as it relates to children and is generic in nature, processing all manner of first tier proceedings – such as licensing and petty criminal offences; as it relates to children it is designated the Children Court and deals with both civil and criminal issues.

- The District Court

This court is required to deal with maintenance, guardianship, custody, access, domestic violence, and other applications. The volume and range of cases has given rise to concern

> for example, in one court on one day, in a District where there was just one sitting judge, there were 139 cases listed, consisting of crime, general civil law, family law and child care. This clearly poses considerable difficulties in dealing appropriately with cases that could be difficult, like child care.[80]

When sitting as the Children Court, it deals with all charges against children in respect of minor offences and may deal with an indictable offence where the child consents.

- The Circuit Family Court

The bulk of family law cases are processed through the Circuit Family Court. An appeal against an order of the Circuit Family Court lies to the High Court and from there to the High Court, to the Court of Appeal, or to the Supreme Court on a point of law or in the context of cases of constitutional or European significance. It is also possible to refer to the European Court of Justice (ECJ) on an issue surrounding the interpretation of European law.

The Children Court and criminal proceedings

Children charged with criminal offences are subject to legal processes governed by the Children Act 2001, as amended by the Criminal Justice Act 2006, the Children (Amendment) Act 2015, and to a lesser extent by other legislation. The

80 See Coulter, C., *District Court Child Care Proceedings: A National Overview* (March 2019), at p 1, at: www.childlawproject.ie/wp-content/uploads/2019/03/CCLRP-regional-report-2019_fINAL.pdf.

Irish Youth Justice Service, established in December 2005, requires that children alleged to have committed a crime be brought before the Children Court.[81]

Representation for children

The UN CRC, Article 12(2), provides that

> the child shall in particular be provided the opportunity to be heard in any judicial and administrative proceedings affecting the child, either directly, or through a representative of an appropriate body, in a manner consistent with the procedural rules of national law.

This right is imperfectly realised in the Irish legal system. In 2016 the CRC expressed its concern that 'under the Children and Family Relationships Act 2015, parents must bear the cost of an expert to hear the views of the child in family law proceedings.'[82]

Representation of child welfare/rights in court

The Joint Oireachtas Committee on Justice and Equality *Report on Reform of the Family Law System* found that "the right of the child to be heard is not being adequately fulfilled—with inadequate facilities, legislative gaps, adversarial proceedings and a lack of appropriately trained staff all proving to be major barriers to upholding the constitutional obligation" as set down in Article 42A.4.[83]

- Consent/views of the child

Article 42A established a constitutional duty, resting on the court, to ascertain the views of children, though for some years there had been a recognition that under Article 40.3 children had a procedural right to be heard in cases affecting them.[84] More recently, Baker J in *A O'D v. Judge Constantine G O'Leary*[85] concluded that a child has a right to have "decisions made in regard to its guardianship and custody taken in the interests of its welfare [as] a personal right of the child

81 See, further, Kilkelly, U., 'Youth Courts and Children's Rights: The Irish Experience', *Youth Justice*, Vol 8, No 1, 2008, at pp 39–56.

82 UN Committee on the Rights of the Child, Concluding Observations of the Committee on the Combined Third and Fourth Periodic Reports of Ireland, 2016, at para 31.

83 See the joint Oireachtas Committee on Justice and Equality, *Report on Reform of the Family Law System* (October 2019) at p 32, at: https://data.oireachtas.ie/ie/oireachtas/committee/dail/32/joint_committee_on_justice_and_equality/ reports/2019/2019-10-24_report-on-reform-of-the-family-law-system_en.pdf.

84 See *FN v. CO* [2004] 4 I.R. 311, per Finlay Geoghegan J at p 322.

85 [2016] IEHC 555.

within the meaning of Article 40.3 of the Constitution"[86] and that the provisions of Article 42A "must be seen as enhancing the rights of the child."[87] In fact the courts have a solid record of defending the right of a child to be heard on matters affecting their welfare. So, for example, when deciding to hear from a six-year-old child, Finlay Geoghegan J stressed that "anyone who has had contact with normal six year olds knows that they are capable of forming their own views about many matters of direct relevance to them in their ordinary everyday life."[88] In *UA v. UTN*,[89] the court was strongly influenced by a clear and cogent desire expressed by boys aged seven and nine years old to stay with their mother and refused to order their return to their jurisdiction of habitual residence. In *RP v. SD*,[90] a child of four years and eleven months of average maturity was found *prima facie* not to be of an age where she was capable of forming her own views in relation to relevant matters. Nonetheless, the Special Rapporteur reports that in relation to child protection cases under the Child Care Act 1991, "the evidence suggests that the tendency to date has often been to not ascertain the views of children until closer to adolescence."[91] He also notes the intention to insert a new s 24A into the 1991 Act, which would impose a general duty on courts in child care proceedings to ascertain the views of the child; a requirement which falls well short of granting a child any right to contribute to decision-making.

- Paramount weighting of child's welfare interests

The Child Care (Amendment) Bill 2021 proposes to insert a new s 24 into the Child Care Act 1991 to provide that, in proceedings under the Act, the court shall regard the best interests of the child as the paramount consideration. It sets out a non-exhaustive list of seven factors to be taken into account in determining what is in the best interests of the child including 'the child's age, maturity and any special characteristics of the child,' and 'the views of the child where he or she has chosen to express such views.'

- Representing a child's welfare/rights

The Child Care Act 1991, in its present form, makes the representation of a child's welfare/rights a forced choice: either by a GAL or by a solicitor.

Section 24 of the 1991 Act requires that a court, 'in so far as is practicable, give due consideration, having regard to his age and understanding, to the wishes of the child,' but it provides only two mechanisms to achieve this: under s 25, it may make the child a party to proceedings (in which case a solicitor will be appointed

86 Ibid, at [89].
87 Ibid, at [90].
88 *N v. N* [2008] IEHC 382.
89 [2011] IESC 39.
90 [2012] IEHC 188.
91 Annual Report of the Special Rapporteur on Child Protection 2020, op cit, at p 92.

for the child); or alternatively, under s 26, a GAL may be appointed to report to the court on the child's views and best interests.[92] Essentially, this amounts to a discretionary power, rather than a duty, confining the appointment of a solicitor to the court and leaving the GAL to otherwise act as the child's representative. The Special Rapporteur suggests that

> the evidence to date is that the power to appoint a solicitor to represent the child is rarely used, while the rates at which GALs are appointed varies widely: appointments are commonplace in some districts and infrequent in others, creating something of a postcode lottery for children.[93]

The role of a GAL, while neither legislatively defined nor the subject of regulatory clarification, has been judicially described as: consisting of a dual responsibility, reporting to the court on the child's views and on the child's best interests;[94] and as 'the best way of ensuring that there is an independent voice in court to convey the views of the child and articulate submissions on his behalf';[95] further, that 'the GAL would look at the case in its entirety and not merely act as a conduit for the child's voice, although of course that is an essential part of the GAL's role.'[96] The Child Care (Amendment) Bill 2021 proposes to clarify, consolidate, and extend the role of the GAL as child advocate in care and protection proceedings and to provide a GAL with an entitlement, in certain circumstances, to legal representation. A new s 35B(5), will oblige District Court judges who decide not to appoint a GAL to give reasons for this decision; and where the court is satisfied that a child is capable of forming his or her own views in the proceedings, to determine the means by which to facilitate the expression by the child of those views. A new s 35H will permit dual representation by a GAL and a solicitor in child care and protection proceedings; but, again, at judicial discretion. A new s 35E will essentially restate in fuller form the earlier judicial interpretation of a GAL's responsibilities with an additional requirement to represent a child's interests in proceedings. Moreover, further changes will see a GAL service established as a government funded body, independent of all other agencies. Cumulatively, these statutory changes to the role of the GAL will significantly advance the representation of a child's welfare interests in court.

- Welfare interests in public and private proceedings

In Ireland these are two distinctly separate sets of proceedings. In those which are private, the judicial power to appoint a GAL or other expert to ascertain and

92 See, further, *AO'D v. Judge Constantine O'Leary* [2016] IEHC 555, per Baker J at [41]–[46].

93 Report of the Special Rapporteur, op cit at p 93.

94 See *Health Services Executive v. DK* [2007] IEHC 488, per MacMenamin J at (59).

95 See *DH v. Child and Family Agency (Role of Child and GAL in Judicial Review)* [2019] IEHC 459 at [41].

96 Ibid, at [42].

represent a child's welfare interests, is currently discretionary with consequent uncertainty as to how those interests are to be ascertained and represented when such an appointment is not made.[97] This may constitute a lacuna that evades the constitutional obligation of Article 42A and risks non-compliance with the UN CRC.[98]

Of particular note is the fact that the statutory specification of matters held to be indicators of welfare interests, to be considered in any judicial determination, will differ in both sets: in private proceedings there are 11 such indicators;[99] but there are only 7 in public proceedings.[100] The Special Rapporteur has criticised the omission of two specific requirements – to consider the history of the child's upbringing and care, including the nature of relevant care relationship and the respective capacities of applicants to care for and meet the needs of the child – asserting that both are equally important in care and protection proceedings.[101]

Other domestic fora

In recent years a number of government agencies and voluntary advocacy organisations have emerged in Ireland. These include the following.

- Irish Human Rights Commission

Established under the Irish Human Rights and Equality Commission Act 2014, the functions of this independent public body include appearing as *amicus curiae* on behalf of children in the High Court and the Supreme Court. It has done so in some important cases such as *C v. Cork University Hospital and Ors*[102] and *In the Matter of JJ*.[103]

- Ombudsman for Children

Established under the Ombudsman for Children Act 2002, as amended, this official is supported by the Ombudsman for Children's Office to promote and monitor the rights and welfare of children and to investigate complaints made by children, or on their behalf, in relation to the administrative actions, or inactions, of public bodies, schools, and voluntary hospitals, where an action complained of 'has or

97 Guardianship of Infants Act 1964, ss 31 and 32 (as inserted by Children and Family Relationships Act 2015, s 63).

98 UN Committee on the Rights of the Child, *General Comment No 12 (2009): The Right of the Child to be Heard*, UN Doc No CRC/C/GC/12, 20 July 2009 at [35].

99 Guardianship of Infants Act 1964, s 31(2)(b), as inserted by Children and Family Relationships Act 2015, s 63.

100 The Child Care (Amendment) Bill 2021, s 7(2).

101 Annual Report of the Special Rapporteur on Child Protection 2020, op cit, at p 94.

102 [2019] IESC 73.

103 [2021] IESC 1.

may have adversely affected' a child. The CRC has expressed concern regarding the independence of this body and in particular criticised the imposed constraints which prevent the Ombudsman from investigating the actions of public bodies in relation to immigrants and asylum seekers, including unaccompanied minors.[104]

- Special Rapporteur on Child Protection

This office was established following the Supreme Court Decision in May 2006 in *CC v. Ireland*,[105] which held that s 1(1) of the Criminal Law (Amendment) Act 1935, which made it an offence to have unlawful carnal knowledge of a girl aged under 15 years, was unconstitutional. The Rapporteur reviews and reports on specific national and international legal developments for the protection of children, examines the scope and application of specific existing or proposed legislative provisions, makes recommendations to government, and publishes an annual report.

The welfare principle in contemporary practice: public family law; civil jurisdiction

The embedding of the paramountcy principle in Article 42A of the Constitution, is considered to mark a significant turning point in public family law. There have, however, been judicial comments indicating that established values may yet prevail. In *PH v. Child and Family Agency*,[106] for example, Humphrey J commented approvingly on the presumption that marital families afforded the preferable setting for securing a child's welfare interests. On the other hand, McKechnie J more recently acknowledged that Article 42A has significantly lowered the bar for state intervention in circumstances where there has been parental failure endangers a child's safety and welfare.[107] It may be that the constitutional amendment has indeed reconfigured Irish family law around a new focus on child welfare interests, but perhaps this is largely confined to public law.

Prevention

In Ireland, the assumption of a benign state, supported by the pastoral care ethos of the Catholic Church, permeates the Constitution. It was reflected in a tradition of largely consensual modes of intervention in family matters and in the singular characteristic of Irish public family law that most children in state care are admitted with the voluntary agreement of their parents.

104 UN Committee on the Rights of the Child, Concluding Observations of the Committee on the Combined Third and Fourth Periodic Reports of Ireland, 2016, at para 19.

105 Report at: www.gov.ie/en/collection/51fc67-special-rapporteur-on-child-protection-reports/.

106 [2016] IEHC 106.

107 See *In the Matter of JJ* [2021] IESC 1.

State duties to support families in need

The Child Care Act 1991, as amended by the Child and Family Agency Act 2013 and in conjunction with ancillary regulations,[108] provide the current legislative framework of preventative, family support duties borne by public service bodies.

Service provision

Agency responsibilities begin with a duty 'to identify children who are not receiving adequate care and protection and co-ordinate information from all relevant sources relating to children in its area.'[109] The agency, under s 4 of the Child Care Act 1991, continues to offer voluntary care arrangements.[110] This service is most indicative of the consensual and supportive state/family relationship: the duty to take into its care any child requiring care and protection but not 'against the wishes of a parent' *nor* to maintain him or her in its care 'if that parent or any such person wishes to resume care.'[111]

In *PT and AHT v. Wicklow County Council*[112] the applicants sought to rely on the paramountcy principle in Article 42A in their attempt to require a public body to provide services for a child in need; a duty statutorily assigned to Tusla under s 5 of the 1991 Act. It was argued that by leaving a child at real and immediate risk of sleeping rough the County Council was failing to exercise its statutory function in accordance with Article 40.3 and Article 42A of the Constitution. The application was dismissed, the High Court found that there was no mandatory obligation on the Council to house children pursuant to Article 42A; though it could be argued that such a duty did arise under the Children First Act 2015. Conversely, in *POT v. CFA*,[113] the High Court found that a public body – now Tusla – had a duty, under Article 42A, to conduct a child sexual abuse investigation autonomously and expeditiously. Presumably, given that both public bodies had the same statutory duty to provide the services sought, and that for both that duty impacted on the welfare interests of a child, the difference in judicial rulings must rest on an interpretation of Article 42A as being confined to circumstances of direct parental failure; a moot point perhaps.

108 The Child Care Act 1991 (Early Years Services) Regulations 2016 (as amended).

109 Ibid, s 3(2)(a).

110 Around 55 per cent of admissions to state care in Ireland take place pursuant to voluntary care agreements. See, further, O'Mahony, C., Burns, K., and Brennan, R., 'Voluntary Care in Ireland Study (2018–21)' at: www.ucc.ie/en/appsoc/resconf/res/voluntarycareinirelandstudy2018-2021/.

111 Ibid, s 4.

112 [2017] IEHC 623.

113 [2016] IEHC 101.

State intervention: consensual

The Child Care Act 1991, s 3, as amended, states the rationale underpinning state consensual intervention in family matters:

(1) it shall be a function of the Agency [i.e. Tusla] to promote the welfare of children who are not receiving adequate care and protection.
(2) In the performance of this function, the Agency shall—
    (a) take such steps as it considers requisite to identify children who are not receiving adequate care and protection and co-ordinate information from all relevant sources relating to children in its area.

Tusla is required to be proactive in giving effect to that responsibility.

Specific support services

The Child Care Act 1991, s 3(3), states the general duty to 'provide child care and family support services' which is then followed by specific duties relating to voluntary care admission, accommodation for homeless children,[114] provision of an adoption service, arrangements for working with voluntary organisations, and a requirement to report 'on the adequacy of the child care and family support services available.'[115] Part VII of the Act governs the availability of pre-school services such as play groups, day nurseries, creches, and other day-care facilities many of which are grant-aided by health boards. It provides a regulatory regime to ensure maintenance of appropriate standards.

The preventative duties are stated in general terms: the responsibility now resting on Tusla is explicit but the methods for giving effect to it (with the exception of references to adoption, pre-school services, etc.) are largely left to agency discretion.[116]

- Children with disabilities

The Ombudsman for Children's Office has expressed concern about the lack of adequate respite services available for children overall and more specifically for children in care with disabilities.[117]

114 See Department of Housing, Planning and Local Government, annual *Homelessness Reports* which show that: in October 2019, 10,514 individuals were in emergency accommodation, of whom 3,826 were children; representing a 3 per cent increase in the number of children in emergency accommodation since October 2018; and a 24 per cent increase since December 2017. Also, see, the Joint Oireachtas Committee on Children and Youth Affairs *Report on the Impact of Homelessness on Children*, published in November 2019.

115 Ibid, s 8(1).

116 There is an absence of specified relevant services such as home help, parent training, or in-home creative child play and development programmes.

117 Ombudsman for Children's Office, *Molly Two Years On: Have Tusla and the HSE Delivered on Commitments to Children with a Disability in the Care of the State?* 2020, at p 5, at: www.oco.ie/app/uploads/2020/01/Molly-Two-Years-On.pdf.

- Traveller children

There can be little doubt that the children of the Traveller community suffer from multiple social disadvantages. Perhaps most importantly – because it is the gateway to opportunities in later life – they are marginalised in the national school system and tend to leave under-educated. Census data for 2016, for example, reveals that 57 per cent of Traveller men and 54 per cent of Traveller women left school with no formal qualifications, compared with 14 per cent and 12 per cent, respectively, in the general population.[118] The welfare interests of Traveller children are compromised in many respects but, as this report shows, much of the cultural distancing they experience flows from the initial experience of being made to feel unwelcome at school. In 2016, the CRC expressed concern regarding 'the structural discrimination against Traveller and Roma children and their families, including alleged impunity for publicly expressed discriminatory remarks by public representatives.'[119]

Promotion

Under the Child Care Act 1991, Part II, as amended by the Child and Family Agency Act 2013, Tusla has the statutory duty, as stated in s 3, 'to promote the welfare of children who are not receiving adequate care and protection.'[120] To some extent, it gives effect to this responsibility by working in collaboration with voluntary and community organisations – empowered to do so under ss 9 and 10 of the 1991 Act – to provide local sports, recreational, and other such programmes to engage young people.

Protection

The majority of the Child Care Act 1991 (Parts III, IV, and V) deals with coercive state intervention in family matters on behalf of children in need of protection, as reinforced by the National Standards for the Protection and Welfare of Children.[121] In 2001 the judiciary took the view that such intervention was only justified in circumstances where there was an immediate threat to the child's life;

118 See, further, the government sponsored report *Out of the Shadows*, at: www.gov.ie/en/policy-information/531ef5-co-ordination-of-traveller-education/#out-of-the-shadows-traveller-roma-education-voices-from-the-communities-published-november-2021.

119 UN Committee on the Rights of the Child, Concluding Observations of the Committee on the Combined Third and Fourth Periodic Reports of Ireland, 2016, at para 27.

120 Established in 2014, this government agency has statutory responsibility for child protection, children in care, adoption, early intervention, and family support services. See, further, at: www.tusla.ie.

121 The Health Information and Quality Authority, *National Standards for the Protection and Welfare of Children*, 2012, at: www.hiqa.ie/sites/default/files/2017-01/Child-Protection-Welfare-Standards_2.pdf.

an immediate threat of serious injury; or an immediate threat to the child's capacity to function as a human person.[122] However, the ECtHR in *O'Keefe v. Ireland*[123] found that threshold to be inadequate: the mere risk of abuse, rather than actual abuse, triggered a duty to intervene; and not to do so violated Article 3 of the ECHR. The Irish judicial view now is that Article 42A has lowered the bar to permit,[124] and indeed to require, state intervention at an early stage.[125]

State intervention: coercive

Determining whether the protection threshold has been breached, violating the welfare interests of a child, falls to the District Court – at least in the first instance – the generic jurisdiction of which accommodates a minority of child protection cases.[126]

Mandatory reporting

The Children First Act 2015 places a legal obligation on mandatory reporters – DSHS employees, law enforcement officers, social workers and professional school personnel – to report to Tusla any knowledge, belief or reasonable suspicion that a child has been harmed, is being harmed, or is at risk of being harmed.

Emergency care order

An Garda Síochána, when alerted to an immediate and serious risk to the health or welfare of a child, are empowered under s 12 of the 1991 Act to enter premises and remove him or her, by force if necessary, to a place of safety. The child is then delivered into the care of Tusla. Alternatively, Tusla may apply to court, under s 13, for an emergency care order in respect of a child at home or removed by the gardaí. The order permits Tusla to have care and control of the child for up to eight days or a shorter period if so specified in the order. These orders are most frequently sought in relation to babies.[127]

122 *North Western Health Board v. HW* [2001] 3 IR 622. Also, see, *MQ v. Gleeson* [1998] 4 IR 95.

123 Application No. 35810/09, (2014).

124 See, for example, *TR v. Child and Family Agency* [2017] IEHC 595.

125 See *In the Matter of JJ* [2021] IESC 1.

126 See, generally, Coulter, C., 'An Examination of Lengthy, Contested and Complex Child Protection Cases in the District Court', (2018), at: www.childlawproject.ie/wp-content/uploads/2018/06/CCLRP-Examination-of-Complex-Child-Protection-Cases-March-2018.pdf.

127 In 2017, of the 150 orders granted, 20 per cent were in respect of children less than 12 months old. See, further, at: www.irishtimes.com/news/social-affairs/more-emergency-care-orders-sought-for-babies-than-any-other-age-group-1.3822125.

Care proceeding

Care proceedings – for an emergency care order, a care order, or a supervision order – are commenced under the Child Care Act 1991, as amended by the Child and Family Agency Act 2015, and are heard in a District Court.

Care plan

The Rules of Court require a 'care plan' to be drawn up by the Child and Family Agency for submission to the court in advance of the first Case Management Hearing, and for circulation to the parents/guardians, the solicitors for the parents/guardians, and the Guardian *ad Litem*. The specification of a care plan is explicitly and extensively stated in Appendix 1.[128]

Care order

Under s 18 of the 1991 Act, the District Court may grant Tusla a care order where it is satisfied that:

(a) the child has been or is being assaulted, ill-treated, neglected or sexually abused, or
(b) the child's health, development or welfare has been or is being avoidably impaired or neglected, or
(c) the child's health, development or welfare is likely to be avoidably impaired or neglected,

and that the child requires care or protection which he is otherwise unlikely to receive. This tier of grounds constitutes a high threshold: there must be compelling reasons why the child's welfare cannot be secured within the family; being 'satisfied' requires more than having 'reasonable cause to believe,' the test for an interim care order. A care order entrusts a named child to the care of Tusla which will accommodate him or her most probably in foster care, but possibly in residential care or in a consensual adoption placement. The care order may be permanent – until the child reaches 18 years of age – or temporary.

Special care order

Under the Children Act 2001, s 16, and following a Tusla convened family welfare conference, the High Court may make a special care order if satisfied that: the child's behaviour poses a real and substantial risk to his/her health, safety, development, or welfare, and the child needs special care and protection which he/she

128 See, Case Management in Child Care Proceedings, at: https://www.courts.ie/content/case-management-child-care-proceedings.

is unlikely to get without such an order. The order commits the child to Tusla's care for as long as it remains in force and authorises that agency to provide appropriate care, education and treatment and, for that purpose, to detain the child in a special care unit. A 'special care order' generally subsists for –three to six months but may be extended, and can be varied by the court on its own initiative or by request of Tusla (see, further, below).

Supervision order

Under the Children Act 2001, s 19, the District Court may issue a supervision order where there are reasonable grounds for believing that a child: has been or is being assaulted, ill-treated, neglected, or sexually abused; or their health, development, or welfare has been or is likely to be avoidably impaired or neglected; and it is desirable that the child be visited periodically by Tusla. It enables a child to remain at home while giving Tusla the authority to visit and monitor their health and welfare and advise the parents as necessary. The court may give such directions as it sees fit as to the care of the child, which may require the parents of the child or a person acting *in loco parentis* to cause him to attend for medical or psychiatric examination, treatment, or assessment at a hospital, clinic, or other place specified by the court. A supervision order may be made instead of a care order or while waiting for a decision on a care order. Alternatively, Tusla may apply to the court for a supervision order instead of a care order. The order is for a fixed period of time up to a maximum of 12 months but may be renewed.

Interim orders

Under s 17 of the 1991 Act, the District Court may grant Tusla an interim care order where 'there is reasonable cause to believe that any of the circumstances mentioned at paragraph (a), (b) or (c) of section 18(1) exists or has existed' and that this 'is necessary for the protection of the child's health or welfare.' The order is valid for 28 days but extensions may be granted.

State care

A notable jurisdictional characteristic is that state care in Ireland has traditionally been provided mainly on a voluntary basis; which may sometimes last for years. Tusla statistics indicate that this continues to be the case: in 2014, 70 per cent of children in care were admitted pursuant to a voluntary agreement made under s 4 of the Child Care Act 1991; falling to 55 per cent in 2018.[129] It perhaps should be noted that because such children are not subject to statutory orders their cir-

129 See, further, O'Mahony, C., Burns, K., and Brennan, R., 'The Voluntary Care in Ireland Study: Key Findings and Recommendations for Law Reform and Social Work Practice in Ireland', *Irish Social Worker*, Winter 2020, at pp 7–16.

cumstances are not subject to guardian *ad litem* assessment – nor is the consent of an older child of any legal consequence – which may endanger their welfare interests and violate their rights under the UN CRC. The Special Rapporteur has recommended that "section 4 of the Child Care Act 1991 should be completely overhauled to provide for safeguards."[130]

Foster care: partnership, rehabilitation, and concurrent planning

As of 2020, there were approximately 6,000 children in care, of whom 91 per cent were in foster care, 7 per cent in a residential placement, and the remaining 2 per cent in other care placements. Because of the limited access to adoption for children from marital families, constrained by the 1988 Act, a far higher proportion of the Irish child care population remained in long-term foster care than was the case in other modern western jurisdictions. State care has not always proved safe for the children involved as illustrated, for example, by the eight case reviews held in 2019 in respect of children known to, or in contact with, Tusla who experienced serious abuse (one case) or who had died (seven cases – three through natural causes, three following tragic accidents, and one suicide).[131] Nor does state care provide a range of appropriate placements. As the CRC noted in 2016, there is an 'insufficient alternative care services for children with special needs, which has resulted in the need for such children to be accommodated in alternative care institutions outside the State party.'[132]

Foster care

Tusla is the sole national statutory foster care service provider with some 4,124 registered foster homes. Agency policy requires children to be placed, where possible, in foster care convenient to their family homes so as to facilitate ongoing parental contact, schooling, and friendships. Where possible this is achieved through kinship foster care.

The particular welfare needs of children with disabilities can be overlooked when they are in foster care, as was revealed in the report on *Molly's case* issued by the Ombudsman for Children in 2018.[133] The Special Rapporteur then commented:

> the report found that there was a lack of co-ordination between Tusla and the HSE which meant that services and supports provided by both organisations

130 Annual Report of the Special Rapporteur on Child Protection 2020, op cit, at p 84.

131 See reports published by the National Review Panel, as cited in the *Annual Report of the Special Rapporteur on Child Protection 2020*, op cit, at p 15.

132 UN Committee on the Rights of the Child, Concluding Observations of the Committee on the Combined Third and Fourth Periodic Reports of Ireland, 2016, at para 43.

133 See, Ombudsman for Children's Office, *Molly's case: How Tusla and the HSE Provided and Coordinated Supports for a Child with a Disability in the Care of the State* 2018, at: www.oco.ie/app/uploads/2018/01/OCO-Investigation- Mollys-Case-Jan-2018.pdf.

were insufficient. Neither agency saw Molly as a child in care and also a child with a disability.[134]

Until very recently, the absence of the adoption option – for those the subject of care orders but from marital families – has meant that long-term foster care has been the mainstay of service provision for such children in state care. There has been a steady increase in the proportion of the child care population placed with foster parents: in 1996, the proportion was 76.2 per cent; in 2011, 90 per cent; reaching 91 per cent by 2020. This has been accompanied by a corresponding increase in the annual number of children adopted by their foster parents.

- Partnership and rehabilitation

Given the constitutional and statutory endorsements of parental care as the preferred setting for furthering child welfare interests, alongside the abovementioned and well used s 4 voluntary care provision, it is unsurprising that Tusla has an established practice of working closely with parents of children in the agency's care. An added statutory onus to do so came with the amendment of s 54 of the Principal Act requiring the Child and Family Agency – now Tusla – to offer support to birth parents that have had their child taken into foster care with the hope of increasing the chances of a 'positive' family reunification. The agency must be satisfied that every reasonable effort has been made to support the parents of the child before that child can be available for non-consensual adoption. *Meitheal*,[135] a 'wraparound-inspired' national practice model that has involved considerable restructuring of national services for children has been operational since 2014 and is indicative of the focus on supporting parents to protect the welfare interests of their children.

One example of such a focus was *Health Service Executive v. JG & Anor (Care Order – Physical Abuse)*,[136] a vigorously contested case concerning an infant – of respectable middle-class parents – hospitalised with serious head injuries which the mother eventually conceded could have been caused by her husband. Ultimately, the judge determined that the child and her sibling should remain in foster care with a relative but a staged programme of reunification should be commenced with the parents under a 'Resolutions' model of rehabilitation. More recently, *Child and Family Agency v. IB and HB (Placement in Care – Parental Capacity Assessment)*[137] concerned a Tusla application, opposed by the parents, to place two of their three children (RB, aged nine, and CB, aged seven, who had been subject to physical chastisement and exposed to domestic violence) in care

134 See *Annual Report of the Special Rapporteur on Child Protection 2020*, op cit at p 18.

135 'Meitheal', an Irish word that equates to the concept of 'team around the child,' refers to a Tusla-led national practice model of working with vulnerable families.

136 [2013] IEDC 16.

137 [2019] IEDC 1.

until they reached 18 years of age. Explaining that she "does not believe that such an order would secure the welfare of RB or CB and/or is a necessary and/or proportionate interference with family life in this case," Quirke J, having noted that no child protection concerns had been raised in respect of the third child, directed that both children should have a phased return to their parents' care under the authority of a supervision order.

- Termination of parental rights

Where there is compelling evidence of parental abuse or neglect amounting to an abandonment of parental responsibilities, this may result in an application to the High Court by Tusla under s 53 of the Adoption Act 2010 for an order terminating parental rights. Under s 54 of that Act the court will make such an order, thereby permitting an adoption placement, if the grounds of parental failure due to 'physical or moral reasons' are established. Case law has shown that parental inaction will be sufficient to convince a court that parents have 'failed in their duty towards the child.'[138] Intent is not a requirement:[139] the grounds may be satisfied even if the parent concerned is without blame and the failure is attributable to their suffering from a learning disability.[140] In *Southern Health Board v. An Bord Uchtála MO'D & MO'D*,[141] the IESC ruled that this required three distinct steps to be satisfied:

- whether the parents have, for physical or moral reasons failed in their duty towards the child;
- whether such failure will continue without interruption until the child attains the age of eighteen; and
- whether the failure constitutes abandonment.

Moreover, the 'abandonment' must have lasted for a minimum of 36 months and be likely to continue without interruption until the child reaches the age of 18. The courts have looked to past conduct as evidence of probability of continued parental failure and have had no difficulty finding that where conduct has satisfied the grounds of s 54 of the 2010 Act then it is likely to continue to do so throughout childhood.[142] The grounds also require the court to be satisfied that the state, as guardian of the common good, should supply the place of the parents. This places

138 Previously under s 3(1)(I)(A) of the 1988 Act. See, for example, *The Southern Health Board v. An Bord Uchtála* [2000] 1 I.R. 165 where the court was satisfied that while the father had actually committed the acts of abuse the mother was also culpable as she had failed to protect her child.

139 *The Southern Health Board v. An Bord Uchtála,* per Denham J.

140 See *NAHB v. An Bord Uchtála* [2003] 1 ILRM 481.

141 [2001] 1 I.R. 165.

142 In this context, it is perhaps worth noting the proportion of children aged 17 who were adopted in 2018, for whom presumably there was no difficulty in predicting that 'abandonment' would continue throughout the remainder of their childhood. To what extent was this a factor in the delayed proceedings?

an onus on the court to examine first whether it can do so and second whether, in the circumstances of the particular child, it ought to do so. Only if convinced on both counts can it then make an order providing for permanent alternative care. The marital status of the parents is no longer a determining factor.

In short, the formulation of the grounds for terminating parental rights as a precursor to nonconsensual adoption has been worded so as to ensure compatibility with, and subservience to, constitutional principles with their emphasis on the 'inalienable and imprescriptible rights'[143] of the family. As mentioned earlier, since 2015 this has been counterbalanced by Article 42A.4.1(ii) which inserts the principle that 'the best interests of the child shall be the paramount consideration' in proceedings relating to the 'safety and welfare of any child.' So, although judicial termination of parental rights is less constrained – now that the 31st Amendment has replaced Article 42.5 with Article 42A – it nonetheless remains more so than in the UK and correspondingly more difficult to utilise adoption as a means of giving priority to the welfare interests of children.

- Concurrent placements

The dual function of such placements has not been part of child care policy, law, or practice in Ireland. Here the placements of children subject to care orders have been along parallel but quite separate lines: a small minority being voluntarily relinquished for adoption and placed accordingly in families assessed for that purpose; and the remainder, by far the majority, being placed with foster parents similarly exclusively assessed. This changed with the Adoption (Amendment) Act 2017 which introduced the adoption option for children from marital families failed by parental care and in Tusla long-term foster care placements. While there have always been a few children – usually adolescents, with unmarried birth parents, and in the same placement for most of their lives – adopted by their foster carers, this has now become a realistic prospect for many more children. However, it remains to be seen whether this change in law will translate into corresponding changes to established Tusla policy and practice[144] and to judicial precedents.

Residential care

A small minority of all children entrusted to Tusla are placed in residential care, mostly those with behavioural or health care needs, where their welfare interests are monitored in accordance with the Child Care (Placement in Residential Care)

143 See Articles 41 and 42 of the Constitution.

144 See Moran, L., McGregor, C., and Devaney, C. 'Outcomes for Permanence and Stability for Children in Long-term Care', Galway, 2017, at: www.childandfamilyresearch.ie/media/unescochildandfamilyresearchcentre/documentspdf/2017_Outcomes-for-Permanence-and-Stability-for-Children-in-Long-term-Care_2017_Digital.pdf.

Regulations 1995 and the National Standards for Children's Residential Centres 2001. The Centres are staffed on a 24-hour basis by social care workers and supported by a range of health care professionals including psychologists and psychiatrists, etc.

Secure accommodation

A small proportion of the residential care population, between 12 and 17 years of age, are placed in Special Care Centres due to behaviour issues which may endanger themselves or others. These placements are time limited and intensively supported with on-site education and vocational training, a psychology service, and detailed programmes of care and intervention aimed at supporting the child's return to their Residential Centre, foster parents, or family home.

Adoption

Paradoxically, as the Irish adoption process sharply contracts, the role of the state in relation to it is becoming more complex. While the annual number of children exiting state care by way of adoption is small – of the 79 adoptions in 2019, 21 were in respect of children in long-term foster care – they generate considerable legal complications for the Adoption Board. The Board has also become increasingly involved in information disclosure and contact arrangements.

Domestic voluntary adoption

Ireland, in common with other western nations, has seen a steady annual decline in the number of children voluntarily relinquished by their parent/s for adoption. The placements of those few – usually babies – are made with prospective adopters, approved and placed on a waiting list by Tusla, either by the latter or by a registered adoption agency. Following placement, the duties of the state are largely to undertake or delegate: placement supervision; appropriate pre- and post-adoption support for the adopters, the child, and the birth parent/s; and to ensure appropriate access to information for the parties concerned at a later date. The Adoption Board is responsible for the legal proceedings and for responding to information disclosure requests.

Post-adoption contact, information disclosure, and state support services

While the parties concerned may enter into a voluntary agreement for post-adoption contact, there is as yet no basis for this in Irish law; although it has been the subject of a government funded inquiry.[145] The absence of statutory

145 Department of Children and Youth Affairs, 'Review and Consultation in respect of the Potential Introduction of Open or Semi-Open Adoption in Ireland', 2019, at: https://assets.gov.ie/38717/3defc42d3e84425ea00e621d1610f800.pdf.

provisions to authorise a practice proven to be beneficial to adoptees in other jurisdictions must constitute a failure to respect the welfare interests of adopted children in Ireland.

Similarly deficient has been the ability of adoptees to access identifying information. In fact Irish law has never provided a right for adopted persons to have automatic access to their birth certificates, neither has there ever been a legal right to access agency records for information[146] on an adopted child's family of origin, nor a reciprocal duty to disclose such information.[147] However, the legislative provision for tracing and re-unification services changed, as Geoffrey Shannon comments, when the Birth Information and Tracing Bill 2022 becomes law.[148] This was largely in response to the CRC recommendation that 'the State party consider incorporating provisions on information disclosure, family tracing and post-adoption support measures, in accordance with international practice, into the Adoption Act 2010.'[149]

In *I.O'T. v. B. and the Rotunda Girls' Aid Society and M.H. v. Rev. G.D. and the Rotunda Girls' Aid Society*[150] the IESC considered consolidated actions brought by two women informally adopted before legal adoption became available. The applicants had sought an order directing the agency that facilitated the placements to disclose the identities of their birth mothers. While these cases concerned informal adoption, the Supreme Court made a number of references to legal adoption. Keane J, in considering the right to privacy, stated:

> I find it difficult to imagine an aspect of human experience which falls more clearly into the constitutional area of privacy … than the circumstances of the natural mothers in the present case.

In short, the Supreme Court recognised a person's unenumerated constitutional right to know the identity of his/her birth mother, but said that this had to be balanced against the birth mother's right to privacy: neither set of rights was absolute. Consequently, in 2019, a fifth of all adoptees who applied for access to their original birth certificate, and to the identifying information recorded on it, were refused by the Adoption Authority on the grounds that the birth parents had not consented to such disclosure.

146 However, a High Court judgment in 1993 determined that, where an adopted person is seeking information under s 22(5) of the Adoption Act 1952, then the Board is obliged to inform itself about the circumstances of the individual case and to decide whether to release or withhold the information sought.

147 Section 22(5) of the 1952 Act generally prohibits public access to the Adoption Index. The prior permission of the Adoption Board is required before any information is released from the Index. Section 8 of the 1976 Act prevents a court from ordering the release of any such information unless satisfied that this is in the best interests of the child in question.

148 Note to author: 25.05.2022. The Birth Information and Tracing Act 2022 became law in June 2022.

149 UN Committee on the Rights of the Child, Concluding Observations of the Committee on the Combined Third and Fourth Periodic Reports of Ireland, 2016, at para 46.

150 [1998] 2 IR 321. Also, see, Kelly, R., *Motherhood Silenced: The Experiences of Natural Mothers on Adoption Reunion*, Dublin, Liffey Press, 2005.

Again, there is no legislative right to access post-adoption support services, nor any specification for such services, though some are provided by voluntary agencies[151] and by Tusla. Child care adoptions are an exception and these may also qualify for a continuation of boarding-out payments; a purely discretionary matter for the Child and Family Agency. Given the above difficulties, together with the fact that there are very few child care adoptions, it is questionable whether the Irish adoption process is wholly governed by the paramountcy principle and prioritises the welfare interests of children in need.

Unaccompanied migrant minors

According to Eurostat[152] 160 unaccompanied children sought asylum in Ireland between 2016 and 2020. In that same period, 115 unaccompanied young people were sent to the Child and Family Agency, Tusla, for assessments as to whether or not they could access support services under the Child Care Act 1991. However, Tusla's data for that period shows that only 48 of the 115 were ultimately assessed to be children and allowed to access child support services, the rest were found to be adults. This discrepancy has given rise to speculation that many child migrants are not receiving the services they need.[153]

Trafficking

The U.S. State Department, in its *Trafficking in Persons Report* for 2019, listed Ireland at Tier 2, as it does not fully meet the minimum standards for the elimination of trafficking but is judged to be making significant efforts to do so.[154] It reported that 'human traffickers exploit domestic and foreign victims in Ireland and traffickers exploit victims from Ireland abroad. Traffickers subject Irish children to sex trafficking within the country.'[155] It was also highly critical of Ireland's treatment of victims, noting that there was no legally mandated psychological assistance and a lack of specialised services to address the physical and mental health needs of victims.

151 Barnardos, for example, has provided a post-adoption service (including counselling and mediation) since 1977, see, further, at: www.barnardos.ie/what-we-do/our-services/specialist-services/adoption.html.

152 See, further, at: https://appsso.eurostat.ec.europa.eu/nui/show.do?dataset=migr_asyunaa&lang=en.

153 See, further, at: https://ec.europa.eu/migrant-integration/news/ireland-issues-age-assessment-unaccompanied-child-asylum-seekers_en.

154 See U.S. State Department, *Trafficking in Persons Report* (June 2019), at: www.state.gov/wp-content/ uploads/2019/06/2019-Trafficking-in-Persons-Report.pdf.

155 Ibid at p 253.

The welfare principle in contemporary practice: public family law: criminal jurisdiction

As in England and Wales, allegations of child involvement in criminal activity are processed through the youth justice system which provides that all such alleged offences, as governed by the Children Act 2001, are heard in the Children Court.[156]

Children, crime, and the law

The law relating to the criminal activities of children was not fundamentally reformed until the introduction of the Children Act 2001, followed by the Report on the Juvenile Justice Review.[157] Subsequently, the Irish Youth Justice Service, (part of the Department of Children and Youth Affairs), declared that its policy was focused on 'diverting children from crime and the criminal justice system, promoting restorative justice, enforcing community sanctions, facilitating rehabilitation and, as a last resort, providing for detention.'[158] Law and practice are now governed by the Children Act 2001 and implemented through a number of agencies: primarily an Garda Síochána, the Probation Service, Irish Prison Service, Irish Youth Justice Service, Oberstown, and Tusla.

Children who pose a threat to the welfare of self or others

As McGrath J noted, in *CK v. Child and Family Agency (Threshold for Special Care Order)*,[159] part of any assessment of what might constitute the welfare interests of a particular child "must take into account behaviour of the child which poses a risk to others."[160]

Age of criminal responsibility

In Ireland, the age of criminal responsibility, which stood at 7 years until 2006, is now set by s 52 of the Children Act 2001 at 12 years; as amended by the Criminal Justice Act 2006 (s 129). However, exceptions are made for those aged 10 or 11 charged with murder, manslaughter, rape, or aggravated sexual assault.[161] The

156 See, further, Kilkelly, U., *Youth Justice in Ireland: Tough Lives, Rough Justice*, Irish Academic Press, 2006.

157 Department of Justice Equality and Reform, *Report on the Youth Justice Review*, Dublin, Stationery Office, 2006.

158 See Irish Youth Justice Service, *Report on the Implementation of the National Youth Justice Strategy 2008–2010*.

159 [2019] IEHC 635.

160 Ibid, at [72] citing the similar approach adopted by Whelan J in *Child and Family Agency v. ML* [2019] IECA 109.

161 In 2016, The CRC reiterated its previous concern (CRC/C/IRL/CO/2, para 66) that, pursuant to the Criminal Justice Act 2006, the age of criminal responsibility has been lowered to ten years for serious crimes (op cit, at para 71).

Special Rapporteur has called for the age limit to be raised to 14 years[162] and has also pointed out that current practice in Ireland does not comply with the UN CRC requirement that the relevant age for the purposes of determining whether youth or adult justice procedures should apply is the age of the child when the offence was committed, and not the age at the time of the trial.[163]

The Children Court

This court deals with criminal proceedings relating to a child, defined under the Children Act 2001 as a person under the age of 18 years (s 3). The Act is based on the philosophy that children in conflict with the law should only be detained by the state as a last resort and a range of community based measures must be explored and exhausted before detention can be considered. Such measures are indicated by s 95(6), which requires that the best interest principle be taken into account when sentencing.[164] As O'Malley J, once pointed out:[165]

> Children differ from adults, not just in their physical development and lesser experience of the world, but in their intellectual, social and emotional understanding. It is for this reason that it has long been recognised that it is unfair to hold a child to account for his or her behaviour to the extent that would be appropriate when dealing with an adult.

The Children Act 2001 requires the parents or guardian of the child concerned to attend any court proceedings involving their child, unless the court rules otherwise.

Community orders

The welfare principle, in a youth justice context, is represented in a range of non-custodial disposal options that may be utilised instead of punitive measures.

The Probation of Offenders Act 1907 allows the court to make a probation order in circumstances where the facts have been proven but the existence of mitigating factors and the offender's remorse give a court the discretion to issue a probation order for a period not to exceed three years.[166] Alternatively, an offender may either: be issued with a supervision order;[167] or given a community service

162 Annual Report of the Special Rapporteur on Child Protection 2020.

163 Ibid, at p 151, citing Committee on the Rights of the Child, *General Comment No 24 (2019) on Children's Rights in the Child Justice System*, UN Doc No CRC/C/GC24, 18 September 2019 at [20].

164 See *DPP v. Donoghue* [2014] IESC 56 and *G v. DPP* [2014] IEHC 33.

165 *G v. DPP*, ibid.

166 See Probation of Offenders Act 1907 (ss 1 and 2); the Criminal Justice Administration Act 1914 (ss 8 and 9); and the Children Act 2001 (s 115ff).

167 See the Criminal Justice Act 2006, s 99, as amended by the Criminal Justice Act 2007, s 60, and the Criminal Justice (Miscellaneous Provisions) Act 2009, s 51.

order requiring him or her to do between 40 and 240 hours of unpaid work in the community, for a period of one year, if they are over 16 years of age and have been convicted of an offence which otherwise would have involved a jail sentence.[168] A fine may be levied.

Custodial orders: special care

The welfare principle also has a role to play in the custodial disposal options.

Special care orders authorise Tusla to provide appropriate care, education and treatment and, for that purpose, to detain the child in a special care unit. As Flaherty J commented in *Child and Family Agency v. MO'L (Review of Special Care Order after Expiry)*,[169] "the very basis for the making of such orders or directions is the welfare of the child."[170] *Child and Family Agency v. ML (Otherwise G) (Threshold for Special Care Order)*[171] concerned a young teenage girl convicted of assault and criminal damage who was assessed at severe risk particularly of self-harm and suicide. Whelan J was of the view that a special care order was in her welfare interests as it offered her "the necessary therapeutic interventions to enable her development to be adjusted so that she can develop the capacity to participate in society and live her life to the fullest extent possible."[172] He concluded that "the vindication of her best interests required a special care order being made for the purposes of protecting her welfare development, and indeed her life."[173]

Custodial orders: detention

The Children Act 2001, as amended by the Criminal Justice Act 2006, provides that detention should be used 'only as a measure of last resort.'[174] This is in line with standards set out in the UN CRC and in General Comment No 24.

Under the Children Act 2001, s 142, a court may impose a period of detention on a child: those aged between 10 and 16, and 17-year-olds sentenced after 31 March 2017, are sent to the Oberstown Children Detention Campus. In practice, children are remanded in custody in Ireland for a variety of reasons including 'breach of bail conditions, the seriousness of the offence, or the inability of the defendant to provide surety for bail.'[175]

168 See the Criminal Justice (Community Service) Act 1983 and the Children Act 2001, s 115.

169 [2019] IEHC 781.

170 Ibid, at para 89.

171 Ibid.

172 Ibid at [138], citing *DG v. Eastern Health Board* [1997] 3 I.R. 511, *DG v. Ireland* (2002) 35 EHRR 33, and *SS v. Health Service Executive* [2008] 1 I.R. 594.

173 Ibid at [175].

174 See O'Connor, J., 'Reflections on the Justice and Welfare Debate for Children in the Irish Criminal Justice System', *Irish Judicial Studies Journal*, Vol 3, No 19, 2019.

175 See Judge, S.J., 'Youth Justice' in *Making Rights Real for Children: A Children's Rights Audit of Irish Law*, Children's Rights Alliance, 2015, at p 164, at: www.childrensrights. ie/sites/default/files/submissions_reports/files/MakingRightsReal2015.pdf.

A long-standing issue is the shortage of adequate placements in Ireland for troubled teenagers. This was illustrated again in the case of *AF (A Minor) v. Child and Family Agency*[176] when O'Regan J was faced with the respondent agency's claim that it had no placement available for AF and was unable to give any indication as to when a placement would be available, despite the acknowledged ongoing immediate risk to AF. The Child Care Law Reporting Project has documented how in numerous cases, adequate facilities and/or staffing are not available in this jurisdiction and children are consequently often transferred to facilities elsewhere 'out of the country, out of their communities and away from such families' which is clearly not conducive to promoting their welfare and may well violate their rights.[177]

The welfare principle in contemporary practice: private family law

The continued shelf-life of much of the Offences Against the Persons Act 1861 speaks volumes in terms of those areas of family law where legislators have feared to tread. Indeed, resistance to change has been a feature of Irish family law in general but particularly as regards its more private aspects.

Children and re-constituted families

Although the traditional marital family unit, as upheld and protected by the Constitution, continues to provide the primary framework for raising children in Ireland it is in a process of gradual decline as the proportion of non-marital families (one in four families are led by a single parent)[178] and families re-constituted from marital breakdown increase. Moreover, the decline in fertility rates in the western world means that in Ireland, as elsewhere, family life for many is now being generated more so than previously by recourse to adoption, IVF, or surrogacy.

Matrimonial

In Ireland, in common with the rest of the developed world, family breakdown is now as likely to occur in non-marital as in marital families, often more than once, with serial paternal roles and newly constituted groupings of children, not always genetically related, becoming more common.

176 [2019] IEHC 435.

177 See Colfer, L. and Coulter, C., 'High Court Oversight of Children's Complex Care Needs' (January 2020), at: www.childlawproject.ie/publications/high-court-oversight-of-childrens-complex-care-needs/.

178 See, further, the 2016 national census at: www.cso.ie/en/census/census2016reports/.

Divorce, nullity, and judicial separation

Not until the introduction of the Family Law (Divorce) Act 1996 did divorce become available in Ireland; and even when available, for many years it was seldom availed of due to the associated social/religious taboo.

Where the proceedings for judicial separation or divorce are contested in relation to custody and access arrangements then, under s 47 of the Family Law Act 1995, the court will normally appoint a child expert to carry out an assessment and make recommendations to the court regarding the best interests of the children concerned. Also, in all such proceedings, the court – under ss 28 and 25 of the Guardianship of Infants Acts 1964–97 (both inserted by s 11 of the Children Act 1997) – may, respectively, appoint a guardian *ad litem* and take into account the child's wishes having regard to their age and understanding. However, the exercise of both powers is wholly a matter of judicial discretion.

A child remains dependent under Irish law until he or she has attained the age of 18 years, or 23 if they continue in full-time education, and parents continue to share rights and responsibilities for them following family breakdown whether or not it had been a marital family. However, in non-marital cases the mother is the sole legal guardian and custodian of the child/children and if she does not appoint the father guardian by statutory declaration then, if he wants to be legally authorised to contribute to decisions affecting the welfare interests of their child, he must apply for guardianship and/or custody and access orders. Following the introduction of the Children and Family Relationships Act 2015, an unmarried father will automatically become guardian where he and the mother have been cohabitants for at least 12 consecutive months.

The welfare checklist

Under Part V of the Children and Family Relationships Act 2015, in cases where orders directing joint custody are made by the court these are generally on the basis that primary care and control is with one parent, with days and times of access for the other set out in detail, or, in less contentious cases, by using the formula 'as agreed between the parties from time to time.'

Where the parties contest custody/access arrangements the court will make its determination on the basis that the welfare of the children is the first and paramount consideration.[179] In so doing, while not required to hear directly from the child, it is required to consider:

- the benefit to the child of having a meaningful relationship with each parent and any other relatives and persons who are involved in the child's

179 As usefully outlined by Jennifer O'Brien of Jennifer O'Brien Solicitors, Irish Family Law Chambers, in *Practical Law*, Thomson Reuters at: https://uk.practicallaw.thomsonreuters.com/3-622-2687?transitionType=Default&contextData=(sc.Default)&firstPage=true.

upbringing and having sufficient contact with them to maintain such a relationship (except where such contact is not in the child's best interests);

- the views of the child, bearing in mind the possibility of these being the result of undue influence and the discretion to ascertain such views by appointing an expert under s 32 of the 2015 Act;
- the physical, psychological, and emotional needs of the child concerned, taking into consideration the child's age and level of development and the likely effect that any change in circumstances will have;
- the history of the child's upbringing and care, including the nature of the relationship between the child and each parent and other relatives and persons involved in the child's upbringing, and the desirability of preserving and strengthening such relationships;
- the child's religious, spiritual, cultural, and linguistic upbringing and needs;
- the child's social, intellectual, and educational upbringing and needs;
- the child's age and any special characteristics;
- any harm that the child has suffered or is at risk of suffering, including harm as a result of household violence, and the protection of the child's safety and psychological wellbeing;
- where applicable, proposals made for the child's custody, care, development and upbringing, and access and custody arrangements, while considering the wishes of the parent or guardian of the child in agreeing to and co-operating with such proposals;
- the willingness and ability of each of the child's parents to facilitate and encourage a close and continuing relationship between the child and the other parent, and to maintain and foster relationships between the child and other relatives;
- the capacity of each person in respect of whom an application is made under the Act to care for and meet the needs of the child, communicate, and co-operate on issues and exercise the relevant powers, responsibilities, and entitlements to which the application relates.

Under s 31(2) of the 2015 Act, the court must also have regard to any household violence that has occurred or is likely to occur and consider: the safety of the child and other members of the household concerned; the child's personal wellbeing, including psychological and emotional wellbeing; the victim of such violence; and the capacity of the perpetrator of the violence to properly care for the child and the risk, or the likely risk, that the perpetrator poses to the child.

Court orders

The court can make orders regulating custody and access under the provisions of the Family Law Act 1995 (as amended) for cases of judicial separation and under the Family Law (Divorce) Act 1996 for cases of divorce. It can also make 'standalone' orders for both married and non-married parents under the provisions of the Guardianship of Children Act 1964 to 1997, as amended by the Act of 2015,[180] and it can make an 'unfit parent' order in appropriate circumstances where the welfare of the child necessitates doing so.

There is no provision for a 'clean break' in Irish law whether in the context of judicial separation or divorce.[181] In both sets of proceedings the court has a duty to ensure that 'proper provision' is made for the spouses and any dependent children. An application for child maintenance can be made independently or ancillary to judicial separation/divorce proceedings in respect of a dependent child. A child, or someone authorised to act on their behalf, can make a claim for child maintenance, during the lifetime of either or both parents. The level of maintenance is determined on the basis of the income and assets of each parent, the needs of the child, and – in the marital context – the standard of living enjoyed by the parties before separation.

Guardianship

This centuries old mainstay of proceedings relating to substitute parental care in common law countries has continued its prominent role in private family law arrangements for children in Ireland. Guardianship, long recognised as inherently vesting in parents as regards their marital child and solely in an unmarried mother, has more recently been legislatively broadened to accommodate birth fathers and others, subject to certain conditions.

Court appointment

As mentioned above, the court may make guardianship orders under the Guardianship of Children Act 1964, as amended by the Act of 2015. Such appointments are most likely to occur in circumstances where a child has been orphaned, where one or both birth parents are absent or incapacitated, or following a decree of nullity in respect of a voidable marriage, or in favour of an unmarried father or other person bearing direct care responsibility for a child. Article 42A requires that in guardianship proceedings – as in adoption, custody, or access – the welfare interests of the child must be treated as the paramount consideration (see, further, below).

Adoption

Adoption is a national public service delivered by Tusla and regulated by the Adoption Authority, but has traditionally been dominated by religious organisations, several of which continue to provide services through their registered, denominational, adoption agencies. The introduction of the Adoption (Amendment) Act 2017, giving effect to Article 42A, made several significant

180 The Circuit Court Rules (Family Law) 2018 (SI 427/2018) apply in the context of applications for judicial separation and/or divorce.

181 *G v. G* [2011] IESC 40.

changes to adoption as a private family law procedure: married couples could place their child for adoption in circumstances where both consent; same-sex couples were enabled for the first time to jointly adopt children and step-children; step-parents were permitted to become sole adopters without the necessity to do so jointly with the birth parent; and the paramountcy principle was inserted into s 19 of the Principal Act to govern all matters arising in adoption proceedings.

Adoptions have declined from 1,500 in 1967 to 1,115 in 1980, dropping to 222 in 2006 and down to 79 in 2019. Of those 79, the majority were step-parent applicants, only six related to infants placed for domestic adoption.[182] Of the total, almost all – 74 – were issued with the voluntary consent of birth parents.

Until the introduction of the Adoption (Amendment) Act 2017, the law only permitted the placement of an orphaned child (with no available relatives) or the child of unmarried parents for adoption either with their consent or where so permitted by the Child Care Act 1991; the placement of a child of married parents for adoption, even if the latter gave consent, was only possible in very limited circumstances – in effect requiring evidence of a total abandonment of parental rights. Since the introduction of the 2017 Act, voluntary adoption placements of children with married parents has been possible.

Step-parent adoption

For some decades, this has been the most common form of Irish adoption. In 2018, of the 72 adoption orders granted, half (35) were in favour of step-parents and in 2019 that was the case for two-thirds (51 of the 79 orders granted).[183] A consistent feature of the Irish adoption process has been that most adoptions are in favour of birth parents; a complete reversal of the underpinning legislative intent.[184] Long regarded as an inappropriate use of adoption by the regulatory body, it was stopped by the availability of guardianship orders and the changes introduced by the Adoption (Amendment) Act 2017 which finally ended this anomalous situation by permitting a step-parent to adopt without the necessity of being joined by the birth parent.

Cultural/religious affinity

Identity issues, inherent in the status of an adoptee, are more problematic when accompanied by an overlay of cultural/religious difference. In fact the likelihood of any such differences have been greatly reduced in this jurisdiction by: placements being traditionally made on a religion-specific basis by denominational adoption societies; the continuation of the legal right of birth parents to determine

182 See, further, at: https://aai.gov.ie/images/AAI_Annual_Report_2019_FINAL.pdf.

183 See, further, at: https://aai.gov.ie/images/Annual_Report_2019.pdf.

184 The child's birth certificate is replaced with an adoption certificate on which the birth mother is recorded as the child's adoptive mother.

the religious upbringing of their adopted child (now qualified but not removed),[185] and the preference exercised in ICA for white Caucasian children. It is perhaps fair to comment that any filters applied to select children on the basis of a perceived 'fit' with prospective adopters could be open to the criticism that such matching is putting the needs of adopters before the welfare interests of children and clearly works to the disadvantage of the children thereby filtered out.

Intercountry adoption

For prospective third party adopters ICA has, to some extent, been a forced option due to the lack of domestic alternatives. Ireland has seen a drastic reduction in the number of infants voluntarily relinquished by their unmarried mothers due to a reversal of the associated stigma which now attaches to such mothers. This situation has been exacerbated by the virtual absence of non-consensual adoption from the public care system, together with the non-availability of children from a marital family. Although once regarded as a provident solution to such trends, annual intercountry adoptions has in recent years dropped sharply: from 307 in 2009 to 117 in 2012, falling to 41 in 2018 and to 33 in 2019.

The constitutional incorporation of the paramountcy principle in Article 42A established that issues arising in an ICA context should now be resolved by applying that principle. This was emphasised by the Court of Appeal ruling in *AMQ v. KJ AND IHREC*[186] which upheld the High Court decision to refuse a father's request for the return to Pakistan of his two children following their unlawful removal by the mother. As the court then stated:

> It is clear that this a mandatory legal rule which must inform the application of our recognition rules vis-à-vis a foreign judgment of this kind, so that, regardless of questions of judicial comity or the smooth application of the rules of private international law, the Court can make no order which would not be in the best interests of the children.

Again, at much the same time, MacMenamin J in the IESC relied upon the paramountcy principle in *CB and PB v. AG*[187] when he declared that the welfare interests of the children had to prevail over all other considerations – to authorise the ICA adoption of two girls.

Surrogacy

Surrogacy agreements remain unenforceable, despite recommendations made more than a decade ago by the Commission on Assisted Human Reproduction in

185 The Adoption Act 2010, s 32.
186 [2018] IECA.
187 [2018] IESC 30.

Ireland.[188] Most such children have been born to surrogate mothers overseas, in countries such as Ukraine, where there is no specific legislation governing surrogacy.[189] Consequently, it is estimated that there are now several hundred children living in Ireland born to surrogate mothers whose legal status is uncertain and their welfare interests insecure.[190]

Surrogate, child, and the commissioning parents

The traditional presumptions favouring the marital family and the respective gender ascribed roles of parents lingered on well into the twenty-first century in Irish family law. They were evident, for example, in *McD v. L & Another*[191] when the Supreme Court, while finding that a sperm donor who wanted to play a role in parenting – despite opposition from the same-sex couple parenting a child conceived by AID – should be granted some visiting rights, also took the opportunity to re-state the core elements of that presumption. It criticised the views of the High Court judge who had ventured an opinion that a same-sex couple with such a child could be construed as a 'de facto family' – as could a heterosexual unmarried couple with a child – for the purposes of Irish law, bearing in mind Article 8 of the ECHR. The IESC asserted that the judge had failed to recognise the innate rights of a biological father and had attached insufficient weight to his claim for a parental role. Fennelly CJ remonstrated that, notwithstanding the bearing of the ECHR Act 2003, "the learned trial judge had no jurisdiction to consider the claims [of the parties] under Article 8 of the Convention." More recently, in *M.R. & Anor v. An tArd Chlaraitheoir*,[192] Justice Abbott ruled against commissioning parents who sought to have the birth certificates of twins altered to substitute their names for that of the surrogate as parents. Relying on the maxim *mater semper certa est* (the mother is always certain), in refusing to alter the register, he held that the genetic mother rather than the gestational mother should be registered as the mother under the Civil Registration Act 2004. He had this to say about 'motherhood' in Irish law:[193]

> Any step which suggests that the birth mother is not the mother of the children opens a range of prospects. If it then becomes the law that the birth

188 See the Report of the Commission on Assisted Human Reproduction, Dublin, 2005 which recommended that a child born through surrogacy should be presumed to be that of the commissioning couple. The Commission also recommended the establishment of a regulatory body for assisted human reproduction. These recommendations have not yet been incorporated into Irish law.

189 See, further, at: www.citizensinformation.ie/en/birth_family_relationships/adoption_and_fostering/surrogacy.html.

190 See, further, at: www.aclsolicitors.ie/news-events/current-news/legal-status-of-surrogacy-in-ireland/.

191 [2009] IESC 81.

192 [2013] IEHC 91.

193 Ibid, at para 90.

> mother is not the mother of the children, then it is simply not possible to control the outcome of that for all of the other persons affected. Such persons include those who have borne children by donor gametes, who now may have issues about the status of their children at a number of levels, which hitherto they did not have by virtue of birth mothers recognition as lawful mothers.

While his iteration of the problem cannot be faulted, his decision can and was. The Supreme Court declined to endorse the significance attached by Abbott J to the maxim *mater semper certa est*. Denham CJ, stated that the maxim was not part of Irish common law nor of statute law but simply reflected a pre-ART approach to motherhood in which the woman who gave birth was deemed to be the mother. She noted that there was no definitive definition of 'mother' in the Constitution and thus no constitutional impediment existed to prevent the legislature from clarifying the respective rights of the parties in such surrogacy arrangements: this legal lacuna was a matter for the legislature not the courts. In allowing the appeal, the IESC ruled that the genetic, commissioning mother was not entitled to be registered on the twins birth certificate as their legal mother, a decision which will stand as a disincentive for any Irish women considering surrogacy as a route to motherhood.

This traditional judicial approach may well present problems for those children in the care of same-sex or trans persons seeking to secure their parenting arrangements.[194] In the meantime, while the Children and Family Relationship Act 2015 has come into effect and the General Scheme of Assisted Human Reproduction Bill 2017 remains pending, the law continues to be uncertain as does its bearing on the welfare interests of the many children conceived via AID and surrogacy. The CRC recommends that appropriate measures be taken to 'ensure that children born through assisted reproduction technologies, in particular with the involvement of surrogate mothers, have their best interests taken as a primary consideration and have access to information about their origins.'[195]

It might be added that if the paramountcy principle is to prevail, in the post–Article 42A era, then *mater semper certa est* (which survived the 2015 Act) and the more general presumption favouring consanguinity – as much as any other such presumptive rule – will have to give way.

Abduction

Increasingly, abduction takes the form of the removal of a child by one parent without permission of the other. It involves taking the child to a different

194 See, further, https://lgbt.ie/advocacy/campaigns/.
Also, see, LGBT Ireland at: https://lgbt.ie/advocacy/submission/.

195 UN Committee on the Rights of the Child, Concluding Observations of the Committee on the Combined Third and Fourth Periodic Reports of Ireland, 2016, at para 34.

jurisdiction and it is a criminal offence.[196] In that event, the relevant legal framework is provided: domestically, by the Non-Fatal Offences against the Person Act 1977, s 16, and the Child Abduction and Enforcement of Custody Orders Act 1991,[197] together with the Protection of Children (Hague Convention) Act 2000 which makes provision for the recognition and enforcement of access orders between signatory states; and internationally – in relation to Hague Convention signatory states – by the Brussels II Regulation, governing abduction between EU states (supplemented by the Hague Conventions of 1980 and 1996), which aims to prevent parental child abduction between member states, and establishes a system to ensure the prompt return of an abducted child to their member state of habitual residence (see, further, Chapter 4).

Returning an abducted child

International conventions and the Brussels II Regulation[198] require: the prompt return of the child to their jurisdiction of habitual residence; and they nominate the courts of that jurisdiction as providing the appropriate forum to determine custody and ancillary issues in the light of what is in the best interests of the child. The Hague Convention on the Civil Aspects of International Child Abduction, Article 13, stipulates that a court is not obliged to order the return of a child if to do so would expose him or her to physical or psychological harm, or otherwise place them in an intolerable situation.

In such cases, a child expert will usually be appointed under s 47 of the Family Law Act 1995 (or for future purposes, s 32 of the 2015 Act). The court will sometimes appoint a guardian *ad litem* (appointed to act on behalf of a child or other person who is not considered capable of representing themselves) to carry out an assessment for the purpose of: informing the court of the child's wishes and feelings; and to make recommendations as to the best interests and welfare of the child in all the circumstances.

Arguably, in responding to Hague based requests for the return of a child 'snatched' by one parent from the other, Ireland has tended to look more towards its domestic custody laws than to Hague requirements. This seemed to be the approach taken, for example, in *HI v. MG.*[199] It was also evident in *WPP v. SRW*,[200] which concerned a mother who had legal custody but took the two children from the United States, where they had lived their entire lives, to her native Ireland, thereby breaching court orders granting the father visitation rights, the IESC dis-

196 The increasing rate of child abductions, into and from Ireland, is well documented. See, for example, at: www.thesun.ie/news/4195401/100-children-abducted-strangers-estranged-family/.

197 The 1991 Act incorporates both the Convention on the Civil Aspects of International Child Abduction 1980 (Hague Child Abduction Convention) and the European Child Abduction Convention 1980 into Irish law.

198 EU Council Regulation (EC) No. 2201/2003 (the 'Revised Brussels II Regulation').

199 (1999) 2 IRLM 22.

200 [2000] IESC 11.

missed the latter's appeal. It ruled that to order the return of the children to their place of habitual residence, merely so as to entitle the non-custodial parent to exercise his rights of access, was not warranted by the terms of the Convention. It would seem that for the court greater weighting was due to custody rights than to Hague requirements and the welfare interests of the children.

The Article 13 defence to an order for the return of an abducted child has been termed the "grave risk" defence by Barron J in *K (R) v. K (J) (Child Abduction: Acquiescence)*.[201] In circumstances where the 'grave risk' is one of physical or psychological harm then, as confirmed by the Court of Appeal in *R v. R*,[202] the onus rests on the party objecting to the return to adduce evidence substantiating that risk. As Fennelly J has stressed, the threshold for establishing such a risk is high.[203] The 'grave risk' test was recently applied by Simons J in proceedings which concerned the legality of the removal from Poland of a seven-and-a-half-year-old boy by his mother who brought him to Ireland in 2018, where both had lived ever since.[204] Mr Justice Simons J found that the removal of the child to Ireland was a "wrongful removal" and then considered – the "grave risk" defence – whether the return of the child would expose him to physical or psychological harm or otherwise place him in an intolerable situation. He formed the view that to require the boy to engage in international travel during the coronavirus pandemic would expose him to a grave risk of contracting the disease. Noting that the Irish government had advised against all unnecessary travel, he stated that such an order would place the mother in the "invidious position" of either exposing herself to a risk to her health by accompanying him to Poland, or else having him travel without her, depriving him of his primary carer at a time of significant change in his life. This would place the child in an "intolerable situation": uprooted from what has been his home for 18 months; to either be placed in the care of a father with whom he has no meaningful relationship and against whom his mother has made serious allegations; or travel with his mother in circumstances where her health would be put at risk. The application for the child's return was dismissed.

Proportionality

In a family law context, this principle's potential application is often suggested in cases where the exercise of statutory powers in respect of a child's welfare

201 [2000] 2 IR 416 when he cited with approval the formulation given in *Friedrich v. Friedrich*, 78 F.3d 1060 (6th Cir. 1996): "first, there is a grave risk of harm when return of the child puts the child in imminent danger prior to the resolution of the custody dispute, e.g. returning the child to a zone of war, famine or disease; second, there is a grave risk of harm in cases of serious abuse or neglect, or extraordinary emotional dependence, when the court in the country of habitual residence, for whatever reason, may be incapable or unwilling to give the child adequate protection."

202 [2015] IECA 265.

203 *AS v. PS (Child Abduction)* [1998] 2 IR 244.

204 *G (Child Abduction: Retained Jurisdiction Following Non-Return Order)(Approved)* [2021] IEHC 20.

interests breaches the constitutional guarantees given to respect the inalienable and imprescriptible rights of the family. For example, *Nottinghamshire County Council and K.B. and K.B. v. HSE*[205] concerned an appeal by an English married couple against an order requiring the return of their children to a local authority in England. The circumstances were that they had left their place of residence with their two children, following the serving of notice of care proceedings, and arrived in Ireland where the children had been admitted to the care of the HSE. In due course an application, pursuant to Article 12 of the Hague Convention, had been lodged requiring the HSE to return the children. The parents refused to co-operate claiming that they, together with their children, constituted a family for the purposes of Article 41 and 42 of the Irish Constitution and that return of the children would be in breach of those provisions because the law of the United Kingdom permitted adoption of the children of married couples in circumstances which would not be permitted in Ireland. In response to that claim the Attorney General argued that the principle of proportionality could be applied. Thus, even if the parents were entitled to invoke the provisions of Articles 41 and 42, and even if they and/or their children could be held to have rights under those Articles, any such rights were not absolute and could be restricted and controlled in the interests of the common good by proportionate means. It was argued that the return of the children to a jurisdiction with a highly sophisticated system of child and family law having at its core the best interests of the child constituted only a very limited interference with the constitutional rights of the respondent parents and could not be seen as disproportionate.[206] Fennelly J, giving judgment on behalf of the IESC, was not convinced of the relevance of that argument but, nonetheless, dismissed the parents appeal. This decision accords with the rationale followed in other similar cases.[207] As Ms Justice Mary Finlay Geoghegan expressed it during the High Court hearing, it is presumed that in the English courts "any decision to place the children, or for their adoption, will be taken in accordance with their best interests and in accordance with what their welfare dictates."[208]

Child's wishes

In *MN v. RN*,[209] Ms Justice Finlay Geoghegan ruled that under Article 13 of the Convention it was appropriate to hear the views of a six-year-old child in determining whether he should be returned to his habitual residence in another EU state. She was clear that the issue as to whether or not the court should give a child an opportunity to be heard was a separate and distinct matter from the appropriate

205 [2011] IESC 48.
206 *Nottinghamshire County Council*, op cit at para 11.
207 *Sanders v. Mid-Western Health Board* IESC (Unreported), 1987.
208 *Nottinghamshire County Council v. B & Anor* [2010] IEHC 9 at para 49.
209 [2008] IEHC 382.

weight, if any, to be given by the court to those views.[210] The court found that a child's views "on everyday matters as to the circumstances in which he was living before he came to Ireland, or his wishes as to his future care including what should happen on return" might be taken into account when considering whether or not to make an order for return pursuant to Article 12 of the Hague Convention.

The welfare principle in contemporary practice: public/private family law

Unlike the corresponding UK jurisprudence, family law in Ireland demonstrates an innate capacity to resist state intervention. The authority of the family protection provisions in the Constitution may have been somewhat diluted by contemporary amendments but their general effectiveness is evident in the continuing traditional sets of proceedings, accompanied by conservative court orders and in the comparatively few crosscutting principles, procedures, and hybrid orders.

Public/private family law

The difference between public and private family law is more sharply delineated in Ireland than in the UK. This would appear to be a natural consequence of the status granted to the legal autonomy and integrity of the family unit in the Constitution, to the accompanying guarantees of protection from unwarranted state intrusion, and to the resulting body of case law demonstrating the high bar set for legal challenges to the traditional roles of family members.

Public service matters

An adequate framework of public services has the potential in Ireland, as elsewhere, to support the coping capacity of socially disadvantaged families to provide 'good enough' parenting. A high national level of poverty would seem to provide a counter-indicator of the likelihood of such an outcome. The Poverty Ireland 2021 report, based on 2019 data, reveals a total of 630,000 people living in poverty of whom 190,000 – or one in four – were children.[211] This clearly indicates an insufficiency in public services that can only serve to jeopardise the welfare interests of many children.

Public health, education, and safety concerns have always transected private family rights – perhaps most obviously in relation to employment – but in this

210 Echoing the rationale offered by Baroness Hale in *Re D (A Child) (Abduction; Rights of Custody)* [2007] IAC 619.

211 See, Social Justice Ireland, the 'Poverty Ireland 2021 report' at: https://www.socialjustice.ie/system/files/file-uploads/2021-09/2019-04-15-sjipovertyfocus2019final.pdf and the Borgen Project, 'The State of Poverty in Ireland' at: https://borgenproject.org/the-state-of-poverty-in-ireland/.

jurisdiction the intersects have been accompanied by a pronounced religious dimension.[212]

Employment

For many generations of Irish women, the legal and social expectations were that they would prioritise the welfare of their children by rejecting opportunities for employment. Article 41.2 of the Constitution declared that 'by her life within the home a woman gives to the State a support without which the common good cannot be achieved,' and guarantees to protect mothers from having to work outside the home 'to the neglect of her duties within the home.' This state proclamation, prescribing how maternal care – exclusively – benefitted child welfare, must have had a bearing on shaping how 'welfare' was interpreted in that society. Again, and for many more generations, in what until the mid-twentieth century was a largely rural and agricultural society, there was an expectation that children would help their parents and the community by working in the fields, or in cutting and stacking turf for heating the home in winter. In a country where the agricultural industry comprised many hundreds of small farms, functioning at little more than subsistence level, it was customary for children to 'help out' before and after school; and frequently instead of, at harvest time.

The Protection of Young Persons (Employment) Act 1996 bans the employment of children under 14 years of age and prohibits those under the age of 16 from regular full-time jobs. The ECSR has recently expressed its concern regarding state failure to ensure that the provisions of this Act are enforced so as to prohibit the employment of children under the age of 15 years or subject to compulsory education.[213]

Health

The national health care system in Ireland has been delivered through an infrastructure containing many hospitals and health care facilities built, and continuing to be managed by, Catholic bodies and consequently the availability of medical treatment has at times been subject to associated religious beliefs. This has particularly constrained women's reproductive rights: abortion, contraception, and IVF being areas where religious sanctions have generated most social controversy; with obvious implications for family planning, including for the welfare

212 See, for example, *Re Article 26 and the Employment Equality Bill 1996*, [1997] 2 I.R. 321,which found that s 12 of the Bill – providing for the prohibition of religious discrimination – would not apply to the selection of nurses or primary teachers for employment in any 'religious, educational or medical institution which is under the direction or control of a body established for religious purposes.'

213 See European Committee of Social Rights, *Conclusions 2019: Ireland*, at: https://rm.coe.int/rapport-irl- en/16809cfbc0.

of unplanned children (and those births resulting from rape or affected by a diagnosed congenital disability).

The increasing permeability of the child welfare principle across both public and private sectors of family law was clearly demonstrated 20 years ago in *North Western Health Board v. H.W. and C.W*,[214] when the IESC considered whether the parents of a 14-month-old child could be required by court order to permit the Health Board to conduct what was a routine 'voluntary' medical procedure – the PKU test – on their child. The Board had notified the parents that

> there is no risk whatever in having the test done but on the other hand the absence of the test can have catastrophic consequences for the child should he or she suffer from one of the metabolic conditions which the test is designed to screen for.

The parents refused on the grounds that 'It is our strong religious belief, that nobody is allowed to injure anybody else.' Ultimately the court found that to issue the order sought by the Board would, in effect, be to make the PKU test mandatory, something the legislature had refrained from doing. In the absence of any immediate and serious risk to the life or health of the child, it found that the decision was one which the parents were constitutionally entitled to make without state interference. Murphy J explained that the parental refusal to co-operate could not be

> categorised as such a default by the parents of their moral and constitutional duty so as to bring into operation the supportive role of the State. If the State had an obligation in the present case to substitute its judgment for that of the parents, numerous applications would be made to the courts to overrule decisions made by caring but misguided parents.

Although this decision preceded the deletion of Article 42.5 and the substitution of Article 42A, as the provision that the state intervenes to take the place of parents only in 'exceptional circumstances' remains intact, so too does the rationale of this judgment which rests on a presumption that – in the absence of any conclusive evidence to the contrary – a child's welfare interests are best left to parental protection.

Education

In Ireland, state education remains mainly faith based, very largely Catholic in nature and perpetuates a Catholic religious ethos aided by the fact that all teacher training colleges are denominational. Some 97 per cent of primary schools and perhaps 50 per cent of secondary schools are state funded but managed by religious

214 [2001] IESC 90.

organisations: 90 per cent of all primary schools are controlled by the Catholic Church;[215] reinforced by the Education Act 1998, s 15(2)(b), which conferred authority on school 'patrons' to whom Boards of Management are accountable for upholding the ethos of a school; an ethos which has difficulty in accommodating the pluralism of contemporary Irish society. This disconnect has been evident in issues regarding rights of access to schools for non-Catholic children and for those teaching staff whose lifestyle is perceived as non-compliant with Catholic values and beliefs. It is evidenced also, and most clearly, in the record of historical abuse of children by Catholic clergy in residential educational establishments.[216]

Legal proceedings

There is evidence of a creeping permeability between the public and private sectors of Irish family law.

Adoption from state care

Private adoptions of children in public care is one such procedure that crosscuts both sectors of family law. Although in theory this was possible, under s 36(1)(c) of the Child Care Act 1991, as Tusla – formerly the HSE – was empowered to place a child 'with a suitable person with a view to his adoption,' such an outcome was seldom achieved. Nor did matters improve with the introduction of the Adoption Act 2010. This was due to the necessity for an application to be made to the High Court, by either the Adoption Authority or the prospective adopters, requesting the court to dispense with the need for parental consent and the consequent stringency with which the test of parental failure – the justification for dispensing with consent – was then applied. As McGuinness J stated in *Northern Area Health Board v. An Bord Uchtála*[217] "there has to be a complete failure to carry out the day-to day-care of the child." The Supreme Court, in *In Re JH (An Infant)*,[218] found that state intervention is only justified if it is established that there are "compelling reasons" why the welfare of the child cannot be met in the custody of the parents. This was reaffirmed in *N v. Health Service*

215 Op cit, which clearly established that the state could support denominationally controlled education in discharging its obligation to provide for free primary education.

216 Letterfrack in Co Galway – opened in 1887, closed in 1974 – and run by the Christian brothers, in which some 147 children died and many more suffered physical and sexual abuse, was one such establishment. See, further, *Report of the Commission to Inquire into Child Abuse* (the Ryan Report), Dublin, Stationery Office, 2009.

217 [2003] 1 ILRM 481. Also, see, *North Western Health Board v. HW* [2001] 3 I.R. 622 where parental refusal to consent to the administration of the PKU test in respect of their newborn child was upheld by the Supreme Court. In this case, the state was not permitted to rely on Article 42.5 to step into the parental role because it was held that the parents of the child had not failed in their duty either for moral or physical reasons.

218 [1985] I.R. 375.

Executive[219] where the Supreme Court decided that "exceptional circumstances" did not exist to justify allowing an infant girl to remain in an adoption placement without parental consent.

The introduction of the Adoption (Amendment) Act 2017, which gave effect to Article 42A and applied the paramountcy principle, significantly changed the law relating to the adoption of children from state care: s 24 amended s 54 of the Adoption Act 2010 to lower the threshold that must be reached before adoptions can be authorised without parental consent. It permits nonconsensual adoption in circumstances where the High Court is satisfied that: the parents have failed in their duty towards their child for a continuous period of 36 months or more; it is likely that such failure will continue; and where the applicants have had care and custody for a continuous period of at least 18 months; in effect, increasing the feasibility of adoption by long-term foster parents. As the court must also be satisfied that the proposed adoption will be in the best interest of the child, it remains to be seen whether the judiciary will use the broader opportunities provided by the legislature to so interpret 'best interests' and correspondingly increase the number of adoptions from state care. Moreover, since the introduction of the 2017 Act, same-sex couples have been able to jointly legally adopt which has increased the pool of approved adopters resulting in a corresponding increase in the number of children whose welfare interests will be promoted by being adopted from the care system.

Post-adoption support

There is no legislative right to access post-adoption support services nor any specification for any services that may be available. In practice no more than 20 per cent of adopters receive post-adoption support. Perhaps the only consistent exception arises in the context of child care adoptions. An important point of difference between the standing of child care and all other adopters is that the former may qualify for a continuation of boarding-out payments. This is a purely discretionary matter for Tusla. As there are very few child care adoptions the proportion of adopters receiving such support is small.

Wardship

Wardship has been described as an 'exercise of a *parens patriae* jurisdiction [but also] as the implementation of the constitutional obligation on the courts to vindicate, as far as possible, the welfare and personal rights of a child."[220] It may only be called upon when statutory powers are unavailable or inappropriate.

219 [2006] IESC 60.

220 *O'Farrell v. Governor of Portlaoise Prison* [2016] 3 I.R. 169, per McKechnie J at p 709 citing decision of Murray CJ in *N. v. HSE* [2006] IESC 60.

As MacMenamin J warned, in *AM v. Health Services Executive*,[221] the "inherent jurisdiction must not be used as a first port of call when, by legislation, the Oireachtas has spoken on the matter."[222] Currently, the Assisted Decision-Making (Capacity) Act 2015 provides the relevant statutory framework,[223] ensuring that wards have their capacity assessed, are thereafter assisted in making decisions about their welfare, property and affairs, but that the responsibility for such decisions lies with the President of the High Court.

Most recently, *In the Matter of JJ (Unapproved)*,[224] the IESC had an opportunity to review the jurisdiction of wardship in the light of Article 42A. This case concerned an appeal by the parents of a boy, with permanent and devastating brain injuries, seeking to ensure that they, rather than the hospital, had control over his medical treatment. The case was acknowledged to raise 'difficult, troubling and complex' issues about when the state may intervene, including by taking a child into wardship, to permit decisions to be taken about the welfare interests of children by third parties contrary to parents' wishes. The IESC took the view that in the absence of a specific statutory procedure to resolve disputes about a child's future treatment, the wardship jurisdiction may be used to determine if the court – in performance of the state's duty under Article 42A of the Constitution – should supply the place of the parents and provide consent to treatment. In such circumstances, the legal test was to consider what a loving and considerate parent would do once apprised of all the relevant information. That parent would take into account the views of the child, if expressed, and the child's character, and decide the best interests of the child in that context. The court would not, however, presume to place itself in the position of the child and be guided by their subjective perception as to what – if capable of understanding their condition – would be in their best interests. Attention was drawn to the fact that

> the retention by the court of all decision making and of power to give directions over all aspects of the ward's welfare can seem to lie uneasily with the constitutional, ECHR and statutory recognition of the right and corresponding duty of the parents to make choices and decisions regarding the welfare of a child, and indeed the rights of the child that those decisions be made by his or her parent.[225]

A statement that omitted to mention any right of the child to have his or her wishes independently represented and taken into account, let alone the possibility that the consent of the child, where practicable, might be sought.

221 [2019] IESC 3.
222 Ibid, at [89].
223 Jurisdiction in respect of adults and minors without legal capacity was transferred to the High Court under the Courts of Justice Act 1961, s 9.
224 [2021] IESC 1.
225 Ibid, at para 37.

In overriding a decision of parents, the IESC declared that it must be satisfied by clear and convincing evidence that such a decision prejudiced the health and welfare of the child to such an extent as to constitute a failure of parental duty. In this case, it was so satisfied and it dismissed their appeal. It held that the hospital would not be acting unlawfully if it considered it to be in the child's best interests to withhold life-prolonging treatments, including mechanical ventilation, in certain circumstances. Stressing the appropriateness of maintaining "the possibility and primacy of parental decision making in this case," the court stated that its declarations and permission for treatments would only become effective if, in each instance, the parents' consent was sought and refused. Baker J, on behalf of the IESC, added that in her opinion the earlier High Court decision to take the child "into wardship for all purposes was an overreach which was not justified in the circumstances."[226] While in her opinion the recourse to wardship was itself justified, because of the clash between parents and hospital as to what constituted the child's best interests, the High Court should have narrowly circumscribed its intervention in a manner that minimised its displacement of parental rights.

Commercial surrogacy

Only altruistic surrogacy is recognised and permitted in Ireland. However there are now perhaps several hundred surrogate children within the jurisdiction who have been born outside it as a consequence of commercial surrogacy arrangements made by Irish couples. The uncertainty surrounding their legal status and their rights to access information regarding the circumstances of their birth have implications for their welfare interests. This is a matter that will increasingly become one subject to hybrid public/private family law proceedings.

Guardianship

The relevant law is currently provided by the Guardianship of Infants Act 1964 as amended by the Children and Family Relationships Act 2015.

The contemporary role of guardianship in a private family law context allows those such as an unmarried father, step-parent, civil partner, a cohabitee, or a grandparent to be vested with parental rights and duties. However, recent changes to the law have extended it – if only marginally – into the public sector by broadening the pool of potential guardians to include anyone who has borne direct care responsibilities for a child. The legislative intent being that foster parents should be encouraged to seek legal security, independent of Tusla, to continue in their proven role as guardians and promoters of a child's welfare interests in circumstances where adoption is not appropriate.

226 Ibid, at para 38.

Court orders

Essentially, the court orders available with a bearing on a child's welfare interests in a civil law context fall into two blocks: those that govern care arrangements in respect of a child viz. guardianship, custody and access, and their enforcement;[227] and those that offer protection from domestic violence for a caring parent and their child. This limited and very traditional range of orders would seem gauged to licence blunt and restrict modes of state intervention in family matters and prevent exercises of judicial discretion. They are both also very clearly separate from the criminal law jurisdiction as it relates to children.

Custody order

A custody order vests responsibility for the day-to-day care, residency, and upbringing of children in a named person or persons. This traditional statutory measure – aggregating parental responsibilities – has been largely replaced in the UK by single function orders, each specifying a particular aspect of care that is to be entrusted to someone. Most usually this occurs in cases of judicial separation or divorce, when one parent is granted custody, but it may be issued in any situation where there has been a breakdown in the parental care of a child. The Children and Family Relationships Act 2015, s 57, makes provision for relatives or other persons to apply for custody of a child in specified circumstances.

Access order

An access order grants a specified right of direct or indirect access – visiting or by letter, respectively – to a named child. It is granted in recognition of the right of a child to maintain contact with someone, usually a parent but sometimes a grandparent[228] or other person with whom the child does not reside but with whom they have a meaningful relationship. It can include arrangements for overnight care and/or holidays.

Guardianship order

The newly inserted s 6C of the 2015 Act gives the court power to appoint a person other than a parent as guardian in certain circumstances. The court can also appoint a temporary guardian under s 6E specifying any limitations that the qualifying guardian wishes to impose on the rights and responsibilities of temporary guardianship. This is to deal with circumstances where a parent is temporarily unavailable.

227 See s 18A of the Guardianship of Infants Act 1964 as inserted by s 60 of the Children and Family Relationships Act 2015.

228 The Guardianship of Infants Act 1964 as amended by the Children Act 1997, s 9.

Other

Family protection orders of a hybrid nature, being equally applicable in a public or a private family law context, are much in evidence in this jurisdiction. The Domestic Violence Act 2018 provides for the issue of: a 'barring order' prohibiting a named person from entering the family home, from behaving in a violent or threatening manner, and from attempting to communicate with the parent and child; a 'safety order' which prohibits a named person from violent or threatening behaviour and excludes them from coming within a specified distance of the custodial parent and child; and a 'protection order' which is a temporary safety order offering protection pending a full hearing for a barring order or safety order. Maintenance orders, requiring a non-custodial parent to make regular payments for the maintenance of their child, are clearly also important.

Conclusion

The dismal record of Ireland's earlier failure to protect its children, as referenced in this chapter and recounted by many academics and others, will stand as an enduring reminder of the risks involved in blind compliance to a fixed set of values, such as those then jointly upheld by church and state, but has perhaps also come to serve as a prompt to put in place safeguards providing better future protection for children.

The constitutionally underpinned imperative to respect the autonomous rights of the marital family as the foundation of society was of central importance for most of the twentieth century. It was attended by the corollary of social and legal rejection of those who, due to choice or circumstances, did not conform to all that it represented. A paternalistic, patriarchical, and culturally homogenous society, cohering around a pervasive Catholicism, did not readily accommodate difference. Constitutional principles and the associated set of values seemed to filter entry into family law proceedings, assign the exit routes, and often approved the institutional facilities which, at the outcome, provided care for the children deemed to have been variously failed by their parents. The welfare interests of very many children suffered as a result.

Irish society, over the past half century, has been transformed into a not untypical modern, western, largely urbanised nation, embracing diversity and multiculturalism and assimilating the principles and judicial rulings of international human rights law as required by its EU membership and by being a signatory to many treaties, conventions, and protocols. This, not coincidentally, has been accompanied by a barrage of changes to the Constitution: 38 amendments in total from 1939–2019; 28 since 1992; of which 10 were directly related to family law. Incremental adjustments to the Constitution, in conjunction with the influence of rulings made under Article 8 of the ECHR and of UN CRC principles, have spurred on the modernising of Irish family law. One significant indicator of the implications this has had for promoting the welfare interests of children lies in the nation's endorsement of 'the Children's Referendum'[229] in 2012 while a corresponding indicator of the further progress needed lies in the absence of any legal necessity for the consent of a child in many of the decision-making processes affecting those interests.

229 The Thirty-first Amendment of the Constitution inserted Article 42A into the Constitution.

Part IV

Jurisdictional analysis of a child's welfare/rights

A thematic approach

7 Themes and a comparative jurisdictional analysis

Introduction

This chapter undertakes a comparative analysis of the welfare principle's role and functions in England and Wales and in Ireland as outlined in Chapters 5 and 6, respectively. It trawls through that material, focusing on key aspects of the principle, identifying significant differentiating national characteristics, and tracing some broad contemporary patterns/trends of commonality and difference. In doing so, it follows the structure of those chapters to build a workable template to be used to facilitate a similar analysis of other jurisdictions in the future books of this series.

It begins, therefore, by dealing consecutively with matters of policy and principles, then with legislation and the court system: giving consideration, in the latter instance, to both domestic and international law. It identifies and examines differences in public family law as it relates to the welfare of children in the nations concerned, first in the civil law then in the criminal, before repeating the exercise in relation to private family law. Finally, the chapter points to a convergence in the similar and increasing use of hybrid court orders – applicable across both the public and private sectors of family law – and considers the significance of this development. In so doing, it reflects on the bearing of principles established in the wider framework of international law.

Policy, principles, and the legal system

In both jurisdictions, the law and policy relating to the welfare interests of children underwent radical change at the turn of the century. In Ireland the nature and extent of this change, constrained for decades by constitutionally entrenched principles requiring the state to protect and support the marital family, seemed to be part of a more general transformation of society as the inter-generational influence of the Catholic Church suddenly waned in response to a sequence of official reports detailing many decades of clerical abuse. In England and Wales the change was driven by pressure from the rising rate of family breakdown and an associated rapid increase in the volume of child care and protection cases.

DOI: 10.4324/9781003268642-12

Policy

In both jurisdictions, while there is a clear distinction between private and public family law and a further distinction in the latter between civil and criminal law, in England and Wales the public/private boundary, there is still no legislative right to access post-adoption support services nor any specification for such services. The line is becoming more blurred as the increased weighting given to the welfare principle forces a legal focus on protecting and promoting the wellbeing of children transcends the traditional categorisation of proceedings.

Public family law relating to children: civil jurisdiction

Government policy relating to family law in England and Wales has for some years been dominated by child protection concerns, to a much greater degree than in Ireland.

The provisions of the Children and Young Persons Act 1989 continue to provide the main pillars of the public law framework for the welfare interests of children in England and Wales as does its counterpart, the Child Care Act 1991, in Ireland. While both strengthen state interventionist powers and make a similar clear demarcation between civil and criminal matters, in Ireland the constitutional provisions provide the family – within its definitional constraints – with an additional layer of protection.

The prevention/protection balance

Despite an equivalence in statutory requirements to invest in preventative measures, there has been a heavier emphasis in England and Wales on coercive rather than consensual intervention in family affairs. This, for example, is reflected in the respective jurisdictional use of voluntary admissions to care which have always been a strong characteristic of state support for vulnerable families in Ireland, whereas in England and Wales the same offer of support, on the same terms, is often regarded with suspicion by such families who fear that a voluntary admission could lead to non-consensual adoption. Moreover, the frequency of scandals associated with adolescent girls in residential care in that jurisdiction is in itself a disincentive for parents in need of relief.

While both jurisdictions rely heavily on foster parents and on kinship placements for children admitted by care order to the public care system, the practice of using non-consensual adoption as the preferred exit strategy for such children has – for many years – been much more pronounced in England and Wales, is more deliberately facilitated through synchronised child care and adoption legislation, and is now a firmly established government policy. Arguably, in that jurisdiction, the introduction of the Children Act 1989 signalled the beginning of the end of extensive state policing of the welfare threshold. As traditional family structures and accompanying social mores ceded ground under pressure from the myriad challenges of modern society, resulting in an unprecedented volume of family law cases coming before the courts, bringing with them a disparate range of attendant parenting disputes, the state began its staged withdrawal from intervention in families where child protection was not a presenting issue. When such issues required state intervention it seemed to be accompanied by a policy that favoured investing resources in alternative long-term care arrangements in approved safe families – adoption or foster care – rather than in risky rehabilitation efforts with families judicially determined to have failed to safeguard the welfare interests of their children.

Both jurisdictions have reduced their reliance on residential care, though this change is more marked in England and Wales as, by the end of the twentieth century, the scandals attached to that resource in Ireland resulted in it being proportionately less used, preference being given instead to kinship care.

Public family law relating to children: criminal jurisdiction

Irish law and policy relating to the delinquency or criminal activities of children have, for most of the state's history, been governed by a legacy of British colonial legislation, principles, and institutions. By the turn of the last century, welfare interests were certainly not a determining criterion – nor even much more than a marginal factor – for the courts of both jurisdictions, when considering disposal options following the conviction of children for criminal offences.

The welfare/justice balance

In England and Wales, as in Ireland, the gravitational pull of these two reference points for responding to the criminal behaviour of children had, by the beginning of the twenty-first century, strengthened in favour of justice. Welfare had become an add-on factor, along with others, to be taken into account by those with responsibility – judiciary, police, prison officers, probation officers, etc. – for children found guilty of criminal conduct.

Private family law relating to children

In Ireland, as has been pointed out, "the regulation of sexuality, gender roles and reproduction has been a mechanism for defining Irish political identity … while the Catholic Church has been an influential force in the politics of gender and motherhood."[1] Although much has changed in recent years, the resistance to embracing emerging social mores is still apparent in the time lag that continues to constrain legal changes in relation to private family law matters such as divorce,

1 Allison, J., 'Enduring Politics: Legislating Assisted Reproduction Technologies in Ireland', *Reproductive Biomedicine & Society Online*, 2016, at p 4, at: www.researchgate.net/publication/311620332_Enduring_politics_the_culture_of_obstacles_in_legislating_for_assisted_reproduction_technologies_in_Ireland/link/5851685708ae7d33e012a54b/download.

abortion, assisted procreation, adoption by same-sex couples, surrogacy, and trans issues. This contrasts strongly with the position in England and Wales where for some decades a more objective functionality has prevailed in the equivalent law and social policy relating to family and reproductive matters.

Matrimonial

Matrimonial law in England and Wales is characterised mostly by state withdrawal from adult decisions on marital status accompanied by a sharper focus on ensuring that such decisions are conditional upon arrangements being made for the continuation of parental responsibility and for the protection of the welfare interests of any child involved; though, arguably, the latter has faded with the introduction of the Divorce, Dissolution and Separation Act 2020. For many decades matrimonial law and policy reflected the deep religious/cultural jurisdictional differences but the introduction of the Irish Family Law Act 2019 had done much to close the gap between the divorce laws of Ireland and England and Wales.

Guardianship and wardship

Guardianship, the most ancient and all-encompassing means for entrusting the welfare of a child to a non-parent has been greatly reduced in legal significance in England and Wales by the range of orders now available to the courts for vesting specific aspects of parental responsibility in a named person, but has retained its traditional significance in Ireland due to the lack of alternative orders. Similarly, wardship – the most authoritative court order for securing the welfare interests of a child – has retained its traditional role in Ireland but is now statutorily barred in England and Wales from being used where another order would be suitable.

Adoption

The jurisdictional differences in family law have been starkly apparent in adoption: in Ireland it has always been almost exclusively a consensual process; whereas in England and Wales a much higher proportion of all adoptions are non-consensual. While adoption as a private family law process is now greatly reduced in both jurisdictions, due to the decline in numbers of voluntarily relinquished children and to the global contraction of ICA, it has been further diminished in both by the introduction of special guardianship orders specifically designed to divert step-parent applicants away from adoption.

Family planning, abortion, surrogacy, IVF, etc.

Until relatively recently, there were also strong jurisdictional differences in relation to the availability of family planning services. In both, pregnancy for the infertile has become a stronger possibility due to improved techniques of artificial insemination and to the international availability of surrogacy, while abortion is now also available in Ireland – though access can be difficult – as it has been in England and Wales for many decades. These developments clearly increase the proportion of births that are 'wanted' and, correspondingly, increase the number of children whose welfare interests are likely to be promoted.

Principles

While the welfare principle is prominent in the relevant law of both jurisdictions – reinforced by their joint adherence to the ECHR, the UN CRC, and the rulings of the ECtHR – there are jurisdictional differences in the principle's role and weighting which are accentuated by differences in the interpretation given to ancillary principles.

The paramountcy principle

In England and Wales this principle, first introduced in the latter half of the twentieth century through use of wardship and since consolidated in child care and adoption legislation, has now ended the uncertainty associated with the fine distinctions previously made between different statutory definitions of the welfare test. From being one among many factors to be judicially considered in proceedings 'welfare' was elevated to become the primary objective – in matters affecting 'upbringing' – and was rapidly established as the governing benchmark in all such decisions taken in a public family law context. Unlike the corresponding position in Ireland, the issues that have arisen are not so much with regard to the principle's function in determining the outcome of proceedings, but more about whether it should have a role as a precursor, determining if proceedings can be instigated (hence, freeing orders and placement orders in relation to adoption from care) and indeed as a sequel (in terms of information rights for adoptees, etc.).

In contrast, paramountcy is a very recent newcomer to Irish law, having been restrained by the constitutional primacy given to the marital family. Not until 2015, when Article 42A amended the Constitution, did this principle become relevant in relation to: public family law as regards the 'safety and welfare of any child'; and to private, 'concerning the adoption, guardianship or custody of, or access to, any child.' It remains to be seen how exactly this constitutionally enshrined principle will be given effect in statutory proceedings and in judicial practice. In particular, it is uncertain whether it will function – as in England and Wales – to bridge the gap between the law of child care and protection and adoption law.

Paramountcy: child consent

Despite the increased legal weighting now given to the welfare interests of a child in both jurisdictions – and despite requirements of the UN CRC – there are virtually no circumstances in which the consent of the child concerned is a legislative requirement for a decision affecting his or her welfare.[2] However, in England and Wales, the *Gillick* decision[3] has provided legal authority for the rule that a child – less than 16 years of age – with sufficient maturity and discernment to understand an issue and its consequences, is entitled to give or withhold their consent in relation to it.

The parental responsibility principle

This principle suggests that such responsibilities are exclusively an attribute of parenthood which may be temporarily met by other persons or bodies but can never be wholly shed by a 'parent' to whom, by definition, they must continue to attach.

The 1989 Act unequivocally established 'parental responsibility' as a key legal construct in family law in England and Wales, thereby consigning the concepts of 'parental rights' and 'parental duties' to history. In Ireland, despite Article 42A, there remains some room for ambiguity as to the standing of this principle relative to the entrenched constitutional protection for the marital family unit accompanied by the corollary that the status of parent in any other form of 'family' must attract less protection. Much now depends on the introduction of the legislation necessary to give effect to Article 42A and on how the judiciary interpret and balance what are competing constitutional principles.

Parental responsibility and corporal punishment

In England, if not in Wales, the introduction of parental responsibility – both concept and court order – left unchanged the ingrained parental right to administer 'reasonable chastisement' in respect of their child. In Ireland, this right was specifically repealed in 2015.

The consanguinity principle

In both jurisdictions a feature of the law relating to children has been the considerable weighting attached to the blood-link as a judicial determinant of the welfare test when making decisions regarding arrangements for a child's custody or upbringing. In Ireland, this long-standing characteristic has been repeatedly re-affirmed while in England and Wales, despite the ruling in *Re G (Children)*,[4] it would seem probable that the judiciary now regard the blood-tie as no more than one factor among the many which must be considered when making such decisions, all of which are subordinate to the paramountcy principle.

2 Note, also, the Article 8 requirements of the General Data Protection Regs.

3 *Gillick v. West Norfolk and Wisbech Area Health Authority*, [1986] 1 AC 112, [1985] 3 All ER 402, HL.

4 [2006] UKHL 43 [2006] FLR 629.

Consanguinity and adoption

Traditionally, in both jurisdictions, there has been a presumption that the prospect of a child being retained within his or her family – by means of adoption or foster care, with relatives – must be preferable to a third party adoption. While this remains a guiding principle in Ireland, it no longer has any traction in England and Wales where the policy is to divert such applicants from adoption to special guardianship.

The proportionality principle

The 'principle of proportionality,' as the ECtHR declared 40 years ago, means that any state interference must correspond to a pressing social need, and be proportionate to the legitimate aim pursued, if it is to be 'necessary in a democratic society.'[5] This principle is central to Article 8 of the ECHR, both jurisdictions are equally required to take it into account in their decision-making and the judiciary in both make constant references to it. However, arguably, the interpretation and application of the principle is in practice subject to cultural context considerations.

Proportionality and adoption

In Ireland the principle would seem to be have been referenced as justification for not pursuing the interventionist measure of non-consensual adoption in respect of children in the public care system, though that may now change if only to a limited degree. The same issue in England and Wales generates warnings of caution from the judiciary, most notably in *Re B-S*,[6] but may not slow local authority recourse to pursuing adoption as the preferred exit strategy for children in the public care system.

The legal system and the public sector: legislation, courts, welfare/rights, and representation

The legal system model is much the same in these two common law jurisdictions: the hierarchical court structure, the classification of legislation, and the ancillary regulatory and advisory bodies are not dissimilar.

Legislative framework

The private/public and criminal/civil legislative divisions are again strikingly similar in both jurisdictions. A singular difference, however, is that Ireland has

5 *The Sunday Times v. United Kingdom*, Application No. 6538/74, (1979).
6 [2013] EWCA Civ 1146.

a Constitution and one that is heavily weighted with provisions requiring state protection and support for the family.

International law

Both jurisdictions are equally bound by much the same commitment to international law. Essentially – for the purposes of child welfare – this consists of the United Nations Convention on the Rights of the Child 1989, the International Covenant on Civil and Political Rights 1966, and the European Convention for the Protection of Human Rights and Fundamental Freedoms 1950.

Domestic legislation

While both jurisdictions have in place a modern platform of appropriate child welfare legislation, in England and Wales it is more comprehensive and thorough, mainly because it is built around the formative provisions of the 1989 Act. By stating the matters held to constitute a checklist of welfare interests and by providing a menu of court orders with broad applicability to family issues, this Act enabled a new, more uniform and objective application of this inherently subjective concept which did much to integrate and bring coherence to the public and private sectors of family law. By introducing the concept of parental responsibility and requirements on local authorities to provide services for children in need it placed a new emphasis on measures to prevent children entering the public care system. In contrast, the blend of constitutional and statutory provisions in Ireland – as they relate, variously, to children, parents, and the family – produces less consistency and little coherence. Irish legislation does, however, state as a fundamental principle that it is generally in the best interests of the child to be brought up in their own family which perhaps results in a firmer focus of resources to that end than is the case in England and Wales.

Courts and regulatory framework

The unified Family Court in England and Wales, operational since 2014, consolidates public and private family proceedings and the functions of county courts and magistrates' courts. This reorganisation has made the court system more 'child friendly' and navigable in terms of transferred proceedings. It has permitted a concentration of training, skills, and experience which has undoubtedly greatly facilitated the development of judicial expertise in relation to the welfare interests and rights of children. There is no equivalent in Ireland.

International judicial and regulatory bodies

Although both jurisdictions are equally amenable to rulings of the ECtHR, the extent to which England and Wales will remain so in respect of the ECJ and other

European bodies following BREXIT is open to question. Ireland, in contrast, will continue its current relationship with all such bodies.

Domestic judicial and regulatory bodies

The Irish national framework of courts and regulatory bodies is much the same as in England and Wales except that in relation to children there is no structure or culture of 'family courts' with specialist judiciary and ancillary support staff.

Family Court and family proceedings

It would seem that the sharp divide between the powers of court and local authority, characteristic of proceedings in England and Wales since *A v. Liverpool City Council*,[7] is less so in Ireland. The Irish judiciary, like their counterparts in England and Wales, have been repeatedly forceful in their condemnation of a lack of family support resources and have at times directed that action be taken to provide appropriate facilities. However, there is no Irish equivalent to the range – and mix of private and public orders – available to the judiciary in England and Wales.

Youth Court and criminal proceedings

Both jurisdictions maintain a clear separation of civil and criminal proceedings relating to children but while the Youth Courts in England and Wales are specialist courts, in Ireland the criminal offences of children are heard in the generic listings of the District Court. Although the latter is notionally re-purposed as the Children's Court, when determining such offences, that in itself is insufficient. The manner of processing care and protection and criminal proceedings in the Irish legal system is clearly inimical to the welfare interests of children.

Representation for children

For the welfare interests and rights of children to be given full recognition and weighting in the many fora in which decisions affecting them are taken, it is essential that they are represented by relevant professionals with the expertise to mediate on their behalf.

In England and Wales the child is normally a party in public law proceedings, and therefore a guardian and most usually a solicitor will be appointed, but not in the majority of private proceedings which are uncontested unless there are significant issues. In Ireland, there is less probability of a child being granted equivalent representation.

7 [1982] AC 363.

Consent of child

While in England and Wales there are no statutory provisions that provide a child – someone under the age of 18 years – with a right to give or withhold a legal consent, since the *Gillick*[8] ruling this will always be sought and respected where the child concerned shows sufficient maturity and discernment to grasp the issue and appreciate the consequences of their decision. In Ireland, the traditional rule requiring the views to be sought and taken into account prevails: there is neither statutory provision nor caselaw granting a child the right to make legally binding decisions.

Public bodies

The governments of both jurisdictions – as in a growing number of other countries – now signal the importance they attach to the needs of children by appointing ministers and establishing advocacy bodies with a specific brief to promote their rights and welfare interests.

Government departments for children

In England and Wales, the short-lived Department for Children, Schools and Families (DCSF) was established in 2007 under a designated Secretary of State. Its functions were largely directed towards schools but it also generated research to inform government policy on children's issues[9] until superseded by the present Department of Education in 2010. A not-dissimilar Irish government body was established in 2011 (as the Department of Children and Youth Affairs) under a Minister for Children and, following inter-departmental transfers of various functions, continues in effect as the Department of Children, Equality, Disability, Integration and Youth. It states its business as focusing on

> harmonising policy issues that affect children and young people in areas such as early childhood care and education, youth justice, children in care, child welfare and protection, adoption, family support, children and young people's participation, research on children and young people.[10]

8 *Gillick v. West Norfolk and Wisbech Area Health Authority*, [1986] 1 AC 112, HL.

9 See, for example 'Safe to Learn: Embedding Anti-bullying Work in Schools – Cyberbullying', at: www.thenbs.com/PublicationIndex/documents?Pub=DCSF.

Also see, 'The Protection of Children in England: A Progress Report' (March 2009) and 'The Protection of Children in England: Action Plan' (May 2009) at: https://assets.publishing.service.gov.uk/government/uploads/system/uploads/attachment_data/file/327238/The_protection_of_children_in_England_-_action_plan.pdf.

10 See, further, at: www.gov.ie/en/organisation/department-of-children-equality-disability-integration-and-youth/.

It too has published reports with important policy implications for the welfare of children in Ireland[11] but the fact that it continues in existence, having proven its worth in co-ordinating government business in relation to children, now establishes it as signifying an important differentiating jurisdictional characteristic.

Children's Commissioner/Ombudsman/Rapporteur

Both jurisdictions have their own domestic independent bodies with a brief for child welfare – the Children's Commissioner in England and Wales and the Ombudsman for Children in Ireland – together with national Human Rights Commissions and both are equally subject to monitoring by UN Special Rapporteurs. In addition, Ireland has its own Special Rapporteur for Child Protection. These specialist advisory bodies perform valuable functions in terms of auditing performance of statutory agencies, publishing guidance, and drawing attention to service deficits.

The welfare principle in contemporary practice: public family law: civil jurisdiction

In the main this is governed by the Children Act 1989 in England and Wales and in Ireland by the Child Care Act 1991, as amended by the Child and Family Agency Act 2013.

Prevention

In Ireland, the relationship between state and family was constitutionally consolidated on the basis that the former would protect and support the latter; although the latter was presumed to be a marital unit. In England and Wales there is a long-standing statutory requirement that every local authority shall take reasonable steps to identify the extent to which there are children in need within its area and make available statutorily specified services to their families. One telling indicator of jurisdictional difference in the preventative role of the state, and of an acceptance of that role as a public service, is that in Ireland most children in state care are admitted with the voluntary agreement of their parents.

State duties to support families and children in need

The Child Care Act 1991, as amended, requires Tusla – the Child and Family Agency[12] – to provide such services as may be appropriate to assist parents and avoid the need for state care. The equivalent duty under the Children Act 1989 explicitly states the preventative responsibilities of local authorities and specifies

11 See, for example, 'State of the Nation's Children' (2020) at: www.gov.ie/en/campaigns/1f703-state-of-the-nations-children/.

12 See, further, at: www.tusla.ie.

the services that should be made available but in practice the obligation to do so is mostly interpreted as being discretionary.

State intervention: consensual

Traditional constraints on the Irish definition of 'family' has very probably restricted entitlement to state support. In contrast, the fact that the 1989 Act extends recognition to persons bearing direct care responsibilities for a child – regardless of whether or not that person is related in any way to the child – as being thereby entitled to local authority assistance, greatly widens the potential of the welfare principle to consolidate the *status quo* care arrangements of children in circumstances which may be far removed from that of the marital nuclear family.

The preventative provisions of the 1989 Act, reinforced by the Children and Social Work Act 2017 and those of the Care Act 2014, have no Irish equivalent. In both the latter statutes the legislative intent was to require local authorities to focus on assessing the needs of children and young persons, especially those being discharged from care, to consider how such needs impact their wellbeing, and to specify the intended outcomes of their intervention. However, in response to the steadily increasing volume of child protection cases, local authorities are constantly having to divert scarce resources from prevention towards more coercive forms of intervention.

Specific support services

The specification of a range of family support services is another indicator of the positive legislative influence on the modern role of the welfare principle. It constitutes an objectification of incidences of welfare, allowing them to become a listing of duties owed to children. However, again, many are discretionary.

The relevant legislation in both jurisdictions specifies some services – voluntary care admission, accommodation for adolescents, and day care for pre-school children – the provision of which is mandatory, and others which are discretionary; though in practice even mandatory provision does not necessarily guarantee access. Children with a disability and their families are in particular need of services and in both jurisdictions there are statutory requirements mandating provision, but in Ireland service access is variable and often provided by voluntary organisations.

Protection

Both jurisdictions are facing rising numbers of care and protection cases and in both the legislation imposes strict duties on the relevant authorities. Whether due to insufficient resource investment, inability to cope with the scale of family breakdown, or resistance to consensual state intervention, the numbers of children committed to state care and remaining there until they 'age out' has been increasing rapidly for some decades.

State intervention: coercive

Within the broad boundaries of family law the most basic indicator of the welfare interests of the child lies in the statutory grounds for child abuse and neglect which, in England and Wales, is fixed by the fact or risk of significant harm.

The orders

The threshold for a care order is at first sight much the same in both jurisdictions. In fact, however, the Irish threshold is higher: there must be compelling reasons why the child cannot remain within parental care; and he or she must require care or protection which they are otherwise unlikely to receive. There is no equivalent to the specification of 'welfare' as set out in the checklist in s 1 of the 1989 Act. In addition, there would not appear to be the same incidence of sexual abuse cases as in England and Wales, and no suggestion that, as in the latter jurisdiction, 'a balance of probabilities test' would suffice to ground a care order.

State care

In both jurisdictions, children are either admitted to state care with parental consent or are committed without it under the authority of a care order. They are then placed either: with family members in 'kinship care'; in foster care; in an adoption placement; or in residential care. A notable jurisdictional difference is that in Ireland most children, if decreasing in number, are in state care on a voluntary basis.

Foster care: partnership, rehabilitation, and concurrent planning

In Ireland, as in England and Wales, retention in foster care, under the authority of a care order, is now the accepted basis for ensuring a safe and permanent home environment for children in the public care system. This continues to be viewed as being most conducive to promoting a child's welfare interests because it enables him or her to retain links with their parents, facilitated by contact arrangements, which best ensure that he or she maintain an authentic sense of identity and of belonging to their family and community of origin.

Partnership and rehabilitation

The ECtHR has stressed in *YC v. the United Kingdom* that

> family ties may only be severed in very exceptional circumstances and that everything must be done to preserve personal relations and, where appropriate, to 'rebuild' the family. It is not enough to show that a child could be placed in a more beneficial environment for his upbringing.[13]

13 Op cit, at para 35.

Further, *Gorgulu v. Germany*[14] provides authority for the view that the child's welfare must be seen in a long-term context and this may even require terminating a third party adoption placement, however satisfactory, if local authority intervention is to meet the test of 'proportionality.'

However, there has for some time been a distinct difference in the jurisdictional response to this judicial statement of principle on a central child welfare issue. Current UK judicial guidance[15] diverges from both ECtHR benchmark cases and from practice in Ireland. In England and Wales there have been clear policy statements that adoption is to be preferred to long-term foster care, a policy facilitated by legislative provisions aligning the grounds for care orders and adoption orders, by the practice of concurrent placements, and by the use of freeing orders and placement orders. In Ireland the constitutional protection afforded a marital family unit has traditionally blocked access to adoption for children in state care from such families. While this block has in theory been removed by constitutional amendment it would seem that the judiciary is responding with great caution to the prospect of non-consensual adoption. Partnership with parents and rehabilitative work may have been something of a forced option, but it has now become established practice and is unlikely to change radically.

Residential care

Residential care provision in both jurisdictions, once the mainstay of the statutory child care system, has greatly diminished due in large part to the reputational damage inflicted by the number of official reports associating such care with a high incidence of child abuse. This was particularly the case in Ireland, where institutional care was most often in facilities owned and staffed by religious organisations, but both jurisdictions abruptly tapered off their use of children's homes in preference for family-based care. By the closing decades of the twentieth century, this form of provision had virtually disappeared except for a few small specialist units.

Secure accommodation

Safeguarding the welfare interests of children requires the provision of secure residential facilities to ensure the protection of those whose behaviour presents a threat to themselves or to others. While both jurisdictions rely to some degree on such provision, the scale of need is greatest in England and Wales.

14 Application No 74969/01, ECtHR, 26.02.2004. Also, see, *P, C and S v. UK* (2002) 35 EHRR 31, *K and T v. Finland* [2001] 2 FLR 707, and *Johansen v. Norway* (1996) 23 EHRR 33.

15 See *Seddon v. Oldham MBC* [2015] EWHC 2609 (Fam) and *Re W (A Child)* [2016] EWCA Civ 793.

Unaccompanied migrant minors and trafficking

The phenomenon of children travelling long distances without parents – who may be dead or missing – crossing borders, usually with unrelated adult migrants, until eventually arriving in England and Wales or in Ireland, where they are detained, is no longer unusual. Unquestionably, the challenge of addressing the welfare interests of such children is considerable but there would appear to be little in the way of significant jurisdictional difference in the approach taken. While efforts are made to locate birth family members, and protect them from possible traffickers, the children are most usually: assessed by relevant professionals; medically examined; then placed in foster homes and enrolled in local schools.

Adoption

The traditional role of the state in relation to children voluntarily relinquished for adoption by their parent/s continues in both jurisdictions, even if greatly reduced in scale and more complicated by statutory support duties.

Non-consensual adoption from state care

As mentioned above, the non-consensual adoption of children has for many years been a central part of government policy for those in state care in England and Wales. It is a policy that by utilising concurrent placements results in young children being adopted by their dual approved (for adoption and fostering) foster parents after a relatively short time in the care system. In Ireland, while there is no corresponding established policy, a few children do currently exit public care by way of adoption, those that do tend to be adolescents being adopted by their long-term foster parents. Recent changes in the law will facilitate the future possible adoption of children from marital families, but this is unlikely to develop into a central policy objective.

Domestic consensual adoption

In both jurisdictions there are now very few voluntary adoptions and fewer every year: improvements in welfare benefits, housing entitlement, etc., coupled with the virtual disappearance of any associated stigma (though not among ethnic minority groups), has almost eradicated voluntary relinquishment as the only option available to an unmarried mother. Nonetheless, the volume of consensual adoptions – by step-parents and others following family breakdown – as a means of legally re-constituting families, has been a particular characteristic of adoption practice in England and Wales where it has placed a burden on the local authorities which are required to provide the court with social work reports on the families concerned.

Adoption support and post-adoption services

Local authorities in England and Wales, like their counterparts in Ireland, have adoption support duties as required by the Hague Convention, including in respect of intercountry adoptions. The provision of relevant services is a statutory requirement in the former jurisdiction, under s 3(2)(b) of the 2002 Act, but is not statutorily specified in Ireland. The Adoption Passport scheme plays a significant role in relation to the adoption of children from the care system: the provision of considerable financial support for two years post-adoption, together with social work involvement, makes a greater contribution to stabilising a new family than the extension of boarded-out payments does in Ireland. Again in England and Wales, unlike Ireland, there are also statutory duties regarding facilitating post-adoption contact on request and also with regard to the disclosure of identifying information.

The welfare principle in contemporary practice: public family law: criminal jurisdiction

In both jurisdictions the criminal justice system as it relates to children, has been separated from civil proceedings and in both the role and weighting of the welfare principle is quite marginal.

The justice system and children

In England and Wales, unlike Ireland, there is now a legislative framework and a range of professionals and facilities specifically designated to address the criminal conduct of children. While the justice system in both jurisdictions is under a general duty to protect and promote the welfare of children they are both focused primarily on preventing re-offending.

Children who pose a threat to the welfare of others

The social problem of child criminality has been more pronounced, attracting greater media attention and has endured for longer in England and Wales than in Ireland. Consequently, the former jurisdiction now has in place a number of specialist facilities, supported by teams of appropriate professionals, for which there is no Irish – or only an inadequate Irish – equivalent.

Age of criminal responsibility

The age at which a child will be held criminally liable for their actions is too low – by UN CRC standards – in both jurisdictions: 10 years of age in England and Wales and 12 in Ireland.

Children in court

Special courts are designated to hear proceedings concerning allegations of child criminality: the Youth Justice court in England and Wales and the Children's Court in Ireland. In neither is there any guarantee that legal aid and representation by a solicitor will be provided and both require the child to be accompanied in court by their parents.

Role of the welfare principle

The courts of both jurisdictions will have the benefit of a social work report drawing attention to any factors of a mitigating nature. There is a common legislative requirement to take into account matters relating to the welfare of a child when considering disposal options.

Court orders: community sentences

Neither the Youth Court nor the Children's Court are empowered to issue explicitly welfare oriented disposal options; both, for example, are prevented from making care orders in respect of a child found to have committed a criminal offence. The judiciary in both jurisdictions may issue probation orders, community service orders, or supervision orders and may impose fines.

Court orders: custodial sentences

Both jurisdictions have available much the same menu of custodial orders that provide for treatment or training options.

The welfare principle in contemporary practice: private family law

The traditional boundaries of private family law have for some time now been under constant attack, resulting in the customary proceedings for divorce, adoption, etc. being radically adapted to serve new functions.

Children and re-constituted families

The heterosexual family unit, based on 'marriage for life,' is no longer as ubiquitous as it once was, which is not to imply that relationship stability within the traditional marital framework is inherently more durable than in its non-marital counterpart, but it is an indicator of how family life and its associated certainties have changed over the course of only one or two generations.

Matrimonial

Family breakdown – whether marital or not – constitutes by far the greatest risk to the welfare interests of children. In the UK this has risen by 8 per cent over the past decade – largely in the context of non-marital families.[16] In fact it is estimated that

16 See, further, at: https://marriagefoundation.org.uk/wp-content/uploads/2017/03/MF-paper-Annual-family-breakdown.pdf.

this jurisdiction has the highest rate of family instability in the developed world, in particular among cohabiting couples with children under 12,[17] and this has become a settled and accepted characteristic of social life. In Ireland, where the rate of family breakdown is a great deal lower, with divorce rates at approximately half those in England and Wales,[18] there is a correspondingly stronger expectation of stability in family life. Divorce, after all, only became domestically available in 1996. Both jurisdictions now have a modernised body of matrimonial legislation catering for the marriage, divorce, and separation of heterosexual and same-sex couples.

Family breakdown and the welfare principle

In both jurisdictions, where there are children involved in proceedings for judicial separation or divorce, the court will require an assurance regarding the proposed arrangements for their future care and information will need to be submitted for the court to be satisfied that their welfare interests will be safeguarded. In both this is addressed in a fairly perfunctory manner where the parties are not contesting future care arrangements: in Ireland, they state their agreed arrangements in an 'Affidavit of Welfare'; in England and Wales, they make an equivalent written declaration; the court duly notes the fact that arrangements, satisfactory to the parties concerned, have been agreed. Where the parties are contesting future care arrangements then in both jurisdictions the court will most probably appoint a GAL (a CAFCASS appointment in England and Wales) to carry out an assessment and make recommendations regarding the best interests of the children concerned: such an appointment is at judicial discretion in Ireland; and is more likely to be accompanied by the appointment of a solicitor in England and Wales. However, since 2022 when the Divorce, Dissolution and Separation Act 2020 came into force, contested divorce proceedings ceased in England and it remains to be seen how this change will affect the future appointment of GALs in divorce proceedings.

In both jurisdictions there is a legislative requirement that the court apply a 'welfare test' to ensure that the proposed child care arrangements are satisfactory and in both this is achieved by applying a 'welfare checklist' to determine whether or not – or to what extent – the arrangements comply with child welfare indicators. Whereas in Ireland the court may enforce its determination by issuing traditional orders for custody and access, in England and Wales the court has a fuller menu of orders – including child arrangements orders – available to it. In neither jurisdiction is the welfare of a child treated in law as being the matter of paramount importance but in both the views of the child must be ascertained and taken into account.

17 DeRose, L., et al, *The Cohabitation Go-round: Cohabitation and Family Instability across the Globe*, New York, Social Trends Institute, 2017.

18 See, further, at: https://ionainstitute.ie/marriage-breakdown-in-ireland-higher-than-we-think/.

Guardianship

The duties of a guardian include those of care, custody, and maintenance of the child concerned and the entailed right to make decisions regarding their health, welfare, religious upbringing, and education. This ancient judicial power for entrusting the welfare and property of a child to an appointed person until the child 'comes of age' continues to have a prominent role in Ireland, though less so in England and Wales. In both it is seen as vesting in the appointee a degree of responsibility that mediates between that of a foster parent and an adopter. Again in both, a variant known as 'special guardianship' is now commonly viewed by the judiciary as appropriate in circumstances where step-parents wish to have the status and responsibilities of a parent but where the all-encompassing powers of adoption are not justified and could lead to confusion for the child concerned. In both jurisdictions when determining whether or not to make a guardianship order, the court is required to regard the child's welfare as the matter of paramount importance.

Adoption

As a private family law consensual procedure, adoption has greatly diminished in recent years in both jurisdictions.

Step-parent adoption

The adoption of a child by a person or persons related to him or her – mostly step-parents – and known as a 'family adoption,' had become the most common type in both jurisdictions by the early years of the twenty-first century. However, for the welfare interests of a child, the disadvantages of this form of adoption continued: it completely severed all legal links between the child and their birth father together with his extended family; it changed the child's legal identity; and it obscured the biological links between the parties concerned. Consequently legislators in both jurisdictions have, in recent years, introduced a requirement that the courts give preference to alternative orders, such as guardianship or special guardianship, when considering the appropriateness of step-parent adoption applications.

Cultural/religious affinity

Article 20(3) of UN CRC, states that when an out-of-home placement is being considered for a child, preference should be given to one that provides for a cultural affinity between adopters and child as this accords with what is best for the latter's long-term welfare – subject to his or her agreement. This has given rise to much contention regarding the respective merits of 'colour blind' or racially congruent policies but it is, perhaps, beyond contention that for an older child a placement which reinforces his or her existing cultural/religious identity must be the most welfare affirmative. Therefore, the policy decision in England to rescind the requirement in s 1(5) of the 2002 Act that 'due consideration be given to religious persuasion, racial origin and cultural and linguistic background,' would seem to breach the Article 20(3) principle and be potentially adverse to the welfare interests of many children. This legislative initiative also creates a significant point of difference between the adoption law and policy of the two jurisdictions.

Post-adoption contact, information disclosure, and state support services

A characteristic of the adoption process in England and Wales – distinguishing it from its Irish counterpart – is the presumption, prevailing since 1975, that on reaching the age of 18, every adopted person has the right to access their original birth certificate and any information held by the relevant adoption agency. Legally sanctioned post-adoption arrangements facilitating information disclosure for adoptees, permitting contact between the parties, and granting an entitlement to state support services now routinely accompany what was once the most exclusive and private of all family law orders. This marks a sea change in the definition of adoption, one indicative of the greater legal weighting attached to the welfare interests of children relative to the needs of adopters, but while this is underpinned by statutory provisions in England and Wales, there is no comparable Irish legislation.

There is considerable jurisdictional difference in the extent of financial support available to adopters. In Ireland the Adoption Benefit grants adopters an entitlement to 24 weeks of employment leave and a compensatory financial payment from the date of placement; essentially a variant of the similar entitlement available to working birth parents. Equivalent entitlements are available in England and Wales but, in relation to adoption from the state care system, there is no Irish equivalent to the level and duration of financial grants and professional support available in the former jurisdiction which is accompanied by a full package of specified services.

Intercountry adoption

In all developed nations, the correlation between increased recourse to intercountry adoption and decreased domestic availability of voluntary relinquished adoptable children – particularly babies – is unmistakable. Clearly, this development is one with considerable implications for the welfare of the children concerned; particularly those within the developed nations who are older and/or have health or social care issues.

A corollary to the well-developed practice of non-consensual adoption as a public family law process in England and Wales has been a corresponding low reliance on the private process of intercountry adoption. The opposite being true in Ireland. However, both jurisdictions share with other developed countries the experience of a rapidly shrinking ICA market as countries traditionally relied upon cease to make children available, while surrogacy and ART make it increasingly possible to bypass adoption as a means of creating a family.

Surrogacy

In Ireland, as in England and Wales, there are broadly relevant legislative provisions but surrogacy agreements are neither prohibited nor legally enforceable, and although there is no regulatory oversight in the former jurisdiction there is some in the latter. In both, however, there are many hundreds if not thousands of children born by surrogacy arrangements, mostly contracted overseas, for whom there are often issues regarding their legal status.

Surrogate, child, and the commissioning parents

The legal uncertainties that accompany surrogacy arrangements in both jurisdictions – and are most apparent in commercial arrangements made overseas in respect of children who return to be domiciled in either jurisdiction – must clearly be adverse to the welfare interests of the children concerned.

Abduction

Child abduction occurs when a child is removed from a parent or person vested with legal custody, without their permission, and is invariably accompanied by contention if not trauma regarding the welfare interests of the child concerned. With increasing frequency, as globalisation accelerates the volume and rate of international travel, such abduction involves the legal systems of more than one country and the parties concerned find their actions and legal proceedings governed by the Hague Convention on the Civil Aspects of Child Abduction 1980. As of 2022, 101 nations were parties to this multilateral treaty which requires the prompt return of any child wrongfully removed from, or wrongfully retained in, a country that is not their country of habitual residence. As both Ireland and England and Wales are parties to this treaty, any contention regarding the abduction of a child habitually resident there and taken to a country within the framework of 101 nations, will be adjudicated in accordance with Convention provisions.

Returning an abducted child

The Convention is primarily concerned with jurisdictional issues, it provides a mechanism for facilitating the comity of nations, treats the welfare interests of the child as a matter of secondary concern,[19] and provides clear and fixed rules for the return of an abducted child. This differs from the approach adopted in similar circumstances involving a non-Convention country where the welfare of the

19 See, for example, *X v. Latvia*, Application No. 27853/09, (2013).

child can be accorded a greater weighting, as conditioned by the cultural context prevailing in that country,[20] thus allowing for more flexibility and uncertainty as regards the return of an abducted child.

In both jurisdictions the majority of international child abduction cases fall to be determined in accordance with the Hague Convention. This in turn depends on the judicial interpretation given to the grounds providing an exception to the prompt return requirement in Article 12. Of particular importance in this context is Article 13(b) which provides that when to do so would expose him/her to a 'grave risk of harm' or otherwise place him/her in an 'intolerable situation,' then an abducted child should not be returned to their country of habitual residence. While in most cases the facts are such as to permit a clear ruling based on these terms, it is probable that where there is doubt – the country of origin does present a degree of risk or of exposure to an intolerable situation – then the probability is that both jurisdictions err on the side of caution and decide on the basis of the primary, but not the paramount, welfare interests of the child. In conducting such a balancing exercise, both jurisdictions would appear to rely on the proportionality principle – weighing the welfare of the child against the gravity of the risk – in accordance with established domestic caselaw relating to the welfare principle.

Child's wishes

Under the Hague Convention, Article 13, a court is not obliged to order the return of a child if it finds that the child objects and has attained an age and degree of maturity at which it is appropriate to take account of his or her views. Also, the Brussels Regulation provides for the right of the child to be heard during the procedure unless the judge considers it inappropriate due to the child's age and degree of maturity.

In both jurisdictions, the court will hear and take into account any objection of a child to his/her return to their country of origin, even if that child is no more than six years of age.[21] While in Ireland the requirement to do so is subject to the 'take into account' caveat, in England and Wales the *Gillick* ruling ensures that a child, even if aged 16 or less will, if of sufficient maturity and discernment, have an actual right to decide whether it is in their interests to return or not.

The welfare principle in contemporary practice: public/private family law

The family law boom in litigation during the late twentieth century was accompanied by an erosion of the traditional common law regard for the boundaries of private family life, even if this seemed to be offset by the gathering momentum of

20 *Re J (A Child) (Return to Foreign Jurisdiction: Convention Rights)* [2005] UKHL 40.

21 See, in Ireland, *MN v. RN*, [2008] IEHC 382; and in England and Wales, *W v. W (Abduction: Acquiescence: Children's Objections)* [2010] England and Wales High Court 332 (Family Division).

ECtHR rulings, under Article 8 of the ECHR, on the human right to privacy and autonomy.

Public/private family law

Over a comparatively short period of time the welfare principle has evolved to become a free-standing legal tool, to be developed and applied across both public and private family law. Among the consequences has been the emergence of what may be termed 'hybrid' court orders.

Public service matters

Socio-economic living conditions and incidences of poverty will necessarily play a key role in determining the welfare of any nation's children. The extent to which a state provides for equality of opportunity and equity of wealth distribution, thereby raising the floor for the general wellbeing of its citizens and in so doing raising the welfare standards of the nation's children, can neither be overlooked nor be fully taken into account in a study such as this (see, also, Chapter 1). Additionally, the quality and accessibility of state public services will mitigate the deficits of the socially disadvantaged and have a direct bearing on the health and welfare of children. This is most obviously the case in relation to employment, health, and education.

Employment

Government concern to provide basic protection for the many children absorbed into the nation's workforce, most probably originated in England with the onset of the 'industrial revolution' in or around the mid-eighteenth century. This was initially driven by a policy, advocated by social activists such as Mary Carpenter and Octavia Hill, to mitigate the harsh, unsafe and often unhealthy, long working days that characterised child labour at that time (see, further, Chapter 2). With the introduction of mandatory schooling, that initial policy developed to include a concern that children were available to attend school. In Ireland, it is probable that although British legislation extended to Ireland during the nineteenth century, the absence of an industrial workforce generating similar concerns, delayed comparable government intervention until the introduction of mandatory schooling following Ireland's independence in 1922.

In recent years both jurisdictions have been equally obliged to respect EEC directives regarding the working conditions for children which aims to protect their welfare by such measures as: the prohibition of employment for school-aged children and also provisions on working hours, night work, rest periods, annual leave, and rest breaks.[22]

22 See EU Council Directive on the protection of young people at work (94/33/EC), 1994.

Health

Parents have a clear legal duty to ensure that their child's health is protected and are required to do so by availing of relevant public services when their child is in need of health care. In both jurisdictions health services are proactive in protecting the health of children and promoting their welfare by, for example: the domiciliary visits of health visitors and district nurses in respect of very young children; and by conducting regular ophthalmic and dentistry monitoring and treatment programmes. Again, in both, the courts have consistently upheld the right and duty of authorities to intervene when parental refusal or neglect in relation to health and safety matters jeopardises the life of their child. It is possible that free access to treatment, through the National Health Service, incentivises parents in England and Wales to avail of non-stigmatising child welfare services to a greater extent than their Irish counterparts and probable that the opposite is the case in relation to availing of family planning services, access to which in Ireland may be subject to the religious beliefs of service providers.

Education

In both jurisdictions the state education system imposes a strict statutory duty on parents to ensure that a child of compulsory school age – 5 to 16 years of age – attends an authorised school, unless parents have been granted permission to provide home schooling. In Ireland, the education infrastructure and educational content are permeated by Catholicism and to that extent, it may be that the state education system could be said to be not wholly compliant with the welfare interests of children who need to be attuned to the broad social mores of contemporary society.

Legal proceedings

In both jurisdictions there is a clear separation of justice and welfare proceedings as they relate to children. However, in England and Wales the further separation between public and private civil proceedings has become less distinct.

Adoption from state care

The policy of facilitating the adoption of children from the public child care system is very contentious. It is viewed by some as a government strategy to redefine a matter of public policy by: privatising its responsibilities through the transfer of child care costs from the public to the private sector; and endeavouring to assuage the demand, represented by an ever growing waiting list of approved adopters, for adoptable children. There are those who consider it to be wholly immoral to legally cut a child's ties to their birth family, that it must be preferable to keep him or her in a safe home environment while facilitating their links with parents and other family members so as to ensure the child retains an authentic sense of identity. Others feel that to allow a child, failed by parental care, to drift between foster homes and be deprived of opportunities to develop attachments, trust, and a sense of belonging, is to deny the developmental needs of that child and the relevance of the welfare principle.

For some decades the respective policies of the two jurisdictions in relation to the non-consensual adoption of children from state care has been markedly different: in England and Wales it has been actively pursued, it is claimed to be the best way of promoting a child's welfare, and concurrent placements, financial assistance, and other forms of support are being used to facilitate it; in Ireland it has so far only been used in relation to a very small number of children – almost all adolescents – adopted by their long-term foster parents. The latter jurisdiction has, in keeping with its constitutional principles, invested instead in maintaining rather than displacing the link between a child in state care and his or her family of origin. This approach is one that would seem to be in line with that advocated by the ECtHR,[23] which has urged that only after every effort has been made to explore rehabilitation of child and birth family will a default recourse to adoption be compliant with Article 8 of the ECHR.

Wardship

Wardship proceedings are matters for the High Court exercising its inherent jurisdiction. Once commenced, the administration of wardship may be transferred to a lower court. It is now seldom used as the 1989 Act expressly prohibits recourse to wardship where statutory proceedings are available to achieve the same result. However, in practice wardship orders are still occasionally made in circumstances of unusual complexity or urgency.

Wardship never acquired in Ireland any equivalence to the level and range of usage it had in England and Wales where local authorities in the latter decades of the twentieth century resorted to it in a care and protection context because of its convenience, its flexibility, and because it enabled pressurised social workers to share responsibility for risky child protection cases with the High Court.

Court orders

A differentiating characteristic of jurisdictional law, as it relates to children, is that in England and Wales the judiciary and local authority have available a modern and comprehensive set of functionally distinct, issue focused, statutory orders. With the exception of criminal law, family proceedings now provide a fixed menu of orders that transect the public and private sectors, bringing a greater degree of consistency and coherence to the role of the welfare principle than was traditionally the case. Ireland, in contrast, very largely continues to rely heavily on

23 *Haase v. Germany*, Application No. 11057/02, (2005).

the care, custody, and guardianship orders that were once the mainstay of state intervention – consensual and coercive – in the family affairs of both jurisdictions.

Parental responsibility order

Although there are many more child oriented orders in England and Wales than in Ireland, and although in legal reality the use of guardianship in Ireland may not be so different from the former's parental responsibility order, arguably the concept and the order signify an important jurisdictional difference in the law relating to children. Ireland has not shared, neither for as long nor to the same extent, the experience in the other jurisdiction of non-marital families, family breakdown, and re-constituted families. That experience gave rise to a social acceptance that while parents are free to re-negotiate their adult relationships there should be available a legal means whereby they can acquire, or be allocated, the rights and duties of a parent in respect of any child born to them or for whom they have had a full-time caring role. In keeping with the fluidity of contemporary sexual relationships, a parental responsibility order enables a legal link between an adult and child to be acquired or maintained by, for example, an unmarried father, a divorcee, an unrelated mother, or a local authority. The holder of such an order may share joint parental responsibility for a particular child with one or more other holders. This order is important, perhaps more than any other, because it represents the complexities inherent in the role of the welfare principle in a modern developed western society and provides a legal mechanism – transcending public and private divisions in family law – for naming a person or entity as having an ongoing parental role in the life of a named child; which may well be perceived by the latter as crucial to their welfare.

Guardianship order

The legislative intent in both jurisdictions – though more so in England and Wales than in Ireland – would seem to be to divert applicants, who in the past would have initiated adoption proceedings to secure their care relationship with a child, towards guardianship in circumstances where the absolute and exclusionary authority of adoption is unnecessary to provide permanence and security for the welfare of a child.

Other

Orders protecting a custodial parent from the threat of domestic violence are an important means of safeguarding a child's welfare interests. While these are most frequently sought in a private family law context, they are also relevant in the public arena as foster parents and adopters may on occasion be applicants in circumstances where protection is needed from members of a child's birth family. These and other such hybrid orders, transecting public and private sectors of family law, are on the increase in both jurisdictions.

Conclusion

It might have been expected that proximity to its more powerful neighbour – the primogeniture common law jurisdiction – would have led to Ireland sharing in much the same developmental phases as regards the law relating to the welfare of children. That was not the case.

Family law is shaped by cultural context.[24] Well before its constitutionally embedded independence from England in 1937, Ireland was very different in terms of religion/culture and associated social mores from its imperial ruler.[25] Administrative control ensured that both jurisdictions started their legislative family law history from the same common law baseline and some remnants of that history – such as the Probation of Offenders Act 1907 and the now much redacted Guardianship of Infants Act 1886 – stand as reminders of their shared genesis. However, with independence and with its distinctive religious/cultural identity firmly represented in constitutional provisions, the Irish approach to family, to marriage, to the welfare of children, and to related legal issues, was initially markedly different to that of its neighbour and remained so for most of the twentieth century. Catholicism wholly permeated such matters – as it did health and education – which, inevitably, led to jurisdictional differences in public and private family law and to differences in the interpretation and application of the welfare principle.

Nonetheless, there were and continue to be areas of jurisdictional commonality. The low age of criminal responsibility being one such negative indicator of child welfare which both continue to share, as is the absence of any statutory recognition of the need for a child's consent in any decision-making process affecting his or her upbringing. The current distinction between public and private family law and between civil and criminal law as this relates to children is another. The arrangements for the voice of a child to be heard in court, and represented by a GAL and solicitor, are also similar. The continuation of traditional private proceedings such as guardianship and wardship is again something they share.

The areas of jurisdictional difference are, perhaps, more revealing. The use of adoption is clearly different: in England and Wales, the reliance on non-consensual adoption from state care and a corresponding low reliance on intercountry adoption have no counterpart in Ireland. This would seem to be linked to the greater emphasis in Ireland on the use of voluntary care admissions and on rehabilitative work with parents following the admission or committal of their children to public care. Until relatively recently – and continuing though to a lesser degree – as Irish matrimonial proceedings did not include divorce so there was no equivalent to the considerable body of English jurisprudence governing custody arrangements following marriage dissolution. Associated with the much greater volume of public

24 A conclusion reflected in the majority ruling of the ECtHR in *A, B, and C v. Ireland*, Application No. 25579/05, (2010).

25 A not-dissimilar colonial experience to that which occurred in such other common law countries as India, Pakistan, and the Philippines.

and private family proceedings in England was the need for a more coherent family court system, with specially trained judiciary and other staff. This is now well established and represents a significant differentiating jurisdictional characteristic which is reinforced by a sophisticated menu of court orders, many equally applicable across both public and private sectors.

Not until the early years of the twenty-first century were there some indications of jurisdictional convergence, and these were probably due to a shared exposure to an array of influences that shaped a common response. Among the more potent of these were: the inexorable demographic trends forcing a contraction in public spending; a rise in the rate of family breakdown, creating an ever-growing pool of vulnerable children; the emergence of a body of academic research – particularly in the field of developmental psychology – which greatly enhanced and informed a professional understanding of child welfare-related matters; and the steady pressure from international judicial and regulatory bodies – particularly rulings of the ECtHR – encouraging national compliance with principles of international jurisprudence. The first two resulted in both jurisdictions prioritising coercive over consensual state intervention and directing it primarily towards child protection and criminality. The third and fourth generated a recognition that family-based care, where safe and permanent attachments could flourish, was preferable to both residential care and to successive short-term foster placements. The combination of all four has led to the state in both jurisdictions retreating from engagement in family disruption, unless there is evidence of child protection concerns to which most resources are now deployed in a well co-ordinated multi-disciplinary response. This is accompanied by an investment in regulating preventative service provision and in funding the mediatory work of voluntary organisations and of oversight bodies such as Children's Commissioners.

Conclusion

The journey from a concern for the welfare of children to respect for their legal rights has some way to go in the British Isles. Indicators of the distance yet to be travelled are many and varied. One such is the obdurate retention in England and Wales of what is probably the lowest age of criminal responsibility for children in the developed western world.[1] England also continues to uphold a parent's 'right' to physically chastise their child and declines to mandate the reporting of suspected child abuse. In Ireland, the latter is mandatory,[2] the age of criminal responsibility is set slightly higher[3] but the court system remains unmodernised – an 'outlier of poor practice' – and inimical to the welfare interests of children.[4] Both, however, share a similar reluctance to enact legislative provisions that specifically require a child's consent to a decision affecting his or her welfare. These indices, representative of traditional state/family relationships, would seem non-compliant with contemporary international principles as stated primarily in the United Nations Convention on the Rights of the Child 1989 (UN CRC), the European Convention for the Protection of Human Rights and Fundamental Freedoms 1950 (ECHR), and as elucidated in associated case law.[5]

By way of closing the book and identifying exploratory tools to be used in other books in the series, this short conclusion focuses on some of the more indicative aspects of jurisdictional difference as regards the law relating to the welfare/rights of children from a perspective framed by relevant UN CRC principles.

1 Set at ten years of age by the Children and Young Persons Act 1933 (as amended), s 50. See, for example, comments of the UN Committee on the Rights of the Child, *Concluding Observations: United Kingdom Of Great Britain And Northern Ireland*, United Nations, (2008) at para 78. Note that in Sweden, Finland, and Norway the age of criminal responsibility is set at 15 years.

2 Children First Act 2015, s 14.

3 Set at 12 years of age by the Children Act 2001, s 52, as amended by the Criminal Justice Act 2006, s 129.

4 Corbett, M. and Coulter, C., *Child Care Proceedings: A Thematic Review of Irish and International Practice* (Department of Children and Youth Affairs, 2019), as cited in Annual Report of the Special Rapporteur on Child Protection 2020 at p 144.

5 For further information on the instruments contributing to the building of an international rights context for children, see O'Halloran, K., *European Perspectives on Child Welfare and Rights*, Routledge (forthcoming).

DOI: 10.4324/9781003268642-13

The United Nations Convention on the Rights of the Child 1989 (UN CRC)

This Convention, signed by some 196 nations, provides the most relevant and well known international declaration of rights held to be vested in children.[6] It lists 42 substantive rights and requires national courts to ensure that decisions broadly comply with the general and specific obligations set out in the Convention. While it has no designated enforcement mechanism, the Committee on the Rights of the Child (CRC) does make recommendations to states, on the basis of reports filed with it under Article 44, for improvements in national law and practice. For present purposes it would seem to offer a convenient audit mechanism and a useful tool for conducting a comparative analysis of jurisdictional respect for the welfare/rights of a child.

Article 2 – Non-discrimination principle

This directs that all Convention rights are to apply to children without exception and without discrimination of any kind. Article 2(2) requires that all appropriate measures must be taken to ensure that the child is protected against all forms of discrimination or punishment on the basis of the status, activities, expressed opinions, or beliefs of the child's parents, legal guardians, or family members. As regards Ireland, however, the CRC was 'deeply concerned' about 'the structural discrimination against Traveller and Roma children, including as regards their access to education, health, and an adequate standard of living.'[7] In that jurisdiction – despite the prohibition on discrimination in Article 40.1 of the Constitution – for almost the entire duration of adoption as a statutory process, children from marital families were excluded. Although the law has very recently been changed to remove this discriminatory provision, the constitutional protections for such families remain in place and it is not yet clear whether the practice will change in accordance with the law.

Arguably, the fact that the age of criminal responsibility is set at 10 and 12 years of age in England and Ireland, respectively, also constitutes a breach of this principle and, to that extent, in England more so than in Ireland.

Article 3 – Best interests of the child is a primary consideration

Article 3 states the most important principle in the Convention. It requires that 'in all actions concerning children, whether undertaken by public or private social welfare institutions, courts of law, administrative authorities or legislative bodies,

6 Three optional protocols have since been added: an Optional Protocol on the sale of children, child prostitution, and child pornography; an Optional Protocol on the involvement of children in armed conflict; and an Optional Protocol on a communications procedure.

7 UN Committee on the Rights of the Child, Concluding Observations of the Committee on the Combined Third and Fourth Periodic Reports of Ireland, 2016, at para 69.

the best interests of the child shall be the primary consideration': thereby conferring on a child the right to have their welfare interests so treated across a range of fora; additionally, the subsequent articles then establish the particular rights held to be vested in a child.

Historically, in both jurisdictions, the record of child abuse suffered by children committed to the care of the state testifies to the extent of the latter's failure to uphold this principle. Currently, in the criminal law of both jurisdictions as it applies to children, it could not be said that their best interests are the primary consideration.

Protection

The protective function establishes a baseline for state responsibility in relation the best interests of a child. In Ireland, the duty to protect is to be found in the Child Care Act 1991 (Parts III, IV, and V), as reinforced by the National Standards for the Protection and Welfare of Children. Compliance with Article 3 imposes a duty on Tusla to intervene at the mere risk of abuse, rather than actuality of it. That the same applies to a local authority was made clear by the ECtHR ruling in *E v. United Kingdom*[8] though this may need to be read subject to Lady Hale's warning that there must be hard evidence of risk because "the threshold conditions are there to protect both the child and his family from unwarranted interference by the state."[9]

Facilities

Article 3(3) requires State Parties to ensure that 'the institutions, services and facilities responsible for the care or protection of children shall conform with the standards established by competent authorities.' In both jurisdictions there is shortage of adequate placements for troubled teenagers – secure accommodation and facilities for adolescents with mental health issues – but the situation is worse in Ireland where the authorities often look to England and Wales for placements which is clearly not conducive to promoting the welfare of the children concerned and may well violate their rights.

It is clear that in England and Wales – since the Children (Leaving Care) Act 2000 inserted ss 23A, 23B, 23C, and 24A and 24B into the 1989 Act – a 'looked after child' has a right to local authority accommodation if he or she needs it following their discharge from care.[10] Moreover, under s 20(11) of the 1989 Act, if the child has reached the age of 16 then he or she may not be removed from accommodation provided by a local authority without his or her consent.

8 Application No. 33218/96, (2002).
9 *In the matter of J (Children)* [2013] UKSC 9 at para 44.
10 *R(A) v. London Borough of Lambeth* [2010] EWHC 1652; [2010] 2 FCR 539, Admin.

Articles 7 and 8 – Right of the child to know their identity

Article 7 recognises the right of a child to information relating to their parents as the means of establishing his or her own identity. In relation to adopted children, this is a powerful legal acknowledgement that he or she has a right of access to information – in the form of agency records, etc. – that could potentially contribute to consolidating their sense of identity. However, currently, such information is not readily available in Ireland where the law has never provided a right for adopted persons to have automatic access to their birth certificates, neither has there ever been a legal right to access agency records for information on an adopted child's family of origin, nor a reciprocal duty to disclose such information. Moreover, it is questionable whether current practice regarding intercountry adoption is compliant with this principle in either jurisdiction.

Cultural identity

The right to a cultural identity – also given explicit recognition under Articles 8, 9, and 11 of the ECHR, Article 27 of the ICCPR, and Article 12 of UNDRIP – specifically recognises the right of minorities to maintain their own culture, language, and religion. It is reinforced by Article 20(3) which states that 'due regard shall be paid to the desirability of continuity in a child's upbringing and to the child's ethnic, religious, cultural and linguistic background.' In Ireland, related issues often come before the court as a consequence of state intervention in the way of life of the Traveller community and there is evidence that their culture is treated adversely, particularly in schools. In England and Wales, the regulatory body, Ofsted, has found the gender differentiation practices in Muslim faith-based schools to be discriminatory. Also, in the latter jurisdiction, the Children and Families Act 2014, s 3, deleted s 1(5) of the 2002 Act requiring that 'due consideration be given to religious persuasion, racial origin and cultural and linguistic background' when an adoption agency places a child for adoption. This deletion could, arguably, impair welfare interests by licensing a potentially serious infringement of a child's right to have the opportunity to develop an authentic, culturally contextualised identity.

Article 9 – Right of the child not to be separated from his or her parents

Article 9 requires State Parties to ensure that a child shall not be separated from his or her parents against their will, except when competent authorities subject to judicial review determine, in accordance with applicable law and procedures, that such separation is necessary for the child's best interests. In Ireland, where the parties contest custody/access arrangements the court will make its determination on the basis that the welfare of the children is the first and paramount consideration.[11] The court in England and Wales, when determining any question

11 As usefully outlined by Jennifer O'Brien of Jennifer O'Brien Solicitors, Irish Family Law Chambers, in *Practical Law*, Thomson Reuters at: https://uk.practicallaw.thomsonreuters.com/3-622-2687?transitionType=Default&contextData=(sc.Default)&firstPage=true.

with respect to the upbringing of a child is required, under s 1(2A) of the 1989 Act, to presume that the involvement of a parent in the life of the child concerned will further the child's welfare, unless there is evidence to the contrary. However, after some equivocation,[12] the judiciary in that jurisdiction would now seem to be firmly of the view that no right or presumption exists in favour of a child being brought up by his or her family of origin.[13]

Contact

Article 9(3) requires States Parties to 'respect the right of the child who is separated from one or both parents to maintain personal relations and direct contact with both parents.' This principle establishes a child 'contact right' which is prone to being compromised in England and Wales by the practice of concurrent placements and subsequent adoption from care. In that jurisdiction, recourse to a combination of adoption and contact orders accelerated in the wake of the 2002 Act because of: the requirement in s 46(6) that the court consider the necessity for post-adoption contact arrangements; and because of the insertion through the Children and Families Act 2014, s 9, of ss 51A and 51B into the Adoption and Children Act 2002 permitting the making of a contact order at any time, including any time after the granting of an adoption order.

Article 12 – Right of the child to express an opinion in administrative and judicial proceedings

This states that a child has the right to express his or her opinion freely and the right to have that opinion taken into account in any matter or procedure affecting the child. This is subject to the caveat that the child concerned must be capable of forming his or her own views. Due weight, in accordance with the age and maturity of the child, must be given to those views. In both jurisdictions the views of a child are seldom sought or taken into account in uncontested divorce and separation proceedings. In England and Wales there is judicial recognition of a child's right to be heard in proceedings affecting their upbringing[14] and in Ireland Article 42A.4.2. of the Constitution provides similar recognition, but in neither jurisdiction does the child's right to express an opinion imply that the court is obliged to attach any particular weight to it.

12 See, for example, *Birmingham City Council v. S* [2006] EWHC 3065 (Fam) when Sumner J recognised a child's "right to be brought up by her own family." See, also, the ruling in *Re B-S* [2013] EWCA Civ 1146, [2014] 1 FLR 1035.

13 *Re E-R (A Child)* 2015 EWCA Civ 405, per Vincent J.

14 *Re D (A Child) (International Recognition)* [2016] EWCA Civ 12, per Lady Hale at para 44.

Representation in court

While the child is a party by right in public law proceedings in England and Wales, and the appointment of a children's guardian *ad litem* is the norm,[15] in private law proceedings they are rarely parties but may be made so,[16] though usually only where there is 'an issue of significant difficulty.'

Articles 13 and 14 – Right of the child to self-determination, dignity, respect, non-interference, and the right to make informed decisions

The state requirement to ensure that a child has the right to make informed decisions has virtually no legislative recognition in either jurisdiction.

Consent

In England and Wales the Sexual Offences Act 2003 expressly recognises that a child, aged between 16 and 18 years of age, can give a valid legal consent to a sexual relationship. Additionally, the Children (Leaving Care) Act 2000 inserted sections 23A, 23B, 23C, and 24A and 24B into the 1989 Act, requiring a local authority to provide accommodation for those 'looked after children' who need it following their discharge from care.[17] Under s 20(11) of the 1989 Act, if the child has reached the age of 16 then he or she may not be removed from accommodation provided by a local authority without his or her consent. Further, s 22(3) obliges the local authority to safeguard and promote the welfare of any child they are looking after including, under s 22(3A), a duty to promote the child's educational achievement, which would seem to imply the reciprocal right of any such a child to receive a good education.

In England and Wales, since the landmark decision *Gillick v. West Norfolk and Wisbech Area Health Authority*,[18] while a child below the age of 16 continues to be treated in law as non-competent this may be rebutted by evidence based on age and understanding. Where a child is aged 16, or though younger is deemed to be '*Gillick* competent,' the law now requires that his or her consent is sought in relation to the matter at issue. So, for example, such a child could give a valid consent to being placed in secure accommodation.[19] There is no equivalent Irish case law.

15 A guardian must be appointed for the child unless the court is 'satisfied that it is not necessary to do so in order to safeguard his interests' (Children Act 1989, s 41(1)).
16 The Family Procedure Rules 2010, Practice Direction 16A.
17 *R(A) v. London Borough of Lambeth* [2010] EWHC 1652; [2010] 2 FCR 539, Admin.
18 [1986] 1 AC 112, HL.
19 See, *In the Matter of T (A Child) (Appellant)* [2021] UKSC 35.

Articles 18 and 19 – Primary responsibility for the upbringing of a child rests with the parent/s

There is a presumptive right of a child to be cared for by their birth parents in both jurisdictions. In England and Wales this is provided under s 38(6) of the 1989 Act: as amended by s 11 of the Children and Families Act 2014 which inserted s 1(2A) to establish a presumption that the involvement of a birth parent in the life of the child would further that child's welfare; though, as noted above, this has been seriously undermined by recent judicial decisions. In Ireland, the presumption is subsumed within the 'natural and imprescriptible rights' of Article 42.5 of the Constitution.

Article 18 requires State Parties to render appropriate assistance to parents and legal guardians to facilitate the upbringing and development of their children. It is reinforced by Article 18(2) which requires the development of appropriate services for the care of children and by Article 19(2) which adds that such services should include 'effective procedures for the establishment of social programmes to provide necessary support for the child and for those who have the care of the child.' In both jurisdictions there are statutory provisions placing a duty upon the authorities to provide parental support services – specified in England and Wales more so than in Ireland – which gives rise to a reciprocal right to receive such services. As child welfare is not easily separated from parental welfare – the younger the child the stronger that assumption – there is a sense in which the parental right could be viewed as a proxy child right as the services are intended for the latter's benefit (e.g. cash grants for necessities, pre-school facilities).

In both jurisdictions, but particularly in England and Wales, this prevention principle has been subverted by the necessity to divert scarce resources from consensual state intervention to the coercive regime of care and protection. Further, it would seem to be the case that the investment of resources to rehabilitate a child in care with their birth parents is less in England and Wales than in Ireland.

Article 21 – Adoption shall ensure that the best interests of the child shall be the paramount consideration

In Ireland, Article 42A.4.1(ii) inserts the principle that 'the best interests of the child shall be the paramount consideration' in proceedings relating to the 'safety and welfare of any child.' So, although judicial termination of parental rights is less constrained – now that the 31st Amendment has replaced Article 42.5 with Article 42A – it nonetheless remains more so than in the UK and correspondingly more difficult to utilise adoption as a means of giving priority to the welfare interests of children.

While the law is technically compliant with this principle in both jurisdictions, it is arguable that it is breached in Ireland by the constraints on accessing origins information. In England and Wales the positioning of this principle at the point of entry to the process facilitates adoptions from the public care system and differentiates it from the Irish adoption process. Note, however, that the Hague Convention contains no express requirement to make the best interests of the child a primary consideration.

Article 25 – Placements must be subject to periodic review

This Article requires periodic review of placements of all types, including foster care and residential units, to ensure that no child in state care is overlooked. Generally there are regulatory provisions that ensure that such reviews take place in all placement settings in both jurisdictions. However, there is good reason to suggest that the type of review should be adjusted to in accordance with the type of placement, in particular that guardian *ad litems* should be involved in secure accommodation reviews.

Article 27 – Every child is entitled to a reasonable standard of living

States are required to recognise the right of every child to a standard of living adequate for that child's physical, mental, spiritual, moral, and social development. In this context, the concern of the CRC that poverty is a factor in the care admissions in England and Wales must be noted.[20] In relation to Ireland, the Committee was also 'deeply concerned about the significant increase in the number of children living in consistent poverty, including reports that such poverty disproportionately affects children from Traveller, Roma and refugee backgrounds, as well as those who live in single-parent households.'[21]

Articles 30 and 31 – Right of a child from a minority group to practise their culture

As mentioned above, Ireland's treatment of its Traveller community and of the children belonging to that community is often in breach of this principle.

Article 35 – Prevention of trafficking in children

Unquestionably, given the scale of population movement currently and in recent years, child trafficking is a pressing issue throughout Europe. Official reports have expressed a concern that neither jurisdiction is taking adequate measures to address this problem.[22]

20 See UN Committee on the Rights of the Child, *Concluding Observations: United Kingdom Of Great Britain And Northern Ireland*, United Nations 2016, at para 52.

21 UN Committee on the Rights of the Child, Concluding Observations of the Committee on the Combined Third and Fourth Periodic Reports of Ireland, 2016, at para 59.

22 See Committee against Torture, *Concluding Observations on the Sixth Periodic Report of the United Kingdom of Great Britain and Northern Ireland*, 2019, at para 58.

Article 37 - No child to be subject to degrading treatment or punishment

As the CRC has pointed out, the current law in England – unlike in Ireland – permits parental chastisement of a child which the Committee maintains constitutes degrading treatment and is thus in breach of this principle.

Article 40 – Every alleged child offender to be justly treated

There are several different aspects to this principle.

First, just treatment requires legal representation which necessitates legal aid and assistance for those who cannot otherwise afford the costs involved. In both jurisdictions the legal aid scheme is inadequate to guarantee representation and consequently not every child is represented. Second, and again in both jurisdictions, the age of criminal responsibility is set too low to ensure just treatment. Third, if the welfare interests of children are to be respected then the court needs to have a menu of different orders to choose from so as to ensure an appropriate match between the disposal option, the needs of a particular child, and the gravity of the offence. In that respect, the range of custodial and non-custodial options that can be accessed by the judiciary in England and Wales has been compromised by removal of the judicial discretion to use care orders for offenders.[23] Finally, the specialist and modernised court system in England and Wales is a good deal more user friendly, from a child's perspective, than its Irish equivalent. Nonetheless, there have been criticisms of non-welfare oriented practices in the Youth Court such as handcuffing children and locking them in secure docks, even though they are being charged with minor offences.

The right to be treated as a child and have anti-social behaviour judged within welfare rather than criminal proceedings is more constrained in both jurisdictions than elsewhere in Europe, but is particularly restricted in England.

23 Under the Children Act 1989, s 90(2).

Selected Bibliography

Books

Bainham, A., *Children: The Modern Law*, 2nd ed., Brisol, Family Law, 1998.
Bainham, A. (ed.), *The International Survey of Family Law, 1996*, Martinus Nijhoff 1998.
Bean, P. (ed.), *Adoption: Essays in Social Policy, Law and Sociology*, London, Tavistock, 1984.
Bean, P. and Melville, J., *Lost Children of the Empire*, London, Unwin Hyman, 1989.
Bettelheim, B., *Love is Not Enough*, New York, Free Press, 1950.
Bilson, A., *Suffer the Little Children*, London, Legal Action for Women, 2017.
Bowlby, J., *Attachment*, London, Penguin, 1969.
Bowlby, J., *Attachment and Loss*, Pimlico, New York, Basic Books, 1968.
Brady, J., *Religion and the Law of Charities in Ireland*, Belfast, Northern Ireland Legal Quarterly, 1976.
Bromley, P.M., *Bromley's Family Law*, 8th ed., London, Butterworths, 1992.
Buckley, H., Skehill, C. and O'Sullivan, E., *Child Protection Services in Ireland*, Dublin, Oak Tree Press, 1997.
Carpenter, M., *Juvenile Delinquents, Their Condition and Treatment*, Oxford, W. & F. G. Cash, 1856.
Carpenter, M., *Reformatory Schools for the Perishing and Dangerous Classes and for the Prevention of Juvenile Delinquency*, published in 1851, London, Routledge, 1969.
Chesterman, M., *Charities, Trusts and Social Welfare*, London, Weidenfeld and Nicolson, 1979.
Corbett, M. and Coulter, C., *Child Care Proceedings: A Thematic Review of Irish and International Practice*, Dublin, Department of Children and Youth Affairs, Government of Ireland, 2019.
Coulter, C., 'An Examination of Lengthy, Contested and Complex Child Protection Cases in the District Court', *Child Care Law Reporting Project, Dublin*, Dublin, Child Care Law Reporting Project, 2018.
Coulter, C., *District Court Child Care Proceedings: A National Overview*, Dublin, Child Care Law Reporting Project, 2019.
Deakin, N., *In Search of Civil Society*, London, Palgrave, 2001.
Dias, R.M.W., *Jurisprudence*, 5th ed., London, Butterworths, 1985.
Eekelaar, J., *Family Law and Social Policy*, London, Weidenfeld and Nicolson, 1984.
Eekelaar, J. and Dingwall, R., *The Reform of Child Care Law – A Practical Guide to the Children Act 1989*, London, Routledge, 1990.
Erikson, E., *Identity and the Life-Cycle*, New York, Norton, 1980.

Erikson, E., *Identity Youth and Crisis*, London, Faber & Faber, 1968.
Fortin, J., *Children's Rights and the Developing Law*, London, Butterworths, 1998.
Freeman, M., *The Rights and Wrongs of Children*, Pinter Pub Ltd., 1983.
Gilligan, R., *Irish Child Care Services: Policy, Practice and Provision*, Dublin, Institute of Public Administration, 1991.
Goldstein, J., *In the Best Interests of the Child: Professional Boundaries*, New York, Free Press, 1986.
Goldstein, J., Freud, A. and Solnit, A.H., *Before the Best Interests of the Child*, New York, Free Press, 1979.
Goldstein, J., Freud, A. and Solnit, A.H., *Beyond the Best Interests of the Child*, Collier Macmillan, 1973.
Goldstein, J., Freud, A. and Solnit, A.H., *The Best Interests of the Child: The Least Detrimental Alternative*, New York, Simon and Schuster, 1996.
Griffin, E., *Liberty's Dawn*, Connecticut, Yale University Press, 2014.
Hoggett, B., *Parents and Children*, 4th ed., London, Sweet and Maxwell, 1993.
Jones, G., *History of the Law of Charity 1532–1827*, Holmes Beach, Florida, Wm. W. Gaunt & Sons, Inc., 1986.
Judge, S.J., 'Youth Justice', in *Making Rights Real for Children: A Children's Rights Audit of Irish Law*, Dublin, Children's Rights Alliance, p 164, 2015.
Katz, S.N., in Probert, R. and Barton, C. (eds.), *Fifty Years in Family Law: Essays for Stephen Cretney*, Cambridge, UK, Intersentia, 2012.
Kellmer-Pringle, M., *The Needs of Children*, London, Hutchinson, 1980.
Kelly, R., *Motherhood Silenced: The Experiences of Natural Mothers on Adoption Reunion*, Dublin, Liffey Press, 2005.
Kelsen, H., *The Pure Theory of Law* (first published in 1934), New Jersey, US, The Lawbook Exchange, Ltd., 2009.
Kilkelly, U., *Youth Justice in Ireland: Tough Lives, Rough Justice*, Dublin, Irish Academic Press, 2006.
King, M. (ed.), *Childhood, Welfare & Justice*, London, Billing & Son Ltd., 1981.
Klein, M., *The Psycho-Analysis of Children* (first published in 1932), New York, Vintage, 1997.
Layard, R. and Dunn, J., *A Good Childhood: Searching for Values in a Competitive Age*, London, Penguin Books, 2009.
Leonard, E.M., *The Early History of the English Poor Relief*, Cambridge, Cambridge University Press, 1900.
Lowe, N. and White, R., *Wards of Court*, London, Butterworths, 1979.
Maidment, S., *Child Custody and Divorce*, Abingdon, Oxfordshire, Routledge, 1985.
Milotte, M., *Banished Babies: The Secret History of Ireland's Baby Export Business*, Dublin, New Island Press, 2014.
Mnookin, R.H., *In the Interest of Children*, New York, WH Freeman & Co, 1985.
Moran, L., McGregor, C. and Devaney, C., *Outcomes for Permanence and Stability for Children in Long-Term Care*, Galway, The UNESCO Child and Family Research Centre, The National University of Ireland, 2017.
Morris, A., Giller, H., Szwed, E. and Geach, H., *Justice for Children*, Stuttgart, Germany, Macmillan, 1980.
Morris, A. and Giller, H., *Understanding Juvenile Justice*, London, Croom Helm, 1987.
Muncie, J., *Youth and Crime*, London, Sage, 2004.
O'Halloran, K., *The Politics of Adoption*, 4th ed., New York, Springer, 2021.
O'Halloran, K., *The Principle of the Welfare of the Child: A History*, Abingdon, Oxfordshire, Routledge, 2022.

O'Halloran, K., *The Welfare of the Child: The Principle and the Law*, Aldershot, Arena/Ashgate Publications, 1999.

O'Mahony, C., Burns, K. and Brennan, R., 'Voluntary Care in Ireland Study', 2018–21, *Irish Social Worker,* Winter *2020,* Dublin, pp. 7–16.

Piaget, J. and Inhelder, B., *The Psychology of the Child*, London, Routledge & Kegan Paul, 1969.

Pringle, M.K., *The Needs of Children*, London, Hutchinson, 1975.

Redmond, P., *The Adoption Machine: The Dark History of Ireland's Mother & Baby Homes*, Dublin, Merrion Press, 2018.

Rutter, M., *Maternal Deprivation Reassessed*, London, Penguin, 1972.

Rutter, M. and Giller, H., *Juvenile Delinquency: Trends and Perspectives*, London, Penguin, 1983.

Sargent, P., *Wild Arabs and Savages: A History of Juvenile Justice in Ireland*, Manchester, Manchester University Press, 2013.

Skynner, R., *Families and How to Survive Them*, Springville, Utah, Cedar Books, 1984.

Spock, B., *The Commonsense Book of Baby and Childcare*, New York, Duell, Sloan and Pearce, 1946.

Triseliotis, J., *In Search of Origins: The Experience of Adopted People*, London, Routledge & Kegan Paul, 1973.

Utting, D., Bright, J. and Henricson, C., *Crime and the Family: Improving Child-Rearing and Preventing Delinquency*, London, Family Policy Studies Centre, 1993.

Wilkes, J.R., 'Introduction', in Herst, B., (ed), *Permanency Planning in the Child Welfare System*, Ottawa, Sparrow Lake Alliance, Children in Limbo Task Force, pp 4–7, 2002.

Winnicott, D., *The Child, the Family, and the Outside World* (First Published, 1964), London, Penguin Classics, 2021.

Reports

Adoption – A Service for Children, London, HMSO, 1996.

A Child in Trust: The Report of the Panel of Inquiry into the Circumstances Surrounding the Death of Jasmine Beckford, London Borough of Brent, London Borough of Brent, 1985.

Mawhinney, A.J.; Cumper, P. (eds.), *Collective Worship and Religious Observance in Schools: An Evaluation of Law and Policy in the UK*, AHRC Network Report, 2015.

An Action Plan for Adoption: Tackling Delay, London, HMSO, 2012.

Children in Trouble, Home Office, Cmnd 3601, London, HMSO, 1968.

Still Running: Children on the Streets in the UK, London, The Children's Society, 1999.

Commission on the Future of the Voluntary Sector in England, *Meeting the Challenge of Change: Voluntary Action into the 21st Century* (the Deakin Report), London, NCVO, 1996.

Justice Ryan, Chair, *Commission to Inquire into Child Abuse* (the "Ryan Report"), Department of Children, Equality, Disability, Integration and Youth, Stationery Office, Dublin, 2009.

Council of Europe and the EU Agency for Fundamental Rights, *Handbook on European Law Relating to the Rights of the Child*, Strasbourg, 2015.

DHSS, 'Review of Child Care Law: Report to Ministers of an Interdepartmental Working Party', HMSO, 1985.

Department of Children and Youth Affairs 'Review and Consultation in Respect of the Potential Introduction of Open or Semi-Open Adoption in Ireland', Dublin, Stationery Office, 2019.

Department of Health, *Adoption Law Review: Consultation Document*, London, HMSO, 1992.

Department of Health, *Draft Adoption Support Services (Local Authorities)(Transitory and Transitional Provisions)(England) Regulations and Draft Accompanying Guidance*, London, HMSO, December 2002.

Department of Justice and Equality, *Report by the Commission of Investigation into Catholic Archdiocese of Dublin* (the "Murphy Report"), Dublin, Stationery Office, 2009.

Department of Justice Equality and Reform, *Report on the Youth Justice Review*, Dublin, Stationery Office, 2006.

Every Child Matters (Cmnd 5860), London, HMSO, 2003.

Every Child Matters: Next Steps, London, Department of Skills and Education, HMSO, 2004.

Family Justice Council, *Guidelines for Judges Meeting Children who are Subject to Family Proceedings*, April 2010, [2010] 2, *FLR* 1872.

Family Justice Council, *Guidelines in Relation to Children Giving Evidence in Family Proceedings*, December 2011, [2012], *Family Law* 70.

Health Information and Quality Authority, *National Standards for the Protection and Welfare of Children*, Dublin, Stationery Office, 2012.

Home Office: The Child, the Family and the Young Offender, London, HMSO, 1965.

Irish Society for the Prevention of Cruelty to Children Report, A Task Force on Child Care Services, Dublin, Stationery Office, 1980.

Irish Youth Justice Service, *Report on the Implementation of the National Youth Justice Strategy 2008–2010*, Stationery Office, Dublin 1

Jay, A., *Independent Inquiry into Child Sexual Exploitation in Rotherham (1997–2013)*, Rotherham Metropolitan Borough Council, 2014.

Joint Oireachtas Committee on Children and Youth Affairs, Report on the Impact of Homelessness on Children, Dublin, Stationery Office, 2019.

Kennedy, J., 'Report on Industrial Schools and Reformatories' (the "Kennedy Report"), Dublin, the Stationery Office, 1970.

Law Commission Consultation Paper 'Building Families Through Surrogacy: A New Law',London, HMSO, 2019.

Law Commission No 118, *Family Law Report on Illegitimacy*, London, HMSO, 1982.

Law Commission, *Wards of Court*, Working Paper No 101, London, HMSO, 1987.

Law Reform Commission, 'Report on Child Sexual Abuse', Dublin, Stationery Office, 1990.

McGuinness, C., *Report of the Kilkenny Incest Investigation*, Dublin, the Stationery Office, 1993.

Ministry of Justice and Department for Education, *The Government Response to the Family Justice Review: A System with Children and Families at Its Heart*, Cm 8273, TSO, London, HMSO, 2012.

Ministry of Justice, *Family Justice Review: Final Report*, London, HMSO, 2011.

Public Law Working Group, *Recommendations to Achieve Best Practice in the Child Protection and Family Justice Systems*, Final report, 2021.

Report of the Commission to Inquire into Child Abuse (the Ryan Report), Dublin, Stationery Office, 2009.

Blom-Cooper L., Harding J., and Milton E., *Report of the Commission of Inquiry into the Circumstances Surrounding the Death of Kimberley Carlile, A Child in Mind: Protection of Children in a Responsible Society*, Greenwich. Social Services Department, 1987.

Report of the Committee of Inquiry into the Care and Supervision Provided for Maria Colwell, London, Dept of Social Security, HMSO, 1974.

Report of the Departmental Committee on the Adoption of Children (Houghton Report), London, HMSO (Cmnd 5107), 1972.

Report of the Inquiry into Child Abuse in Cleveland 1987 (Cmnd 412), 1988.

Report of the Interdepartmental Committee on Local Authority and Allied Personal Social Services (the Seebohm report),London, HMSO, 1968.

Report of the Royal Commission on the Employment of Children and Very Young People in Mines and Factories, 1842.

Report of the Royal Commission into the Operation of the Poor Laws, 1832.

Review of Child Law: Guardianship and Custody (Law Commission Report No 172), London, HMSO, 1988.

The Law on Child Care and Family Services, Cmnd 62, London, HMSO, 1987.

The Victoria Climbié Inquiry, London, HMSO, 2000.

UN Committee on the Rights of the Child, Concluding Observations of the Committee on the Combined Third and Fourth Periodic Reports of Ireland, Geneva, Switzerland, 2016.

UN Committee on the Rights of the Child, Concluding Observations of the Committee on the Rights of the Child, *United Kingdom of Great Britain and Northern Ireland C RC/C 15Add34*, Geneva, Switzerland, 1995.

UN Committee on the Rights of the Child, *General Comment No. 7, 'Implementing Child Rights in Early Childhood'*, Geneva, Switzerland, 2005.

UN Committee on the Rights of the Child, *General Comment No. 12 (2009): The Right of the Child to Be Heard*, Geneva, Switzerland, 2009.

UN Committee on the Rights of the Child, Concluding Observations on the Fifth Periodic Report of the United Kingdom of Great Britain and Northern Ireland (CRC/ C/GBR/ CO/5), Geneva, Switzerland, 2016.

Utting, D., *Family and Parenthood: Supporting Families, Preventing Breakdown*, Rowntree Foundation, York, 1995.

Waterhouse, R., *Lost in Care: Report of the Tribunal of Inquiry into the Abuse of Children in Care in the Former County Council Areas of Gwynedd and Clwyd since 1974*, London, the Stationery Office, 2000.

Youth Justice – The Next Steps, London, HMSO, 2003.

Index

For Product Safety Concerns and Information please contact our EU
representative GPSR@taylorandfrancis.com
Taylor & Francis Verlag GmbH, Kaufingerstraße 24, 80331 München, Germany

www.ingramcontent.com/pod-product-compliance
Ingram Content Group UK Ltd.
Pitfield, Milton Keynes, MK11 3LW, UK
UKHW021828101126
477531UK00020B/546

* 9 7 8 1 0 3 2 2 1 4 8 9 4 *